D1556884

Picturing
Political Power

IMAGES IN THE WOMEN'S
SUFFRAGE MOVEMENT

PICTURING POLITICAL POWER

Allison K. Lange

The University of Chicago Press

Chicago and London

Publication of this book has been aided by a grant from the Neil Harris
Endowment Fund, which honors the innovative scholarship of Neil Harris,
the Preston and Sterling Morton Professor Emeritus of History at the
University of Chicago. The fund is supported by contributions from the
students, colleagues, and friends of Neil Harris.

The University of Chicago Press, Chicago 60637
The University of Chicago Press, Ltd., London
© 2020 by Allison K. Lange
Published 2020
Printed in the United States of America

29 28 27 26 25 24 23 22 21 20   1 2 3 4 5

ISBN-13: 978-0-226-70324-4 (cloth)
ISBN-13: 978-0-226-70338-1 (e-book)
DOI: https://doi.org/10.7208/chicago/9780226703381.001.0001

Library of Congress Cataloging-in-Publication Data

Names: Lange, Allison K., author.
Title: Picturing political power : images in the women's suffrage
     movement / Allison K. Lange.
Description: Chicago ; London : University of Chicago Press, 2020. |
     Includes bibliographical references and index.
Identifiers: LCCN 2019046670 | ISBN 9780226703244 (cloth) |
     ISBN 9780226703381 (ebook)
Subjects: LCSH: Women—Suffrage—United States—History. | First-wave
     feminism. | Graphic arts—Political aspects—United States. | Women in
     art. | Women—United States—Portraits. | Suffragists—United States—
     Portraits. | Women—Political activity—United States.
Classification: LCC JK1896 .L36 2020 | DDC 324.6/230973—dc23
LC record available at https://lccn.loc.gov/2019046670

♾ This paper meets the requirements of ANSI/NISO Z39.48-1992
(Permanence of Paper).

CONTENTS

I.1: Currier & Ives, *The Age of Brass, or The Triumphs of Woman's Rights*, 1869, lithograph. Courtesy of the Library of Congress, LC-DIG-pga-05762.

INTRODUCTION

In 1869, Currier & Ives, the era's most famous printmaker, published *The Age of Brass, or The Triumphs of Woman's Rights* to depict what would happen if women won equality (figure I.1). This print depicts a group of elite white women as they gather to cast their ballots. Some wear enormous bows around their necks and towering, unwieldy hairstyles. To wear such absurd feminine fashions, the picture implies, they must be irrational and ignorant of important issues. Other women in the image have a masculine aesthetic—top hats, bloomers, morning jackets—to prompt laughter from viewers at their cross-dressing antics. On the right, an angry woman, whose glasses signal her education, scolds her shocked husband, the only man in sight. To viewers used to idealized images of women, she would have appeared ugly. Instead of caring for her family, as she should according to the day's social norms, the woman abandons her baby with her husband in order to engage in politics. To reiterate that women's rights would lead to the submission of men, a sandwich board advises women to cast their ballots for "Susan Sharp Tongue," the "celebrated man tamer."

Cartoons like this one dominated popular representations of political women throughout the nineteenth century. According to opponents, if women won rights, they would disdain family life and transform American society. Adversaries of women's votes believed that men already represented the interests of their families. This print, and the many others that came before and after it, depicted female voters as a joke. Women had gained property rights and greater access to education by 1869, but surely they would never win the vote. Currier & Ives sold the print to audiences who wanted to laugh at their fears and at these reformers.

Female voters may seem unremarkable today, but the majority of Americans—men and women alike—vehemently opposed them for most of the nation's history. The Currier & Ives print illustrates the real anxiety that many felt about changes to voting rights. When this print was published in 1869, Americans were deciding who would have political power after the Civil War. Congress passed the Fifteenth Amendment to grant the ballot to black men. Many Americans wondered: If formerly enslaved men could vote, who was next? That same year, the territory of Wyoming granted women the ballot. Reformers also established the first national organizations to advocate for women's suffrage, the right to vote, throughout the United States.

From the colonial era through the present, satirical images consistently represented political women as power-hungry, masculine-looking activists who deserted their families to pursue fame and end traditional family values. Pictures that circulated publicly often portrayed elite white men as powerful, revered leaders, but comparable imagery of women and people of color barely existed. Nevertheless, reformers persisted. While opponents relied on old tropes, suffragists coordinated the first visual campaigns to transform notions of political womanhood. Visual politics—the strategic use of images to promote a cause or candidate—proved central to their efforts to change Americans' expectations for political women. Suffragists adopted tactics from other campaigns and pioneered their own strategies to create one of the first extensive visual campaigns in American history.

By the late nineteenth century, in direct response to cartoons like this one, suffragists coordinated visual campaigns that painted white female citizens as virtuous mothers and wives. The National American Woman Suffrage Association (NAWSA), the most powerful suffrage group, argued that women could balance domesticity with political participation and professional goals. Women's votes, the organization contended, would actually *reinforce* traditional gender norms and make society more moral: men could remain political leaders and heads of households without becoming domestic, and voting women would not disrupt heteronormativity or white supremacy. This campaign, with its message designed by publicity professionals and carried out by a generation of educated female journalists and artists, won widespread support.

The vision had appeal, but it did not reflect the realities of women's lives or the movement's diversity. Competing suffrage groups promoted alternatives. The National Association of Colored Women (NACW) presented an image of refined, elite black women, while the National Woman's Party (NWP) distributed photographs of pretty young white women protesting in the streets. Although the latter's campaign differed from that of NAWSA, both groups' visual campaigns emphasized that suffragists were white.

Although they promoted different visions, suffragists pioneered the use of images in modern political campaigns, and their success likely spurred the US government's creation of visual propaganda during World War I.

Reformers secured the necessary support to pass the Nineteenth Amendment, which barred voting restrictions based on sex, in 1920, but white suffragists chose not to advocate for women of color who were unable to cast a ballot due to state-level restrictions.[1] Their choice not to address racial stereotypes or impossible literacy tests forced people of color to fight for the ballot until the passage of the Voting Rights Act in 1965. Native American, Puerto Rican, and Asian women did not win the ballot with the Nineteenth Amendment, either.

Suffragists constructed popular ideals for modern American political women more than a century ago. The dominant groups' representations of themselves as virtuous white women in their visual propaganda led many contemporaries to expect that women would cast their votes as a bloc to improve society. The suffrage message proved so effective that because no such bloc ever emerged, even scholars have argued that women's ballots did not make much difference. To this day, the suffragists' successful visual campaign to associate political womanhood with family values has obliged prominent women to negotiate their public images in terms of their statuses as mothers, wives, daughters, and potential mothers.

The dominance of the suffragists' vision for political womanhood was not inevitable. In 1872, three years after the Currier & Ives print, Victoria Woodhull declared herself the first female candidate for president of the United States. Even though she had no chance of winning, she wanted to claim political power by running for office rather than working with suffragists to ask for it. She did the same in her profession: along with her sister Tennie C. Claflin, she became the first female stockbroker on Wall Street and the first female editor of a weekly newspaper.

Woodhull knew her choices bucked the norm, and so did the public. In the late 1860s or early 1870s, as she pursued her string of "firsts," she posed in the studio of the celebrity photographer Mathew Brady. In the image in figure I.2, Woodhull wears a top hat with a bow and military-style jacket, mimicking the women in cartoons like *The Age of Brass*. Unbuttoned, the jacket allows room for her breasts and suggests that she wears men's clothing. A faux bow tie completes the ensemble. She leans against a wooden desk in an ungraceful, unladylike pose. By appropriating the costumes and poses from caricatures of political women, she demonstrates her power over these ideas. Woodhull teased Americans who feared that political women would become masculine. In 1872, Thomas Nast, the influential *Harper's Weekly* cartoonist, even portrayed her as a winged devil.[2]

Almost 150 years after Woodhull's presidential run, Hillary Clinton's

I.2: Studio of Mathew Brady, *Victoria Claflin Woodhull*, 1866–1873, cabinet card photograph. Courtesy of Special Collections, Fine Arts Library, Harvard University.

journey to become the first female presidential nominee of a major political party looked very different. First a lawyer and later a senator and secretary of state, she chose a path well worn by generations of men to the office. Like Woodhull, Clinton preferred a traditionally presidential, masculine aesthetic that made her look powerful, not pretty. Instead of fashionable tailored dresses, Clinton wore short hair and pantsuits balanced against bright feminine colors rarely worn by male politicians. The pantsuits attracted derision from her opponents, but her supporters designated them a symbol of female power and wore them on election day in 2016.

Throughout Clinton's presidential campaign, references to the suffrage movement were everywhere. In June 2016, the US Treasury announced a new design for the ten-dollar bill featuring portraits of five suffragists. The next month, it became clear that Clinton was the Democratic Party's nominee. She delivered a speech with a video, *History Made*, which began with the Seneca Falls Convention and included film footage of parading suffragists. Afterward, a slew of articles analyzed the white pantsuit she wore to accept the nomination, focusing not on its style but on its reference to the suffragists who had marched in white. Writers chronicled the joy of centenarians, who had been born before the passage of the Nineteenth Amendment. They believed that they would elect the first female president. On Election Day, the media covered the stories of those who pressed their "I Voted" stickers onto Susan B. Anthony's gravestone. The election of the first female president seemed like the fulfillment of a goal set long ago.

As excitement about Clinton crested, so did the enmity of her opponents. Clinton is only one recent example of a female politician who attempted to win support by performing a balancing act between motherly, feminine beauty and masculine political authority.[3] Cartoonists caricatured Clinton for looking too manly, but her stylists knew she needed a commanding air.[4] Her opponent, Donald Trump, declared: "Well, I just don't think she has a presidential look. And you need a presidential look. You have to get the job done."[5] He articulated a conclusion of recent studies, which suggest that people associate masculinity with leadership and power.[6] Trump also called her a "nasty woman," an epithet that summed up centuries of disgust for women seeking power. Detractors labeled Clinton's criticism of male opponents as "ball-busting" and sold nutcrackers in her likeness. Like the baby held by the man in the 1869 print, Clinton's presence on the debate stage was itself emasculating. She was the sharp-tongued "celebrated man tamer" that female voters wanted to elect.[7] The hashtag #RepealThe19th trended just before the election.[8] The twenty-first-century debate about political women has not changed much since the publication of the Currier & Ives print 150 years ago. By looking to the past, we can understand the roots of the relationship between gender, images, and power that shapes the fight for female leadership in the present.

This book analyzes over a century of public political images that Americans continue to respond to, negotiate with, and challenge. From eighteenth-century woodblock engravings through twentieth-century photographic halftones, political leaders took advantage of improvements in image technology and the public's fascination with pictures to revolutionize politics. From engraved cartoons to lithographic posters, suffragists developed strategies for each new visual medium. Widely distributed pictures offered a fast, inexpensive way to influence Americans throughout the expanding nation. This book examines popular pictures, rather than personal ones intended for family and friends, because they reveal shared ideas. These public images were at the heart of the development of a shared national visual language, composed of symbols and gendered conventions.[9] This language helped fuel the rise of mass society and the highly visual culture of twenty-first-century life.

Images are political. We acknowledge this truth today, but they are often an overlooked register of political argument in the past. The pictures that flooded into parlors defined and reflected popular conceptions of power.[10] Engravings and photographs do not simply illustrate a person or historical event. Artists, editors, and publishers printed them to make arguments, and public pictures conveyed those arguments to many. An image's content, medium, and relationship to contemporaneous pictures point to a broader story. The images that suffragists and their opponents sold are just as important as the pamphlets they wrote.[11]

Female reformers launched one of the longest and earliest coordinated visual campaigns. They combatted negative representations peddled by opponents and strategically controlled visual representations of themselves for political ends. Throughout much of the nineteenth century. women rarely had enough power or money to counter pervasive and profitable sexist imagery. During the mid-nineteenth century, individual activists led piecemeal efforts, but by the 1890s, suffragists enlisted press committees and professionals to distribute imagery across the nation. As suffragists honed their visual campaign and constructed an appealing image of political women, mainstream publications gradually began to feature their propaganda. By the 1910s, most publications featured imagery that suffragists designed, influenced, or staged (as in the case of protest photographs). Building on recent studies of race and visual politics during the antislavery and civil rights movements, this book highlights the relationship between gender and visual politics over the course of a century.[12]

Picturing Political Power offers the most comprehensive analysis yet of the connection between visual culture, gender, and power.[13] Suffragists needed to change minds about the bounds of female citizenship before they could change laws. To gain power, an individual must be visible, and in the nineteenth century, prominent figures often won visibility with portraits. Suffragists recognized that popular pictures defined notions of gender and power for a broad audience. Disparaging cartoons made reformers visible, but the artists and editors controlled the way suffragists appeared.

So suffrage leaders distributed their own portraits to claim power. But it was nearly impossible for suffragists to be both visible and virtuous women. Women were supposed to embrace the feminine private sphere, but public portraits symbolized their crossing into the public, political, and masculine one.[14] Gendered imagery has shaped—and continues to shape—the relationship between women and the state.

Public visual debates about gender and power provide an expansive lens for looking beyond the internal movement politics that have long defined suffrage histories.[15] It is difficult to understand the fight for women's votes without understanding the powerful opposition. The sexist satirical pictures that dominated popular culture entrenched ideas about gender and politics. Female reformers forged innovative strategies to refute the style of attacks leveled at them.

Public, political pictures point to a diverse story of women's activism that builds on recent literature. From Phillis Wheatley and Sojourner Truth to Mary Church Terrell and Ida B. Wells-Barnett, black women stand out as public image innovators.[16] Racist stereotypes prompted the public images that these activists developed. Prejudice also prompted white suffragists to differentiate themselves from black women. The visual campaigns by the National American Woman Suffrage Association and National Woman's Party addressed fears that women's equality would lead to racial equality by backing a vision of political womanhood that was white, motherly, and virtuous. However, imagery in civil rights publications and the black press highlighted black suffrage leaders. Black women had even more to gain—and lose—than white reformers did.

Suffragists used images to define the ways that contemporaries understood the movement, and they guide the way we remember their struggle today.[17] For example, the women whose portraits were selected to appear on a new ten-dollar bill in 2016—Lucretia Mott, Elizabeth Cady Stanton, Sojourner Truth, Susan B. Anthony, and Alice Paul   secured their place by defining public images of political womanhood over a century ago. These women developed visual campaigns that continue to shape ideas of political women.

Picturing Political Power tracks the ways that women gradually transformed public images of gender and political power. The story begins with portraits of Phillis Wheatley, Martha Washington, and Mary Wollstonecraft in late eighteenth-century America. These women secured power with the help of men—in this case, owners, patrons, and husbands. Their exceptional public portraits contrasted with conventional symbolic images of women, which emphasized their anonymity and idealized beauty. The era's most popular pictures connected elite white manhood and political leadership, which laid the foundation for American visions of power. In the 1850s, spurred by the rise of illustrated newspapers and women's rights conventions, opponents of women's rights distributed graphic satire. They based their cartoons on long-established visual conventions to mock the reformers. Women's rights advocates sought greater visibility, and in response their opponents made Martha Washington iconic as an ideal political hostess and wife, a foil to female reformers.

The next two chapters outline women's first significant efforts to deploy portraits as their representatives to the public. Chapter 3 situates the damaging cartoons alongside portraits of Lucretia Mott and Sojourner Truth, who learned visual strategies from the antislavery movement and Abraham Lincoln's presidential campaign. Female reformers circulated their photographic portraits to demonstrate their femininity and advance their cause. The pictures made them famous, but their similarity to portraits of male politicians only proved that political women would transform American values. Chapter 4 analyzes the efforts of Susan B. Anthony and the first national suffrage organizations to create the movement's iconography, especially through the *History of Woman Suffrage*. These projects entrenched divisions between white suffragists and suffragists of color, who established their own organizations and iconography.

Even suffragists disagreed among themselves about what political women would look like. Were they respectable older leaders or young picketing activists? Caring white mothers or refined black intellectuals? The final two chapters detail the national visual campaigns developed at the turn of the century. Chapter 5 centers on Mary Church Terrell, who became the first president of the National Association of Colored Women. She and the NACW articulated a vision for respectable, educated black political women. Black suffragists largely relied on an often ambivalent black press to distribute their pictures. Comparatively well-funded white suffragists formed press committees to design propaganda that pictured them as beautiful, patriotic mothers, obscuring black women's activism. Chapter 6 contrasts the emphasis on idealized femininity embraced by leading white and black women with the demonstrations carried out by their militant counterparts. Borrowing publicity tactics from labor activists and British suffragists, Alice Paul and the National Woman's Party staged parades and pickets to ensure media coverage. Suffragists took advantage of new halftone technology, which allowed newspapers to print photographs cheaply for the first time.[18] They won support by winning over the popular press, keeping the cause in the news with dramatic public protests, and mounting propaganda campaigns that transformed dominant representations of female citizens. Visual debates about gender and politics continue today.

1.1: *Phillis Wheatley, Negro Servant to Mr. John Wheatley, of Boston*, 1773, engraving on paper, published as the frontispiece in Phillis Wheatley, *Poems on Various Subjects, Religious and Moral* (1773). National Portrait Gallery, Smithsonian Institution.

1: SETTING THE STANDARDS

Poet Phillis Wheatley was the first female author in the American colonies whose portrait appeared in her book (figure 1.1).[1] Wheatley arrived in Boston in 1761 around the age of seven or eight. John and Susannah Wheatley purchased and named her after the ship that had carried her from Africa. The Wheatleys gave her an unusually good education for a woman, especially an enslaved one. As a teenager, the poet published for audiences on both sides of the Atlantic and interacted with leaders like George Washington and Benjamin Franklin.[2]

As a representation of an enslaved woman, Wheatley's public portrait was especially rare and necessary. The patrons of her 1773 book, *Poems on Various Subjects, Religious and Moral*, paid for the engraving to prove that an African woman had written it. One of Wheatley's supporters, the Countess of Huntingdon, Selina Hastings, wrote to the Wheatleys that she "desir'd … to have Phillis' picture in the frontispiece" because it would contribute to "the Sale of the Book."[3] In the oval portrait, Wheatley pens a few lines with her quill at a desk. She contemplates her next phrases with her chin in her hand. The pose and profile view make her resemble a classical thinker. The book by her side references Wheatley's education and engagement with elite intellectual circles, while the text around the portrait's frame—"PHYLLIS WHEATLEY, NEGRO SERVANT TO MR. JOHN WHEATLEY, OF BOSTON"—reminds viewers that she is enslaved.[4] The publisher chose a metal plate, likely copper, for the portrait because it could produce five hundred to a thousand fine impressions. An artist engraved a reverse of the image on the plate before inking it and pressing it onto paper. Looking closely, one can see the fine, dense lines that form the poet's dark face.

Wheatley's famous face matters because few women—and even fewer black women—had portraits that reached wide audiences. To modern eyes, public portraits of women may seem unremarkable. This chapter reminds us that living, individual women lacked public visibility in early America, which reflected and reinforced their lack of political power. An individual's visibility signaled their power. Late eighteenth-century public portraits often asserted the political power of elite white men.[5] Portraits of Queen Elizabeth, the biblical Mary, and Joan of Arc also circulated, but the powerful, divine, and dead statuses of these women meant that no one accused them of selling their portraits to promote themselves, an unwomanly act. Men designed most of the pictures that Americans encountered, and they preferred to produce pictures of generic, idealized white female figures who represented abstract ideas, like liberty or genius. Furthermore, women held few public positions, so profit-driven printers knew their individual portraits would never sell.

Early American popular pictures defined the conventions for representing political power that lasted through the nineteenth century and still influence modern ones. Wheatley, Martha Washington, and Mary Wollstonecraft—an enslaved female poet, a first presidential spouse, and a female intellectual—had very different social statuses, but these exceptional women won an exceptional degree of visibility. Their portraits demonstrate the rare examples of living women in public imagery that later female leaders could model. These three women did not design their portraits to win political power. Owners, patrons, and printers—nearly all male—employed their portraits to sell books, share ideas, and secure respect for a new nation. In the late nineteenth century, when suffragists designed their own imagery and portraits, they challenged these long-standing norms by claiming visibility and power that had once almost solely belonged to men.

Improvements in technology and the appeal of inexpensive pictures facilitated the beginnings of a shared visual language. Standards for depicting power were rooted in European—especially British—imagery and dependent on its artists for decades after the American Revolution. Americans especially desired printed portraits because they wanted to see the faces of their favorite public figures.[6] Because of the expense, only an estimated 1 percent of the colonial population ever had their likenesses painted.[7] Even fewer had portraits engraved and sold. Shipped throughout the Atlantic world, printed portraits often reproduced paintings of elite, white Europeans by prominent artists. These engraved pictures replicated the conventions for depicting race, class, gender, and religion for a wide audience. Most considered paintings of elite white women to be best suited for private family parlors. Women had some control over their own painted portraits, but since they rarely acted as publishers and printers, they had little influence over which pictures were most visible.

Wheatley had little choice about her portrait, but she might have approved of it because it challenged social hierarchies.[8] The portrait marked her as different because most authors did not print their portraits in their books at that time; even white female authors did not regularly include their portraits until the mid-nineteenth century.[9] Wheatley's portrait aimed to convince a skeptical audience that a black woman was a refined intellectual and a virtuous woman.[10] Likely for the first time, the *Boston Gazette* called the portrait of a black woman "elegant."[11] Wheatley's elegance stands out because even antislavery pictures often reflected racist stereotypes. For example, the popular 1787 Wedgwood medallion *Am I Not a Man and Brother?* features a kneeling, half-clad enslaved man (for a version featuring a woman, see figure 3.3 on p. 57).[12] Wheatley's patrons also called her "an uncultivated Barbarian from *Africa*."[13] They worked to assure readers of Wheatley's modesty, writing that she "had no Intention" to publish her work, but she did so because of her "best, and most generous Friends; to whom she considers herself, as under the greatest obligations."[14] The portrait and book won her unprecedented visibility but also threatened any claim she might have had to feminine virtue.

Unlike Wheatley's exceptional engraving, portraits of George and Martha Washington exemplify the era's popular pictures. George's likeness often accompanied Martha's to remind viewers that he was the reason for her prominence. Joseph Hiller Sr. published mezzotints, fine and expensive prints, of the pair around 1777 (figure 1.2). *Lady Washington* may be Martha's earliest public portrait. These pictures decorated the homes of the revolution's elite supporters. To create a mezzotint, an artist covers a metal plate with thousands of tiny dots before engraving the picture. The dots produce rich tonal variations—like the folds in Martha Washington's dress—that make mezzotints look more like paintings than line drawings.

Portraits of George and Martha Washington announced gendered republican virtues that defined norms for generations.[15] Though not everyone could or wanted to achieve these idealized visions, all were measured against them. In this portrait, Martha leans against a window ledge and stands in a contrapposto pose, similar to classical statues. She is supported by elaborate columns wrapped with flowering vines that allude to her fertility, a common symbol in women's portraits.[16] The interior space and view of a domesticated landscape through the arched window contrast with the smoke billowing from the fires behind George. Martha is sheltered from war, but George must face it. Hiller copied the stance, uniform, and background from portraits of military leaders to affirm his power for colonial and European audiences alike.

After the American Revolution, American artists incorporated European visual conventions even as they sought to define their own. In 1796, seven

1.2: Joseph Hiller Sr., *Lady Washington* and *His Excellency George Washington Esqr.*, ca. 1777, mezzotints. New York Public Library.

years into Washington's presidency, Gilbert Stuart painted a portrait later copied by many engravers (figure 1.3).[17] Stuart based the composition, Washington's pose, and luxurious setting on Allan Ramsay's 1762 coronation portrait of King George III. Unlike the monarch with an ermine robe and jewels, Washington wears an elegant, plain black velvet suit.[18] Glowing light bathes George III, suggesting his divine right to rule. In contrast, Washington gestures to a gilded desk with a few books titled *American Revolution*, *Constitution of the United States*, and *Journal of Congress*. The president derives his power from his knowledge and the nation's founding documents. His authoritative pose suggests his physical strength, and his sword symbolizes his military leadership. Washington's wealth and power needed to be legible to American citizens and foreign officials.

Washington's portraits connected elite American political power to white manhood.[19] Citizens purchased printed portraits, ranging from expensive mezzotints to cheap woodcuts, to display their own republican virtue.[20] Americans associated Washington's face with his achievements and with abstract virtues like honor and sacrifice.[21] By the late eighteenth century, displaying George and Martha Washington's portraits in one's home became a component of political participation.[22]

Wheatley's portrait, in contrast, subverted visual conventions to provide evidence of black women's potential.[23] After her death in 1784,

1.3: Gilbert Stuart, portrait of George Washington, 1796, oil on canvas. National Portrait Gallery, Smithsonian Institution; acquired as a gift to the nation through the generosity of the Donald W. Reynolds Foundation.

British and American reformers adopted her portrait as an antislavery icon. Wheatley was emancipated soon after her book's publication, but, without her patrons' support, she never published another volume. In 1837, the abolitionist paper the *Liberator* praised Wheatley's "beautiful" portrait and noted that her work demonstrated "the amount of genius which slavery is murdering" (figure 1.4).[24] Her new portrait, published in the book *Memoir of Phillis Wheatley*, was a lithograph, a popular medium by the 1820s and 1830s. The black, white, and gray tones make lithographs resemble paintings, but they were inexpensive, which made them available to a broader audience.[25] In 1850, the *Anglo-African Magazine*, a monthly aimed at educated free black people, suggested that black women should have such a copy of Wheatley's portrait. They "would do well to make the head of Phillis Wheatley a study." The author appealed to the phrenology craze and analyzed Wheatley's skull to describe her character, noting her

1.4: Pendleton's Lithography, *Phillis Wheatley*, 1834, lithograph, published as the frontispiece in B. B. Thatcher, *Memoir of Phillis Wheatley, a Native African and a Slave* (1834). Courtesy of the American Antiquarian Society.

"finely formed" forehead, "large" brain, and "well set" eyes that made her face "an index of healthy intellectual powers."[26] The portrait empowered African Americans in a world that privileged white faces over black ones.

While portraits established norms for representing men and women, cartoons policed gender.[27] In 1775, Londoner Philip Dawe engraved a mezzotint in response to the news that fifty-one American women had agreed to boycott British tea.[28] Entitled *A Society of Patriotic Ladies, at Edenton in North Carolina*, the print depicts a woman leaning over the table—an unladylike stance—to sign the boycott (figure 1.5). A man whispers into the ear of a seated woman, charming her into signing the document. At the end of the table, a woman with a hook nose, double chin, and extravagant hairstyle lifts a gavel as if she were holding court. A black woman next to her, probably enslaved, holds a quill and an ink bottle. She looks eager to sign too. A standing woman drinks from a bowl filled with an alcoholic punch. Three women on the left pour out their tea canisters into receptacles held by two eager men. Men helped orchestrate the women's boycott. Along with the masculine woman ruling the gathering, they persuaded impressionable women, by means of alcohol and romance, to support the rebellion.

This mezzotint, printed in London for Loyalists throughout the Atlantic

1.5: Philip Dawe, *A Society of Patriotic Ladies, at Edenton in North Carolina*, 1775, mezzotint. Courtesy of the Library of Congress, LC-DIG-ppmsca-19468.

world, contended that the rebellion in the American colonies disrupted the natural order. When the patriarchy was under threat, slavery—and white supremacy—was too. The women's elaborate styles emphasize the decadence that had led them to prefer politics to motherhood. The neglected child under the table symbolizes the consequences of their boycott. Everyone ignores the child, except for a dog that licks the child's face and urinates on discarded tea canisters. Dawe designed several mezzotints that portrayed unruly mobs and women at the revolution's helm.[29] His expensive prints appealed to elite audiences, who most feared changes to the social hierarchy. Cartoons often caricatured specific male leaders because artists assumed the public would recognize them from their portraits. But graphic satire lampooned anonymous women, deriding them as a class to undercut their efforts.[30]

Many believed that the patriarchy needed to remain in place or the entire social hierarchy would collapse. Abigail Adams wrote to her husband, John Adams, in 1776 to "Remember the Ladies" as he helped to devise the nation's laws.[31] John feared that granting women rights would prompt social upheaval. He wrote "that Children and Apprentices were disobedient—that schools and Colledges were grown turbulent—that Indians slighted their Guardians and Negroes grew insolent to their Masters." John attempted to placate his wife by adding, "We know better than to repeal our Masculine systems. Altho they are in full Force, you know they are little more than Theory.... We are the subjects."[32]

After American independence, restrictive laws like coverture, which prevented married women from owning property and signing contracts, remained in place. Women could not vote, except in New Jersey from 1790 until 1807. Men who did not meet property requirements could not vote either.[33] Even without the ballot, men and women asserted themselves in political conversations. They signed petitions, published, and joined in political celebrations.[34] Elite white women like authors Mercy Otis Warren and Judith Sargent Murray wrote to advocate for a broader role for women, but the vote was not yet a goal. The wives of politicians, like Martha Washington and Abigail Adams, hosted gatherings to facilitate relationships and lobby in favor of their husbands' agendas.[35]

The ranks of educated women grew, especially after 1792, when Enlightenment philosopher Mary Wollstonecraft published *A Vindication of the Rights of Woman*. The book inspired conversations about women's rights on both sides of the Atlantic.[36] With better education, the British author argued that women could become men's intellectual equals and "truly useful members of society."[37] Wollstonecraft labeled fears about masculine women a "bugbear."[38]

To celebrate her ideas, *The Lady's Magazine*, published in Philadelphia, featured an allegorical engraving (figure 1.6). Americans most often encountered representations of idealized, symbolic white women, like the three women here, in their pictures.[39] They would have easily recognized the seated figure with a liberty pole as the personified Liberty. The stand-

1.6: Thackara & Vallance, *Frontispiece*, 1792, engraving, published as
the frontispiece in *Lady's Magazine and Repository of Entertaining
Knowledge* (1792), vol. 1. Courtesy of the American Antiquarian Society.

ing woman, labeled the "Genius of Emulation," holds a trumpet and laurel crown. The third woman, designated by the editors as the "Genius of the Ladies Magazine," kneels and presents Liberty with Wollstonecraft's book.[40]

The allegorical scene signaled the editors' preference for conventions. A portrait celebrating the female author would have been too transgressive. They wanted *The Lady's Magazine* to mold women into "that greatest of all treasures—a GOOD WIFE."[41] An article declared that women could write, but that overexposure threatened feminine virtues. The author concluded, "However highly we may prize her productions, we must pity the error in judgment which could engage her in pursuits repugnant to female delicacy, so derogatory to the natural character of her sex."[42] The editors valued Wollstonecraft's education plan to improve family life, but they discouraged readers from emulating her.

Wollstonecraft never published her portrait with her work, but artists still painted copies for sale. In 1797, John Opie painted her portrait when she was pregnant with her second daughter, Mary Shelley, and it became the author's most famous (figure 1.7).[43] Wollstonecraft gazes at the viewer with her face in a three-quarter view. She wears a white empire-waist gown, a fashionable silhouette. A dark headpiece covers her unpowdered brown locks. While an earlier portrait depicts her writing, nothing alludes to her work here.[44] In some ways, the portrait resembles those of polite women, but her simple dress and thoughtful expression link her to the era's male thinkers. Artists often copied this portrait for prints and later publications, and a century later, suffragist Susan B. Anthony hung a version above her desk.[45]

Wollstonecraft's fame points to a moment of tentative support for women's rights as well as the consequences of overexposure. Revelations about her life scandalized the public soon after the portrait's completion.[46] Wollstonecraft died after she gave birth in 1797. The following year, her husband, William Godwin, published *Memoirs of the Author of "A Vindication of the Rights of Woman,"* which detailed Wollstonecraft's affairs with married men, suicide attempts, and child born outside of marriage. The book featured the engraving of Opie's 1797 portrait. To many, Wollstonecraft demonstrated that public, educated, political women rejected domestic life as well as Christian values. She may have looked respectable, but the text and the public picture signaled her rebellion against accepted norms.

As Americans rejected Wollstonecraft and her ideas, they reinforced separate gender roles. By the 1830s, political parties and universal white male suffrage entrenched governing as the province of white men. Women,

1.7: In 1804, Vice President Aaron Burr, who educated his daughter
based on Wollstonecraft's principles, commissioned this copy of
Opie's second portrait for display in his home, the only known painting of the author in the United States. John Keenan, after John Opie,
oil portrait of Mary Wollstonecraft, 1804, oil on canvas. Courtesy of
the Carl H. Pforzheimer Collection of Shelley and His Circle, New York
Public Library.

especially white women from elite and middle-class backgrounds, were
most valuable as homemakers, mothers, and moral figures.[47] Since many
Americans assumed women were virtuous, enterprising women reframed
their efforts as moral ones to operate outside of formal politics. They
formed benevolent societies, promoted temperance, combatted prostitution, and won approval for their efforts to create a better society.[48]

1.8: James Akin, *A Downwright Gabbler, or A Goose That Deserves to Be Hissed*, 1829, lithograph. Courtesy of the Library of Congress, LC-USZC2-599.

Artists continued to design familiar sexist cartoons that mocked women who veered from this path. The number of skilled American artists rose, producing ever more pictures to entrench gendered norms.[49] When the British reformer Frances Wright went on a lecture tour of the United States in 1828 and 1829, she became one the first women to speak publicly to audiences composed of both men and women. She denounced slavery and organized religion, while she advocated for controversial reforms like birth control and women's rights. In 1829, James Akin published a lithograph entitled *A Downwright Gabbler, or A Goose That Deserves to Be Hissed* (figure 1.8). Wright, whose name Akin integrated into the title, is portrayed as a thoughtless "gabbler." She stands with the head of a goose, colored blue. Wearing black robes and a white shawl—a feminine version of a minister's robes—she reads in front of a table topped with candles, books, and a water glass. A man, perhaps the preacher whose place Wright occupies, stands next to her with his hand over his heart. He holds her feathered bonnet and waits for her command. By countering the patriarchy and Christianity, Wright threatened American society.

Washington, Wheatley, and Wollstonecraft were among the few women whose printed portraits circulated during their lifetimes. Representations of female authors like Wheatley and Wollstonecraft remained unusual in comparison to allegorical white women and portraits of the Washingtons. Portraits of Martha Washington demonstrate the widely accepted conventions for idealized, virtuous elite white women. Artists emphasized her virtues and support of her husband, not her own accomplishments. Wheatley and Wollstonecraft's portraits praise their work but also signal the authority of their owners, patrons, and husbands over their public image. A desire for fame, implied by the circulation of one's portrait, remained beyond the pale even for Wollstonecraft. Her overexposure and unconventional life damaged support for women's rights for decades. These portraits once marked these women as unusual, but today, displayed in elite museums, they celebrate their lives.

Gender norms established and reinforced by artists and printers in early American pictures presented a challenge for female reformers for over a century. Public portraits cemented the association between elite white men and power. Political leadership required visibility, but women were not supposed to seek it. When they did distribute their portraits to the public, they earned accusations of manliness. Cartoonists ensured that images like *A Downwright Gabbler* dominated. Gender roles were ideals rather than reality. They constantly needed reinforcement, and printed pictures proved a quick, inexpensive way to convey messages to wide audiences. Rather than rely on husbands and patrons, later women's rights advocates designed pictures to alter popular constructions of womanhood, win visibility, and secure political power. White leaders also worked to disconnect gender equality from racial equality.

As women organized in the 1840s, artists created a flood of familiar satirical cartoons in response. Technological advancements, consumer desire for illustrations, and growing numbers of trained artists and printers facilitated the beginnings of a shared visual language. The improvements that gradually made it possible for female reformers to coordinate their own public image also facilitated a barrage of negative pictures. Artists etched, publishers printed, and consumers purchased and hung popular pictures to reinforce the patriarchy.

2.1: J. Rogers after John Wollaston, *Mrs. George Washington (Martha Dandridge)*, 1855, engraving, published in Rufus Griswold, *The Republican Court, or American Society in the Days of Washington* (New York: D. Appleton, 1855), frontispiece. Emmet Collection, Miriam and Ira D. Wallach Division of Art, Prints and Photographs, New York Public Library, Astor, Lenox, and Tilden Foundations.

2: DOMINANT IMAGES OF GENDER AND POWER IN ANTEBELLUM AMERICA

While she lived, Martha Washington resisted attention, but within decades after her death, printmakers made her one of the most visible American women of the nineteenth century. In an 1855 engraving by J. Rogers, Washington stands in a lush garden (figure 2.1). She wraps her fingers around a cluster of blooms and gently pulls it toward her. Despite the gray tones, the detailed greenery suggests the garden's richness, which represents the fertility of this twenty-six-year-old mother. The picture copied British émigré John Wollaston's painting of the wealthy Virginia matron, part of a series of likenesses of her family that included her two children and first husband.[1] Wollaston's 1757 painting captured her the year of her first husband's death and just before her second marriage. She gazes with a blank expression at the viewer. Tiny, widely spaced dots emphasize the whiteness of her skin, while deeper lines and more concentrated markings define her eyebrows and lashes. She wears her wealth, symbolized by fine lace and the shine of expensive silk.

In the nineteenth century, artists often copied Wollaston's portrait of Washington. By 1855, when readers first encountered Rogers's engraving at the front of the book *The Republican Court*, few needed the identifying caption. In 1825, printers replaced copper engraving plates with steel ones. The new plates allowed them to produce tens of thousands of prints from a single plate and sell inexpensive pictures to more Americans than ever before. Portraits of the first lady and president hung on the walls of homes and filled popular books.

The features of her face mattered less than the ideas that her portrait represented. Viewers likely experienced a wave of pride upon seeing the nation's founding mother. Alongside her portrait, biographers told the story of Martha Washington, née Dandridge. Born in 1731, she grew up in one of Virginia's largest landholding families. She married her first husband, Daniel Parke Custis, at eighteen. In 1757, he died and left her with two small children, one of the largest estates in Virginia, and hundreds of enslaved people. Two years later, Martha married George Washington. Her marriage portion made him one of Virginia's richest men and fueled his rapid rise to prominence in the colony's affairs. As George Washington became a leader in the revolution, Martha Washington acquired a public persona too. In 1789, when her husband was elected president, she moved with him to New York and established the role later called first lady. The president's wife, then in her late fifties and early sixties, organized weekly levées for local elites and distinguished guests. She defined the office of the first lady as a hostess and facilitator of political discussions.[2] In 1797, after two terms in office, the couple retired to Mount Vernon, located outside the new capital of Washington, DC. Martha Washington died in 1802, three years after her husband.

At midcentury, artists, authors, editors, and publishers told the story of First Lady Martha Washington to establish her as a model for white feminine political power in the United States. She represented abstract concepts that ranged from virtue, beauty, and motherhood to wealth and loyalty. Since most imagery depicted women as allegorical figures, Martha Washington's relatively generic portraits easily referred to the ideas associated with her in texts. She served as a signal example of a woman who indirectly participated in politics by acting as a hostess for her husband's political affairs, caring for the household, and looking after children. Books like *The Republican Court* suggested that women had always had this role; women's influence on politics was an American tradition. Wives of other early presidents, such as Abigail Adams and Dolley Madison, sometimes represented similar ideals, but the number of Washington's pictures dwarfed theirs throughout the nineteenth century.[3]

As women's rights activists petitioned and organized in the 1830s and 1840s, Martha Washington represented an alternative to the reformers' direct political involvement. Opponents promoted Washington to entrench restrictive ideas of womanhood. The mostly male engravers, authors, publishers, and editors who produced circulating texts and images fought against women's rights. They composed a loose, unorganized network that warned Americans against changes in gender roles. Opponents had two main visual strategies. First, they constructed their preferred form of traditional political womanhood through portraits of respected elite white women, especially Martha Washington. Second, they distributed sexist imagery that portrayed female activists—and women in public more generally—as masculine monsters who rejected family life and threatened American values. Their messages galvanized their predominantly anti–women's rights audience to resist changes to established notions of political power.

The images published by the informal coalition of artists and editors proved more effective than the efforts of loosely organized female reformers. After years of petitions and lectures, in 1848, reformers met in Seneca Falls, New York, to call for a women's rights movement. Even so, female reformers were losing their battle to ensconce a fresh vision of gendered political power. The proliferation of influential public pictures was new, and, at first, reformers did not realize they needed such a vision. They needed to circulate visual evidence to counter widespread anxiety about masculine women, but they faced significant challenges. Women were supposed to avoid the public eye, so distributing portraits only affirmed the leaders' "manly" tendencies. When reformers looked fashionable, critics deemed them frivolous. When they dressed more simply, detractors labeled them unwomanly. At midcentury, women could not win. They did not have money, a national organization, or enough clout to challenge dominant visions of political power.

POPULAR REPRESENTATIONS OF GENDER AND POWER

By the mid-nineteenth century, Americans recognized that images could "explain" ideas in a way that words could not. In 1856, *Ballou's Pictorial Drawing-Room Companion*, an early illustrated newspaper, stated, "Pictorial representations of persons, plans, and things, are no longer regarded as mere ornaments."[4] The article continued, "No one would think of purchasing a cyclopedia that was not amply illustrated, and yet twenty-five years ago, a voluminous cyclopedia would be issued without a single explanatory engraving."[5] Between the 1840s and 1860s, illustrations became an important part of everyday life. Americans encountered images in everything from newspapers and advertisements to books and broadsides. The visual shift resulted from the increased demand for pictures, the emergence of new image mediums, and the lower costs of industrialized production and distribution. Popular pictures constructed and reinforced social structures for the masses.

Ballou's Pictorial Drawing-Room Companion represents the rise of weekly illustrated newspapers in the 1840s and 1850s. Pictorial papers favored illustrations over text. They featured pictures of current events, political cartoons, illustrated stories, and instructive engravings of novel technology and faraway places. The weekly *Illustrated London News*, first printed in 1842, became a model for American papers.[6] Some penny press newspapers featured engravings in the mid-1830s, but daily newspapers rarely printed time-consuming, expensive illustrations until the 1870s.[7] Newspapers relied on engravings because they were the cheapest and easiest type of image to reproduce.[8] The stereotyping process allowed printers to impress images and text together on a single metal plate, which increased the number of uses a printer could get out of a single image.[9] Americans subscribed to pictorial periodicals just like their text-based counterparts. City dwellers bought them from newsboys and stores. Some viewers never purchased them; instead, they borrowed papers from friends and neighbors or encountered them in parlors, coffeehouses, clubs, or saloons, where discussing them was a group activity.[10]

In comparison to earlier decades when few could buy expensive prints, by midcentury many Americans could afford to adorn their parlors with them. In 1855, *Ballou's Pictorial Drawing-Room Companion* proclaimed that it had over 100,000 subscribers, even more than the *Illustrated London News*.[11] That year, *Frank Leslie's Illustrated Newspaper*, and, two years later, its main competitor, *Harper's Weekly*, came out. The two papers pushed *Ballou's* out of business and dominated the illustrated press through the end of the century. Publishing, printing, and manufacturing became concentrated in New York, Philadelphia, and Boston. Printers increased efficiency and began to use paper made of cheap wood pulp instead of cotton rag.[12] The number of lithography firms grew fivefold from 1850 to 1860.[13] Printers had steam-powered lithographic presses that increased the number of prints they produced per hour, from twelve to almost one thousand.[14] Urbanites purchased prints—engravings, lithographs, and eventually photographs—in local print shops and galleries, while their rural counterparts ordered them through catalogs and itinerant salesmen. Improvements in transportation and the postal service (including decreased postage prices) made prints more accessible too.[15] Chromolithographs, colorful lithographs made with layers of ink, became widespread by the 1840s.[16]

Americans learned to read pictures as they encountered more of them. A viewer did not have to be literate to see the picture, understand the message, and discuss it. Images required a visual literacy that involved recognition of popular figures, symbols, and local and national discussions. Early illustrated newspapers offered instructions to help readers pick up on cues. Their articles reveal the enduring interest in physiognomy (reading a person's character by examining her face) and a growing attention to phrenology (interpreting one's character based on the contours of the skull).[17] An 1856 article in *Ballou's Pictorial Drawing-Room Companion*, for example, emphasized that popular portraits of George Washington "serve a better purpose than the gratification of mere idle curiosity." Instead, "the contemplation of those mild and benignant, yet dignified and firm features, keep up a conception of the character of the Father of his country."[18] The *Anglo-African Magazine*, a short-lived monthly aimed at educated free black people, agreed. The author of an 1859 article wrote that a picture, when "looked at, calls up associations, emotions, and produces troops of thought that paint the memory afresh with hues the most beautiful, touching, beneficial, and lasting."[19] Washington's portrait "recalls to mind the American Revolution, and the early history of the Republic," while Thomas Jefferson's reminded viewers of the Declaration of Independence. Even in papers aimed at black audiences, pictures linked white men and political power.

Pictures provided face-to-face encounters in an increasingly mobile and geographically diffuse world. In 1856, *Frank Leslie's Illustrated Newspaper* covered its first presidential election and the bitter contest over the future of slavery. Their July 12, 1856, issue printed six portraits: three candidates for president and three for vice president. On the front page, above a portrait of Millard Fillmore, an author noted that few voters saw the candidates in person, yet a natural desire existed "to see the men upon whom we set a high estimate." So *Frank Leslie's* aimed to fulfill this public good and "make their faces familiar from the Atlantic to the Pacific shore." The author added that the pictures answered an oft-asked question: "Are we, as a people, handsome?" He wrote, "If the personal appearance of presidential candidates is to be taken as a criterion ... then we have cause for self-congratulation; for we believe that it would be difficult to bring together six better made, or, generally, more attractive looking men."[20]

Presidents represented the nation, and *Frank Leslie's* portraits influenced impressions of the candidates. Although the issue did not explicitly endorse a candidate, the newspaper implicitly supported former president Millard Fillmore. Writers described him with the warmest words because, they argued, he offered an alternative to sectionalism (figure 2.2). Wreaths surround all of the candidates, but Fillmore's features a bald eagle, wings outstretched, proffering a laurel victory garland. Oak leaves and acorns suggest the prosperity of his past and future presidencies, especially in comparison to the foreboding dark, knotted branches that surround John Frémont's face. The portraits represent the conventions for depicting political power. All six men appear in three-quarter view, not profile and not the full face, and look into the distance. They wear fine clothes, but the likenesses emphasize their faces, not their fashions. The caption under each states that artists copied ambrotypes, an early form of photograph, by the famous photographer Mathew Brady. The note deemed the portraits faithful representations by which readers could judge these men.

George Bingham's painting and subsequent engraved print *The County Election, 1852* similarly linked political participation to white manhood

2.2: *Millard Fillmore, American Candidate for President.—Ambrotyped by Brady*, 1856, engraving, published in *Frank Leslie's Illustrated Newspaper*, July 12, 1856, page 72. Courtesy of the American Antiquarian Society.

(figure 2.3).[21] A country town with some two-story buildings, a church steeple, and a few horses galloping through the streets creates the backdrop. White men of all classes congregate around a porch to vote. Farmers in wide-brimmed hats interact with the political candidates wearing sleek black top hats. An African American man appears in the margins. He pours what is likely an alcoholic beverage, perhaps hard cider, into the cup of a plump man who appears to have had too many already. A well-dressed man in the center, presumably a candidate, props up a man so he can vote,

2.3: John Sartain after George Bingham, *County Election*, 1854, engraving. Courtesy of the American Antiquarian Society.

even though he is too unwell—or drunk—to stand. Another man seated on the right with a bandaged head conveys the potential for violence in this passionate, inebriated crowd. Young boys play in the foreground, soaking up the political process in which they will participate soon.

By the time Bingham completed his painting, antislavery activists and women's rights supporters were attacking his vision of political life, and Americans feared it might disappear. The image obscures these anxious debates. Though the print probably angered teetotalers, the romanticized scene might have appeared idyllic and amusing to many Americans in the 1850s. The lack of women and the marginalization of the African American man reinforce their lack of political power.

In contrast to popular pictures of powerful male leaders and voters, images linked white women with beauty, virtue, motherhood, and domesticity. As in earlier eras, female symbols (such as Columbia, Liberty, or Justice), religious figures, and fictional characters remained popular. Visually, women's lack of power was most often defined by their absence and anonymity. Publishers had few reasons to sell the portraits of individual, unknown women. Many white middle-class Americans prized women as wives and homemakers rather than as politicians. Piety, purity, submissiveness, and domesticity characterized this type of True Womanhood.[22] Men and women might not achieve these ideals, but they constantly engaged with them.

Popular pictures, such as those in *Godey's Lady's Book*, often idolized anonymous white women as beautiful, domestic figures. For four decades starting in 1837, Sarah Josepha Hale edited the magazine for middle-class white female readers. The publication featured fashions, sewing patterns, stories, and editorials and had the highest circulation rate of any magazine before the Civil War.[23] In an engraved fashion plate from 1850, called *Mutual Admiration*, two women show off dress styles (figure 2.4).[24] A fan in one hand, a standing woman holds the hand of a seated woman, signifying their close friendship. The woman on the left wears a gown with a tiered, embellished skirt and fashionable hairstyle. The other woman wears a plainer dress with a bonnet and muff. Their demure expressions imply the pleasantries they are exchanging in the plush parlor. While *Frank Leslie's* hinted that the presidential candidates were considering the nation's future, the women in *Godey's* look away from the viewer to suggest their modesty.[25] Given the money required for this lifestyle, working women and women of color could only hope to achieve this ideal and the respectability associated with it.

Most women did not publish their portraits because they believed they should embrace domesticity rather than publicity. Americans wondered: should a woman ever want her face inked on a well-worn piece of paper passing through unknown hands? At midcentury, women with famous faces were often actresses or singers. Jenny Lind, the "Swedish Nightingale," toured America with P. T. Barnum in the early 1850s. Portraits of Lind circulated widely and often represented her with her eyes demurely averted, wearing conservative dresses, and with her hands folded in her lap.[26] Even though she won fame for her talent, she (along with Barnum, who excelled at garnering public interest) wanted to remind audiences of *Godey's* idealized women. One gift book depicts her returning home to her husband and children, which likely allayed concerns about her status as a public woman.[27]

Besides female performers, Americans often encountered pictures of Queen Victoria, who ruled Britain beginning in 1837. Like representations of queens before her, Queen Victoria's portraits combined representations of masculine power with feminine symbols to emphasize her majesty, elegance, and command.[28] She wore fashionable attire and posed in domestic settings as a devoted mother with her children.[29] But the queen—like any political leader—endured public scrutiny, and political cartoonists

2.4: *Mutual Admiration—Godey's Fashion Plate for the Month*, 1850, engraving, published in *Godey's Lady's Book*, February 1850, page 154. Courtesy of the American Antiquarian Society.

2.5: Alfred Hoffy, *Ellen Jewett*, 1836, lithograph. Courtesy of the American Antiquarian Society.

mocked her too.[30] Since European and American society did not prize women in the public eye, women like Queen Victoria and Jenny Lind occupied complicated places. They balanced representations of their work with depictions of themselves as virtuous women.

Women avoided circulating their portraits because public women were most often associated with prostitution, not political power.[31] Helen Jewett, a prostitute murdered in New York in 1836, became the subject of numerous images in the flash press, newspapers aimed at men that covered everything from sports and crime to prostitution. Erotic pictures of prostitutes and lower-class women perceived as sexually available covered the pages. They provide examples of how respectable women did not want to appear.[32] Alfred Hoffy designed a print of Jewett's murder in the style of flash press pictures. The caption notes that the lithograph reveals "a correct likeness & representation of this unfortunate female" (figure 2.5).[33] Jewett lies among her burned bedclothes that strategically hide and expose. Titillating rather than tragic, her round breasts peek out above the blanket that covers the rest of her torso and reveals her legs. Pictures of Jewett remained popular for over a decade after her death. Advertisements featured an engraving of her face and breasts, all encircled by a snake—a common depiction of the devil from the biblical story of the fall of man.[34]

While prostitutes were objects of sexual desire, women who performed

2.6: Portrait of Madame Restell, 1847, engraving, published in *Wonderful Trial of Caroline Lohman, Alias Restell* (3rd ed., 1847), opposite page 38. Courtesy of the National Library of Medicine.

abortions became associated with evil. In 1847, an engraving—an "allegorical of the 'Female Abortionist'"—depicted Madame Restell, a woman put on trial in New York (figure 2.6). The portrait appeared in the *National Police Gazette*, a popular weekly that reported on crime and scandals, and in publications of her trial.[35] Restell's torso rises above a winged demon whose fangs crush a limp baby. She looks away from the viewer with a defiant expression. She also resists the day's fashions. The accompanying text noted that the demon was "a device which the genius of our artist has selected as typical of her infernal mystery." The "mystery" was how a woman in a society that prized motherhood could facilitate abortions. Restell was "a fiend" whose "name [was] never mentioned without a curse."[36]

Mid-nineteenth-century popular pictures facilitated the spread of a shared national visual language that signaled social and political hierarchies. Images standardized stereotypes based on identities like gender, race, class, religion, ethnicity, and locale. They became shorthand for a range of ideas, and Americans quickly learned to interpret them with only a caption or no accompanying text at all. Illustrations connected white men with political power and virtuous white women with idealized femininity. As illustrations of Helen Jewett and Madame Restell demonstrated, public women who did not embody these ideals faced consequences.

LAMPOONING POLITICAL WOMEN

Female reformers faced an impossible task as they advocated for rights and aimed to maintain a high social standing. Women who had the means to live up to ideal femininity, but chose not to, prompted anxiety. Ultimately, one of the main tasks of the women's rights movement was to justify their steps outside accepted gender roles and, eventually, change these roles. But without power, money, or organizational strength, activists could not change the way Americans conceived of political women. Cartoons that derided reformers proliferated during the years after the Seneca Falls Convention. Almost a century after the 1775 cartoon of tea boycotters (figure 1.5 on p. 17), artists continued the tradition of representing political women as ugly, masculine threats to American values, including gender norms, white supremacy, and heteronormativity.

The women's rights movement grew out of women's activism on behalf of other people. In the 1830s, women, especially white middle- and upper-class women, participated in and led antislavery and moral reform societies.[37] They signed petitions, raised money, and read the *Liberator*. Abby Kelley Foster, the Grimké sisters, and Lucy Stone traveled the country to deliver public lectures.[38] Rather than leading organizations, they hoped to leave behind towns of supporters who organized on their own.[39] By the end of the decade, their outspokenness angered even their fellow antislavery supporters. In 1840, the World's Anti-Slavery Convention in London, for example, refused to seat female attendees.[40] Discussions of women's rights were part of local conversations years before women brought them to the national stage. In 1844, a group of men in New Jersey petitioned the state constitutional convention to grant women the vote.[41] Two years later, three groups petitioned the New York constitutional convention to enfranchise women.[42] One, a group of women from Jefferson County, asked for more than the ballot. They wanted "to extend to women equal, civil and political rights with men."[43]

In July 1848, about three hundred people, including prominent abolitionists Lucretia Mott and Frederick Douglass, met in Seneca Falls, New York. They sparked national conversations about women's rights and set an agenda. At the end of the two days of proceedings, one hundred attendees signed a statement of their aims, the Declaration of Sentiments.[44] The main author was Elizabeth Cady Stanton, a thirty-two-year-old highly educated mother. In the manner of the Declaration of Independence, her Declaration of Sentiments affirmed that "all men and women are created equal." Attendees called for rights ranging from women's education and employment opportunities to the right to own property and control their money. Reformers included the right to the ballot, which they viewed as a tool to gain other rights and enact temperance and antislavery laws. In 1851, the attendees of the convention in Worcester, Massachusetts, resolved that "the Right of Suffrage for Women is, in our opinion, the corner-stone of this enterprise, since we do not seek to protect women, but rather to place her in a position to protect herself."[45] They addressed their opponents' arguments, which contended that fathers, husbands, and sons represented their female counterparts.

Unlike petitions to local governments, the Declaration of Sentiments established specific goals to launch a movement. Stanton's document asserted, "We shall employ agents, circulate tracts, petition the State and national Legislatures, and endeavor to enlist the pulpit and the press in our behalf." They wanted their meeting to prompt "a series of Conventions, embracing every part of the country."[46] Between 1848 and 1860, they held national conventions every year (except in 1857).[47] Organizers concentrated their national meetings in the Northeast and Midwest, but local groups held gatherings throughout the United States.

Public calls for women's rights prompted a backlash. Artists, editors, and publishers seized upon fears of political women and produced a powerful new wave of cartoons to caricature them.[48] They policed gender roles and undercut reformers. In 1849, David Claypoole Johnston, a popular engraver based in Boston, published a page of five scenes in his periodical, *Scraps* (figure 2.7).[49] His cartoons exemplify the negative press that plagued activists. One of the pictures on the top right, *Women's Tonsorial Rights*, depicts a

2.7: David Claypoole Johnston, detail from *Women's Rights*, 1849, engravings, published in *Scraps* (1849), page 2. Courtesy of the American Antiquarian Society.

woman about to be shaved in a barbershop. To her right, a woman stands in an unladylike manner with her hands in her coat pockets and a cane propped against her chair. Another female customer reads the *Woman's Rights Advocate* newspaper as she sits with her feet up on a chair. On the left, a woman shaves her face. The scene recalls pictures of barbershops filled with men, with their hats and canes set aside, socializing as they are shaved.[50] Even the picture hanging on the wall depicts female boxers. Johnston's other images reveal that these scandalous women might feel empowered to propose marriage and smoke in public. He suggested that women would become like men physically and usurp men's separate spaces and rites if they gained rights.

Artists and editors presented the movement as a ridiculous threat to established values. Similar to Johnston, in August 1851, *Harper's New Monthly Magazine*, aimed at an educated Northern audience, combined several of these sexist tropes into their engraving called *Woman's Emancipation* (figure 2.8). The illustration depicts six women wearing bloomer styles

2.8: *Woman's Emancipation*, 1851, engraving, published in *Harper's New Monthly Magazine*, August 1851, page 424. Courtesy of the American Antiquarian Society.

with top hats or bonnets, carrying canes, and smoking. The bloomers have short skirts, much shorter than those actually worn, and one woman on the right pulls up her pant leg, boldly revealing an ankle. Another woman on the left wears a bulky overcoat with her hands in her pocket in a relaxed, masculine stance. The only man in the picture wears a broad-brimmed hat and holds a whip, an allusion to true manhood. He turned his back to the women and rides away hauling a cart; perhaps he is a farmer who has just finished his dealings in town. He is leaving the city with its "emancipated" women for a more traditional rural community. Two of the women link arms, perhaps a suggestion of their preference for female partners, and watch him go.

An accompanying satirical letter underscores the idea that political women challenge values ranging from gender norms to heteronormativity. The letter, supposedly written by the "strong-minded American woman" Bostonian Theodosia Bang, declared that women were emancipating themselves from the "feudal" systems, symbolized by the term "Lady," and from traditional "European" clothing. Bang continued, "The American female delivers lectures, edits newspapers, and similar organs of opinion" so that the "degrading cares of the household are comparatively unknown to our sex."[51] Emancipated women were distinctly American, and the fictional character announced that she planned to proclaim these ideas in Europe next.

Artists, editors, and publishers expected audiences to laugh at these women. Without context, to twenty-first-century eyes, pictures of women living nontraditional lives might suggest that *Harper's New Monthly Magazine* supported women's rights. Today, Americans regularly see images of women smoking, wearing pants, and taking part in same-sex relationships. However, knowledge of the era's visual context makes the ridicule apparent. Neither cartoon represents the reformers as respectable women. *Scraps* was a comic publication, and the satirical letter in *Harper's Weekly*'s clarified the picture's message. Women's rights supporters were easy targets and subjects for entertainment since most Americans opposed their cause.

In their pictures, artists stressed that gender equality would lead to racial equality. Pictures most often lampooned the white women who tended to hold the most visible positions. However, some artists noticed the emergence of black female reformers, such as Maria Stewart, Sojourner Truth, and Harriet Forten Purvis and her sister Margaretta Forten. One print, published in 1851 in New York City, was part of a satirical series that featured multiple plates about women's rights and dress reform (figure 2.9).[52] This lithograph, entitled *Bloomerism in Practice: The Morning after the Victory*, depicts two smiling bloomer-clad reformers. The white woman, wearing a knife, holds a sign that says "NO MORE BASEMENT AND KITCHEN!" with a fork at the top of the pole. The black woman's sign reads "NO MORE MASSA & MISSUS." It implies that if white women abandon their domestic work, then black women will resist enslavement and oppression too. These women are eager to fight for Mrs. Turkey, seated in the center, to become president. Her name, the turban, and the water pipe reference a popular alternate name for bloomers: "Turkish dress." This female politician abandoned her child, who wants his breakfast. Mrs. Turkey pets her husband, who hunches over like an old woman and mends his coat. Society praised women for their domestic tasks, but the same chores degraded men. An earlier plate in the series notes that he wears bloomers too, per his wife's orders.[53] *Bloomerism* was more than a fashion, the cartoons said; it was dangerous.

By 1851, Americans had encountered images like these for almost a century. Images *showed* audiences a future that many feared. If women won rights, then black women would as well. One shift in the hierarchy would endanger the entire social and economic system. Women's rights even

2.9: Adam Weingärtner, *Bloomerism in Practice*, published in *Humbug's American Museum Series* (1851), plate 17. Courtesy of the Boston Public Library Print Department.

threatened to tip the balance in debates about slavery and white supremacy. Since Americans conceived of political power as masculine, manly women's rights activists fit established visual conventions. To maintain a balance, men, opponents posited, would need to become feminine, take on more domestic responsibilities, and heed their wives' orders. Rather than create fresh commentary, artists relied on familiar visual tropes to keep women in their place.

In 1845, thinker Margaret Fuller bemoaned cartoons like these in *Woman in the Nineteenth Century*. The transcendentalist book rejected the dominant gender norms. Fuller observed that opponents contended that if women became political, "The beauty of the home would be destroyed, the delicacy of the sex would be violated, the dignity of the halls of legislation degraded." This fear, Fuller argued, resulted in the "ludicrous pictures of ladies in hysterics at the polls, and senate chambers filled with cradles."[54] In response, she countered that "woman can express publicly the fulness [*sic*] of thought and creation, without losing any of the particular beauty of her sex."[55] Unfortunately, reformers lacked any power to prove Fuller's point.

Fuller knew that graphic satire damaged impressions of female reformers. Pictures most often disparaged women as a class, but sometimes they lampooned specific reformers. Even before listeners went to see Lucy Stone lecture, they had a negative stereotype of her in mind. Stone encountered angry audiences when she started lecturing in 1847. Once, a man with a club protected her from an unruly crowd, but other times the audience launched eggs, spitballs, and even a hymnal at her.[56] Crowds disliked her message, but they also disliked the messenger. An 1853 engraving in the *Illustrated News* (a short-lived publication by showman P. T. Barnum), supposedly copied a photograph by Mathew Brady. Stone appears in bloomers, short hair, and a frumpy jacket, reinforcing the idea that she appeared masculine.[57] Two years later, *Ballou's Pictorial Drawing-Room Companion* commented, "Lucy Stone is lecturing on the subject of woman's rights in Michigan. Her appearance is said to be quite manly."[58] In response to criticisms like these, reverend and women's rights supporter Thomas Wentworth Higginson wrote in a suffrage tract, "Lucy Stone said, 'woman's nature is stamped and sealed by her Creator, and there is no danger of her unsexing herself, while his eye watches her.'"[59]

Popular pictures criticized women who wore bloomers, but they also made fun of women who wore fashionable dresses, suggesting they were incapable of rational thought.[60] Clothes served as a visual signifier for gender, class, occupation, and country of origin.[61] In the early 1850s, American women increased the circumference of their skirts by adding layers

MR. JONES, BY HOOKING HIS UMBRELLA ROUND THE LAMP-POST, ATTEMPTS TO SHAKE HANDS WITH MISS PHIPPS, BUT DOESN'T DO IT

2.10: *Mr. Jones, by Hooking His Umbrella round the Lamp-Post, Attempts to Shake Hands with Mrs. Phipps, but Doesn't Do It*, 1857, engraving, published in *Frank Leslie's Illustrated Newspaper*, January 10, 1857, page 92. Courtesy of the American Antiquarian Society.

of heavy petticoats. European fashions often influenced American styles, and magazines like *Godey's Lady's Book* kept moneyed women aware of the latest styles.[62] The tightest corsets and most voluminous skirts signified a woman's elite social status. Farming, domestic and factory work, exercise, and travel were challenging in such clothing. Even Southern slaveholders invested in dresses and petticoats for enslaved women, though trousers would have kept them safer as they tended kitchen fires.[63]

Popular pictures reveal that fashionable women provided as much entertainment as women in bloomers did. In 1856, the introduction of the crinoline, a skeletal undergarment resembling a cage, made skirts even wider.[64] *Frank Leslie's Illustrated Newspaper*, priced at six cents, included scores of images between 1857 and 1864 that mocked the crinoline (and more ridiculing other women's fashions). In an 1857 engraving, a man wraps his umbrella around a lamppost in an attempt to shake hands with a woman wearing an expansive, tiered skirt (figure 2.10). Her dress separates her from the man and, implicitly, from society. On the right, a man looks at the scene in disbelief. His reaction may suggest the dismay that some Americans felt about women's fashions. She cannot participate in an activity as mundane as greeting passersby. Some engravings mocked women who attempted to garden in crinolines, while others joked that women in crinolines would blow away like hot-air balloons.[65]

Nick-Nax for All Creation, an inexpensive comic monthly, printed a nearly identical version of this illustration a month later.[66] Publishers shared engraving plates to keep costs low. *Nick-Nax* changed the caption to tell a story of a man meeting his betrothed after his long absence.[67] Later that year, the paper published a poem that put the cartoon's message into words. The lines alerted readers: "For be sure that your dresses the wider they get, The more narrow the mind they disclose."[68] Such pictures amused Americans throughout the nation. While *Nick-Nax for All Creation* was printed in New York, responses to puzzles indicated they had readers from Canada, Florida, Santa Fe, and Cape Cod.[69]

In 1851, Lucy Stone, Elizabeth Cady Stanton, and Susan B. Anthony donned bloomers to signal their rejection of dominant gender norms.[70] Stanton contended that "woman is terribly cramped and crippled in her present style of dress."[71] Some utopian societies in the United States had already adopted pants for women to enhance their ability to contribute, but governments across the country passed laws against cross-dressing in the 1850s.[72] The outfit implicitly argued that elite white women wanted more than to act as decorative representatives of family wealth. Women could wear trousers and loose-fitting clothes while performing domestic chores, but wearing the outfits in public threatened the men whose needs trousers were designed to meet.[73] Trousers, still relatively new, symbolized democratic, capitalist progress, and women could not participate equally.[74]

Bloomers put women's bodies on public display and challenged feminine values like modesty.[75] The mainstream press dismissed bloomers, and they became a symbol of the reformers' unwomanly nature.[76] *Nick-Nax for All Creation* featured a picture titled *The Attractive Points of a Woman's Rights Lecture*, which showed the outline of a woman's legs, clad in bloomers.[77] An 1856 article in *Frank Leslie's Ladies' Gazette* called "hideous" bloomers "an outrage" that prompted "a common laugh of derision." The costume supposedly dated back to the French Revolution, when the "fashion of the male for one month was frequently adopted for the mode of female for the next." This "extravagance"—the flexibility of the visual signifiers of gender—would culminate in revolution.[78] Activists later recalled that opponents associated bloomers with unpopular ideas, such as "free love," "easy divorce," "strong-minded[ness]," and "amalgamation" of the races.[79]

Public disapproval prompted activists to wear dresses again. After just under two years of ridicule, Stanton abandoned the costume in 1853 and convinced others to do the same "for the sake of the cause." She believed that "physical freedom" was less important than "mental bondage."[80] In 1855, Stanton publicly defended her stance in response to fellow women's rights reformer (and Stanton's cousin) Gerrit Smith, who argued that if women wore masculine clothes, man "would confess her transmutation into his equal."[81] In an 1857 letter to the Reform Dress Association, Smith said that female activists "in their hoops and jewelry" reminded him "of pictures I have seen of amateur lady farmers, raking hay in the whitest gloves, and feeding pigs in flounces and furbelows."[82] Stanton retorted, "Dress is a matter of taste, of fashion ... but institutions, supported by laws, can be overturned but by revolution." Women "have no reason to hope that pantaloons would do more for us than they have done for man himself." Men had not won rights simply by donning pants. Wearing dresses, which Stanton called "a badge of degradation," would nevertheless help reformers secure more support.[83]

By 1865, American imagery had successfully connected women's dresses with a lack of power. Jefferson Davis, the president of the Confederacy, became a laughingstock when artists depicted him in a crinoline. Cartes de visite, lithographed prints, and illustrated papers portrayed Davis disguised in his wife's dress when the United States captured him after the Civil War. One comic monthly, *Phunny Phellow*, generally oriented toward a Northern audience, printed an engraving of his arrest in July 1865 (figure 2.11).[84] Two soldiers capture Davis, whose skirt is tipped up to confirm that he wears a crinoline over a pair of trousers.[85] Davis accuses them of arresting a harmless woman, but his boots and disheveled skirt assure the soldiers they have the right man. Publishers knew audiences would find a man in women's clothes amusing, but they also saw an opportunity to depict Davis as dishonorable and powerless. Davis's defenders denied that their leader had ever worn a dress.[86]

Whether the women were in bloomers or crinolines, editors and artists mocked them in popular pictures to reflect and reinforce gender norms and American values. Authors, editors, artists, publishers, and printers— often men—controlled visual content. They used images to argue that women should not participate in politics.[87] Americans who opposed women's rights—the majority of the population—bought these sexist images and, implicitly, their ideas about women. Only an elite few activists wrote and read works on the intricacies of political reforms, but these pictures were part of popular conversations.

2.11: *The Capture of Jeff. Davis of the C.S.A.*, 1865, engraving, published in *Phunny Phellow*, July 1865, page 1. Courtesy of the American Antiquarian Society.

MARTHA WASHINGTON: A MODEL OF TRADITIONAL POLITICAL WOMANHOOD

Cartoons presented a future most Americans wished to avoid, but portraits of Martha Washington provided an idealized vision of a past that many wanted to revive. Washington stood as a model for women's indirect political participation as good wives, hostesses, and mothers. From the antebellum period through the revolution's centennial in 1876, her portraits and biographies emphasized her performance of these roles. Opponents of women's rights turned her into an icon, an alternative to the vision advanced by reformers.[88]

As with her husband, books that featured Martha Washington's portrait articulated the ideas that became associated with her face. Rufus Griswold, a prolific author and editor, articulated his vision of traditional political womanhood in *The Republican Court, or American Society in the Days of Washington*. The book, published in 1855 and reprinted seven times through 1867, discussed the elite men and women who, like their counterparts in European royal courts, had political and social prominence.[89] Griswold argued, "Nothing would have a more happy influence on the politics of this day ... than a study of the private and public characters and actions of those who founded our constitution."[90] He yearned for the founding era, when men were public figures and women participated behind the scenes.

Griswold promoted Washington as a female ideal that would have this "happy influence" on politics. Upon opening his book's elegant cover, the reader encountered Washington's engraved portrait (figure 2.1 on p. 24). Washington was in her late fifties by the time she became first lady, but this engraving, like many others from that era, depicted her as a young woman. All of the pictures in Griswold's book portrayed the wives of prominent men as youthful beauties. Their portraits decorated a text that largely detailed their husbands' accomplishments. Beauty helped women provide pleasant company and support for their husband's political ventures.

The Republican Court argued that indirect political participation did not affect the charms of America's founding mothers. Griswold wrote, "Women unhesitatingly evinced their sympathies with whatever was generous and honorable in public conduct, but rarely if ever in forgetfulness of the requirements of feminine propriety." Washington topped the list of ideal political women who, Griswold wrote in the final lines of his book, "had no desire, as Montaigne expresses it, 'to cover their beauties under others that were none of theirs.'"[91] Rather than coveting men's rights, these women embraced their feminine nature. Montaigne, a French writer, referred to women's positive attributes as "beauties" instead of acknowledging women's intellectual capacity. Women who embraced Griswold's vision of femininity earned the attentions of men who politically represented them. In contrast, the author called women's rights activists "shameless females" and "curious monsters."[92] They did not desire "delicacy and grace" or to be "women worthy of men."[93]

Smaller, cheaper gift books promoted Washington as an ideal for more diverse audiences. Families displayed these annual volumes in their parlors and, as the name of this genre suggests, frequently gifted these publications.[94] Gift books included illustrations as well as short stories, poems, and essays penned by popular female authors. In 1851 and 1852, the gift book *The Golden Keepsake* featured its own frontispiece engraving of Washington based on Wollaston's portrait. The editor, Mrs. S. T. Martyn, wrote a piece titled "What Constitutes a Lady?" and upheld Washington, the English evangelical Christian writer Hannah More, and the English prison reformer Elizabeth Fry as "models of excellence for all coming gen-

2.12: Alexander Hay Ritchie, *Lady Washington's Reception*, 1865, engraving. Courtesy of the American Antiquarian Society.

erations."[95] Like Griswold, she warned against "masculine women," whom she considered "nature's worst anomalies."[96]

Popular prints reinforced Washington's iconic status and illustrated her hostess skills. An 1865 engraving entitled *Lady Washington's Reception* depicts her as a hostess and first lady, a mother to the nation, during one of her levées (figure 2.12). In 1861, Alexander Ritchie commissioned Daniel Huntington for this painting, and Ritchie engraved a plate based on the canvas.[97] The print features a crowd of founding figures wearing elegant clothes in a lavishly decorated room. The classical ornamentation—including the Corinthian columns and marble statues—references styles popular during the earliest republican experiments in Greece and Rome. An accompanying pamphlet references Griswold's *The Republican Court* and includes a key to identify the figures.[98] George Washington speaks to a young Harriet Chew (a socialite from a wealthy Philadelphia family), while Thomas Jefferson stands next to future first lady Dolley Payne (who married James Madison).

On a platform to the left, a queenly Martha Washington wears an extravagant dress that draws the viewer's attention. Closer to the center of the scene, the president—clad in a dark suit—mills among the people. He stands in a pose resembling that of Gilbert Stuart's Lansdowne portrait (figure 1.3 on p. 15) as he introduces his wife to the crowd. Martha Washington presides over her court. Unlike portraits of her as a young mother or grandmotherly founding mother, Ritchie's portrait depicts her with an air of poise and feminine power. Washington's idealized facial features, white hair, and veiled cap give her a matronly yet commanding presence. Portraiture of Queen Victoria likely provided a model for Washington's depiction. Since her contemporaries scrutinized the administration for monarchical leanings, no image from life shows Washington with such obvious references to monarchical power because she discouraged it.[99] Ritchie's print cost between fifteen dollars for a "plain" print and fifty dollars for an artist's proof, but cheaper imitations abounded, and the scene became iconic.[100] Through the nation's centennial in 1876, women wore early nineteenth-century costumes to replicate this scene for their own receptions.[101]

Washington's portraits made her one of the most visible American women during the nineteenth century. Her pictures presented a lasting vision of femininity and demonstrate the acceptable conventions for representing respectable women in American visual culture. Portraits depict Washington as a beautiful young mother, a prestigious founding mother, and a powerful republican queen. A respectable woman needed to be elite, white, beautiful, and eager to support her husband and family. Opponents of women's rights applied a lot of ink to print Washington's portraits and praises to encourage women to emulate the first lady.

LESSONS LEARNED

Cartoons and portraits of idealized women dominated American imagery and established strong visual arguments to resist the advances of female reformers. Straying from these visual conventions signaled women's rejection of popular norms. Washington became an icon after her death, which protected her from accusations of ambition or neglect of domestic duties. Living female reformers faced a difficult choice. They could attempt to bridge the public-private divide by selling copies of their portraits, but this act only confirmed that they eschewed private domesticity. Public images, like public speaking, exposed women to untold onlookers. On the other hand, not publicizing their faces allowed opponents to depict them any way they pleased.

During the 1840s and 1850s, women's rights activists made few attempts to counter negative pictures. They distributed some portraits that presented their vision for female leadership. In 1857, Leopold Grozelier designed a lithograph with seven oval portraits of prominent female antislavery and women's rights activists (figure 2.13). Punningly entitled *Representative Women*, the print depicts exceptional, not typical, women.

2.13: Leopold Grozelier, *Representative Women*, 1857, lithograph. Sophia
Smith Collection, Smith College.

At midcentury, they were among the few well-known American women.
Harriet Beecher Stowe, Abby Kelley Foster, Lucy Stone, Lydia Maria Child,
Antoinette Brown Blackwell, and Maria Weston Chapman form a circle
around the central portrait of Lucretia Mott.[102] Four of the seven women
avert their eyes in a show of modesty. Stowe (the author of *Uncle Tom's
Cabin*), Blackwell (the first ordained female minister), and Mott (a prominent reformer), however, stare straight ahead, engaging the viewer. The
stray curls dangling in Stowe's portrait give her the frazzled air of an artist,
and her cross necklace reminds the viewer she is the daughter of promi-

nent minister Lyman Beecher. Blackwell wears a feminine lacy collar and small brooch, but still appears commanding. With her simple Quaker clothing, Mott looks determined. The choice made by these women to publicize their likenesses challenged social norms.

Representative Women paralleled Grozelier's lithograph of male reformers that included William Lloyd Garrison, Ralph Waldo Emerson, Theodore Parker, and Gerrit Smith.[103] The title referred to a series of Emerson's lectures from 1850. In *Representative Men*, Emerson contemplated great men such as Shakespeare and Napoleon, and wrote, "Men have a pictorial or representative quality, and serve us in the intellect.... Men are also representative; first, of things, and secondly, of ideas."[104] Like others in this era, Emerson argued that portraits of exceptional individuals served to remind viewers of their ideas. As in his print *Representative Men*, Grozelier featured extraordinary women whose portraits were supposed to remind viewers of their own contributions.

Popular pictures designed and distributed mostly by men deemed women, whether in bloomers or crinolines, unsuitable for politics. Since women's rights activists exerted little control over their public image, they left their movement vulnerable to the destructive pictures that circulated far beyond the chapels where they lectured. Made possible by new technology and consumer desire, the barrage of pictures that derided activists and crinoline-clad women formed models of femininity that wielded power that Americans were only beginning to understand. Martha Washington's portraits and the ideas she represented—beauty, motherhood, domesticity, support for her husband, influence instead of political power—dominated. Nearly two decades after the 1851 engraving *Woman's Emancipation* in *Harper's New Monthly Magazine*, in 1869 Currier & Ives printed a remarkably similar lithographic print called *The Age of Brass, or The Triumphs of Woman's Rights* (figure I.1 on p. vi). The political landscape changed dramatically during those decades, but these pictures reveal consistent fears of masculine political women as threats to American values.

Some portraits, like those by Grozelier, demonstrated that political women did not look like the figures in their opponents' cartoons. Reformers sought to strike a balance between attractive femininity and public, masculine authority. After enduring ridicule during the antebellum period, women's rights leaders began to construct their own public image. They came to believe that visual evidence of their femininity, sincerity, and adherence to more familiar conventions of womanhood—at least for the sake of appearances—might attract public support. As female reformers learned that pictures influenced political power, they learned to wage their own war.

SOJOURNER TRUTH.

3.1: Portrait of Sojourner Truth, 1850, engraving, published as
the frontispiece in *Narrative of Sojourner Truth*. Courtesy of the
American Antiquarian Society.

3: PORTRAITS AS POLITICS

Born around 1797, Isabella Baumfree grew up enslaved in Ulster County, New York. She endured separation from her parents at age thirteen, multiple different owners, and an incident that resulted in the loss of part of her finger. In 1826, she freed herself by running away to New York City. She became a follower of the Prophet Matthias, a religious leader who claimed the Holy Spirit spoke through him.[1] Isabella did not attain the spiritual enlightenment she hoped for in 1836, the year Matthias had predicted the world would end. Instead, she fashioned her own fresh start. In 1843, at the age of about forty-six, she adopted the name Sojourner Truth and became an itinerant preacher. She moved to Northampton, Massachusetts, joined a network of reformers, and eventually became a traveling lecturer.[2]

In 1850, Truth began to sell a book, with her story and portrait, to introduce herself to a broader public. Five years earlier, Frederick Douglass, who had also freed himself from slavery, had published his own autobiography. His book's success inspired Truth to publish the *Narrative of Sojourner Truth*, which similarly recounted slavery's horrors in order to win antislavery supporters. Truth printed her book seven times through 1884. She sold the work through the mail and at her lectures.[3] Both publications featured their author's engraved portrait as the frontispiece. Truth's depicts her almost fully facing forward, with her head tilted (figure 3.1). She wears a determined expression and meets the viewer's eyes. Her face conveys a toughness rare in women's portraits. A white cloth, which she often wore in her pictures, covers her hair. The head wrap, as well as her plain dress, alludes to her former enslavement and her continued status as a working woman.[4]

Portraits of Truth and Douglass signal a significant difference between the two: Douglass could read and write, but Truth had neither skill. Her amanuensis, fellow antislavery activist Olive Gilbert, had transcribed the book for her.[5] Douglass's picture also appealed to well-known associations between masculinity, visibility, and power. The two have similar poses and expressions, but Douglass's carefully coiffed hair, elegant suit and tie, and crisply pressed white shirt suggest that he is among the educated elite

3.2: Portrait of Frederick Douglass, 1845, engraving, published as the frontispiece in *Narrative of the Life of Frederick Douglass*. Courtesy of the American Antiquarian Society.

(figure 3.2).[6] Douglass, who cultivated his public image throughout his life, also hired an engraver with much finer skills than the artist of Truth's portrait.[7] In contrast to the harsh lines and blocky clothes in Truth's portrait, the fine, delicate marks that compose Douglass's contribute to the impression of his higher status. More than seventy-five years after the publication of Phillis Wheatley's portrait, Truth was still one of the few women—one of even fewer women of color—whose portrait reached a wider public. While Wheatley's portrait emphasizes her authorship (figure 1.1 on p. 10), Truth's accentuates her status as a worker and downplays her work as a lecturer. By emphasizing their subjects' individuality and humanity, portraits like these challenged popular racist stereotypes.

Photographic portraits became essential political tools in reform movements and presidential campaigns in the 1860s. By then, the distribution of cheap photographs had become possible. Portraits became extensions of activists themselves, acting as agents for causes across the United States.[8] Americans associated the medium with truthfulness, so photographs provided evidence that engravings, with their visible marks of an artist's hand, did not. Unlike the variable performances of traveling lecturers, photographs conveyed a consistently poignant message. Douglass and Truth enlisted photographs to define their public image and spread their messages to the widest possible audience. However, engravings still dominated publications because photographs could not yet be reproduced alongside text. Photography still transformed these engravings. For example, artists sometimes copied photographs to produce engraved images. To capitalize on the association between photography and truth, captions to these images often noted that the artist had based the engraving on a specific photograph.

Truth modeled strategies for using photographic portraits to change the way people understood race and public, political women.[9] Her portraits countered racist cartoons as well as sexist ones that envisioned political women as threats to society. She started to develop her public image during the antislavery movement and brought it with her to the later women's rights and civil rights movements. Leaders of the new suffrage organizations, founded in 1869, integrated strategies forged by Truth and fellow antislavery reformers as well as presidential campaigns. By the 1870s, suffragists circulated photographic portraits to challenge the popular cartoons and cultivate a public image for their increasingly cohesive movement. During this era, antisuffrage imagery still dominated, but gradually suffragists turned their nascent visual campaign into a formidable weapon.

A VISUAL CAMPAIGN AGAINST SLAVERY

By the time Douglass and Truth published their books, antislavery advocates had been distributing imagery to win supporters for over fifty years.[10] The mature movement was armed with numerous organizations, international conventions, and powerful leaders. Supporters enlisted imagery to convey two ideas: the cruelty of slavery and the humanity of those enslaved. Initially, they employed engravings to spread their message, but reformers soon integrated photographs into their campaigns. Reformers who began their careers in the antislavery movement learned from these strategies and incorporated visual politics into the women's rights movement.

Advocates who supported early women's rights efforts sometimes based their pictures on existing antislavery imagery.[11] Originally, the seal adopted by the Society for Effecting the Abolition of the Slave Trade in 1787, *Am I Not a Man and Brother?*, became an antislavery icon. Josiah Wedgwood sold a medallion based on the seal, which became popular in England and its former colonies.[12] Benjamin Franklin, head of the Pennsylvania Antislavery Society, thanked Wedgwood for his work and wrote, "I am persuaded it [the medallion] may have an Effect equal to that of the best written Pamphlet, in procuring Favour to those oppressed People."[13] Decades later, the 1837 antislavery book *Slavery Illustrated in Its Effects upon Woman and Domestic Society* featured an enslaved woman in the place of the man in Wedgwood's design (figure 3.3).[14] In *Am I Not a Woman and Sister?*, the enslaved woman wears a flowing pant as she kneels in chains to plead for assistance. Her face appeals to the era's physiognomic and phrenological ideals to signal her humanity. Deprived of civilized femininity, the artist shows her baring her chest to stress her sexuality and vulnerability to rape. The book's author, George Bourne, argued that slavery created an immoral society, "one vast brothel," in which enslaved women could not fulfill their feminine duty to care for their own families.[15] Furthermore, the engraving subtly asked viewers to consider the shackles that bound every American woman. As women's rights gained momentum, the supplicating enslaved woman appeared on more printed materials.[16]

Angelina Grimké, a women's rights and antislavery activist, recognized the importance of these pictures. Born to a slave-owning family in Charleston, South Carolina, Grimké became the first southern white woman to speak out against slavery. In her 1836 *Appeal to the Christian Women of the South*, she wrote that "they [antislavery images] are powerful appeals and have invariably done the work they were designed to do, and we cannot consent to abandon the use of these until the realities no longer exist."[17] Pictures of chained people made the practice real. She wrote, "Until the pictures of the slave's sufferings were drawn and held up to public gaze, no Northerner had any idea of the cruelty of the system, it never entered their minds that such abominations could exist in Christian, Republican America."[18] The following year, the first Antislavery Convention

3.3: *Am I Not a Woman and a Sister?*, 1837, engraving, published as the
frontispiece in George Bourne, *Slavery Illustrated in Its Effects upon
Woman and Domestic Society* (1837). Courtesy of the American Antiquarian Society.

of American Women passed a resolution that endorsed the use of images
in their work.[19]

Antislavery pictures that encouraged empathy for people of color challenged racist images that dominated the visual sphere. American imagery,
still largely produced by white men, often illustrated the perceived dangers
of freed black people that white consumers feared. Prints depicted black
men marrying white women, and white men acting as their servants.
Others signaled that, no matter how hard they tried, black people would
never integrate into American society. For example, in the late 1820s, Philadelphia engraver Edward Clay printed a series of cartoons called *Life in
Philadelphia* to respond to anxieties about the city's growing freed black
population (figure 3.4).[20] In plate 4 of the series, Clay depicts a black man
standing before a black woman, both dressed in outlandish, frivolous versions of fashionable clothes. He sports an oddly proportioned jacket, while

3.4: Edward Williams Clay, *Life in Philadelphia, Plate 4*, 1828, etching. Courtesy of the Library of Congress, LC-DIG-pga-13802.

she wears puffy sleeves and an oversized hat covered with ribbons and flowers. The man asks, "How you find yourself dis hot weader Miss Chloe?" She responds, "Pretty well Mr. Cesar only I aspire too much!" The cartoon suggested that they could aspire to be respectable and middle-class but would never achieve this goal. Their faces do not reflect physiognomic ideals seen in *Am I Not a Woman and Sister?*, and their language stresses their lack of education. Engravers in New York and London copied the prints and added their own to the series, which demonstrates the shared fears about slavery's end. Pictures that caricatured women's rights entrenched the patriarchy, while racist cartoons reinforced white supremacy. As women's rights activists knew, some cartoons did both.

In 1861, Frederick Douglass argued that visual politics could do more than prompt pity for enslaved people: images could advance racial equality. He delivered one of his lectures, entitled "Pictures and Progress," in Syracuse and Boston.[21] His speeches and publications attracted supporters and people curious to hear the eminent African American. In Boston's Tremont

Temple, he asserted: "The picture making faculty … is a mighty power—
and the side to which it goes has achieved a wondrous conquest."[22] If activists harnessed this "power" for their cause, they would likely succeed. Even
"the dullest vision can see and comprehend at a glance the full effect of
a point," Douglass argued.[23] Images required cultural literacy rather than
formal education for viewers to understand them. Douglass continued:
"The picture plays an important part in our politics and often explodes
political shams more effectively, than any other agency."[24] Portraits of a
refined black man like him challenged racist stereotypes.

Pictures had power because they reached the masses. Douglass told
his audience that "the great cheapness, and universality of pictures must
exert a powerful though silent influence, upon the ideas and sentiment of
present [and] future generations."[25] Technological innovations made this
visual conversation possible. Improvements in electrotyping expedited the
printing process and facilitated higher print runs of engraved material.
Pictorial publications like *Harper's Weekly* and *Frank Leslie's Illustrated
Newspaper* became widespread.[26] Between 1860 and 1880, the number
of engraving operations in the United States nearly doubled. Engravings
dominated because printers could reproduce them alongside text. As in
other industries, the labor of engravers became increasingly subdivided.
An engraving would once have been a week-long project for one person,
but now workers each completed only a small section of a picture. Together, they finished full-page illustrations in about eight hours.[27]

Engravings became cheaper, and the new visual medium of photography provided reformers new opportunities to counter stereotypes with an
image that looked like proof. In the mid-1850s, photographers started to
expose their images onto glass plates that became photographic negatives.
Professional studios implemented this wet-plate process, which allowed
them to reprint photographs from glass negatives as long as they remained
intact. Photographs could not yet be printed in newspapers or books, but
they could be reproduced as prints and sold in great numbers for the first
time. By the early 1860s, cheap photographs became staples in American
households. Photographs, which artists also copied to create engravings
for publications, made the faces of prominent figures recognizable to the
largest audience ever.

Douglass employed photographs to counter racism. He regularly sat for
them and became the most photographed American of the nineteenth century, claiming the visibility expected of leading men.[28] The reformer represented himself as a well-dressed, educated, and respected man. Around
1862, Douglass delivered a lecture on the importance of photographs,

which he lauded for their "faithfulness ... in delineating the human face and form." The truthfulness of photographs helped reformers to defy damaging stereotypes. Unlike an engraver, a photographer could not add stereotypical features to a subject's face. However, as Douglass probably knew well, photographs did not actually capture truths. Instead, photographs made truths. Douglass appeared intelligent and well groomed, and this performance made him so. He told his audience, "The portrait makes our president. The political gathering begins the work and the picture gallery ends it."[29] A portrait made a man like Abraham Lincoln into a respected president. Without his inclusion in galleries filled with pictures of important leaders, Lincoln could never have held a prominent place in the American mind.

The Civil War made photographs an essential part of American life.[30] The conflict prompted a need for this transportable, realistic, and inexpensive form of remembrance. Before they left home to fight or nurse the wounded, men and women flocked to photographers to capture their likenesses for loved ones. In 1862, a writer for a professional photography journal noted that "America swarms with the members of the mighty tribe of cameristas, and the civil war has developed their business in the same way that it has given an impetus to the manufacturers of metallic air-tight coffins and embalmers of the dead."[31] Photographers pitched makeshift studio tents next to army camps and were "thronged from morning to night."[32]

By the end of the war, purchasing and exchanging portraits became an established practice across social classes. Urban consumers bought prints and photographs from studios, printshops, bookstores, and newspaper offices. Mail-order catalogs and itinerant agents sold pictures, and newspapers published notices about prints and photographs available for purchase. The postal service helped photographs reach even rural areas.[33] Cartes de visite photographs especially set off a craze.[34] This type of print was small, roughly two by three and a half inches. They were sturdy, transportable, and, most important, cheap. They cost two to three dollars per dozen, or less than twenty-five cents per photograph, about the price of two copies of *Frank Leslie's Illustrated Newspaper*.[35] In 1863, author and scholar Oliver Wendell Holmes noted their popularity in the *Atlantic Monthly*. He wrote, "*card-portraits* ... as everybody knows, have become the social currency, the sentimental 'green-backs' of civilization."[36] Like greenbacks, the new national currency, cartes de visite distributed valuable information and indicated cultural capital.

Consumers collected the faces of people they found noteworthy and added them to albums that held the portraits of prominent figures and loved ones.[37] Even Northerners wanted a picture of Confederate President Jefferson Davis so that they could see what he looked like.[38] Consumers created their own collections of important people, and their albums demonstrated their cultural authority. The range of albums made them accessible to many families. Small ones cost as little thirty-seven and a half cents, while others were larger and finer.[39] An 1864 article in *Godey's Lady's Book*, the magazine with the highest circulation before the Civil War, called albums "a necessity for the people."[40] The "trifling expense of photographs," the author wrote, "put within reach of the public the faces of all those we love, all we esteem, and all we admire and revere of our own family, of great men; the hero, the patriot, the sage, the divine." The author concluded, "The American family would be poor indeed who could not afford a photograph album."[41]

Photographs became important sources of information because, to nineteenth-century Americans, they resembled science more than art.[42] Illustrated newspapers, for example, noted when artists had copied photographs, to convince readers of the accuracy of their engravings. In 1859, a writer for the abolitionist newspaper *National Era* wrote of photographs: "[There] is no allowance to be made for the imagination of the artist. They are facts. The sun is a faithful biographer.... He gives us men as he saw them."[43] The emotional experience of seeing photographs differed as well. An 1862 *New York Times* article affirmed that photographer Mathew Brady's Civil War photographs made the war feel immediate. The author wrote, "We [Northerners] recognize the battle-field as a reality, but it stands as a remote one." Photographs destroyed the distance. The article continued, "Mr. Brady has done something to bring home to us the terrible reality and earnestness of the war. If he has not brought bodies and laid them in our dooryards and along the streets, he has done something very like it."[44]

Reformers employed this new realistic medium to spread their message about slavery's brutality. The widely reproduced photograph entitled *The Scourged Back* or *A Map of Slavery* highlights the raised scars on the bare back of a man named Gordon (figure 3.5). Viewers see his face in profile, but his features lack definition. The picture represents the scars that mark his body and asks the viewer to imagine the torture that produced them. A writer for the New York *Independent* declared that the "Card Photograph should be multiplied by the 100,000 and scattered over the states. It tells a story in a way that even Mrs. [Harriet Beecher] Stowe cannot approach because it tells the story to the eye."[45] Photographs could convince more people of slavery's horrors than even the most popular book of the period,

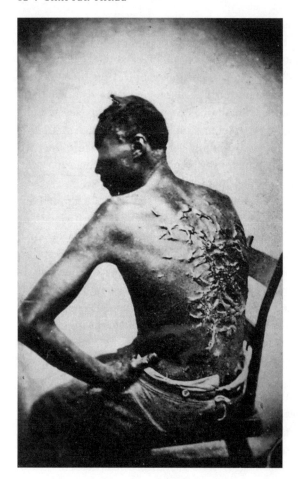

3.5: *Overseer Artayou Carrier Whipped Me. I Was Two Months in Bed Sore from the Whipping. My Master Come after I Was Whipped; He Discharged the Overseer. The Very Words of Poor Peter, Taken as He Sat for His Picture. Baton Rouge, Louisiana*, 1863, carte de visite photograph, Photographic Prints in John Taylor Album, compiled ca. 1861–ca. 1865. National Archives photo no. 533232 (Records of the War Department General and Special Staffs, 1860–1952).

Uncle Tom's Cabin. Engravers copied the photograph for publication in *Harper's Weekly* and other illustrated papers.[46] Such pictures won sympathy, but, similar to contemporaneous anthropological photographs of enslaved people, they also objectified their subjects by diminishing their individuality.

Political parties quickly integrated imagery into their campaigns too.

3.6: Mathew Brady Studio, *Lincoln on the Day of His Speech at the Cooper Union, February 27, 1860*, 1860, carte de visite photograph. Courtesy of Special Collections, Fine Arts Library, Harvard University.

Likely well aware of antislavery imagery, Abraham Lincoln became the first presidential candidate to circulate his portrait to build his public image. When Lincoln ran for president in 1860, few voters knew about the Illinois lawyer, and even fewer could recognize his face. So when the newly established Republican Party announced his nomination, they distributed numerous engravings of their candidate to introduce him to voters across the expanding nation.[47] One of Lincoln's most famous campaign photographs captured him on the day of his speech at the Cooper Union in New York on February 27, 1860.[48] Photographers paid famous subjects— politicians, actors, military leaders, and authors—to sit for them so that they could sell their portraits. Lincoln stopped by Mathew Brady's New York studio to pose.[49] In this photograph, he stands erect and looks at the viewer (figure 3.6). He places his right hand on two books that reference his education and experience as a lawyer to emphasize his preparedness for high office. His clothes appear wrinkled and his hair tousled from travel. Still, Lincoln's jaw is firmly set, and he has an air of confidence, even arrogance, that he can achieve the position he seeks. Having already posed for dozens of photographs and seen portraits of other presidents, he had an idea of how he wanted to look to convince voters that he possessed the character for the job. Brady sold the portrait as a carte de visite, and artists copied it on campaign materials and for newspapers. By the time Lincoln died in 1865, he probably had the most recognizable face in America. Brady reported that Lincoln had told him that his Cooper Union speech and this portrait had won him the presidency.[50]

Even without the funds and organizations available to political parties, individual women could distribute portraits to enter the public sphere and influence their image on a limited scale. Many suffragists started out as antislavery activists. Before mainstream publications like *Harper's Weekly* started printed antislavery imagery, the movement relied on enterprising individuals to distribute much of its visual propaganda. Female leaders had added antislavery icons to stationery and seen the value of having a famous face, and they started to incorporate these strategies into the suffrage movement. They could have their photograph taken, but, like antislavery activists, they needed to distribute imagery on their own. In comparison to portraits of famous men, Brady's studio sold few images of women. Women rarely occupied the high-profile positions that made selling their portraits lucrative.

Lucretia Mott was among the earliest women's rights and antislavery advocates to distribute her public image. Born in 1793, Mott was a well-known Quaker preacher in Philadelphia. Like Angelina Grimké, she was criticized for delivering lectures to mixed audiences of men and women in the 1830s.[51] Mott presented herself as a serious, dedicated, and respectable advocate. She cared more about winning supporters than privacy and domesticity. Regardless of the medium, she represented herself with similar expression, pose, and clothing throughout her life. In 1851, Marcus Root took one of Mott's earliest photographs (figure 3.7). By that time, she was a leading reformer, yet Mott projected an image of herself as a woman who preferred simplicity and feminine modesty. She sits, arms crossed, with her face positioned in a three-quarter view. She wears a plain Quaker dress with a shawl and bonnet. Since this daguerreotype could not be reproduced, Mott likely intended it for family and close friends, or she could have sent it to engravers to copy.[52] In 1865, she portrayed herself in a similar manner (figure 3.8). In the later portrait, she looks more directly

3.7: Marcus Root, portrait of Lucretia Coffin Mott, 1851, half-plate daguerreotype. National Portrait Gallery, Smithsonian Institution.

at the viewer but wears the same stern expression. Her age, in combination with her plain, unfashionable attire, endows her with a sense of wisdom.

Mott's portraits helped viewers picture her a respectable reformer, not a masculine shrew. Root understood the familiar visual conventions for representing gender. In 1864, he wrote about them in his book *The Camera*

3.8: Frederick Gutekunst, portrait of Lucretia Mott, 1865, albumen silver print carte de visite photograph. National Portrait Gallery, Smithsonian Institution; gift of Irwin Reichstein, Ottawa.

and the Pencil. He quoted a painter named Barry, probably the eighteenth-century Irish painter James Barry, who noted "the female form ... gives the idea of something rather passive than active" and with "softer, milder qualities." In contrast, the "male form ... indicates an aptness and propensity to action, vigorous exertion, and power."[53] Though Lincoln's portrait conveys a sense of excitement about the path ahead, Mott appears to be waiting.

Mott allowed her portraits to reach large audiences, but she never promoted them as Sojourner Truth did. In 1863, two articles made Truth famous to a wider public. Harriet Beecher Stowe, author of the wildly popular *Uncle Tom's Cabin,* wrote an article about Truth as the "Libyan Sibyl" in the *Atlantic Monthly.*[54] Stowe represented Truth as a vibrant woman whose "conversation" was "strong, simple, shrewd." But her article, based on one meeting with Truth a decade earlier, incorrectly stated that Truth was from Africa and that she had recently died.[55] Later that month, women's rights activist Frances Dana Gage praised Truth's speaking gifts in the New York *Independent.*[56] She wrote that in 1851 Truth's "magical influence" had "turned the whole tide" in favor of women's rights at one of the first conventions.[57]

Stowe and Gage had fashioned mythical versions of the preacher, and Truth wanted to popularize her own truth. She took advantage of her new fame and sat for the first photograph that she would sell.[58] Her photographs made her appear modest and intelligent as they emphasized her blackness. A year after her first sittings, she selected a preferred pose and props.[59] In one photo, at around age 67, Truth sits next to a table with her knitting needles and work in her left hand (figure 3.9). Her right hand (with the scarred finger) grips the tail of her yarn, which snakes down her skirt as if the photographer had interrupted her midstitch. Knitting implied feminine domesticity but also represented a vital, practical skill for any working woman who sought to keep her family warm. The bouquet of flowers and table imply a domestic setting, while her book and wire-rimmed glasses (a "novelty," according to a contemporary) reference her intelligence and inclusion in elite, educated circles.[60] Her signature white head wrap, simple dark-colored dress, and modest shawl resemble Mott's Quaker attire.[61] The blank background in combination with her white head wrap and shawl draw the eye to her face. The light shining on her dark skin illuminates her serious expression. This Truth is no myth; she has survived by relying on her own strength of character. Truth had her portrait taken at least seven times between 1863 and 1875, resulting in at least fourteen different versions.[62] The poses vary slightly, but she consistently composed herself according to conventions for representing middle-class women who never thought of selling their portraits.[63] The pictures implied that she subscribed to mainstream notions of femininity, even though her political speeches suggested no such thing.

In 1873, Truth replaced the old portrait of her as a laborer with one based on the above photograph in new editions of *Narrative of Sojourner Truth* (figure 3.10). The old portrait remained in her book, but closer to the end. The artist simplified the composition of the new engraving, taking out props like knitting needles and flowers. Truth's expression is even gentler than the one in her photograph. Both the engraved and photographed versions demonstrate a black woman embodying a feminine, domestic ideal. In the context of contemporaneous imagery that represented black women as unintelligent servants, curiosities, and scientific specimens, Truth's portrait provides a different vision of blackness in America.[64]

Truth personally managed her public image. Rather than selling rights to a photographer, she sold her own photographs and managed the profits. Most unusual, she copyrighted her portrait, allowing her to maintain full

I Sell the Shadow to Support the Substance.

SOJOURNER TRUTH.

3.9: "Sojourner Truth," 1864, carte de visite photograph. The caption reads, "I Sell the Shadow to Support the Substance. SOJOURNER TRUTH." Courtesy of the Library of Congress, http://hdl.loc.gov/loc.rbc /lprbscsm.scsm0880.

SOJOURNER TRUTH,
" THE LIBYAN SIBYL. "

3.10: *Sojourner Truth,
"The Libyan Sibyl,"*
1875, engraving, pub-
lished as the frontis-
piece in *Narrative of
Sojourner Truth.* Cour-
tesy of the American
Antiquarian Society.

control over it.[65] In a letter to the New York *World*, Elizabeth Cady Stanton wrote that Truth always brought her photographs when she traveled,
instead of clothes or rations. She said that Truth told her, "I don't want
my shadow even to be dogging about here and there and everywhere, so
I keep it in this bag."[66] While she sold some of her photographs in the
larger cabinet size, most were smaller cartes de visite. Purchasers added
her portrait to their albums or private collections. She appeared alongside
portraits of family members, politicians, and favorite actors.

Just as he inspired her *Narrative*, Frederick Douglass might have
sparked Truth's interest in photography. Truth explicitly associated her
portraits with her causes. Backing cards for her photographs included the
text "I sell the shadow to support the substance." The term "shadow" was
a common term for a photograph, since sunlight created the image on the
glass plate. The phrase referred to the selling of her portrait to support
her "substance," meaning her physical self and the substantial reforms
she advanced. The *Revolution*, a newspaper run by Susan B. Anthony and

Elizabeth Cady Stanton, printed an article noting that Truth had said "some might like to see her shadow after she had gone." The "shadow" was an extension of Truth, the "substance." Her portrait traveled far beyond her hands to share her message. The *Revolution* writer added, "As the substance had often been sold, it was quite a pleasure for her to sell the shadow herself."[67]

Fellow reformers paid for Truth's first photographs, and friends helped her sell them. Purchasing Truth's portrait associated the buyer with her causes. Papers like the *National Antislavery Standard* and *Antislavery Bugle* ran sale announcements.[68] Prominent reformers, such as the lecturer Anna Dickinson, urged supporters to purchase them and sent Truth the proceeds.[69] Advertisements for Truth's lectures noted that attendees could purchase her portrait at the event. At one talk in Detroit, Truth made twenty-one dollars from sales.[70] She could more easily travel the lecture circuit with hundreds of photographs than hundreds of books. Furthermore, if she sold all of her portraits, she could have new prints made at a local studio.

Portraits of Mott and Truth stand out because most white female reformers never sold their likenesses to the public. The style of feminine politics associated with idealized versions of Martha Washington and other elite white women, which focused on their support of their husband's ventures, still dominated American culture. Female reformers kept their likenesses private to maintain their respectability in a society that frowned upon public, political women. Truth did not have the same inherent respectability that a middle-class white woman had, but she carried out her own personal visual campaign that illuminated a positive vision for women of color and won her respect that continues to this day. Phillis Wheatley's patrons commissioned her portrait to claim Wheatley's education and refinement, while Truth chose to claim this power for herself. Mott and Truth chose to look like women who acquiesced to a place in the public eye, critical to displays of visual femininity. Unlike popular racist and sexist caricatures of women in elaborate costumes, they wore plain clothing and stern expressions. Both women composed their portraits in similar manners throughout their lives.

During the 1860s and 1870s, portrait photographs became essential tools to define—and win—political power. The antislavery movement's powerful pictures helped to secure support to end slavery. Having learned from that campaign, presidential candidates and reformers integrated pictures into their own efforts. Printed portraits acted as extensions of the individuals and their ideas. However, popular illustrations still provided no positive models for women who wanted to vote or run for office. Women's rights advocates who had distributed antislavery imagery, and perhaps Lincoln's likeness as well, started to integrate pictures into their own movement. They could circulate their portraits to establish their own models and counter negative stereotypes. Female reformers did not have the coordination or funds to compete with mainstream publications, but they could use the power of photography for their own advantage.

FROM PORTRAITS TO SUFFRAGE ICONS

Mott and Truth modeled strategies to define the public image of the women's rights movement. Initially, Truth became so valuable that even when the suffragists split in 1869, she participated in efforts on both sides.[71] In response to decades of cartoons that lampooned political women, suffrage leaders embraced new visual technology—photographic portraits—to present an appealing face for their cause. Activists did not need funding to distribute cheap pictures to eager supporters. Their portraits defined them as leaders and demonstrated that they were not cartoonish, masculine shrews.

In August 1865, Susan B. Anthony employed images to win support for newly freed people. She stood before a meeting of the Women's Loyal National League, which she had founded two years earlier to support the abolition of slavery. Anthony "held up two photographs to the view of the audience." One featured "the bare back of a Louisiana slave," while the other depicted Truth.[72] According to a report in the *National Antislavery Standard*, "Many of the audience were affected to tears." They saw that "the Louisiana slave's back bore scars of whipping," and the paper incorrectly noted that Truth had lost three fingers while enslaved. After holding up the portraits, each perhaps no larger than a roughly four-by-six-inch cabinet card, Anthony might have passed them around for a closer look. The newspaper recounted that she pleaded with her audience, telling "every one [sic] to suppose that woman was her mother, and that man her father." Rather than relying on Reconstruction-era politics to dictate the fates of formerly enslaved people, she wanted to raise money to support them. Anthony and others had spoken in favor of this motion earlier in the meeting without success. Immediately after the group saw the photographs, however, fundraising resolutions "were at once unanimously passed."[73]

Anthony hoped to touch the hearts of those in her audience, and she chose her pictures well. The exact prints she selected remain unknown. The descriptions, though, offer enough detail to be matched with popular images. The "Louisiana slave" was likely Gordon, pictured in *The Scourged Back*, who was enslaved in Baton Rouge (figure 3.5 on p. 62). Similarly, Truth's portraits remained remarkably consistent and likely resembled her 1864 carte de visite (figure 3.9). As a freed woman, she had more power over her likeness than Gordon did over his. Truth's photographs referred to her past, but, unlike Gordon's, they also represented her claim on an entirely different future.

Anthony displayed these photographs to raise awareness and money, and she brought these visual strategies to a new phase of the suffrage movement. After the Civil War, women received some recognition for their work, but not enough to win the vote. In 1866, activists founded the American Equal Rights Association to advocate for universal suffrage. The following year, the Republican Party prioritized the ballot for black men. Some women, including Anthony and Elizabeth Cady Stanton, felt furious. They made racist arguments that black men should not have the vote before white women.[74] When Kansas called for a referendum on women's and black men's suffrage later that year, the pair campaigned to win the ballot for women, but not black men. Both measures failed, mostly due to Republican infighting and a lack of funds, but reformers blamed Anthony and Stanton because of their refusal to campaign for black male suffrage.[75]

In 1869, the conflict over the Fifteenth Amendment, which granted the vote regardless of race or previous enslavement, prompted the collapse of the American Equal Rights Association and the end of the universal suffrage campaign. Instead, women founded the first national groups focused on women's suffrage. Angered by the enfranchisement of black men and women's exclusion, Stanton and Anthony formed the National Woman Suffrage Association. In response, longtime civil rights and women's rights leader Lucy Stone and her husband, Henry Brown Blackwell, founded the American Woman Suffrage Association. The group attracted those who supported the amendment and wanted to ensure that women would vote next.[76]

At first, the leaders considered a truce. As months and years wore on, though, they developed platforms in opposition to each other. Stone's American Association advocated for local organizations to win the ballot for women in each state. In contrast, Anthony and Stanton's National Association wanted to coordinate a campaign to secure a constitutional amendment that forbade sex-based voting restrictions. The American Association made Boston its headquarters, but the National Association had offices in New York City. The American Association selected Reverend Henry Ward Beecher as the first president, and men made up half of the group's officers.[77] In contrast, the National Association wanted only female leaders. Local suffrage groups from across the country allied themselves with these umbrella organizations.

Each association founded a publication to outline organizational structures and goals, articulate strategies for large audiences, and establish leaders. The *Revolution*, created by Anthony and Stanton in 1868, served as a "mouthpiece of women."[78] Though the paper only lasted through 1872, the *Revolution*, as the title suggests, argued for swift, sweeping—and often controversial—improvements. In addition to suffrage, the paper discussed religion, race, financial reforms, dress, and labor. The National Association did not have enough money or supporters to introduce portraits of its leaders to the public, but it could do so for supporters. The paper reprinted writings by forerunners like Mary Wollstonecraft and Margaret Fuller, whose portraits the organization also sold to honor them as the movement's founders. Daily newspapers still printed few engravings, if any. Illustrated papers like *Harper's Weekly* remained distinct from text-based papers. Instead, suffrage newspapers advertised the sale of their leaders' portraits, offered them as benefits for subscribers, and described their display at events.

Printed in New York, the *Revolution* circulated widely. Press notices and letters to the editor reveal that people read the paper from Maine to California, from South Carolina to Minnesota. Its peak of three thousand subscribers, however, did not make up for the paper's $10,000 debt.[79] In May 1870, Anthony sold the paper, and the content immediately became more moderate. The new editor still discussed women's rights, but puzzles, children's stories, and household tips crept into the pages. The National Association, however, kept its controversial platform.

The American Association's *Woman's Journal*, which began publication in January 1870, also prompted the *Revolution*'s demise. Established by Stone, Henry Brown Blackwell, Julia Ward Howe, Mary Livermore, William Lloyd Garrison, and Thomas Wentworth Higginson, the *Woman's Journal* became the voice for more measured activists. The paper entered the divide between the *Revolution* and traditional ladies' magazines like *Godey's Lady's Book*. Editors focused on "woman's legal and political equality," rather than the range of gender inequalities discussed in the *Revolution*, to attract as many supporters as possible.[80] Anthony was not impressed. She complained that the *Revolution* (under its new management) and the *Woman's Journal* were "dull" and "absolutely dead, dead, dead." Though Anthony detested it, the moderate tone of the *Woman's Journal* made it far more successful.[81] From its debut, the *Journal* had stable financial backers

3.11: *Portraits of Stanton and Anthony Together*, ca. 1870–1895, carte de visite photograph. Schlesinger Library, Radcliffe Institute, Harvard University.

and attracted a longer subscriber list.[82] Editors printed updates from state organizations, political tracts, and letters from all over the country that reflected the paper's reach.[83]

Now in charge of an organized social movement, Stanton and Anthony challenged the status quo with their own vision of political power. Perhaps inspired by Truth, they started by promoting portraits of the movement's founding mothers and of themselves. On August 19, 1870, Stanton and Anthony went to Napoleon Sarony's photography studio in New York City. Anthony wrote in her journal that they "sat for pictures in all forms & positions."[84] Their session resulted in a series of individual portraits and photographs of the pair. In several versions, the two sit at a small circular table, a studio prop with elaborate twin cast iron legs and a book open atop it. In one of the portraits, Anthony sits on the left and Stanton sits on the right (figure 3.11). Stanton's stare (or glare?) directly at the viewer is the most striking detail. Perhaps she is impatient for the session to end, but that is unlikely since she would have known the importance of the portraits. Anthony looks at the viewer as well. Both women lean intently—perhaps aggressively—on the table. In an 1868 book about female reformers, one writer commented that "they often stimulate each

3.12: *Elizabeth Cady Stanton and Her Daughter, Harriot—from a Daguerreotype 1856*, print made between 1890 and 1910 of a daguerreotype taken in 1856. Courtesy of the Library of Congress, LC-USZ62-48965.

other's aggressiveness.... I know of no two more pertinacious incendiaries in the whole country! Nor will they themselves deny the charge."[85] Indeed, the women look formidable. They wear dark dresses, not the bloomers that cartoonists still portrayed them in. Dark lace floats atop Stanton's white, delicately curled hair and shrouds her shoulders. Long necklaces loop around her neck, one with a large cross pendant weighing against her chest. Anthony wears a cameo pinned to her white collar. An open book affirms their participation in educated circles.

To modern eyes, Stanton and Anthony look like ordinary women dressed up for the camera, but these portraits constituted a statement about their friendship and agenda. The pair's choice to take multiple portraits together was unusual. Photographs of unrelated women posing together—suffragists or not—was not common. Instead, friends like Stanton and Anthony would have exchanged photographs. Popular public photographs rarely depict prominent men with political partners.[86] Representations of Lincoln's cabinet circulated, for example, but as engravings rather than photographs. Stanton and Anthony's portrait represented their movement.

The pair rejected gendered visual conventions to present a fresh, positive image of political women. They knew that they flouted traditional representations. Stanton, for example, had posed many times before with various combinations of her seven children, just as other mothers did. In a reproduction of a daguerreotype originally made in 1856, Stanton sits with her infant daughter and future suffragist, Harriot (figure 3.12). She pulls Harriot close, partially out of motherly love but also in effort to still the baby during the long exposure time. The composition recalls Christian representations of the Madonna and Child. In a frilly bonnet and an elaborate dress, Stanton offers a closemouthed smile. Later generations could reproduce daguerreotypes, but she could not have had circulation in mind when she sat for the intimate photograph. Stanton could have been pictured with her children in the 1870 portrait to reiterate her status as a wife and mother, but Anthony, who remained single and without children, could make no such claim.

When Stanton and Anthony approached this session, they knew their likenesses would be public. If they did not already have a deal to sell their pictures, they made one quickly after their session. Sarony printed cartes de visite and cabinet cards following their sitting. Though cartes de visite photographs often lack dates, extant prints have backing cards with a variety of Sarony's addresses and partners from over the years. Some photographs were printed starting during his affiliation with Campbell, which only lasted until early 1871.[87] The large collection of portraits from this session suggests that Sarony found them profitable enough to reprint for a long time.

Mott and Truth cloaked their public, political personas behind more traditional feminine modesty, but Anthony and Stanton displayed their revolutionary vision of female political leadership. In 1869, a year before this portrait session, Stanton wrote that the press had once called suffragists, "old, and ugly, and badly dressed.... So we dried up our tears, schooled our dolorous facial muscles to express cheerfulness and content, and polished up our words and wardrobes."[88] Even so, papers continued to ridicule them. These portraits suggest that the two reformers decided not to try to appease critics anymore. The photographs depict two women emanating confidence about themselves and their work.

The book *Eminent Women of the Age* illustrates the complicated combination of images and rhetoric that the heads of suffrage groups espoused as they established their leaders for the public. First published in 1868, the book consisted of forty-seven biographies and fourteen engraved portraits of white women. Stories of singer Jenny Lind, sculptor Harriet Hosmer, and actress Adelaide Ristori mingled with those of nurse Florence Nightingale, philosopher Margaret Fuller, and lecturers Anna Dickinson and Stanton.

Women were rarely, if ever, eminent at that time, so the book presented the possibilities open to a rising generation. The authors wanted an "au-

3.13: H. B. Hall Jr.,
E. Cady Stanton, 1868,
engraving, published
in *Eminent Women of
the Age* (1868), facing
page 332. Courtesy
of the American
Antiquarian Society.

thentic and attractive record" that would "make an impression for good
upon the young women of our land, and upon the whole American public." Like Mary Wollstonecraft's *A Vindication of the Rights of Woman* (1792),
they argued that society, not biological differences, limited women's
potential. *Eminent Women* "will tend to develop and strengthen correct
ideas respecting the influence of woman, and her share in the privileges
and responsibilities of human life."[89] The subjects, after all, were eminent *women*, not ladies. Ladies did not write theory like Margaret Fuller
or travel the country to lecture like Anna Dickinson. The book (along with
similar reform-minded publications) redefined the term "woman"—and
the women's rights movement associated with it—as empowering rather
than degrading.

    Eminent Women of the Age complicated ideals of womanhood with its
portraits. In the nearly profile engraving of Stanton, her eyes look away
from the reader (figure 3.13). She wears a brooch on her dark dress, and
her white hair curls like a crown around her head. Supporters often
emphasized the similarities in the appearances of Stanton and Martha
Washington. *Eminent Women* noted: "Mrs. Stanton's face is thought to

resemble Martha Washington's, but is less regular and more animated."[90] Similarly, a *Chicago Evening Post* article, reprinted in the *Revolution*, wrote about the "beautiful presence of Mrs. Stanton, who looks as though she had stepped out of a picture painted in the days of Martha Washington" with her "matronly face, beautiful even now, when she has passed her half century of life."[91]

The idealized Washington remained among the most visible American women, but Stanton wanted to present a new vision for political womanhood. She wanted the public to see that these prominent white women cared for families even as they led political movements. The strategy continued to emphasize that political power should be reserved for elite, white Americans, but it challenged the entrenched idea that women should not participate in politics. Stanton's biography in *Eminent Women*, by her friend and fellow reformer Theodore Tilton, labeled her "aggressive" and "incendiary."[92] But he also affirmed her familiarity with the "sacred lore of motherhood." He asserted, "Pity is her chief vice; charity, her besetting sin."[93] She was not just a leader; she was a mother with womanly virtues. In the fifteen biographies of women's rights "champions" that Stanton authored for the book, she, too, balanced descriptions of their activism with dominant cultural expectations for white women.

Eminent Women of the Age hoped future generations would follow this path. The book reached a wide audience and went through six printings between 1868 and 1879. Companies in Hartford, Chicago, St. Louis, and San Francisco published the work, and hired agents to sell it. Two advertisements in *Godey's Lady's Book* from January 1871, for example, called for agents ("male or female") and claimed the work had sold forty thousand copies.[94] The *Revolution* promoted the book and boasted of its "excellent engravings." An article noted, "Every woman in the country should give this volume a place in her library."[95] The *Revolution* printed excerpts and sold copies of the portraits from *Eminent Women*.[96] Anyone who recruited ten subscribers received Mott's likeness. The editors wrote of her portrait, "It is a *wonderful likeness* of our *great leader*. It should be a household picture in every family—favoring Woman Suffrage."[97] The print did not just represent Mott; it symbolized support for the movement.

A letter penned to a cousin and reprinted in the *Revolution* and the *Woman's Journal* demonstrates the book's reach. The teenage son and clerk of Esther Morris, a recently appointed justice of the peace in Wyoming, wrote that the book gave him hope for the future. In comparison to the female activists in the past who "had to endure public ridicule and much worse, were sometimes scorned, hissed at and mobbed," he thought that

3.14: L. Schamer, *Representative Women*, 1870, lithograph, L. Prang and Company. Courtesy of the American Antiquarian Society.

"the way for their followers now seems comparatively very smooth."[98] He was overly optimistic.

Similarly, in 1870, a new artist updated the 1857 print *Representative Women* (figure 2.13 on p. 50) to reflect the updated vision for white female leadership (figure 3.14). Only Lucretia Mott and Lydia Maria Child made it onto the revised print. Mott appears at the top, while Stanton, Mary Livermore (an editor of the *Woman's Journal*), Child, Susan B. Anthony, and writer Grace Greenwood circle Anna Dickinson. Only Mott and Livermore engage the viewer, while four of the seven women did in the earlier version. The others avert their gaze and appear to contemplate their plans for the future. Their three-quarter-view portraits resemble those of male politicians. Their long hair (pulled back and curled according to the day's styles), cameos, necklaces, and frills emphasize their femininity. Even Anthony, who generally disdained frivolity, wears a lacy hairpiece like Stanton's.

The print excludes black women and members of the American Association, reflecting the divisions among suffragists. *Representative Women*, following the cues of suffragists, erases black female leaders in favor of white ones to win support for the cause. Additionally, the print features National Association leaders Stanton, Anthony, and Mott but excludes Lucy Stone, founder of the American Association, who appeared in the 1857 version. Though Livermore, who is present in the later print, also helped lead the American Association, the Boston-based print publisher, Louis Prang and Company, might have insisted on representing the local leader and author of the famed Civil War song "Battle Hymn of the Republic."[99] Prang surely would have been aware of the omission of Stone, another local. The firm sold many popular lithographs, which suggests they believed they would profit from this print. A contingent of suffragists might have worked with Prang to compose this piece, or the publisher could have chosen the grouping on their own. Stone might even have refused to be included.

Suffragists hung prints like this one to highlight their movement's leaders. The large size of this print—over nineteen and a half by almost seventeen inches—implies that Prang and Company intended for purchasers to display it. Visitors to the *Revolution*'s headquarters noted the many portraits. One letter to the *Cincinnati Commercial Gazette* noted that "engravings and photographs hung thickly." The walls featured portraits like that of "Mary Wollstonecraft's looking into futurity with earnest eyes" and "Lucretia Mott's saintly face, beautiful with eternal youth."[100] After holding an open house for reporters in 1870, the *Revolution* reprinted seven articles from local papers like the *New York Tribune*, *World*, and *Herald*. Five articles mentioned the "fine, appropriate engravings" and photographs of women that hung in the *Revolution*'s offices. The *Brooklyn Daily Union*, however, ignored the women portrayed and mentioned only the men, such as Reverend Henry Ward Beecher, Frederick Douglass, William Lloyd Garrison, and Theodore Tilton, whose likenesses illustrated their support for the cause.[101]

Stanton and Anthony's National Association eagerly distributed portraits of female leaders, but the American Association did not. Livermore's portrait appeared in *Representative Women*, but leader Lucy Stone circulated

3.15: Warren, *Portrait of Lucy Stone*, ca. 1875–1885, carte de visite photograph. Schlesinger Library, Radcliffe Institute, Harvard University.

few likenesses of herself. Several portraits of Stone, printed as cartes de visite and larger cabinet sizes, came from a session at a Boston photography studio between 1875 and 1885. In one, Stone wears a plain (for Victorian dress) dark jacket over a white blouse with a circular pin (figure 3.15). She averts her gaze from the camera with a pensive expression. Unlike Truth, with her abundant references to domesticity, Stone makes no effort to appeal to feminine ideals. She almost seems to dare the viewer to bother her with frivolous fashions. Her portrait suggests a different truth: a white woman did not need to work as hard to claim femininity in her portrait. In comparison to most white suffragists, Truth exaggerated her domesticity and respectability. The *Woman's Journal* criticized suffrage opponents who preferred for women to "*shrink from the notoriety* of the *public eye*" because they felt "restrained by that modesty," which they believed was their "chiefest ornament."[102] Yet the American Association chose not to present their own vision of suffrage leadership by selling portraits of Stone. As a result, the portraits promoted by the National Association dominated.[103] Stone's face never became as familiar as Anthony's.

These pictures represent the earliest efforts to promote a suffrage iconography. The National Association distributed portraits to define the movement's founders and contemporary leaders and normalize women as public, political leaders. The fact that they put their limited resources behind such efforts demonstrated that they needed a new vision of political womanhood to win support for their cause. Their pictures did not have the same reach as *Harper's Weekly*'s cartoons, but they represented a wave of resistance to those damaging illustrations. The American Association had no such strategy, so Stanton and Anthony defined the movement's vision of female political leadership. They portrayed suffragists as white middle- and upper-class women. Gradually, they erased Sojourner Truth, who had modeled strategies for winning supporters and money, from the leadership. Neither association advertised her portraits. Suffrage portraits made it clear that these associations focused on securing the ballot for white women.

BACKLASH

The 1872 election marked a turning point in the movement's visual campaign. As organized political women became visible and ambitious, attacks by opponents became more incisive. Leading up to the election, suffragists encountered unprecedented opportunities. In 1869 and 1870, women in the territories of Wyoming and Utah gained the vote. The fledgling suffrage organizations had not waged campaigns to win these laws, but they counted them as positive signs.[104] In 1872, the Republican Party platform became the first to include a women's rights plank. The support, however, remained vague. Republicans belatedly recognized women's efforts during the Civil War and stated that women's "admission to wider fields of usefulness is viewed with satisfaction, and the honest demand of any class of citizens for additional rights should be treated with respectful consideration."[105] The platform did not endorse any specific legislation, suggesting that the party wanted to attract reformers without losing votes.

Taking advantage of this momentum, the National Association articulated a strategy called the "New Departure." They argued that the Fourteenth Amendment, ratified in 1868, already enfranchised women. The amendment guaranteed the rights of citizens, and—they argued—all citizens had the right to vote. Although Sojourner Truth preferred to work with the American Association, she liked this strategy. In 1872, Truth, along with hundreds of women across the nation, attempted to register to vote and cast a ballot.[106]

Three white women secured more fame than Truth during the presidential election. Victoria Woodhull became the first woman to run for president. When she announced her decision, she declared: "While others of my sex devoted themselves to a crusade against the laws that shackle the women of the country, I asserted my individual independence ... and proved [men and women's equality] by successfully engaging in business."[107] While many suffragists banded together, Woodhull worked for herself. She did not seek to change dominant ideals of womanhood; she ignored them. Her photographic portraits even emphasize a masculine aesthetic, borrowing tropes from caricatures of political women (figure I.2 on p. 4). Woodhull confirmed the fears of Americans concerned that political women challenged the accepted social order.

Even before Woodhull ran for president, Elizabeth Cady Stanton had become disgusted with attacks on Woodhull for her disregard for feminine norms. In 1871, Stanton wrote to Lucretia Mott, "We have had women enough sacrificed to this sentimental, hypocritical prating about purity. This is one of man's most effective engines for our division and subjugation." Stanton continued, "He creates the public sentiment, builds the gallows, and then makes us the hangman for our sex."[108] Stanton wanted women to stop holding each other to men's ideals for women. She concluded, "If Victoria Woodhull must be crucified, let men drive the spikes and plait the crown of thorns."[109]

Though Woodhull briefly aligned herself with Stanton and Anthony, she refused to fall in line behind them.[110] In 1872, just before the presidential election, she brought scandal to the cause when she named the famous preacher Henry Ward Beecher an adulterer. She publicized his affair with Elizabeth Tilton, wife of prominent reformer and editor Theodore Tilton, in her paper, *Woodhull & Claflin's Weekly*.[111] Beecher had been president of the American Association, and Tilton frequently wrote in support of suffrage. The public scrutinized Woodhull and fellow suffragists in the wake of her revelation, so the National Association shunned her. For Stanton and Anthony, the time for individual suffragists who worked outside of organizations—especially theirs—had passed. The National Association thought they wanted revolution, but their rejection of Woodhull signified their limits. They needed to moderate their demands to win public support.

The 1872 election also spotlighted Susan B. Anthony, the most famous woman to cast her ballot. Unlike many of her counterparts, she was allowed by officials to vote. Soon afterward, though, she was arrested, and her national fame guaranteed publicity. A judge found Anthony guilty of voting illegally and fined her $100 plus the costs of the trial. She refused to pay it. In 1873, a couple of weeks before her trial, the *Daily Graphic* featured a cartoon of Anthony on its front page (figure 3.16). The caption identified her as *The Woman Who Dared*. In earlier decades, cartoonists had caricatured nameless activists. By the 1870s, portraits had made the movement's leading women familiar. Artists assumed viewers could identify Anthony. Her hairstyle, a center part with her hair pulled back, and her lacy collar and cameo copied the photographs from her 1870 session with Stanton (figure 3.11 on p. 74). A star-spangled hat resembling Uncle Sam's sits askew on her head. Anthony's face, unlike her hair, is barely recognizable with its furrowed brow and exaggerated frown. The artist, Thomas Wust, even illustrated how one of Anthony's eyes sometimes moved from her point of focus, which she often hid by sitting for profile portraits. Her expression offers anger rather than feminine passivity. She stands with a fist on her hip and an umbrella at the ready, like a man with a sword. Her short dress shows off her boots and spurs. Anthony wears her shawl like a classical toga, referencing her belief that she led a democratic movement. On the left, a policewoman surveys the scene. Eight women speak from a raised stage (decorated with a banner reading "We favor Union to a Man") to a female audience. The cartoon suggests that these political women forced men into domesticity: on the right, one man clasps an upset child, while the other carries a basket of groceries.

Suffragists were making efforts to improve their public image, but negative portrayals like this one prevailed. Engraver Thomas Wust and many other artists—still a male-dominated group—relied on old tropes of swapped gender roles to prompt laughter at these women. Even photographers incorporated these themes to sell their work.[112] But by then, suffragists had actually participated in the scenes that earlier cartoonists had only imagined. Pictorial papers featured engravings of Woodhull casting a ballot and Stanton speaking to the Senate Committee on Privileges and Elections.[113] Suffragists did not yet orchestrate such public demonstrations as the rally in *The Woman Who Dared*, but viewers likely feared these protests might be next. Modern viewers might see the women in the picture as feminist precursors to twenty-first-century female protestors, but the scene appeared dystopian to Wust and his viewers.

While Anthony could not appeal her case to a higher court, one National Association leader, Virginia Minor, did. After being prevented from

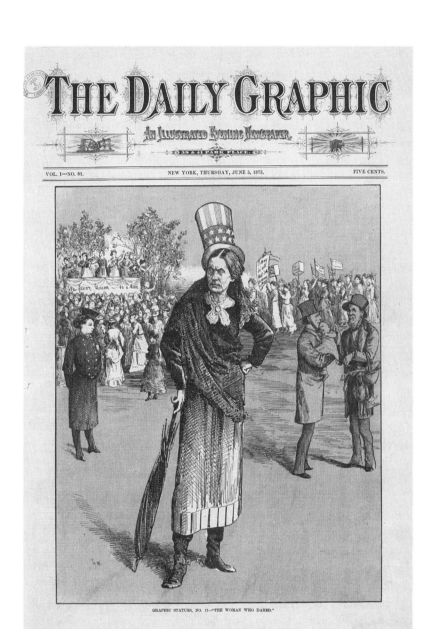

3.16: Thomas Wust, *Graphic Statues No. 17, "The Woman Who Dared,"* 1873, engraving, published in the *Daily Graphic*, June 5, 1873. Courtesy of the Library of Congress, LC-DIG-ppmsca-55836.

registering to vote in Missouri by a county registrar named Reese Happersett, Minor took her case to the Supreme Court. In 1875, in *Minor v. Happersett*, the Supreme Court ruled that voting was not a right of citizenship. Therefore, the Fourteenth Amendment had not granted women the ballot. The case clarified the legal relationship between citizenship and voting rights that continues into the present. Suffragists would be forced to choose a new strategy: take on the monumental task of lobbying for a constitutional amendment, or divide their limited resources among state-level campaigns.

White suffrage leaders continued to refuse to feature black women in their imagery, even though black suffragists also led the movement. Mary Ann Shadd Cary, a National Association member, also attempted to register to vote as part of the New Departure strategy. Unlike Sojourner Truth, Cary, born to a free black family, had an elite education, having attended law school at Howard University. In 1872 she addressed the Judiciary Committee alongside Stanton and Anthony. Cary argued that during the Civil War, black women had "fed, and sheltered, and guided in safety the prisoner soldiers of the Union." They had shown their patriotism and wanted to "be governed by their own consent."[114] Yet her words were not published with the testimony of her fellow white suffragists.[115] Eight years later, Cary established the Colored Women's Professional Franchise Association with a range of demands: the ballot, education for black children, and financial institutions that made loans to both sexes. Her group advocated for the needs of black women more than the National Association or American Association did.

Until she died in 1883, Sojourner Truth worked to win rights for women and people of color. Upon her death, Frederick Douglass praised her "independence and courageous self-assertion" that made her "an object of respect and admiration to social reformers everywhere."[116] Despite her work alongside leading suffragists, they had already started to erase her from their movement's iconography. Their choice signified their shift away from the cause of universal suffrage, with its implicit aim to enfranchise women of color. They separated women's rights from racial equality because they believed they might win support for white women's votes. Suffrage imagery promoted by Stanton and Anthony presented a vision of elite, white political women to the public. Despite their efforts—or perhaps because of them—black activists later made Truth's portrait into the icon that it is today.

During the 1860s and 1870s, the growing popularity of images gradually created a national visual language of recognizable people, places, events, and symbols, establishing a shared consciousness. The combination of cheap illustrated newspapers, photographs, and prints gave suffragists opportunities to experiment with visual politics, but it gave their opponents opportunities as well. Suffragists started to implement this visual language to define a fresh conception of political women. But they could not circulate their portraits as widely as Abraham Lincoln's. Furthermore, while antislavery pictures had documented horrific conditions and provoked sympathy, suffragists lacked a consistent, compelling message. Comparatively, the women's rights movement was young, and their fledgling organizations did not have the apparatus or funds to coordinate a visual campaign. Conflict prevented suffragists from creating a unified narrative.

Stanton and Anthony deployed pictures to win more supporters and model their idea of female political leadership. The Woodhull episode and the backlash against voting women, however, stressed the power of the press. Suffragists needed to appeal to the public, not give them fodder for ridicule. The National Association leaders enlisted controversial politics and imagery in the early 1870s, but they quickly realized that they needed a vision with wider appeal to win backers. Suffragists also needed their vision to reach beyond their supporters to a broader public. They learned much from their initial efforts to create a visual campaign, and these experiences formed the foundation for the campaign they gradually built.

4.1: F. Gutekunst, *Elizabeth Duane Gillespie as Martha Washington*, 1873, cabinet card photograph. Portrait also published in Gillespie, *A Book of Remembrance* (1901). Historical Society of Pennsylvania Portrait Collection.

4: A "FINE LOOKING BODY OF WOMEN"

Female Political Leaders on the Rise

By 1876, Susan B. Anthony knew suffragists needed a better strategy for a positive public image. Over the previous five years, their situation had worsened. Victoria Woodhull ran for president in 1872 and won only infamy. She seemed to embody all of the evils associated with suffrage. Portraits of Anthony and Elizabeth Cady Stanton depicted them as defiant women, and cartoons reinforced this characterization. In 1873, Anthony went to trial for casting a ballot and saw harsh caricatures of herself in the press. Two years later, the Supreme Court rejected the suffragists' claim that all citizens had won the vote with the protections guaranteed by the Fourteenth Amendment. Animosity remained between the leaders of the National Woman Suffrage Association and the American Woman Suffrage Association, and the breach seemed impossible to overcome.

Anthony and her fellow suffragists saw the nation's centennial in 1876 as an opportunity to present a new vision of political womanhood. They hoped the celebrations of independence and democracy would inspire support for women's equality. Visitors from all over the world gathered in Philadelphia at the Centennial Exhibition to see art, historical displays, innovative technology, and new products.[1] The elite local women on the committee that selected items for the Women's Pavilion, however, preferred to honor women's influence on American politics rather than advocate for the ballot. At fundraisers, committee members, led by Elizabeth Duane Gillespie (a descendant of Benjamin Franklin), dressed as Martha Washington to remind potential donors of the woman who remained a beloved icon (figure 4.1).[2] Gillespie later recalled that each member wore a "Martha Washington cap and kerchief," which sparked the popularity of "Martha Washington tea parties."[3] In their pavilion, issues of Lucy Stone's *Woman's Journal* appeared alongside other periodicals edited by women, but not as a suffrage display.[4] Stone had sent an exhibit entitled *Protests of Women against Taxation without Representation*, but the committee deemed it inappropriate. They removed the large title and placed the display on a high shelf out of view.[5] Although not officially an antisuffrage organization, the committee acted like one.

Despite having no official presence at the fair, Anthony and her fellow National Association leaders rented rooms nearby to establish a suffrage headquarters. Local law prevented married women from securing contracts, so Anthony signed the paperwork. At age 56, she was one of the movement's few unmarried leaders. In her twenties, she had taught to support herself and her siblings. By the time she turned thirty in 1850, she had dedicated her life to reform work.[6] Anthony advocated for causes that ranged from abolition and temperance to women's economic and political equality. She lectured throughout the country, edited a newspaper, led conventions, and founded one of the first national suffrage associations. Biographers noted that she even rejected marriage proposals to preserve her focus on her work. To opponents, the single, childless activist represented the negative changes that women's votes would inaugurate. Mary Anthony, her sister, took care of daily domestic tasks in Rochester, New York. Mary's work made it possible for Susan to become the face of the suffrage movement.

The suffrage headquarters served as a space for meetings as well as housing for Anthony and others.[7] From there, they made plans for the July Fourth celebrations. On the fairgrounds, Anthony read and distributed copies of a "Declaration of Rights of the Women of the United States." Like the Declaration of Independence that the holiday celebrated, the document affirmed the equal rights of individuals. Anthony proclaimed to her audience that the "aristocracy of sex" in the United States "imposes upon the women of this nation a more absolute and cruel despotism than monarchy."[8] The government taxed women without representation and did not allow them to be tried by their peers.

Though suffragists sought a new future, the centennial highlighted the utility of the past. Soon after the exhibition, Anthony, Stanton, and Matilda Joslyn Gage—all National Association officers—announced that they would write a one-volume history of the women's rights and suffrage movements.[9] They could tell their own story of American political womanhood, illustrated with portraits of their icons.

The *History of Woman Suffrage* proved to be the first comprehensive project to transform the movement's public image.[10] Publishers and engravers were still predominantly men, but suffrage leaders began to hire them for their own ends. In 1882, Stanton wrote to fellow suffragist Olympia Brown to ask for her portrait because she and her fellow editors had decided, "We wish posterity to know that we were a remarkably fine looking body of women!!"[11] Despite the immense cost of collecting and engraving images, they wanted their history to feature portraits of their founders for the public and later generations to admire. Of the three editors, Anthony proved especially dedicated to transforming the public image of political women. Her work to define herself and her colleagues as leaders ensured her own prominence in twenty-first-century suffrage iconography on everything from postage stamps and coins to history textbooks and exhibitions.

During the 1870s and 1880s, image distribution shifted as women who had once been individual reformers became the leaders of national organizations. Anthony recognized the movement's increasing cohesiveness as she cultivated its public image. In 1885, she wrote to a fellow suffragist: "25 & 30 years ago—Each woman went on her own hook—without thought of any other one's caring what she said or did!! While now—each one who speaks or writes or acts—there is a large constituency of thinking, intelligent, earnest women who feel themselves honored or disgraced." Suffragists had become a social type, and the appearance and actions of their leaders contributed to the way Americans imagined them. In contrast to previous decades, Anthony said, "mutual understandings & agreements . . . are vastly important to-day—as never before."[12]

In the 1880s, the National Association mobilized to present the movement's finest face to the public. Since their founding in 1869, they had aimed for their images to reach a broader audience than those of the competing American Woman Suffrage Association. The first volumes of the *History of Woman Suffrage* represented leaders according to conventions for depicting powerful men. Over time, however, suffragists decided to directly counter political cartoons that mocked them as masculine and saw them as threats to the social order. They featured more portraits that adhered to traditional conventions for representing femininity, to convince Americans that political women could remain womanly. By the end of the century, pictures of feminine suffragists became a key component of their visual campaign.

THE *HISTORY OF WOMAN SUFFRAGE* IN PORTRAITS

Soon after the Centennial Exhibition, Anthony went to Stanton's home in Tenafly, New Jersey, to start writing the *History of Woman Suffrage*. The editors sifted through their collections of letters, news clippings, and photographs. According to the *Chicago Daily Tribune*, Stanton had "scores of daguerreotypes, photographs, and steelplate engravings on the walls of her library."[13] Anthony, Gage, and Stanton probably looked through her collection to inspire the selections for their volumes. The National Association editors aimed to shape the way contemporaries and later generations would think of their movement.[14] While scholars have offered close readings of the text, they have not studied the images. The series continues to influence suffrage scholarship because it is the most complete—if distorted—visual and textual record from that period.

In 1881, five years after they announced their plan to write the *History of Woman Suffrage*, the editors published the first book of what became a six-volume series. The preface stated: "Our object has been to put into permanent shape the few scattered reports of the Woman Suffrage Movement still to be found, and to make it an arsenal of facts for those who are beginning to inquire into the demands and arguments of the leaders of this reform."[15] The book included twelve engraved portraits of women's rights leaders. In 1882, they published a second volume with thirteen portraits. They printed twenty-two in their third book four years later. By 1922, six roughly one-thousand-page volumes, with nearly one hundred images in all, covered the span of the movement. Each volume focused on about two decades. This section examines the first three volumes, all published in the 1880s by the original editors.

The portraits in the *History of Woman Suffrage* emphasized three main goals for a new vision of political womanhood. First, the public portraits implicitly eschewed the idea that women were supposed to prefer privacy. Next, they looked more like male politicians—even presidents—than beautiful, feminine, domestic women. Suffragists needed a public iconography of the movement's leaders. Finally, though editors had worked closely with reformers of color for decades, they linked their movement with elite white womanhood. In doing so, they relied on prevailing ideas about white women's superiority to make their demands. Their strategy to separate gender equality from racial equality aimed to assuage fears that the two were linked and thereby to win more support. The faces of white female leaders provided an example of political womanhood for rising generations to follow.

The editors rejected the idea that women should prefer privacy. Before the movement, their introduction stated, women did not have the "courage to compare their opinions with one another, nor to publish them." Recent activism, however, made public speaking and writing the new bulwarks of engaged femininity. They continued, "It requires philosophy and heroism to rise above the opinion of the wise men of all nations and races, that to be *unknown*, is the highest testimonial woman can have to her virtue, delicacy and refinement."[16] Political women had been "uniformly ridiculed, misrepresented, and denounced in public and private." The editors aimed to end the "odium" that "has ever rested on those who

4.2: J. C. Buttre, *Elizabeth Cady Stanton*, 1881, engraving, published in *History of Woman Suffrage*, vol. 1 (1881), facing page 721. Reproduction from Wellesley College, Library and Technology Services, Ella Smith Elbert Collection.

have risen above the conventional level." Suffrage leaders were "women of superior mental and physical organization, of good social standing and education" who combined "domestic virtues, knowledge of public affairs, and rare executive ability."[17]

Words and pictures could prove suffragists' "superior mental and physical organization." From the first volume, the editors modeled the vision of political womanhood they promoted. Stanton's portrait, a three-quarter view that depicts her from the shoulders up, might have provided an example for others (figure 4.2). She wears a black lace mantilla (a common accessory in her portraits) over her curled white hair. Stanton, in her late sixties when she edited the *History*, appears as a picture of modesty in venerable age. Anthony's portrait, in contrast, shows her in nearly full profile (figure 4.3). Only nine of the forty-eight portraits from the first three volumes feature women in this pose. Profiles recall the sculpted heads of male leaders from the classical era.[18] They distance the viewer from the subject and imply a position of power that was not associated with women. Unsmiling, Stanton and Anthony look into the distance away from the viewer. Like most of the era's sitters, they sought to capture their essential selves for posterity, not their transitory emotions.[19]

The editors looked to familiar presidential imagery that defined visual conventions for representing authority. Suffragists wanted the public to take them as seriously as they did their male leaders. A presidential campaign poster from 1880, the year before the publication of the *History*,

4.3: G. E. Perine & Co., *Susan B. Anthony*, 1881, engraving, published in *History of Woman Suffrage*, vol. 1 (1881), facing page 577. Reproduction from Wellesley College, Library and Technology Services, Ella Smith Elbert Collection.

4.4: Currier & Ives, *Grand National Republican Banner 1880*, 1880, lithograph. Courtesy of the Library of Congress, LC-DIG-pga-00739.

features the Republican candidates James Garfield and Chester Arthur (figure 4.4). Because it is a lithograph rather than an engraving, the poster has more finely graded coloring than the *History*'s engravings. The portraits represent the men at bust length, from the shoulders up. Garfield's portrait is a three-quarter view, while Arthur's face is almost full front. Arthur's directness was appropriate for a general and vice president, but

4.5: J. Hoover, *Heroes of the Colored Race*, 1883, chromolithograph.
Courtesy of the Library of Congress, LC-DIG-pga-01619.

less so for a female reformer. Flags and an eagle emphasize their patriotism and position as national leaders. Their military service strengthened their claim to power. Opponents of suffrage frequently argued that women should not vote because they could not fight for their country.

Some artists represented newly enfranchised black men according to the same visual conventions because, like the suffragists, they wanted to counter dominant stereotypes. During Reconstruction, which lasted from 1865 through 1877, the federal government ensured that African American men could exercise their rights in former Confederate states. Many ran for and won political office. One chromolithograph, made in Philadelphia by Joseph Hoover, depicts the *Heroes of the Colored Race* (figure 4.5). Frederick Douglass, who began cultivating his public image four decades before, appears in the center. The first two black United States senators, Blanche Bruce and Hiram Revels, flank him. Revels is in full profile, while the other two portraits are three-quarter views. Like Garfield and Arthur, the well-groomed trio wears elegant suits. They are surrounded by patriotic stars and stripes. These three powerful officials offered a model for fellow black men to follow. The style of their portraits matches that of the three presidents, Lincoln, Garfield, and Ulysses Grant, in the ovals above them. The portraits countered popular racist cartoons that represented black men as uneducated, unruly brutes who were incapable of holding office. The vignettes in the four corners present a history of black Americans, from slavery, war, and emancipation to education for full citizenship. Though the white printmaker likely supported black voters, he also expected the inexpensive chromolithograph to yield a profit.

The editors of the *History of Woman Suffrage* presented a female version of male leaders. They discussed men who supported the ballot for women, but they included none of the men's portraits. The editors could have selected Henry Brown Blackwell, who cofounded the American Association and the *Woman's Journal* with his wife Lucy Stone. Frederick Douglass supported the Declaration of Sentiments at the 1848 Seneca Falls convention, and Parker Pillsbury edited the *Revolution*. Male and female officers led the American Association, but the National Association still had only female leadership. Portraits of these male leaders would have been familiar to the public, but the editors prioritized their vision of political womanhood over telling a complete story.

Anthony published uniform portraits that resembled those of male politicians and signaled her ambition. The choice of portraiture was itself a statement. Portraits singled out individuals. Stanton and Anthony had already made their faces familiar to the public, and they endeavored to make the faces of other leading reformers recognizable too. Anthony could have hired an engraver to produce a view of women speaking to Congress, but images of women acting—rather than just looking—like leaders would have suggested that the dystopian world promised by antisuffrage cartoons was on the horizon, prompting anxiety for many Americans. For the first volume of the *History*, engravers copied older family photographs that the sitters never expected to circulate beyond their parlors. The pictures, as a result, have greater variation. Six suffragists face the viewer, four appear in three-quarter views, and two are in profile. In 1882, a year after the publication of the first volume, Anthony wrote to Elizabeth Boynton Harbert that she wanted a "Cabinet size" portrait that showed "just the head shoulders [*sic*]" in "about three quarters profile—not a full front—nor yet an entire profile—about halfway between."[20] In the second volume, ten of the thirteen portraits depict the women in a three-quarter view.

The *History* presented the most comprehensive collection of suffrage portraits yet, the movement's first visual canon. The editors as well as lecturer Frances Wright (whose portrait was the frontispiece), Lucretia Mott, and Amelia Bloomer appeared among the twelve subjects in the first volume. By then, the portraits of Mott, Anthony, and Stanton were likely recognizable, especially to supporters. The second volume included portraits of thirteen suffragists, including the famous lecturer Anna Dickinson and American Association officers Julia Ward Howe, Mary Livermore, and Lucy Stone. The twenty-two women with portraits in the third book included contemporaneous suffragists like Woman's Christian Temperance Union leader Frances Willard, Western lawyer and editor Laura de Force Gordon, and writer Lillie Devereux Blake.

The editors spent tremendous time and money on the portraits. Anthony wrote to women all over the United States to request their most flattering photographs.[21] Suffragists could mail multiple photographs for the engraver to use in creating a composite portrait with the most pleasing representation of their features. Anthony told Amelia Bloomer, for example, to specify which photograph had the "best eyes," "best hair," and "best mouth" in order to make the engraving "the best possible."[22] She hired skilled engravers to translate each photograph onto a metal plate. This process was time-consuming and expensive. Printers had not yet adopted a mechanical process for reproducing photographs alongside text in books. The steel engravings for the first three volumes alone cost $5,000 total, or about $100 to $150 each (in today's dollars, around $2,160 to $3,250 each).[23] For suffragists reliant on donors and short on funds, this was no small charge. The price affected the number of portraits in the *History* and determined which suffragists appeared in the work. Anthony wanted suffragists to pay for their engravings, but this strategy meant that she excluded poorer women.[24] She regretted this, writing "I am sorry that we have to come to this—because the women who will pay may be the one's [*sic*] to do the book the least good."[25] Wealthy women became the faces of the movement.

The cost might have contributed to the editors' choice to feature exclusively white women. Leading black activists, such as Sojourner Truth and Frances Ellen Watkins Harper, received no visual recognition in the *History*.[26] The editors did include a short biography of Truth, who, like Anthony, had voted in the 1872 presidential election. They snubbed Harper, who publicly criticized white reformers for ignoring the racism that black women faced.[27] By excluding the likenesses of women of color, the editors erased them from the movement's iconography.

However, if they had really wanted Truth's portrait, the editors could have raised the money, as they did for Clarina Howard Nichols's picture. Nichols, a Midwesterner, had spoken at women's rights conventions since 1850. An exchange between Nichols and Anthony demonstrates the connections many Americans made between whiteness and political power. In

1881, Nichols, then age seventy, responded to a letter from Anthony that requested her portrait for the *History*.[28] Nichols thought the photograph she had was poor. She and her son, George, believed "the lips are niggery" and "I never had such thick lips."[29] Nichols concluded that she would "rather lose it than have the thicklipped picture go into the History."[30] The editors intended to memorialize her for future generations, and the idea that she might resemble the stereotype of a black person repulsed her. She argued for the rights of freed black peoples, but her sentiment demonstrates the racism of even progressive activists.

Nichols wanted to conform to accepted conventions for representing women, not challenge them. She proposed to send a photograph that "all my friends and family call my best because of its truthfulness to the home look." She explained to Anthony, "I would like my picture to strike the reader as a womanly, mother by body; that would suggest nothing like the wooden face my pictures generally present."[31] What portrait she referred to is unclear because she did not include a copy with this letter. But based on other popular portraits of women from this era, the picture likely depicted her with the traditional studio props that suggested domesticity: a comfortable chair and side table draped in a decorative cloth with some flowers. She likely wore her best dress and a passive, yet compassionate, feminine expression.

The portrait that appeared in the first volume of the *History* was one of five featuring women facing full front (figure 4.6). A much younger Nichols sports ringlets on either side of her head—a fashionable style at midcentury—and an unsmiling expression. Perhaps this was the "wooden face" she believed she had. Nichols or the editors apparently did not like the result. They paid for a new one in the 1887 edition (figure 4.7). None of the other suffragists changed their portraits between editions because it was so expensive. In the updated version, Nichols's face appears more symmetrical and rounded. Her hair looks freshly curled without the flyaways of the previous portrait. The white collar and vertical seam up the front of her dress draw the viewer's eye to her face. Nichols's second portrait does not give her the "home look" she prized, but she appears more idealized.

The letters from Nichols illustrate a preference for the aesthetics of whiteness and femininity that grew stronger among suffragists during the 1880s and 1890s. With each volume of the *History*, the white women looked more feminine and wealthier. The number of women wearing head coverings (like bonnets or mantillas) decreased as the modesty they implied fell out of fashion. Suffragists began to wear more jewelry in their

4.6: J. C. Buttre, *Clarina I. Howard Nichols*, 1881, engraving, published in the *History of Woman Suffrage*, vol. 1 (1881), facing page 193. Reproduction from Wellesley College, Library and Technology Services, Ella Smith Elbert Collection.

4.7: J. C. Buttre, *Clarina I. Howard Nichols*, 1887, engraving, published in the *History of Woman Suffrage*, vol. 1, reprint ed. (1887), facing page 193. Courtesy of University of Toronto Libraries.

portraits. Only half of them wore brooches, earrings, or necklaces in the first volume, but seventeen of the twenty-two wore them in the third. Suffragists showed off their finest accoutrements to assure the public of their respectability. The change also reflected the movement's growing base of wealthier women and desire to attract more.

The American Woman Suffrage Association never countered the *History* with their own iconography and, instead, let their story be told by the National Association. The second volume featured three American Association officers and a chapter on their work. Portraits of its leaders— Lucy Stone, Mary Livermore, and Julia Ward Howe—composed nearly a quarter of the volume's images. Despite requests from the editors, Stone resisted contributing her biography or information about her group.[32] In 1876, she wrote to Stanton: "I do not think [the history of the movement] can be written by anyone who is alive to-day.... Your 'wing' surely are not competent to write the history of 'our wing.'"[33] Stone made a reasonable argument. In the 1880s, Anthony's organization was smaller than hers. The National Association campaigned for a federal amendment and social equality, which made them more controversial as well. In contrast, the larger American Association focused mainly on the vote. Their successful newspaper, the *Woman's Journal*, allowed Stone and her fellow leaders to communicate with supporters and coordinate their state-by-state campaigns.

If Stone had realized how much power the *History* and its portraits would give the National Association, perhaps she would have found a way to present her own vision. The American Association distributed few images to the public, which is one reason why its leaders are largely forgotten today. For example, the *Woman's Journal* buried an unenthusiastic announcement in the columns of an 1888 issue: their offices had "a few card photographs of Lucretia Mott, Lydia Maria Child, and William Lloyd Garrison for sale" at twenty-five cents each.[34] Rather than promoting current leaders, editors sold photographs of activists who had achieved prominence in the antislavery movement decades earlier. Mott was even a member of the competing National Association.

Anthony, Gage, and Stanton lacked the support of major publishers and worked hard to ensure their roughly one-thousand-page tomes reached the public.[35] Fowler & Wells, who printed the first two volumes, published almost exclusively for reformers on topics such as the water cure, efficient octagonal houses, and phrenology.[36] The editors used donations to furnish free copies for supporters and politicians, schools, and 1,200 public libraries in the United States and Europe.[37] Free copies significantly widened the reach of the expensive books. The first two volumes cost $5 for a copy bound in sheepskin, while an 1882 biography of Andrew Jackson by scholar William Graham Sumner cost only $1.25.[38]

The investment in portraits paid off. Reviewers recognized that the engravings aimed to establish the movement's "prominent suffragists" and "leading ladies."[39] They thought the engravings made the book more valuable. Reacting to the first volume, a reviewer praised the "very excellent steel-plate portraits of the handsome women." Another said "the admirable portraits in steel ... lend a special charm to the volume, and in themselves constitute a strong inducement to the general reader for its purchase."[40] As Anthony had hoped, the portraits offered flattering images of oft-derided suffragists. A range of periodicals printed reviews of the volumes, from the reform magazine the *Chautauquan* to mainstream publications like the *Washington Post* and *Godey's Lady's Book*.[41] When referring to the second book, one reviewer wrote: "The volume forms a remarkable history, and pictures the growing power of the women of America in the forum, on the platform, and in the earnest discussion before the most august assemblies of the land."[42] While the author meant the term "pictures" metaphorically, the portraits literally demonstrated women's growing power on the political stage.

Though the public offered some approval of the *History*, Stone's *Woman's Journal* did not. In her review of the first volume, Stone asserted that it should not have been written because women had not yet won the vote. Stone argued, furthermore, that the book did not represent the whole movement. She likened the situation to the comparatively radical abolitionists writing a history of the entire antislavery movement before the Thirteenth, Fourteenth, and Fifteenth Amendments had passed.[43] Her scorn did not relent with the second volume of the *History*. The *Woman's Journal* offered only a brief listing in the "Books Received" column.[44]

The *History of Woman Suffrage* became one of the most substantial self-representation projects by the founding generation of suffragists. Anthony, Gage, and Stanton promoted a grand new vision of political womanhood for the public, rather than just for supporters. The portraits broke with traditional American iconography by depicting individual women who resembled presidents, and they gave readers a set canon of the movement's leaders that still influences the suffragists we celebrate today. The portraits, furthermore, entrenched the cause as a fight for white women's political power.

THE "LOVEABLE" FACES OF THE BEST-KNOWN
FEMININE AGITATORS

The *History* stands out because popular imagery rarely represented political women in a positive light. Americans were familiar with women's portraits in private family albums, genre scenes of female domesticity, fashion plates, and caricatures of political women. In the late nineteenth century, more public portraits than ever before recognized the work of individual women, especially authors, reformers, and wives of political figures. Gradually, suffragists veered away from the visual conventions for portraying masculine political authority they had embraced in the *History*. They adopted a more feminine appearance and reinterpreted that femininity as politically powerful.

As the women's committee for the 1876 Centennial Exhibition knew, Martha Washington remained the preferred model of American political womanhood. She was so beloved that the United States Treasury printed her portrait on the one-dollar silver certificate in 1886 and again in 1891 and 1896. Washington became the first (and, at this writing, only) woman whose portrait has appeared on federal paper currency (figure 4.8).[45] Engravers copied the portrait of her in her late fifties and early sixties with a light-colored gauzy cap and shawl. Washington's portrait was among the few popular images of a prominent, older, and respected woman.[46] The notes recognized her as a venerable founder and promoted the version of womanhood she had long represented.[47] By then, she was a familiar, comforting face that provided a nostalgic reminder of the nation's past, when women supported the political activities of their husbands.

In combination with this currency "first," artists continued to mock suffragists using familiar visual tropes. Popular pictures still emphasized that they looked masculine or like fashionable, incompetent women. In the summer of 1894, the popular humor magazine *Puck* chose the latter stereotype for its cover (figure 4.9).[48] The chromolithograph *A Squelcher for Woman Suffrage* depicts an elite woman wearing wide skirts and puffed sleeves. As she approaches the voting booth, she realizes that she cannot fit inside. The illustration recalls cartoons from the 1860s that lampooned crinoline-clad women who could not perform practical tasks. Women's fashions had changed, but, according to cartoonists, they still prevented them from becoming equals. An accompanying article described the suffragist as a "society doll ... stuffed with sawdust" who took up the cause only for "her own amusement." There may not be "harm" in the "chatter" of "society women," the author continued, "but there is harm in tolerat-

4.8: Martha Washington's portrait on a one-dollar silver certificate, 1886. National Numismatic Collection at the Smithsonian Institution.

ing talk among men of shifting men's burden's on women's shoulders."[49] Opponents of suffrage believed that they protected women from such responsibility.

Though most popular images mocked political women, more publications featured their faces. Even editors who supported the cause, however, did not necessarily print flattering images. Anthony kept an eye on the press. In 1883, the *Cincinnati Commercial Gazette* printed engraved portraits of her and Stanton (figure 4.10). Anthony, then in Washington, DC, wrote to the editors that the engravings were "too horrible to have our names written under them."[50] Perhaps she objected to the deep lines on their faces, the extra roundness added to Stanton's cheeks, or the unusual outlines of their hairstyles. They did not look fashionable or pretty according to the era's standards; they also did not resemble male political leaders. Instead, they appeared stern and misshapen.

Anthony wrote that she had seen the same unflattering portraits reprinted in the Philadelphia *Call* less than a week later. She worried that

4.9: Charles Taylor, *A Squelcher for Woman Suffrage*, 1894, chromolithograph, published in *Puck*, June 6, 1894, page 241. The caption reads "How can she vote, when the fashions are so wide, and the voting booths are so narrow?" The sign on the voting booth reads, "Ballots must be prepared in these booths." Courtesy of the Library of Congress, LC-DIG-ppmsca-29110.

SUSAN B. ANTHONY.
THE STRONGEST FEMALE ADVOCATE OF FEMININE
FRANCHISE IN THE UNITED STATES.

ELIZABETH CADY STANTON.
A BRIEF BIOGRAPHY OF THE VETERAN RE-
FORMER.

4.10: Portraits of Susan B. Anthony (left) and Elizabeth Cady Stanton
(right), 1883, engraving, printed in the *Cincinnati Commercial Gazette*,
December 23, 1883, extra sheet page 1. Courtesy of the Library of
Congress.

other papers would borrow the engravings too, a common practice that
kept the cost of illustrations down. Anthony asked the *Gazette* whether
the editors would "be so kind as to destroy [the engraving plates]." She
asserted that Stanton was "a very fine-looking woman." Anthony also joked
about her own sensitivity regarding "being made to look more ugly than
truth absolutely demands." For any future engravings, she told the paper
to ask her for photographs to work from. The *Gazette*'s article praised the
pair for their activism, noting that Anthony did not have an "unseemly or
unkempt radical air" and that Stanton had "the most loveable face of the
best known feminine agitators."[51] The engravings, then, likely resulted
from poor handiwork rather than an editor's attempt to mock them. Still,
Anthony realized that unattractive portraits contributed to negative perceptions of political women.

Opponents of suffrage grew concerned as movement leaders gained
visibility and the number of female voters increased. In the 1880s, women
began to vote in western states.[52] The territory of Wyoming had allowed

female voters since its founding in 1869. In 1890, when the territory became a state, Wyoming became the first to grant women the ballot.[53] Similarly, since 1870, the territory of Utah had allowed women to vote. In 1887, the Edmunds-Tucker Act overturned the law during debates over Utah's statehood, but women won back the vote in 1896. While Utah and Wyoming fully enfranchised women, other states allowed women to vote in certain local elections. By 1890, twenty-four states allowed women to vote in elections relating to schools. Kansas granted women the right to vote in municipal elections, while women in Montana voted in elections related to taxes.[54]

As more western women voted, Americans in the east wondered what enfranchised women really looked like. In the 1880s, the two most popular illustrated papers, *Harper's Weekly* and *Frank Leslie's Illustrated Newspaper*, responded to such curiosity.[55] In 1888, *Frank Leslie's* printed an illustration of women voting in Cheyenne, Wyoming, on its front page (figure 4.11). The engraving depicts seven women in line to vote while a uniformed man, perhaps an election inspector, monitors the scene. The women wear fashionable dresses and hats. One woman on the right has her young son at her side carrying a wicker basket full of the day's groceries. At the far right of the frame, a woman hands a voter a slip of paper, probably in an effort to persuade her on a certain candidate or issue. She wears glasses (signifying her education or interest in knowledge) and looks active (she seems to have been captured midsentence). Even so, this political woman remains within conventional boundaries of respectable femininity.

This decorous scene starkly contrasts with popular cartoons of female voters. Opponents still argued that enfranchised women caused a host of problems, from voter fraud to moral disorder, but they had no major organizations yet.[56] The engraving in *Frank Leslie's* countered their arguments by illustrating that political women had not become manly or abandoned their families. The scene makes public life in Cheyenne look peaceful and suggests that home life remained peaceful as well. The accompanying article emphasized that "ladies" were taken in "elegant carriages" to polls "as orderly as those of any Eastern town." They were "apt political workers" who were more interested in the "moral influence of the candidates" than men were.[57] The illustration, the author reminded viewers, copied a photograph; therefore, the engraving was credible. Not wanting to miss a story, *Harper's Weekly* printed a similar illustration of women voting in Boston's municipal elections a few weeks later.[58]

Positive imagery of political women remained uncommon in mainstream newspapers, but *Frank Leslie's* was a special case. After the death

FRANK LESLIE'S ILLUSTRATED NEWSPAPER

No. 1,732.—Vol. LXVII.]   NEW YORK—FOR THE WEEK ENDING NOVEMBER 24, 1888.   [Price, 10 Cents.

WOMAN SUFFRAGE IN WYOMING TERRITORY.—SCENE AT THE POLLS IN CHEYENNE.
From a Photo. by Kirkland.—See Page 213.

4.11: *Woman Suffrage in Wyoming Territory.—Scene at the Polls in Cheyenne. From a Photo by Kirkland*, 1888, engraving, published in *Frank Leslie's Illustrated Newspaper*, November 24, 1888, 229. Courtesy of the Library of Congress, LC-USZ62-106109.

of Frank Leslie in 1880, his wife legally changed her name to Mrs. Frank Leslie and managed the newspaper.[59] Leslie financially supported the suffrage movement throughout her life and believed in the importance of the press.[60] When she died in 1914, she left half of her estate—nearly a million dollars—to fund suffrage presswork through the Leslie Woman Suffrage Commission.[61]

The rising interest in women's suffrage helped spur the union of the American Association and the National Association. The cause needed the strength it could gain with a united front. In 1890, after three years of negotiations, Alice Stone Blackwell (the daughter of Lucy Stone and Henry Brown Blackwell) mediated the merger. The new National American Woman Suffrage Association (NAWSA) split its efforts between passing a federal amendment and state laws to grant women the vote. The American Association's platform, which focused more specifically on the vote, won the day. As a compromise, Stanton became the first president.[62] Under NAWSA, suffragists created the first coherent public image of their movement. The united group took advantage of their rising profile to present a public face that appealed to a broader range of supporters. NAWSA adopted the American Association's toned-down rhetoric, but they incorporated the visual strategies pioneered by Anthony and her fellow leaders of the National Association.

Suffragists united in an era when American women were beginning to join national organizations in large numbers.[63] In the 1890s, male and female reformers banded together to advocate for social justice and lobby against corruption, political machines, and monopolies. Their activism characterized the period from roughly 1890 through 1920, known as the Progressive Era. Reformers wanted the government to provide regulations that would improve the lives of all Americans.[64] They believed it was the government's responsibility, for example, to ensure that citizens drank unadulterated milk and worked in safe, regulated industries. Reformers wanted city dwellers to enjoy nature in public parks and walk down streets free of trash and human waste.

Women's suffrage became part of the Progressive platform. Gender ideals held that women, especially white women, were morally superior to men. Reformers argued, therefore, that women's votes would ensure the passage of moral legislation, such as laws aimed to decrease government corruption. Progressives incorporated traditional values to advocate for their modern social justice goals. Women's concerns for their families, homes, and schools would simply extend a little further into politics. This message—this "public motherhood" rhetoric—dominated arguments and visual politics through the end of the movement.

Conservative elite and middle-class white women populated many Progressive Era clubs, which gradually pledged to support suffrage. They lent crucial respectability and funds to the cause.[65] As chapter 5 examines further, these women often segregated their clubs by race. Even when national club regulations did not exclude women of color, local chapters could and did. Some black suffragists persisted and worked alongside white reformers, while others formed their own clubs with their own agendas.

As the new organization's leaders, Stanton and Anthony continued to orchestrate the public image of suffrage with portraits at first. In 1891, Stanton, NAWSA's first president, sat with her vice president, Anthony, for a picture. The portrait was taken in a photography studio, and the blank background focuses the viewers' attention on the women (figure 4.12).[66] A spectacled Anthony stands as she rests her hand on Stanton's shoulder and assists her. The two concentrate on the sheet of paper they hold together. The women appear as if the photographer has captured them without their knowledge. The paper might be a letter from Stanton's daughter or a suffrage text. The act of reading makes them look more traditionally feminine in comparison to the *History of Woman Suffrage*'s portraits or their portraits as defiant activists from their 1870 session (figure 3.11 on p. 74). Stanton and Anthony wanted to appeal to a broader audience, and nearly all American women had done the activity their portrait shows.

The photograph suggests that female political leaders could remain caring and womanly even as visible leaders of the suffrage movement. Their poses and aging faces might reinforce the stereotype that these older women were wise and nonthreatening caregivers. James Garfield and Chester Arthur, for example, would not have had themselves photographed in such a maternal pose. And yet, this compelling portrait demonstrates the pair's long friendship and joint activism. In her 1885 speech "The Pleasures of Age," Stanton contended that older women, whose children had grown, should not be passive. Without the responsibility of motherhood, these women had the greatest opportunities to develop themselves and improve society by leading reform movements.[67]

Although the pair did not significantly change their political views, they did moderate their public image to offer a fresh picture of feminine, maternal political womanhood. An article in the Washington, DC, *Evening Star* from 1889 reinforces Anthony's growing preference for a less aggressive presence. The author was adamant that "nothing in her appearance ...

4.12: Elizabeth Cady Stanton, seated, and Susan B. Anthony, standing, three-quarter length portrait, ca. 1890s, carte de visite photograph. The photograph was taken in 1891, and the print dates from 1891 to 1895. Schlesinger Library, Radcliffe Institute, Harvard University.

is manly" or "correspond[s] with the distorted idea of a woman's rights agitator." Instead, she has a "strong and intellectual face" that is "full of womanly gentleness." Her glasses even give her a "motherly" expression, perhaps by suggesting that she is wise.[68] Since Anthony's authorized biography reproduced this article a decade later, the description must have pleased her.[69]

The *History of Woman Suffrage* and cartes de visite like this one represented the end of an era. These portraits are some of the last examples of efforts by individual leaders like Anthony to cultivate their movement's public image. In the 1890s, the founding generation of suffragists began to retire from public life. Starting in 1891, Anthony limited her travel and spent more time in her Rochester home. Stanton, who had often balanced family duties with work, "rejoice[d]" that Anthony was "going to housekeeping ... where you can live and die in peace."[70] The two remained suffrage leaders but delegated more daily tasks to their growing organization.

NEW ORGANIZATION, NEW TECHNOLOGY, AND A NEW POLITICAL WOMANHOOD

In the 1890s, a rising generation of suffragists emerged to lead NAWSA and coordinate a visual campaign to define a positive vision of political womanhood. Instead of individual leaders making decisions, suffragists formed committees to manage representations of their leaders in the press. They also took advantage of new image technology: the halftone printing process. At first, NAWSA continued the tradition of printing portraits of their founding mothers. The imagery served to unite suffragists behind a shared vision of their movement's history as they plotted its future.

In the 1890s, suffragists started to distribute photographic halftones, a visual medium that dramatically altered the American visual landscape.[71] For the first time, photographs could be printed alongside text in newspapers, magazines, and books. Images gradually became standard in all newspapers, not just illustrated ones. More pictures than ever before entered American homes of all income levels. Halftones, like the photographs they copied, offered viewers a sense of authenticity that engravings could not.[72] The printing process breaks up images into a pattern of dots of varying sizes that appear as a unified image when viewed from a distance. Printers mechanized the illustration process and lowered their production costs.[73] The time-consuming, labor-intensive chore of pasting photographs into books by hand had made photograph books too expensive. Halftones

4.13: *Lucy Stone*,
halftone, published in
the *Woman's Column*,
April 15, 1893, page 1.
Collection of the Massachusetts Historical
Society.

did not require the cost, time, skill, or materials that engravings did, either. They became widespread by 1893 and are still printed today.[74]

Progressive Era activists capitalized on the apparent realism of halftones to promote their reforms. In 1890, the journalist Jacob Riis was among the first to incorporate them, in his book *How the Other Half Lives*. Photographic halftones gave evidence of the miserable living conditions of poor New Yorkers. His photographs depict dirty, cramped tenements and children laboring in sweatshops. Riis and his famous photographs helped to convince the public that they needed to regulate housing standards to improve the lives of the poor.[75]

Alice Stone Blackwell wanted her mother, Lucy Stone, to be recognized as one of the movement's founding mothers, and she printed halftones of Stone. Whereas Anthony, Stanton, and the women they trained ensured their legacy, Stone did little to promote herself. Blackwell edited her mother's paper, the *Woman's Journal*, as well as the *Woman's Column*, a biweekly suffrage paper. She frequently highlighted Stone's work and printed portraits of her. Blackwell argued her mother had not sought fame because she embraced privacy over publicity. Stone, she believed, would be "annoyed" when she learned her portrait and biography had been published.[76]

Blackwell helped two of Stone's portraits become familiar. The first

4.14: *Lucy Stone in 1855*, halftone, published in the *Woman's Column*, March 24, 1894, page 1. Collection of the Massachusetts Historical Society.

ran on the front page of the *Woman's Journal* and the *Woman's Column* in April 1893 (figure 4.13). The original photograph dates from between 1888 and 1893 and depicts Stone as an older woman.[77] She wears a lace head covering that gathers at the neck and spreads over her shoulders. Rather than engaging the viewer, she looks into the distance. After Stone died in October 1893, the *Woman's Journal* printed the same portrait on the front page of its memorial issue.[78] The second popular portrait of Stone appeared on the front page of both papers in 1894 (figure 4.14).[79] This version was based on an 1855 photograph that was probably not intended for the public. The picture features a thirty-seven-year-old Stone with a similar expression and three-quarter-view pose. The young woman wears her dark hair neatly pulled back, without the lacy covering from the later portrait.

Suffragists favored the portrait of her as an older woman. In November 1893, the *Column* and *Journal* began distributing Stone's portraits to anyone who recruited new subscribers.[80] Readers could choose between "the likeness taken of her as a woman in the prime of her life, or that which shows her as an elderly woman in a white cap." The notice, probably written by Blackwell, went on to state, "The latter is the favorite with most people."[81] Age enhanced the suffragists' appearance of respectability. Another notice stressed that "a very general expression of desire" existed for Stone's portrait, and that the photographs were made for "permanent preservation."[82]

The year before, both of Blackwell's papers had featured an article that implicitly reinforced Stone's feminine, motherly style. The author, E. M. H. Merrill, cited "the once popular idea that a typical woman suffragist must be a tall, gaunt, and homely female, with aggressive manners, a masculine air and a strident voice." Stone did not fit this mental "picture." According to Merrill, Stone was "small and plump, very quiet, gentle and unassuming in manner" with a sweet voice and "winning charm." Merrill finished the description by noting that her "snowy white cap and fichu of dainty lace" made her "look like the lovely grandmother of all good children!"[83]

Stone and her lacy white cap conjured a striking resemblance to Martha Washington. Suffragists took advantage of the continued popularity of this visual type of feminine political power and reframed the first lady as a suffrage icon. Since the 1860s, commentators had noted a resemblance between the founding generation of suffrage leaders—especially Stanton and her famous white curls—and the founding mother of the republic.[84] They were, after all, among the few women whose faces were familiar to the public.

At the end of the century, during a rise in efforts to preserve the nation's early historical artifacts and landmarks, suffragists linked portraits of their aging founding mothers to Washington and incorporated her portraits into their own iconography. A rare photograph of an 1894 meeting in New York shows a host of speakers, including Anthony and other NAWSA presidents, sitting on a stage (figure 4.15).[85] Seven large portraits hang above the platform. Oval portraits of Martha (left) and George Washington (right) hang from columns on either side. Likenesses on the back wall of the stage include those of Abraham Lincoln, Stanton, and Anthony. The Washingtons represented the founding of the democratic nation, and Northern reformers recognized Lincoln as a human rights advocate. Suffragists even argued that Lincoln had endorsed women's suffrage in an 1839 letter.[86] These pictures served as a history of leaders who supported political equality.

The *Woman's Journal* often described such exhibits of portraits. Suffragists decorated platforms at meetings, printed halftones in newspapers, posted photographs in the windows and on the walls of their headquarters, and sold them to raise money. After Stone died, for example, the Maryville Equal Suffrage Association in Tennessee held a memorial. A local suffragist wrote to the paper that activists had gathered a group of "pictures of her

4.15: Suffrage meeting, probably in New York, 1894, photograph.
Courtesy of the Friends Historical Library of Swarthmore College.

strong and bonny face" (clipped from the *Woman's Journal*) and "encircled" them with flowers.[87] Another club in Galva, Illinois, displayed portraits of Anthony, Stanton, Stone, and Henry Blackwell at a reception. At a NAWSA-sponsored birthday celebration for Stanton in Hampden Corner, Maine, suffragists exhibited large portraits of both her and Anthony.[88]

NAWSA portrait displays helped to recruit new suffragists. The *Woman's Column* encouraged readers to showcase portraits in their home. An 1892 article, "What Southern Women Say," recounted the story of Floridian Mrs. F. B. Chamberlain, who had displayed Anthony's picture "in her home for years."[89] One day she used it to attract "an old colored woman" to support suffrage. She told the African American woman, perhaps a domestic worker, "whose picture it was, and something about what Miss Anthony had tried to do, and what bad things had been said about her." Soon after, Chamberlain saw the woman speaking to the portrait, encouraging Anthony: "You keep right on, for you's right."[90] Chamberlain's story insisted portraits could help attract supporters. Whether the account was true or

4.16: Frances B. Johnston, *Susan B. Anthony at Her Desk*, taken in 1900, copyright 1905, photograph. Sophia Smith Collection, Smith College.

apocryphal, the article encouraged others to follow her example. The story also implied that white women should reach out to more black women.

Although Anthony decided to focus on "housekeeping" in 1891, she remained a committed organizer and often appeared in suffrage publications. She served as NAWSA's president from 1892 through 1900 and worked to ensure her status as a suffrage icon. In 1900, NAWSA printed a calendar illustrated with photographs of her home in Rochester, New York. The eighty-year old leader shared her display of portraits with viewers (figure 4.16).[91] The photograph depicts Anthony in profile seated at her desk.[92] Suffrage paraphernalia covers every surface. Twenty-one portraits are visible in the uncropped version. For the most part, the portraits feature individuals, but one larger group picture features suffragists from an 1888 meeting of the International Council of Women. Though Anthony might have placed additional portraits in the room for this session (such as the ones on her desk), the pictures on the shelves and walls probably always hung there. The engravings and photographs depict prominent women—from Mary Wollstonecraft, Ernestine Rose, Lucretia Mott, and Anna Dickinson to Ida Husted Harper, Anna Howard Shaw, and Stanton.[93]

The portraits represent Anthony's personal relationships with and support for these leading women.

Frances Johnston, one of the first female commercial photographers, took this photograph. She made portraits of politicians (including Theodore Roosevelt) and socialites alike. Johnston grew up in the capital and gained entrée into political society through her family, particularly her mother, who was a political correspondent for the Baltimore *Sun* in the 1870s.[94] The photographer did not campaign for women's rights, but her work paved the way for other women to become commercial photographers. She shifted cultural notions of womanhood rather than legal ones.

Johnston rebelled against traditional conventions for representing women. She even photographed herself in men's clothing.[95] Her portraits of society women pictured them full-length and with soft lighting against neutral backgrounds.[96] In contrast, she portrayed Anthony the way she depicted male political leaders. The portrait emphasizes the suffragist's face and her political work. Anthony sits among the stuff of the movement: letters, papers, volumes of the *History*, and portraits of inspirational women. She had been photographed many times before in studios, but this picture gave viewers a glimpse of her behind the scenes. Johnston highlighted the outline of Anthony's head by draping a dark cloth behind her. Through the powerful profile pose and this suffrage display, Johnston implied her importance was on par with the era's male political leaders. The Anthony Portrait Committee, which commissioned Johnston, noted the photographs from this session had "received Miss Anthony's approval and high praise."[97]

Suffragists hoped to raise money by selling the pictures. Supporters could purchase photographic prints and postcards for fifty cents to a dollar (depending on the size). Or they could pay fifty cents for the 1901 *Anthony Home Calendar*, which included more photographs from Johnston's session (figure 4.17).[98] The halftones and accompanying captions portrayed Anthony as a living legend. One depicted "A Corner of the Famous Attic, Where the Records of Fifty Years of Suffrage Are Stored," while another captured the "Table on Which the Call for the First Woman Suffrage Convention Was Written in 1848."[99] The calendar tempered the political imagery with pictures of Anthony's quilting and needlework.

NAWSA encouraged members to purchase and display suffrage imagery in their homes as Anthony did. Supporters bought images through suffrage periodicals and at bazaars, headquarters, and conventions. NAWSA's 1898 annual meeting, for example, had "suffrage supplies," including leaflets

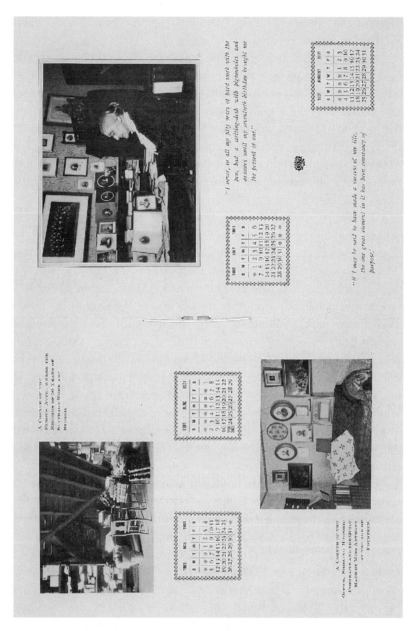

4.17: A cropped and published halftone version of *Susan B. Anthony at Her Desk*. Catharine M. Fleming, *The Anthony Home Calendar*, with illustrations by Frances B. Johnston, 1900, page 5. Schlesinger Library, Radcliffe Institute, Harvard University.

and badges, as well as "miniatures of leading suffragists, photographs and books" for sale in the lobby.[100] The *Woman's Journal* advertised "Beautiful Suffrage Calendars" embellished with sunflower designs and portraits of male and female suffragists for twenty-five cents.[101] NAWSA collected donations in small boxes adorned with portraits of Stone. They also gave away three thousand copies of souvenir books at a suffrage fair that featured Stone, Mary Livermore, and Julia Ward Howe.[102] At the annual meeting in 1900, NAWSA sold five hundred "Susan B. Anthony Buttons" with "a small bow of yellow ribbon" for ten cents each. The buttons—the "badge of the Convention"—probably featured a small portrait of Anthony with a yellow ribbon pinned to it, similar to those that survive from later meetings.[103]

The last volumes of the *History of Woman Suffrage* reflected the expansion of the suffragists' visual campaign. Through the passage of the Nineteenth Amendment, NAWSA used portraits to inspire supporters and remind the public of the movement's long history. In 1902, with Ida Husted Harper, Anthony published the fourth volume with thirty-five inexpensive halftone portraits, more than twice the average number of portraits from the first three volumes. In 1922, Harper completed the final two volumes of the series. Some pages feature small, formal portraits of (mostly) deceased suffrage pioneers (figure 4.18). However, other photographic halftones depict suffragists in action, including NAWSA president Carrie Chapman Catt celebrating the passage of the Nineteenth Amendment (figure 4.19). Together, the last two volumes had only sixteen images.[104] Suffragists no longer relied on these expensive, thousand-page books to publicize their work. The shift in imagery over the course of the *History of Woman Suffrage* series points to the reformers' efforts to incorporate innovative visual mediums and cultivate new outlets to reach broader audiences.

THE END OF AN ERA

By the start of the twentieth century, Anthony and her protégés had enshrined her as a suffrage icon. As she completed the final volumes of the *History*, Harper worked with Anthony on her authorized biography. The pair burned documents that contradicted Anthony's preferred public image.[105] Though Alice Stone Blackwell continued to publicize her mother's legacy, Lucy Stone never became central to the popular suffrage story. Even Stanton lost her footing, especially after she authored *The Woman's Bible* in 1895. The book challenged biblical instructions for women's subservience to men, and NAWSA condemned it.[106] Stanton remained a controversial reformer until her death in 1902.

4.18: *Pioneers of Woman Suffrage*, halftones, 1922, printed in the *History of Woman Suffrage*, vol. 5 (1922), opposite p. 172. The page features portraits of (clockwise from top left) Elizabeth Cady Stanton, Lucy Stone, Millicent Garrett Fawcett, and Lucretia Mott encircling a picture of Susan B. Anthony. Courtesy of University of Toronto Libraries.

4.19: *Mrs. Carrie Chapman Catt*, halftone, 1922, printed as the frontispiece in the *History of Woman Suffrage*, vol. 6 (1922). Courtesy of University of Toronto Libraries.

In contrast, Anthony's politics accommodated the movement's increasingly conservative, middle-class base.[107] An icon while she lived, she became a suffrage saint when she died in 1906. NAWSA regularly featured Anthony's likeness. Her face provided inspiration and represented the historical struggle for women's political equality. Sometimes her photograph appeared alongside an inspirational quote from her last public speech: "Failure is impossible" (figure 4.20).[108] In the 1910s, NAWSA peddled large photographic portraits—up to sixteen by twenty-two inches—of their presidents, with the exception of Stanton.[109] Suffragists eventually nicknamed the Nineteenth Amendment the "Susan B. Anthony Amendment."

By the time Anthony died, she—with the help of her colleagues—had already established the iconography of their movement's founding mothers. The leaders promoted in the *History of Woman Suffrage* remain the movement's most recognizable figures. The mainstream popular press, still run by mostly male editors and artists, continued to print satirical cartoons that suggested the consequences of women having men's responsibilities. Suffragists hired artists, printed materials, and distributed their vision through their own newspapers, events, and publications. The

Susan Brownell Anthony

February 15, 1820—March 13, 1906.

"Failure is impossible"

4.20: *Susan Brownell Anthony, February 15, 1820–March 13, 1906: "Failure Is Impossible,"* after 1906. Library of Congress, Rare Book and Special Collections Division, National American Woman Suffrage Association Collection, http://hdl.loc.gov/loc.rbc/rbcmil.scrp2005301.

first unified national organization used the latest visual technologies and publicity techniques to further their visual campaign. The portraits they circulated celebrated feminine political leadership that prized elite whiteness. NAWSA became ever more invested in ensuring that the public knew that they were, as Stanton once wrote, a "fine looking body of women."

5.1: George Prince
Photography Studio,
portrait of Mary
Church Terrell,
ca. 1896, cabinet card
photograph. Courtesy
of the Moorland-
Spingarn Research
Center, Manuscript
Division, Howard
University.

5: COMPETING VISUAL CAMPAIGNS

One day in 1896 (or perhaps late 1895), Mary Church Terrell, then in her early thirties, selected a dark dress fashioned with stylish oversized sleeves. The popular silhouette gave the impression that Terrell had broad shoulders and made her appear more imposing than she was. In her home in LeDroit Park next to Howard University—the best neighborhood in Washington, DC, for elite black families—she sat in front of her mirror to fix her hair, perhaps with the help of a maid. It needed to look smooth, not a hair out of place. Finally, Terrell selected jeweled drop earrings to sparkle next to her beaded dress. A white flower brooch seemed like the perfect finishing touch for her ensemble. She was ready to have her portrait taken.

Terrell was one of the first black women in the nation to receive a bachelor's degree. She wrote in her autobiography that she had seen plenty of the cartoons by "comedians" who portrayed educated women in "bad-looking, unbecoming hats, long dresses with the hem ripped half out, and shoes run down at the heel." She wanted to "prove all those charges against college-bred women false."[1] Terrell had traveled Europe and kept up with the latest fashions. She wanted people to know it.

Terrell visited George Prince's photography studio at Pennsylvania Avenue and Eleventh Street Northwest. From that corner, she could see the rotunda of the US Capitol building. Terrell could not vote for any of the men who met there; neither could her husband. The district had lost its congressional representatives in 1874. The men who did meet in the building (and their wives) were the city's most powerful people. Prince photographed their faces and the ceremonies they attended. Terrell wanted a portrait that would position her, socially and politically, as a leader who would force them to make changes.

She selected a nearly full-profile photograph to be her representative to the world (figure 5.1). In the tradition of American political portraiture, Terrell looks into the distance and contemplates the future. The angle illuminates the light complexion, which won her greater privilege and respectability than a darker tone would have. She allowed the public to see her face, but they would never fully know her. Terrell was the daughter of formerly enslaved parents, and her skin tone implicitly points to the rape of her enslaved foremothers. She was related to wealthy white Southern families. Yet the era's "one-drop rule," more of a cultural code than a legal one, categorized her and anyone with African ancestry as black. Her profile portrait recalls Susan B. Anthony's popular portraits in the same pose, perhaps suggesting Terrell's similar aspiration to lead. Soon after her sitting, she paid local engraver J. H. Cunningham to translate her photograph onto a metal plate for reproduction in newspapers across the country. Cunningham's copy, as well as less fine versions, appeared in newspapers such as the *Colored American*, the *Woman's Era*, and the *Chicago Daily News*.[2]

Terrell used her image of feminine respectability as a weapon to win favor from the public. In 1896, around the time she took this portrait, delegates from across the country elected her the first president of the National Association of Colored Women (NACW). Terrell never represented only herself. She represented NACW members and their goal to improve the lives of people of color, declared in their motto of racial uplift: "Lifting as We Climb." These elite reformers embraced respectability politics, working to uphold social norms dictated by dominant white society. By speaking and acting like white Americans, they aimed to challenge racist stereotypes of black people. Though often studied as an ideology, appearance and public images were central to this strategy of proving that they looked similar to white Americans. While respectability politics subverted racist tropes, the ideology proved conservative and was even a form of confinement. Advocates aimed to meet standards set in place by the dominant white culture, and doing so required money. To appear respectable, reformers needed to present their best selves. They wanted to show that women of color were intelligent, well educated, elegantly dressed, and virtuous citizens who cared for their families and communities. Terrell's portrait, essentially, needed to resemble those of leading, moneyed white women. She needed to be a refined, visible leader. Terrell and her colleagues had a "double handicap"—a term Terrell used to refer to the disadvantages she faced because of her race and sex—which meant they encountered prejudice on many fronts, including from racist suffragists, antisuffragists, sexist black men, and advocates of white supremacy. In changing the perception of black women, the NACW believed respectability politics would provide a strategy to advance the entire race.

White suffragists, with the help of the mainstream press, distanced themselves from black reformers. Terrell and her fellow NACW members did not have to wait long for racist cartoons to attack them. In June 1897, the cover of *Leslie's Weekly Illustrated*, the descendant of *Frank Leslie's*

Illustrated Newspaper, featured the *First Parade of the New Woman's Society in Possumville* (figure 5.2). A large, dark-skinned woman in the center leads the parade. She has on a double-breasted coat, a crumpled hat, and tall boots and holds a sign that reads: "WIMMINZ IZ NOT THE SLAV OF MAN." The woman next to her wears a blank expression and hunches over a drum. In front, a young girl, crowned with spiky hair, grins mischievously. Perhaps she reminded viewers of the unruly tomboy Topsy, an enslaved character from the bestseller *Uncle Tom's Cabin*. She and the boy on the left wear tattered clothes, evidence that their mothers did not properly care for them. This image contends that these uneducated, unwomanly activists did not deserve respect, and that they were foolish to believe they could do anything to uplift the race. While *Frank Leslie's* had printed favorable images of white women voting, especially under suffragist Mrs. Frank Leslie's management from 1880 until 1889, this picture undermines the efforts of suffragists of color.[3]

In the late nineteenth century, white women systematically excluded black women and focused their campaign on winning the ballot for themselves. If white suffragists had wanted black women to vote, they would have had to fight against laws in each of the Southern states that allowed literacy tests and poll taxes to disenfranchise black men too. White suffragists wanted to focus energy and funds on the vote for women, even if that meant excluding black women. Some even worked to ensure that legislation for white women's votes would not enfranchise African Americans. In the 1880s, Susan B. Anthony and her fellow editors had produced the *History of Woman Suffrage* to portray white female suffragists as political leaders. Projects to entrench associations between suffrage and whiteness continued in its wake, misrepresenting the diversity of the women who sought the ballot. Following the Woman's Christian Temperance Union's model, at the turn of the century the National American Woman Suffrage Association (NAWSA) built up their organization with press committees and professionals to coordinate a national visual campaign. Their pictures stressed that women's votes would bolster established notions of virtuous white femininity, upholding the racial hierarchy. Women of color, in response to their exclusion and to further their own causes, formed organizations to promote their own visions of political womanhood. Histories of women's voting rights often overlook the NACW: technically, the organization did not list women's votes as their priority at their founding. This choice relegates black suffragists to the sidelines, just like NAWSA did. The NACW obviously wanted political power. They elected a suffragist as their first president and sought policies and programs that would improve black communities.

5.2: *First Parade of The New Woman's Society in Possumville*, 1897, engraving, published in *Leslie's Weekly Illustrated*, June 10, 1897, page 375. Courtesy of the Library of Congress, LC-USZC2-755.

Elite black reformers like Terrell took advantage of the latest visual technologies to cultivate a new public image for leading black women. In the popular press, negative representations of black women dominated. In comparison to NAWSA, the NACW had fewer members and less funding. They relied on elite leaders like Terrell, the black press, and reform-minded publications to develop a positive face for the public. White women were already associated with morality and virtue, and black women like Terrell distributed their own portraits to make a similar claim. Terrell employed strategies pioneered by Sojourner Truth and Susan B. Anthony to position herself as a prominent leader and entreat the public to take her platform seriously. By then, popular reproductions of portraits of Phillis Wheatley and Truth were exemplars of black womanhood, especially in the black community. Reformers like Terrell built on the iconography of the earlier women, but she emphasized her own upper-class refinement and lighter skin. These reformers aimed to transform the face of black political womanhood to help advance equality.

WILLS OF THEIR OWN

Terrell was part of a rising generation of women who wanted to have more influence on American society than their mothers had. In the late nineteenth century, women, especially those of the elite and middle classes, had better opportunities for higher education than ever before.[4] They entered new professions, ranging from journalism to photography. Many women became part of national organizations, composed of state and local clubs, that articulated the central ideas of the Progressive Era. They advocated for policies that promoted government intervention to ameliorate problems, from dirty urban streets to corporate corruption. Consequently, the state became more integrated in modern life, and more women identified the ballot as essential to American citizenship. Suffragists used their education, skills, and professional connections to develop a new face for their movement with their first piece of visual propaganda. While Terrell became an icon of elite, refined, and educated womanhood for people of color, white suffragists enlisted the morality and virtue already associated with their skin tone to advance their campaign.

Members of the NACW were not the only ones who subscribed to respectability politics. Other activists helped Terrell establish herself as a prominent woman within the black community before the group's founding. Building on *Eminent Women of the Age*, *History of Woman Suffrage*, and numerous other books that praised influential white women, black reformers authored books about leading women of color in the 1890s. In 1892, Dr. M. A. Majors requested the portrait of the exceptionally well-educated Terrell. He wanted her to hold "a prominent place" in his forthcoming book, *Noted Negro Women*.[5] Majors believed it was necessary to show "the world who our women are and what they are doing ... in order that many others may be stimulated to emulate them."[6]

A year later, Gertrude Mossell, a journalist and suffrage advocate, published *The Work of the Afro-American Woman* to celebrate respectable women of color.[7] One of the earliest in the genre written by a woman, her book became a foundational text for black reformers and thinkers.[8] Competing volumes about black women began with portraits of their male authors; Mossell's opened with a portrait of her with her two young daughters. The dedication offered a prayer that her daughters might "grow into a pure and noble womanhood."[9] Mossell listed women in fields that ranged from sculpture and medicine to business and literature. While she agreed that the home was "undoubtedly the cornerstone of our beloved Republic," she argued that the "woman who has a mind and will of her own" would also have a happy home.[10] Women like Terrell, Ida B. Wells-Barnett, and Fannie Barrier Williams, all of whom agitated for women's political rights and appeared in the book, certainly had wills of their own.

Books by Majors, Mossell, and others emphasized the importance of education. For Terrell, the income from her mother's beauty shop and her father's saloon secured her an exceptional education. She attended Oberlin College, among the first colleges to accept female students as well as students of color. Rather than taking the shorter, less comprehensive women's literary course, Terrell chose the men's classical course. She studied Greek, the Bible, politics, and history. In 1884, she received her bachelor's degree.[11] Her friends warned her that her choice was "unwomanly" and "might ruin [her] chances of getting a husband," but Terrell ignored them.[12] She capped off her education with a grand tour of Europe, a tradition for elite Americans. Terrell considered staying overseas, where she "could enjoy freedom from prejudice," but she believed it was her duty to return and "promote the welfare of the race."[13] She taught first at Wilberforce University and then at M Street High School in Washington, DC. In 1891, she married her colleague Robert Terrell, a fellow women's suffrage supporter. He held degrees from Harvard University and Howard University Law School.[14] Her education had not ruined her chance at marriage after all.

Educated women like Terrell harnessed their growing power by founding local and state clubs coordinated at a national level. These bureaucratic organizations fueled Progressive reforms. NAWSA attracted more members, and new organizations, like the General Federation of Women's Clubs, grew rapidly. During the 1890s, women won the right to vote in four states, and by 1899, NAWSA had an affiliate organization in every state. Many flocked to the Woman's Christian Temperance Union (WCTU), the largest group that endorsed suffrage at the dawn of the 1890s.[15] Its president, Frances Willard, endorsed suffrage because she believed moral female voters would enact laws that prohibited alcohol.

Even as they claimed greater influence, Progressive reformers often relied on traditional ideas of domestic womanhood. Most of these reformers had husbands to support them. Terrell and others in her class—white and black alike—were forced to leave their jobs after marriage. Still, work as a reformer could compare to a professional position. Terrell planned and led conferences, wrote articles, lectured throughout the country, founded local nurseries, and served on the school board in Washington, DC. She could afford help to raise her two daughters and keep an elegant house. Leading reformers wanted to prove women could have it all: a fulfilling home life and the responsibilities of American citizenship.

In 1893, Progressive reformers flocked to Chicago for the World's Columbian Exposition to win greater visibility for their causes. The World's Congress of Representative Women, one of the many conferences held at the fair, attracted activists from all over the world. Over 150,000 people attended the week-long conference.[16] The era's most prominent female leaders "present[ed] their position and work in every field of labor" to demonstrate the progress women had made.[17] Speakers represented NAWSA, the WCTU, and 124 other organizations.[18] Susan B. Anthony and Elizabeth Cady Stanton asked audiences to support women's votes. Women of color, including Hallie Quinn Brown, Anna Julia Cooper, and Fannie Barrier Williams, encouraged reformers to address the discrimination they faced. Besides attending lectures, Terrell recalled seeing "the endless aisles of the long buildings filled with exhibits from nearly every country in the world."[19]

Suffragists took this opportunity to display their first piece of visual propaganda. Henrietta Briggs-Wall, an activist in Ohio and Kansas, designed a four-by-six-foot picture for the Kansas State Building. Executed by Kansas artist W. A. Ford, the large pastel attracted the attention of visitors (figure 5.3). WCTU president Frances Willard appears in the center. Her glasses signal her education, while her white ribbon reminds viewers of her antialcohol agenda. The *Woman's Journal* identified the four men around her. In the top right, the "convict" wears striped clothing. The

5.3: Photograph of W. A. Ford, *American Woman and Her Political Peers*, 1893, cabinet card photograph. Schlesinger Library, Radcliffe Institute, Harvard University.

"American Indian chief" wears an elaborate headdress, implying his re-fusal to assimilate with white culture. In the top left, the "idiot" appears with his mouth agape, a sign that he lacks intelligence.[20] The wide-eyed "insane person" holds a branch on the bottom right. Whereas the men are stereotypes, Willard is an individual.

The seemingly unrelated figures probably baffled viewers, which was the point. Entitled *American Woman and Her Political Peers*, the picture depicted disenfranchised Americans. Briggs-Wall believed that women, specifically the elite white women represented by Willard, were superior to the men in this category. The pastel was among the first pieces of visual propaganda that advocated for women's right to vote. Unlike portraits and political cartoons, visual propaganda conveys complex political arguments to sway viewers. The term "propaganda" did not have the negative conno-tation it does today; instead, many viewed propaganda as an educational tool.

Suffragists had great ambitions for the picture. Briggs-Wall "hope[d]," according to the *Woman's Journal*, that "this visible illustration [would] show in a new way the injustice" of women's disenfranchisement.[21] She called it a "weapon of warfare" that would "win in the war for woman's freedom" because it would "kill prejudices."[22] In December 1893, another article declared, "People were reached who never would go hear a suffrage lecture, or read a suffrage paper" and proclaimed the picture "a complete and unqualified triumph."[23] A male viewer affirmed that *American Woman* was "better than fifty sermons."[24] The *Woman's Journal* also included a letter from Briggs-Wall that told readers where to find the picture at the World's Fair.[25]

Leaders encouraged suffragists to purchase a copy of *American Woman and Her Political Peers* to demonstrate their support for the cause. The burgeoning advertising industry distributed colorful, collectible trade cards, similar in size to modern baseball cards, that marketed products to consumers. Taking a cue from their success, Briggs-Wall photographed her "weapon" for distribution beyond the fairgrounds.[26] Consumers pur-chased cheap cabinet-sized photographs (roughly four by six inches) for twenty-five cents and larger copies (up to fourteen by seventeen inches) for as much as $1.50.[27] Suffragists who did not attend the fair wrote to Briggs-Wall to purchase copies to display on the walls of their homes and meeting places.[28]

Briggs-Wall did not make the image for a specific organization, but NAWSA quickly claimed the picture for their work. In 1894, Dorothy Bewick Colby, editor of the *Woman's Tribune*, presented it to the United States

Senate Committee on Woman Suffrage and declared, "That picture is the best argument in favor of the passage of the joint resolution that we can present to you."[29] Women like Willard, she said, should not "be associated with male idiots and lunatics."[30] Colby appealed to the senators' masculine honor, saying, "We trust that your chivalry and sense of justice will compel you to assist our efforts to release ourselves from this shameful category."[31] Prominent lecturer and soon-to-be NAWSA president Anna Howard Shaw declared at the close of her speech, "I should not feel badly if gentlemen were haunted all their lives by the picture until it was obliterated from the picture itself and borne into the minds of men."[32]

American Woman and Her Political Peers also appalled suffrage opponents, who still had so much widespread support that they needed no formal organization. Ethel Ingalls, who wrote for publications like the *Washington Post* and the *Ladies' Home Journal*, was not pleased.[33] She argued in the *Los Angeles Times* that women were "overwhelmed with mortification and wrath on beholding that monstrosity of art." Ingalls added that "women in Kansas are not considered to be on an equal plane with the stricken humanity"—meaning the men—pictured in this "horror." She called the pastel "the offspring of a depraved and contemptible mind."[34] Even though she hated the picture, Ingalls affirmed its message: white women should not be classed with these men.

Briggs-Wall's picture signaled a shift toward the use of visual propaganda to win the vote for white women. Suffragists aimed to directly counter the satirical imagery that had lampooned political women as manly revolutionaries for generations. Progressive Era reformers wanted to extend their moral, womanly expertise into politics. They portrayed the ballot as an enhancement of, not a departure from, existing domestic duties. Their conservative "public motherhood" message emerged in imagery even before it dominated speeches and texts in the early 1900s, as scholars have long noted.[35] Pictures of attractive reformers and caring mothers appealed to the masses. While suffragists continued to argue that women deserved the vote because they were equal to men, their organizations did not trumpet this message.

No matter how educated, finely dressed, and beautiful, a portrait of Mary Church Terrell could not have appealed to the senators' sense of chivalry as Willard's did. Many associated virtue with white women and assumed black women were sexually promiscuous, stereotyping them as Jezebels.[36] Briggs-Wall chose Willard because she had a "sweet, serene, lovely, and intellectual face" and represented "all the womanhood of this land."[37] A white, educated reformer did not actually represent all American women, but she did represent the white women that clubs wanted to recruit. White suffragists emphasized their whiteness as a political strategy to quell fears that women's votes would alter the existing hierarchy, structured by patriarchy, white supremacy, and elite leadership. Racist ideologies colored even the era's most progressive movements.

THE RISE OF THE BLACK WOMEN'S CLUB MOVEMENT

At the World's Fair in 1893, Fannie Barrier Williams spoke to the World's Congress of Representative Women. The black reformer asked: "If it be a fact that this spirit of organization among women generally is the distinguishing mark of the nineteenth-century woman, dare we ask if the colored women of the United States have made any progress in this respect?"[38] Baptist women of color already coordinated missions and social programs, but Williams envisioned a secular group comparable to the National American Woman Suffrage Association. Her group would encourage women of color to become members and leaders to promote a platform that addressed black women's concerns.[39] Soon after, women founded national organizations to coordinate their efforts with a shared agenda. Already prominent, Mary Church Terrell emerged as a public face of the black women's club movement.

White suffragists excluded African American women from their organizations and focused on white women's votes because they hoped to win support from more officials, especially those in Southern states that sought to diminish black political power. Beginning in 1890 with Mississippi's updated state constitution, Southern states systematically disenfranchised black and poor white men through poll taxes, literacy tests, and other requirements.[40] Mississippi's constitution specifically barred "idiots, insane persons and Indians" from the vote.[41] *American Woman and Her Political Peers* obscured the disenfranchisement of black men, but the legal wording in Mississippi's constitution must have inspired Briggs-Wall's image. White suffrage leaders recognized that enfranchising black women would not win support, so they avoided the imagery and discussions of race as much as possible.

Black women thus founded their own institutions because they had a host of problems to address. In addition to disenfranchisement, in 1896 *Plessy v. Ferguson* legalized "separate but equal" facilities for Americans of color. The Supreme Court decision further entrenched white supremacy by approving the segregation of trains, hotels, and schools. But, as *Brown v. Board of Education* ruled in 1954, separate was never equal. Communities could not count on the government to guarantee equal accommodations, so activists led efforts to improve conditions.

Bostonian Josephine St. Pierre Ruffin, editor of the *Woman's Era*, the first paper aimed at black clubwomen, decided to organize black women to spur progress.[42] An antilynching activist in London forwarded Ruffin a letter from the president of the Missouri Press Association. The letter stated that "the Negroes of this country are wholly devoid of morality" and "the women are prostitutes and all are natural liars and thieves."[43] In 1895, Ruffin sent the letter to black women's clubs throughout the United States to "call all of our women all over the country to act."[44]

Two months after *Plessy v. Ferguson*, women of color gathered in the Nineteenth Street Baptist Church in Washington, DC, to chart a path forward.[45] Black women had started meeting in the wake of Ruffin's letter and formed groups, but now they all wanted to confer. The formerly enslaved activist Harriet Tubman passed the torch to them. The *Woman's Era* reported that it felt like "the clasping of hands of the early nineteenth century and twentieth centuries."[46] Attendees formed the National Association of Colored Women through the unification of two fledgling national organizations that represented fifty-five clubs.[47] Their object was "to awaken the women of the race to the great need of systemic effort in home-making and the divinely imposed duties of motherhood." They wanted to lead "the upbuilding, ennobling and advancement of the race."[48] NACW leaders aimed to uplift less advantaged families by founding kindergartens, orphanages, parks, and playgrounds. Their initiatives supported a rising generation and their working parents. Elite clubwomen wanted to help all black families.

Black women led the NACW and set its agenda. Some white women recruited women of color for their clubs, but they largely chose not to recognize the problems those women faced. Black women wanted to end the convict-lease system, address inequities in the education of their children, and end the practice of public, vigilante murders of black men and women known as lynchings. At the national level, NAWSA did not exclude women of color, but local groups could and did choose to exclude them from membership, meetings, and leadership. In 1895, for example, Susan B. Anthony asked her longtime colleague Frederick Douglass not to attend NAWSA's meeting in Atlanta. She did not want to offend the racist local hosts.[49] Five years later, the General Federation of Women's Clubs refused to seat Josephine Ruffin at their annual meeting because of her race.[50]

"Progressive" organizations led by white women, however, wanted to project the image that women of all backgrounds supported their agen-

5.4: Woman's Temperance Publishing Association, *For God & Home and Every Land, Boston 1891*, 1891, lithograph, published in Mary Greenleaf Clement Leavitt, ed., *Report Made to the First Convention of the World's Women's Christian Temperance Union* (1891), page 12. Susan B. Anthony Ephemera Collection, Huntington Library.

das. In 1891, the Woman's Christian Temperance Union adopted the motto "For God and Home and Every Land."[51] The cover of their annual report featured an illustration of the motto that imagined the first international meeting of the World's WCTU (figure 5.4).[52] Front and center, a white woman with a long list of demands leads a group of diverse women. A woman in a hijab symbolizes Middle Eastern members, while another with a bun and shiny silk kimono represents the group's expansion into Asia. Each woman looks resolved to return to her country to carry out the temperance work. Rather than representing women of color as leaders with their own aims, these reformers seem content to follow the white woman. Rather than threatening white women's leadership, the illustration and organization cemented it. Above the group, illustrations of the Mayflower and 1787 Northwest Ordinance affirmed that "religion and morality are the basis of all good government." Despite this image of diversity, the WCTU focused on the desires of white women to create the change they wished to see. Some black activists, including Frances Ellen Watkins Harper, held leadership positions.[53] Frances Willard, however, rejected calls—made most publicly by Ida B. Wells-Barnett in 1893—to condemn lynching. Willard never disputed the widespread myth that the murders were a form of justice that punished black men for the rape of white women.[54]

Despite these conflicts, black women stated that temperance and suffrage advocates paved the way for them. The NACW's official organ, *National Notes*, cited suffragists as "the pioneer force for woman's emancipation and progress."[55] In 1899, three years after the NACW's founding, *National Notes* announced an official women's suffrage department and "recommended the lives of Susan B. Anthony and Elizabeth Cady Stanton for perusal."[56] The interest in securing women's votes kept white and black reformers involved in each other's work. NACW leaders spoke at NAWSA conventions and recruited white affiliate members, including leaders like Jane Addams, Rheta Childe Dorr, and Crystal Eastman.[57]

The NACW elected Mary Church Terrell as president to represent their vision of black political womanhood and counter dominant stereotypes about women of color.[58] She had to balance the modesty expected of her with her efforts to promote herself and her organization's respectability politics. Women, even prominent reformers, were not supposed to desire fame. In May 1895, Terrell's usual column in the *Woman's Era* celebrated her appointment as the first black woman to the district's board of school trustees. Quotes from the *Washington Post* praised her as "one of the brainiest women of her race."[59] In its next issue, the *Woman's Era*'s noted the quotes had been included in Terrell's column by mistake. No one should think, the anonymous author wrote, "that Mrs. Terrell was indulging in self-praise."[60]

Terrell recognized the high stakes of her position. In 1900, she wrote in *National Notes* that "the dominant race in this country insists upon gauging the negro's worth by his most illiterate and vicious representatives, rather than by the more intelligent and wealthy classes."[61] She wanted to counter this stereotype. The engraving of her photographic portrait appeared that same year on the front page of the *Colored American*, a magazine published in Washington, DC, for African American readers (figure 5.5). The image presented the face by which she wanted Americans to judge women of color. The NACW encouraged members to purchase clothes that made them "appear pleasing." Their newsletter emphasized the importance of "elegant" attire, such as "the pretty shoe, the handsome stocking, the well-fitting glove and the becoming veil.... No one can afford to neglect these little things."[62]

Terrell distributed her portrait widely. She aimed to appear as an idealized lighter-skinned, elite, straight-haired black woman to challenge racist stereotypes, and popular advertisements ensured that Terrell's audiences understood her message. The engraving of Terrell's perfectly styled hair appeared next to advertisements in the *Colored American* for remedies that promised to "make kinky, harsh and stubborn hair grow long, straight, soft, pliable and glossy."[63] Though referring to hair, the terms also referenced stereotypes of black women that she aimed to counter. Terrell had almost certainly seen these kinds of advertisements before, and her hair resembled that of women in the "after" images in ads for hair treatments (figure 5.6).[64] Advertisements promoted a "wonderful face bleach" that would "turn the skin of a black person four or five shades whiter."[65] The ads affirmed the dominance of colorism, a preference for lighter-skinned women like Terrell and discrimination against those with darker skin.[66] Her skin tone was pale enough that she occasionally passed as white—"outwitting those who are obsessed with race prejudice"—to gain access to better facilities.[67] Respectability politics did not change laws, but reformers hoped their appearance would change ideas, which, in turn, would change laws. Physiognomy and phrenology had fallen out of fashion, but scientists and anthropologists built on these ideas about physical characteristics to formulate a racial hierarchy. These credentialed professionals classified people from civilized to uncivilized, and leaders like Terrell aimed to resemble those designated as most refined.

Terrell became an icon of ideal black political womanhood, but she could never represent all women of color. Some opposed efforts to appear respectable according to dominant, white norms. Many could not afford fancy clothes and college degrees. Others did not want the treatments that promised the straight hair associated with whiteness.[68] During the annual conference in 1906, for example, the black press widely reported disagreements over the NACW's presidential election. NACW member Hallie Quinn Brown, who was later president from 1920 to 1924, voiced concerns that her

The Colored American

A NATIONAL NEGRO NEWSPAPER

VOL. 7. NO. 47. WASHINGTON, D. C., SATURDAY, FEBRUARY 17, 1900. PRICE FIVE CENTS

WOMAN'S CASE IN EQUITY

Gracefully and Forcefully Presented by Mrs. Mary Church Terrell Before the Brainiest of Equal Suffragists in America—The Premier Representative of our Womanhood Makes the Hit of the Convention.

The equal suffragists have come and gone. Those who followed their proceedings and digested their arguments will all agree that the cause they advocate with so much earnestness and intelligence is today better understood than ever before, and has been made to command a more and more serious degree of consideration. Woman suffrage, once a subject for ridicule, has ceased to be a joke. It is one of the grave problems of the hour. The wonderful advancement of the feminine sex in business, in the professions, in the industries, and in the world of finance, is giving her an importance in the affairs of life which the sensible man must recognize, and subscribe to a change of laws and customs to accord with the higher conditions that have come about in consequence of woman's broadening influence.

All of the week's sessions were instructive and interesting. Well informed and witty women, thoroughly alive to everything, not only where the advancement of women is concerned, but in all things and events which are under discussion throughout the whole world, addressed the meetings when they were thrown open for that purpose, and delivered their opinions with great force of logic and intelligence. There is nothing about the woman suffragist today to remind one of the agitator of a quarter of a century ago. The mannishly attired, short skirted, short haired woman, who, for so many years, was the butt of the satirist and the cartoonist, has been shoved off of the board and in her place stands the cultured, womanly woman of the twentieth century. In her dress she keeps pace with fashion. She is in many instances a mother, and she boasts of it and the home which she ennobles.

Many of the nation's brightest women took part in the gathering, headed by the veteran Susan B Anthony, but none made a better impression for wisdom, happiness of expression and power of oratory than did our own Mrs. Mary Church Terrell, president of the National Association of Colored Women. As was noted in a former issue

MRS. MARY CHURCH TERRELL,
President of the National Association of Colored Women. Her Address on "Woman Suffrage" the Hit of the Recent Gathering of America's Brainiest Women.

of this paper Mrs. Terrell was announced to speak on "The Justice of Woman Suffrage," the pièce de résistance of the whole convention. We said Mrs. Terrell would meet the highest expectations in handling this trying topic—and she more than did so. Her effort was a masterpiece of argument, scholarly and logically put and was delivered with that ease and grace of bearing, that ineffable charm and magnetism of manner, and dignity and force that are characteristic of all Mrs. Terrell does or says. She was her self—at her best—that's all, and to state that her presentation was "resistless" will convey a perfectly clear idea of its excellence to all who know the leader of Afro-American womanhood. The race may well feel proud of such a splendid representation. By Mrs. Terrell's appearance at this convention both the cause of women in general and the Negro in particular has been incalculably benefited.

We cannot give the entire address but Mrs. Terrell said in part:

(Continued on Fourth page)

A Banquet in Honor of Abraham Lincoln's Birthday.

Baltimore, Md., Special—On last Monday night at the McKinley Club on Druid Hill avenue, a banquet was tendered in honor of Abraham Lincoln's birthday. After a very fine dinner was served, the table being laden with all the delicacies of the season, Hon. Warner T. McGuinn was made toastmaster of the evening. The gathering was largely attended by many of the prominent citizens of the city.

Dr. J. Marcus Cargill responded to the toast, "Abraham Lincoln," Mr. J. E. G. Webb, "The Political Outlook of the Negro," Hon. George B. Mills, "Organization," J. Henry Bayton, "The Field of Journalism," Mr. Lewis Tunsell, "The Hustler," Samuel C. Brown, "The Qualities of a Man" and Mr. Alex. McDaniel, "The Good Work of Abraham Lincoln." The evening was one of great interest, many fine speeches were made. The annual banquet committee was appointed as follows:

Dr. J. M. Cargill, Messrs. Geo. Mills, J. E. G. Webb and W. T. McGuinn. The inclemency of the weather did not at all prevent a goodly number being present, and all seemed to have enjoyed the celebration of the noted and worthy chieftain's birthday, in the personation of Abraham Lincoln.

POLITICS IN CONNECTICUT.

The Patriarchie Meeting in June—Death of a Prominent Woman—Social Horoscopa—News Notes

New Haven, Conn., Special—All colored men who are interested in the political welfare of the race in New Haven should be up and doing. There should be more interest along that line now than ever. There is something in store for the colored man if he will only get out and hustle for himself. We have a great many men who will "blow" around and say what ought to be done, but are never ready to assist. There is also a class of men who go into politics looking only for their own interest and when they find they cannot win out they will try to kill the progress of every other colored man. This spirit must die before the Negro can prosper in New England. The Negro must learn to talk his business with his friends and keep it from the white man the white man is looking for himself everytime, and when he asks any favors of the Negro, the return is always made with a promise. But, ah, the Negro of today has seen the folly and has decided to demand such rights as belong to the Negro, simply by casting an honest ballot next spring.

The Goffe street branch of the Y. M. C. A. is the only colored Y. M. C. A. in New England today and it is very painful to say that there are nearly six thousand Negroes in this city and this association has such small attendance. The young men in New Haven should feel it a duty to support this organization.

The annual Field day and Convention of the New England and New York Patriarchie Union which was to convene in New Haven on the first day of June 1900. All Patriarchies under the jurisdiction of this Union will govern themselves accordingly. For further information address A. Lee Epps, No. 78 Webster street, New Haven, Conn.

Mrs. Josephine Mitchel, of Milford, after returning from church Sunday evening, February 4, met with a very sad death. Early Monday morning she was found in the well by her husband. It proved to be an accidental death from the verdict rendered by the coroner's inquest. Mrs. Mitchell was born in Norfolk, Va , 50 years ago and has lived North for 25 years or more.

(Continued on Fifth Page.)

OUT IN SAN DIEGO.

Dr. Hubbard's Matchless Work—Other Items of News.

San Diego, Cal., Special—Having a reader and admirer of your race journal for the past few years. I consider it a firm, loyal advocate for the Negro, and take this opportunity of commending your worthy and appreciated efforts. While rusticating in the golden sunlight of sunny California on the Pacific coast, I wish to contribute a few words to your valuable columns. The needs of our race are numerous and the press is grasping the opportunity of familiarizing the people with our greatest and most essential desires. And with those who are not prejudiced we can see qualified men and women rising to lead the race, and it is to those who have showed themselves capable that we must follow. One of the most intellectual bodies of Afro-Americans that will convene in the closing of the nineteenth century will be the General Conference of the Africa Methodist Episcopal Church. And while those that have held the banner highest will receive the election of bishopric, let all centralize on the one greatest financiers the Connection has ever known, Rev. P. A. Hubbard, D. D., of Colorado. The California delegation will vote solid for Dr. Hubbard. The press of the entire country should agitate his election, he has a clean record. Dr. Hubbard is an ideal type of the Christian minister, and has not shirked from any of the duties from class-leader to Presiding Elder, the latter he has filled for six years. He is an educated, loyal, moral, Christian minister. Let all who are contesting for the election of Financial Secretary of the A. M. E. Connection throw the strength to Rev. P. A. Hubbard, D. D., of Colorado, and make his election unanimous. It will cast a reflection upon the general assembly to not show appreciation of Dr. Hubbard's work in this way.

Yours for Ethiopia,
MRS. JULIA EMERY.

THE LATE GUY H. BERKELEY,
Pastor of the New Bethel Baptist Church, Washington, D. C.

Politics in Connecticut.

(Continued from First Page.)

She was a member of the Immanuel Baptist church in New Haven, and had always been connected with the church work. After Mrs. Mitchell married she lived in Milford, Conn., and even here in this town she and her husband worked with a greater zeal for the upbuilding of Christ's kingdom. They started a halt to start a Baptist mission, and worked faithfully for its growth, without growing weary. Mrs. Mitchell leaves to mourn her loss a loving husband, a daughter, Mrs. Ada Brinsmade and two grandchildren, besides a host of friends who deeply sympathize with the family in this, their hour of sad bereavement. Rev. A. C. Powell, of New Haven, preached the funeral sermon at the Baptist church in Milford last Wednesday, February 8, 1900, at 2 p. m. The church was packed with sorrowing friends.

Mrs. W. A. Tribbett continues very sick at her home on Orchard St.

Mrs. Mary Goings of 79 Eaton street has been confined to her bed by illness for over a week.

Mrs. John C. T. Alexander, of Starr St., who has been very indisposed for the past week, is now rapidly on the mend.

Mrs. Mildred Smith, of 53 Webster St., who has been very ill for the past few weeks is now improving. She is under the care of Dr. I. N. Poster.

Mr. J. H. Richmond, of 70 Webster St., has returned from Hampton, Va. where he went to bury his sister, the late Mrs. Hattie Hell who died in this city two weeks ago.

Mrs. Eliza Carter, who has been spending some time with her daughter, Mrs. A. O. Powell, of 28 Gill St., returned to her home in Charleston, W. Va., last Thursday.

Mrs. H. W. Fry, of Boston, who has been spending a few days visiting relatives in this city, left last Wednesday for Springfield, Mass., where she will spend a few days with her mother-in-law.

Mrs. Mary Goines, of 79 Eaton St., died Tuesday afternoon at 4.35, at her home. The deceased had been sick for some time. She was a sister of the late William T. Effut. Report of the funeral will appear next week.

Sumner Club No. 2 will hold their business meeting on Monday evening the 19th inst., at their room No. 15 Insurance Building. Every member is expected to be present as there is business of importance to be transacted. By order of the President Dr. I. M. Porter.

Members of the Household of Ruth gave a parlor social on Thursday evening February 8th, at Mrs. Frederick Young's, 92 Eaton street. The proceeds are for helping to purchase a banner for the Patriarchie. The weather being very stormy the attendance was not very large.

This paper will be found every Saturday at Ransom and Waight's Ice Cream Parlor, Hall's Barber Shop, 111 Foot St., and at the Headquarters, 78 Webster St. It will be delivered to any address in the city on application for the same. All customers failing to receive their paper will please notify the agent at No. 78 Webster St.

A. LEE EPPS.

Skin Specialist!

MME. G. A. FINNIE MACK Is located at 1704 10th Street, n. w. She treats and guarantees cure for all Skin troubles, also the Scalp, terms reasonable. She has a preparation for growing the Hair and cultivates the Hair in the same old way. Will be pleased to have her former customers call and be beautified by her new Skin treatment. Bangs and Wigs made to order.

preferred candidate would not be elected "on account of her light color." Some NACW members wanted a "full-blooded Negro" without the "'white taint' in her veins" to represent them.[69] Members believed, according to Terrell, that a dark-skinned woman could be "shown as a proof of the colored people's ability." She disagreed and concluded, "The colored people are their own worst enemies."[70]

Despite some concerns, Terrell made her public image appealing to black and white suffragists alike. In 1898, she addressed NAWSA's annual convention, which commemorated the fiftieth anniversary of the Seneca Falls meeting. She reminded her audience that when the 1848 meeting had occurred, black women could not only "possess no property, but even their bodies were not their own."[71] Terrell and her fellow NACW leaders often embraced the politics of dissemblance.[72] They appeared to support white suffragists in public, but their letters reveal their real opinions. Terrell preferred to advocate for the inclusion of women of color from the main stage of NAWSA's convention rather than to announce her critical opinions of white suffragists.

Although Terrell won some support from white suffragists, NAWSA rarely—if ever—featured her or other suffragists of color in their visual campaigns. NAWSA primarily worked to enfranchise white women, and their public image reflected their choice. Terrell could be a representative black woman on their convention stage, but not in an editorial cartoon sent to newspapers across the country. NAWSA did not promote her or the vision for black political womanhood that she represented. Besides Terrell, the group could have chosen to feature Mabel Lee, a Chinese-born suffragist based in New York City, or Jovita Idár, a Mexican American woman who wrote for a Texas newspaper that advocated for social justice.[73] Even when states granted the ballot to women, the Chinese Exclusion Act of 1882 prevented Lee and her fellow Chinese Americans from citizenship and voting rights. Similarly, Mexican Americans often faced the same voting restrictions that disenfranchised African Americans and poor people in the South.[74] NAWSA knew that enfranchisement of the greatest possible number of American women would not pass, so they prioritized the ballot for the white women who dominated the organization.

Even with limited support from white suffrage groups, Terrell ensured that her addresses attracted attention from diverse audiences. She knew that "such publicity helped a great deal."[75] In 1900, the Colored American featured this caption with her portrait: "Her Address on 'Woman Suffrage' the Hit of the Recent Gathering of America's Brainiest Women." The magazine concluded, "She cannot but serve as a striking example worthy of emulation by the rising womanhood of the Afro-American race." *National Notes* reported praise for their president's speech on "The Justice of Woman Suffrage." The *Washington Post* proclaimed her address "scholarly," and the *Boston Transcript* noted that it was the "most brilliant to which a Washington audience may listen."[76]

Within the African American community, the issue of women's rights proved divisive. Some black men blamed black women for weakening communities by not living up to the respectable domestic ideal.[77] They embraced patriarchal views to argue that wives and daughters needed to create better homes to change black culture and perceptions of it. Not even all black civil rights activists wanted women of their race to vote. Prominent reformer W. E. B. Du Bois emphasized this idea in his address to Spelman College, the first historically black women's college. In February 1902, Spelman's newsletter published his accompanying article, "The Work of Negro Women in Society." Du Bois praised the "wise division of labor [that] has made man the bread-winner and woman the homemaker." He prioritized a woman's "physical function as a mother" and the "ideal of goodness and a reverence for God's truth" that she should infuse into her household.[78] Ultimately, though, he changed his mind. By 1911, he authored articles in support of women's suffrage for the *Crisis*, published by the National Association for the Advancement of Colored People.[79]

Black women used respectability not just to appeal to gendered ideals but also as a tool of resistance against sexual violence and stereotypes of black women's promiscuity. Portraits needed to emphasize Terrell's virtue and de-emphasize her sexuality without turning her into the "mammy" stereotype, which became especially popular after the branding for Aunt Jemima pancake mix was introduced at the 1893 World's Fair.[80] Antebellum photographs of enslaved black women caring for white children, along with popular blackface minstrel shows, became the foundation for the racist visual type. Viewers recognized the mammy as a fat black woman, often with a kerchief tied around her hair, wearing a plain work dress and apron to reference her domestic skill. She was a maternal, comforting figure. Mammies signaled nostalgia for an earlier era, making them part of the rise of the Lost Cause narrative that valorized the antebellum South.[81] The mammy stereotype desexualized black women and linked them with subservience and bondage. In contrast, the NACW wanted to position themselves as virtuous and elegant women. In the words of scholar Brittany C. Cooper, the NACW's brand of black womanhood was "a foil to the sexually deviant Black female specter that haunted the American political imagination."[82] Their version of respectability emphasized motherhood and marriage, as evidenced by the frequent inclusion of their maiden and married names in publications.

Although Ida B. Wells-Barnett, a leading journalist and antilynching activist, did not always side with Terrell and the NACW, the two leaders agreed that black women needed to restrain their sexuality to gain respect. In 1888, Wells-Barnett wrote in the *New York Freeman* newspaper that "the typical girl's only wealth is her character; and her first consideration is to preserve that character in spotless purity." Even her language should be remarkable for its "chastity."[83] Wells-Barnett's understanding of race and sexuality provided the basis for her antilynching activism too. She pointed to widespread assumptions that black men could not control their sexuality, and therefore raped white women, as the false justification for many lynchings.

Many praised Terrell and the NACW, but their model of black political womanhood was not the only one. Terrell was willing to appear to compromise and collaborate with racist reformers, but Wells-Barnett was not. Terrell visited exhibits at the 1893 fair as Wells-Barnett penned an attack on the organizers for excluding exhibitions of black culture.[84] The diplomatic Terrell looked past Stanton and Anthony's often racist positions, writing that "the original suffragists" were not "badly afflicted with race prejudice."[85] Wells-Barnett demanded that the leaders denounce racism. She had a complicated relationship with the NACW officers, who praised her work but not her outspokenness.

Despite differences among black activists, the NACW underscored the importance of visible female leaders like Terrell.[86] Portraits of Terrell, Wells-Barnett, and fellow leading women of color countered popular negative representations of black women and challenged suffrage propaganda produced by white suffrage organizations. But imagery of these leading women of color also often emphasized the lightness of their skin and straightness of their hair. The NACW wanted a specific type of black women to lead.

PROFESSIONAL PRESS COMMITTEES AND STATE CAMPAIGNS

Compared to the new NACW, the Woman's Christian Temperance Union (WCTU) and NAWSA had more members and funding. They were also institutionally mature. During the 1890s, both organizations had local and national committees staffed with professionals to manage their public image and distribute propaganda. While women's rights papers like the *Woman's Journal* remained important to the movement, the paper printed few images, and NAWSA aimed for their propaganda to reach a far broader audience. In contrast, Terrell relied on the black press and civil rights publications aimed at an audience of reformers to promote her public image. Her strategies resembled those employed by Susan B. Anthony from decades earlier when she distributed portraits on her own. Antisuffragists formed organizations too. Throughout the nineteenth century, suffrage opponents functioned as a loose network of prominent individuals, writers, editors, and artists, but women founded the two first state-level groups in 1895. The mainstream press still largely voiced antisuffrage sentiments, and these new organizations campaigned against local voting measures. As suffragists ramped up their campaigns, opponents realized they needed to coordinate their own.

As reformers centralized their work, they put committees in charge of their public image. In 1879, the WCTU led the way with their own publishing association. They printed literature ranging from their newspaper and pamphlets to an illustrated calendar. By 1889, the WCTU had thirty-nine departments, including one dedicated to "influencing the press."[87] With a highly developed organization and 200,000 members, the WCTU was at the height of its power when suffragists established NAWSA in 1890. Though sidelined in the traditional suffrage story, the WCTU modeled for NAWSA how to build their organization and coordinate national campaigns. NAWSA recruited wealthy female donors to found similar departments and their own press committees during the 1890s.[88] In contrast, the NACW relied on innovative leaders like Terrell and the press, especially the black press, to disseminate their vision of black political womanhood. As a NAWSA member, Terrell watched the organization mobilize to produce more presswork. In 1900, she proposed that the NACW needed a press committee too. The executive committee, however, concluded that it was "hardly feasible."[89] They did not have the resources or people to devote to the press.

Even with national coordination, local suffrage clubs affiliated with NAWSA completed significant presswork. Women in Colorado and Idaho campaigned and won the vote in 1893 and 1896. Suffragists allied with the Populists, a political party mostly made up of Southern and Midwestern farmers. Populists advocated for government ownership of the railroads, a graduated income tax, and the direct election of senators. They hoped female voters would support their platform.[90] In 1896, Utah women, who had been disenfranchised in 1887, successfully regained the vote when their territory achieved statehood.[91] Many politicians at the national level did not support women's suffrage. Southern officials, however, advocated against government interference in state voting laws, especially as their states enacted laws to disenfranchise African American men.[92]

Suffrage wins inspired California activists to pioneer presswork during their unsuccessful campaign of 1896. The year before, NAWSA's press committee had reported the "lively progress" of "the great campaign of national education."[93] Their motto was "Publish an antidote wherever the [antisuffrage] poison appears."[94] That meant sending editorial cartoons, articles, and portraits to highlight women's advancement. California suffragists agreed: they saw the press as "essential ... to the cause of woman suffrage" and encouraged local newspapers (such as the antisuffrage *Los Angeles Times*) to feature fewer "ill-natured" cartoons.[95] Activists sold photographs to supporters to promote their cause, but also to make money to support their operations.[96] Suffragists wanted to buy pictures to display their loyalty. Even suffragists without active state campaigns worked with the press. NAWSA praised New Yorkers, who coordinated their publicity at the local, county, and state level and reached "more papers than any other state in the Union."[97]

In 1896, NAWSA experimented with an early form of branding. They printed their first attempt on that year's annual convention report. The feminine icon consisted of their name emblazoned on a ribbon that surrounded a sunflower (figure 5.7).[98] In 1887, suffragists had chosen the yellow flower to commemorate the municipal enfranchisement of women in Kansas, the Sunflower State.[99] In the flower's center, "1848" identified the meeting in Seneca Falls as their founding to lend historical legitimacy to their cause. Most important, they could print the engraved emblem cheaply. NAWSA dropped the icon after the fiftieth-anniversary celebrations ended in 1899, but yellow remained a suffrage color.[100]

Though initially focused on text, NAWSA's press committee, led by Elnora M. Babcock, called for a focus on images at the convention of 1900. By that time, they had made their press committee "a central office for collecting and distributing arguments and practical illustrations."[101] Babcock explained, "Illustrated articles never fail of securing space in an illustrated paper, and are furnished to papers just as often as we can find the women to illustrate." Newspaper editors paid special attention to images because their readers demanded them. Babcock noted that they "furnished some fifty of these articles to the illustrated papers" and to "various press companies, which in their turn furnish many additional papers."[102] She emphasized "the wonderful power of the press" and encouraged suffragists to "realize the importance of utilizing it in every way possible for the education of the people."[103] By referring to her efforts as "education," she

5.7: National American Woman Suffrage Association emblem, 1896, engraving, on the cover of the Rachel Foster Avery, ed., *Proceedings of the Twenty-Eighth Annual Convention of the National American Woman Suffrage Association* (1896). Sophia Smith Collection, Smith College.

and NAWSA framed presswork as a feminine project. Suffragists incorporated the techniques of the growing advertising industry to—as Babcock put it—coordinate "the first systematic press-work throughout the United States."[104] NAWSA learned the value of creating and selling symbols of their cause through these successful visual campaigns.[105]

Suffragists needed new strategies because antisuffragists were launching their own campaigns. It might seem unusual that the cause had female opponents, but, like their male counterparts, they believed suffrage threatened their way of life. Catharine Beecher, a popular author and lecturer, advocated for women's education so that mothers could fulfill their main duty: educating their children and caring for their families. In 1870, Beecher declared to an audience of Bostonians that women's votes were "contrary to the customs of Christian people." Men—"the stronger sex"—shouldered the "cares of civil life, and the outdoor and heavy labor which take a man from home."[106] The ballot would be a form of "oppression" for women. Voting would force them "to assume responsibilities belonging to man, for which they are not and can not be qualified."[107] In her book, *Woman's Profession as Mother and Educator with Views in Opposition to Woman Suffrage*, she offered an even darker view. "This *woman movement*," she believed, "is uniting ... all the antagonisms that are warring on the family state."[108]

In 1895, after decades of informal agitation, women established the first antisuffrage groups in Massachusetts and New York.[109] In Massachusetts, women had voted in school elections since 1879.[110] The state held a non-binding referendum in 1895 to determine whether women should vote in municipal elections. Anyone registered to vote in school elections could exercise the franchise. In response, women founded the Massachusetts Association Opposed to the Further Extension of Suffrage to Women to convince the public that "the great majority" of women did not want the ballot.[111] Instead of going to the polls, antis urged women "to use their influence" to win men to their side.[112] As they hoped, women's turnout was low. Of the women who did vote, 96 percent supported suffrage, whereas only 32 percent of male voters did. In total, 37 percent of all voters favored women's suffrage.[113] The campaign marked an early victory for opponents.

Unlike the suffragists, who made the faces of their leaders and fore-mothers famous, antisuffragists preferred less notoriety, almost anonymity. Their preference for privacy recalled familiar feminine ideals from at least a century earlier. Massachusetts antis did not even elect a president for their first two years.[114] They did, however, print the names of their executive committee in their official publication, the *Remonstrance*. Single women like Miss Sarah Crocker went by their own names, but married women like Mrs. James Codman did not. This choice was an anathema to activists who constantly publicized their female leaders, but antis preferred to highlight their connections to their husbands. Like Catharine Beecher, they believed political womanhood would "lessen their influence for good and imperil the community."[115] Antisuffragists lacked a national infrastructure that resembled NAWSA or the NACW until 1911, but state organizations still thwarted local suffrage efforts.

Although not yet distributed by antisuffrage organizations, popular pictures continued to mock suffragists for abandoning domestic roles. Opponents relied on the tradition of graphic satire because the images remained profitable and popular.[116] In the mid- to late nineteenth century, looking at stereographs had become a common parlor pastime. These photographs appeared three-dimensional when viewed through a stereo-scope. Although they were a different image type from a different era, stereographs portrayed the New Women according to long-established conventions for representing women's rights supporters. At least fifty different versions—and an unknown number of copies—lampooned the "New Woman" stereotype between 1871 and 1907.[117] In an 1899 stereograph, a woman wearing bloomers and a straw hat sits next to a bicycle (figure 5.8).[118] The woman bares her stockinged legs as she reads

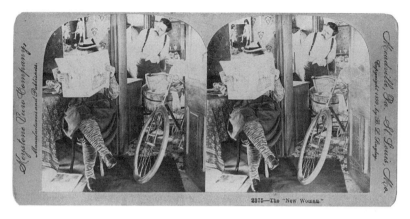

5.8: *The "New Woman,"* 1899, stereograph, Keystone View Company,
Meudville, PA. Library Company of Philadelphia.

a newspaper. On the wall behind her is a picture of two women in their
undergarments—New Women might even be lesbians![119] A man stands
over the washboard in the next room and glares at the seated woman.
Modernity—represented by her bicycle—appears between the couple in
the doorway. By the mid-1890s, bicycles were wildly popular and provided
women greater mobility and independence. Women wore bloomer outfits, similar to those from the 1850s, to ride them. Bloomers resembled
men's trousers and symbolized sexual freedom and availability.[120] The New
Woman, this image implied, preferred the company of other women and
relegated the New Man to drudgery. As the man's face suggests, he was
not happy about it. The stereograph's publisher, Keystone View Company,
expected consumers to laugh happily at the absurdity of the picture.

In the 1890s, Americans who preferred traditional gender roles feared
that masculinity faced a crisis. The rise of the New Woman, organized fe
male activists, and female voters at the state and local levels threatened the
power of elite white men. Labor unions went on strike to contest the power
of wealthy company owners. Furthermore, the 1893 census declared that
the romanticized rugged Western frontier was settled. Native Americans
had been confined to small plots of land. Men could no longer rely on the
West as a proving ground for their bravery. Finally, more Americans lived
in cities than ever before, and urban life supposedly produced weaker men.

Amid these concerns, Theodore Roosevelt became an icon for a new
vital manhood. In 1894, seven years before he became president, his article "The Manly Virtues and Practical Politics" argued that "a peaceful

and commercial nation is always in danger of suffering the loss of the virile fighting qualities without which no nation ... can ever amount to anything."[121] Along with morality, efficiency, and patriotism, he said, men must have "the rougher, manlier virtues, and above all the virtue of personal courage."[122] In 1898, Roosevelt and his backers eagerly supported the declaration of war against Spain to win Cuban independence. The Spanish-American War offered men a new frontier to prove themselves. Since the hierarchy of races crowned Anglo-Saxon men as leaders, they had the responsibility—nicknamed the "white man's burden"—to civilize so-called inferior peoples like the Cubans and spread democracy.[123]

Not everyone thought this aggressive brand of masculinity was the answer. In July 1898, the magazine *Puck* featured an ambivalent image of Roosevelt leading the Rough Riders (figure 5.9). The leader appears larger than life with a gun in one hand and a flag in the other. His stance evokes his physical strength and courage. *Puck*, however, critiqued his brutality. A caption notes that he and his soldiers were "rough on the Spaniards." In the illustration, Roosevelt tramples them. Another man thrusts the butt of his gun toward several small soldiers below. *Puck*'s editorial argued that Americans should not harm locals. People who thought men needed to experience war were wrong, it said; a peaceful nation did "not necessarily degenerate into brainless, sapless, nerveless imbeciles." Instead, the war demonstrated that "some of the finest courage the world has ever known has come right out of a generation that has known only peace."[124]

Many black men strove to achieve a similar masculine style of leadership. Because society viewed African American men as violent, they aimed to be perceived as less physically aggressive. In October 1904, John H. Adams Jr., an artist and professor at Atlanta's Morris Brown College, wrote for the *Voice of the Negro*, a mouthpiece for leading black intellectuals. His article characterized the "New Negro Man" as "tall, erect, commanding" and with a face that is "strong" and "expressive."[125] He is "always studying, thinking, working." Adams featured portraits of individuals that ranged from a dentist who "shows the enterprise of the new Negro man" to the *Voice of the Negro*'s editor, Jesse Max Barber.[126] The men uniformly wear suits, ties, and stern expressions. Adams rejected the "newspapers and the evil men behind them" who "paint[ed] the new Negro" as "a brute and ... [sought] to revert the cast of manhood into cowardly, cringing and willful serfdom." In response to racist rhetoric, the New Negro had to be courageous, yet controlled. Adams's portraits reflected black men's desire for civil rights and their embrace of respectability politics. Ideals were most important, since, as Adams wrote, "Man dies. Manhood lives forever."[127]

5.9: Udo J. Keppler, *The Rough Riders*, chromolithograph, 1898, published in *Puck*, July 27, 1898, cover. Courtesy of the Library of Congress, LC-DIG-ppmsca-28721.

5.10: Charles Dana Gibson, 1899, engraving, published in *Life*, December 28, 1899, page 547. The caption reads, "I often wonder why you don't get married." / "Because I'm too fond of men's society." Courtesy of Widener Library, Harvard University.

As Americans grew concerned about shifting gender roles, reformers styled themselves as more feminine. The Gibson Girl, designed by Charles Dana Gibson in 1894, offered a pleasing model. The Gibson Girl became the archetype of the beautiful, fashionable, and educated white woman. She appeared in illustrated newspapers, magazines, novels, calendars, postcards, plates, and brooches until the flapper replaced her in the mid- to late 1910s.[128] An 1899 illustration for *Life* magazine depicts two women who exemplify the style (figure 5.10). Their corseted waists, fancy gowns, and elaborate hairstyles suggest their status. One woman says to the other, "I often wonder why you don't get married." Her friend responds, "Because I'm too fond of men's society." Prosuffrage author Charlotte Perkins Gilman wrote that the Gibson Girl "represent[ed] a noble type indeed." She asserted, "Women are growing honester, braver, stronger, and more healthful and skillful and able and free, more human in all ways."[129] They did not have to marry immediately; they could go to college, engage in politics, and have careers.[130]

Only elite, educated white women with money and leisure time—the demographics of NAWSA—could be like Gibson girls, so the black press promoted their own New Negro Woman. Three months before his article on the New Negro Man, John H. Adams Jr. wrote that the New Negro Woman had "not only the physical beauty, not only the intellectual graces but also the moral stamina, the purity of heart, the loftiness of purpose and the sober consciousness of true womanhood the same as her white or red or olive sisters."[131] He drew fictional idealized women valued for their "poetic soul" and "rare beauty." In a long tradition of feminine imagery, these symbolic women represented ambiguous ideals rather than specific individuals.

Adams's ideal New Negro Woman (figure 5.11) resembled the portraits that Terrell distributed. Just two months before his article, the *Voice of the Negro* had included Terrell's portrait (figure 5.12). In both images, the standing women wear fashionable, embellished gowns. Their heads turn toward the viewer, but their bodies do not. Each knows she is on display. Adams might not have modeled his New Negro Woman after Terrell, but he had likely encountered plenty of her portraits.[132] For Terrell, his illustrations might have seemed like an affirmation of the public image she cultivated. Terrell kept a copy of Adams's article on the New Negro Man for the rest of her life.[133] Even though she presented herself as a beautiful, refined New Negro Woman, in reality she was as commanding and courageous as Adams's ideal New Negro Man.

Unlike the symbolic New Negro Woman, Mary Church Terrell provided a real figure for women to emulate. In 1900, she finished her three terms as NACW president, and she continued to lead. Four years later, Terrell addressed the meeting of the International Congress of Women in Berlin, Germany, and won widespread fame in reform circles.[134] Upon her arrival at the conference, she overheard attendees "criticizing" those who had lectured in English. Terrell decided to enlist her knowledge of German so that her audience would understand her experience of social injustice.[135] The *Washington Post* reported that prominent NAWSA suffragist Ida Husted Harper had declared Terrell's speech "the hit of the congress."[136] Terrell later recalled, "I wanted to place the colored women of the United States in the most favorable light possible. I represented, not only the colored women of my own country, but, since I was the only woman taking part in the International Congress who had a drop of African blood in her veins, I represented the whole continent of Africa as well."[137]

After her successful speech, Terrell distributed a striking portrait taken in Berlin. Rather than paying an artist to engrave her likeness, she har-

An admirer of Fine Art, a performer on the violin and the
piano, a sweet singer, a writer—mostly given to essays, a
lover of good books, and a home making girl, is Gussie.

5.11: John H. Adams Jr., *Gussie*, halftone, 1904, printed in *Voice of the
Negro*, August 1904, page 326, with the article "Rough Sketches: A Study
of the Features of the New Negro Woman." The caption reads, "An
admirer of Fine Art, a performer on the violin and the piano, a sweet
singer, a writer—mostly given to essays, a lover of good books, and
a home making girl, is Gussie." Courtesy of the Moorland-Spingarn
Research Center, Manuscript Division, Howard University.

MRS. MARY CHURCH TERRELL
of Washington City

Who sailed for Berlin last month, where she has been invited to
address the International Congress of Women in June on
"The Progress of the Colored Women in
the United States."

5.12: *Mrs. Mary Church Terrell*, halftone photograph, 1904, published in *Voice of the Negro*, May 1904, page 216 Courtesy of the Moorland-Spingarn Research Center, Manuscript Division, Howard University.

nessed the power of photographic halftones to spread a more realistic version of the New Negro Woman (figure 5.13).[138] Halftones reproduce photographs, so they convey a sense of authenticity.[139] In the portrait, Terrell stands next to an ornate wooden table. She wears a light-colored coat over her dress with a sculptural hat. It's not an intimate portrait. Others from the session depict her closer up and without outerwear, offering a more personal look. In this one, Terrell is ready to walk out the door to speak at the congress. The pins on her dress are likely her conference badges. Viewers had probably encountered similar images of white women. Terrell's portrait implies that through education and hard work, black women could achieve this level of success and respect.

The NACW incorporated photographic halftones into their work too. In 1902, they published a record of what they had accomplished. Halftone portraits of their officers and engravings of their meeting spaces covered

Mrs. Mary Church Terrell,

The Famous Platform Lecturer, and Member of School Board, Washington, D. C.

This noted lecturer spoke to crowded houses in Europe. She recently spoke in Marshall, Dallas, Fort Worth, Houston and New Orleans. She has inspired all who have heard her. She will lecture at the C. M. E. Church Tuesday night, May 5th, at 8:30 o'clock. Hear her.

ADMISSION, 25 CENTS.

5.13: *Mrs. Mary Church Terrell*, flyer with halftone photograph, early 1900s. Mary Church Terrell Papers, Printed Matter, Oberlin College Library Special Collections.

the pages of *A History of the Club Movement among the Colored Women of the United States of America*. Similar to the *History of Woman Suffrage*, the book told the story of the NACW's founding to advertise and legitimize their work. The portraits defined the movement's leaders and presented a vision of black political womanhood that emphasized respectability, elegance, education, and community. The NACW's lack of power and funds—especially in comparison to NAWSA—made their public image less visible to a white audience, but they still offered a positive vision of black political womanhood.

For all three of these suffrage organizations at the turn of the century, motherhood proved central to their arguments about American political womanhood. Opponents believed the vote would diminish women's power in the home. In contrast, the WCTU, NAWSA, and NACW offered a fresh interpretation of familiar gender roles. With slightly different inflections, each group's imagery and rhetoric stressed that women's votes would lead to social progress. The WCTU offered a version rooted in white Protestant morality, while NAWSA's secular vision relied on virtuous white motherhood to argue that women's votes would simply extend their domestic duties. The NACW, on the other hand, focused on black women's respectability and work to uplift their families and communities. They advocated for women to care for their homes, but, since most black women needed jobs to support their families, they idealized women's domestic sphere less than the other groups.

Suffrage organizations developed strategies to take advantage of new visual technology, such as photographic halftones, to reach broader audiences. They continued to rely on leaders, but committees headed by professionals coordinated national publicity strategies. The rise of photojournalism and the popularity of halftone photographs in the early twentieth century provided suffragists with new publicity opportunities. Women—suffragists and growing numbers of female artists—designed and circulated more visual propaganda. They also produced innovative protests, like parades and pickets, and used halftone photographs to present a vision of political womanhood that Americans had not witnessed before.

6.1: Leet Brothers, *Head of the Suffragette Parade Passing Treasury*, 1913, postcard. Schlesinger Library, Radcliffe Institute, Harvard University.

6: WHITE PUBLIC MOTHERS AND MILITANT SUFFRAGISTS WIN THE VOTE

A photographic halftone, printed on a postcard, captures the excitement and chaos of the first suffrage parade in the nation's capital, in 1913 (figure 6.1). In the picture, women march down the city's most politicized street, Pennsylvania Avenue. The outline of the Capitol Building in the background serves as a reminder of the political representation they seek. They started from that landmark and proceeded to the White House, and the photograph captures the head of the parade about midway through their route.[1] The suffragists wear large hats and long, white dresses, a color that symbolizes purity and innocence, while they ride majestic white horses. One horse pulls a cart with a large sign declaring their purpose, which onlookers near and far—and even viewers of the postcard—could easily read: "WE DEMAND AN AMENDMENT TO THE CONSTITUTION OF THE UNITED STATES ENFRANCHISING THE WOMEN OF THIS COUNTRY." Thousands of men and women crowd together to see, leaving little room for the procession. On either side, American flags and yards of bunting drape buildings, prepared not for the suffragists but for the presidential inauguration the following day. The Leet Brothers, just one of the publishing companies who sold photographs of the parade, produced the postcard to capitalize on popular demand for this visual mode of communication. Suffragists and bystanders could keep or send the postcards as mementos of their participation in this unprecedented protest.

News headlines and photographs presented Washington, DC's, first suffrage parade to Americans across the country. Twenty-eight-year-old Alice Paul had planned the parade to attract this kind of publicity for her aggressive—yet young and beautiful—vision of white political womanhood. Paul, chairman of the National American Woman Suffrage Association's Congressional Committee, worked with her friend Lucy Burns. They had organized a procession through the streets of Edinburgh in 1909 and knew how to make it happen.[2] When Paul asked the local chief of police for a permit, he told her it was "totally unsuitable for women to be marching down Pennsylvania Avenue." He suggested Sixteenth Street, a residential road, rather than a political thoroughfare. Paul and Burns knew "no one would pay much attention" if they processed there, so they used family connections to secure Pennsylvania Avenue.[3] The pair selected March 3, 1913, the day before Woodrow Wilson's presidential inauguration, to guarantee masses of crowds, reporters, and photographers. Congress even voted to halt traffic for them.[4] Their colorful, symbolic pageant resembled the inaugural parade planned for the following day.[5] Instead of a new president, the procession inaugurated a new model for the modern political woman.

As she reflected on her life in 1974, eighty-nine-year-old Paul remembered the parade as a turning point in the movement's public image. She told an interviewer the parade was "the first impression we [suffragists] probably made on Congress." The march demonstrated the "enthusiasm, interest, excitement on the part of women which they probably never imagined."[6] Suffragists forced local politicians and Americans across the country to grapple with this new type of feminine politics. Paul met Burns in Britain in 1909, and they were arrested during a demonstration carried out by suffragists at the House of Commons.[7] The militant suffragists who preferred public protests and clashes with officials—which often helped them make the news—operated under the slogan "Deeds Not Words."[8]

Photographs of processions and elaborate stunts won British suffragists publicity and demonstrated their unshakable conviction for all the world to see. Paul and Burns wanted the same for the American cause, so they modernized campaigns by designing spectacles that would attract professional press photographers, who sold their pictures to newspapers and the public. Nationwide, daily newspaper circulation rose to 22.4 million in 1910, so the medium was an effective way to reach Americans.[9] In the 1890s, the adoption of the halftone printing process facilitated the cheap, mass reproduction of photographs and rise of photojournalism. The engraved newspapers of the previous century, like *Harper's Weekly*, declined in popularity as the public increasingly wanted photographs to illustrate their daily news. Furthermore, halftones offered viewers a sense of immediacy that could not be conveyed in an engraving. Since photographs provide viewers with a sense that they are observing the event, the images often obscure the choices the photographer makes to construct the picture.

Suffragists took advantage of this dramatic shift in visual culture and journalism to create their most expansive, comprehensive, and deliberate visual campaign yet. If they planned newsworthy spectacles, newspapers across the nation printed photographs of them. Any suffragists, not just the sainted founding mothers of an earlier era, appeared under headlines. They hired publicity professionals to ensure that pictures depicted youthful suffragists as modern and fashionable, while a rising generation of female artists and editors ensured that pictures of this new political woman circulated more widely than sexist stereotypes. In addition, suffragists distributed great quantities of cartoons, photographs, posters, and other visual propaganda to the masses. They demonstrated the centrality of imagery to modern political campaigns and paved the way for the government to produce its own visual propaganda to win support for entering World War I.

Pictures of suffragists as refined, white, and moral mothers, part of the suffragists visual campaign since the 1890s, competed with pictures of marchers. These images presented two visions of modern womanhood to the public and pointed to tensions among suffragists. Comparatively conservative leaders of the National American Woman Suffrage Association (NAWSA) and the National Association of Colored Women (NACW) grew concerned about the resemblance of controversial public protests to those of militant British suffragettes and criticized them in the press. Public motherhood rhetoric—visual and otherwise—remained rooted in traditional ideas of femininity. Arguments about women's innate moral qualities and equality coexisted within the movement. The range of arguments helped attract a coalition of supporters. Although NAWSA suffragists could also be feminists, the National Woman's Party (NWP) embraced this platform more fully in their visual campaign. The ballot, NAWSA's visual campaign stressed, would allow educated, white mothers, wives, and daughters to extend their domestic expertise into the public realm. These women would not become manly or challenge heteronormative family values. Alice Paul and her fellow NWP activists, on the other hand, claimed the same rights and spaces as men. These competing visions shared an emphasis on whiteness that signaled leading suffragists' anxiety that altering the gender hierarchy might change the racial hierarchy too.

THE TYPE HAS CHANGED

While Alice Paul was in college and working with British suffragists, NAWSA focused their visual campaign on public motherhood. Although the Woman's Christian Temperance Union proved a powerful advocate of the ballot for women in the late nineteenth century, NAWSA became the dominant suffrage organization in the early twentieth. As president, Carrie Chapman Catt, one of Susan B. Anthony's protégés, oversaw NAWSA's expansion from 1900 through 1904. She stepped down, and Anna Howard Shaw, another of Anthony's protégés, became president. In 1906, Jane Addams, leader of the settlement house movement and a NAWSA board member, articulated the preferred message at the annual convention.[10] She told her audience that "city housekeeping has failed partly because women, the traditional housekeepers, have not been consulted as to its multiform activities." Men were "indifferent to the details of the household" and could not properly perform these tasks. "Public spirited" women would contribute their expertise to help clean up the nation.[11]

NAWSA printed flyers with Addams's address on public housekeeping, and the following year, cartoonist Luther Bradley created a visual representation of her idea for the *Chicago Daily News* that was reprinted in newspapers throughout the country (figure 6.2). A man wearing an apron labeled "The Man Who Votes" stands in a messy "Municipal Kitchen." Liquid from a kettle and pan overflows on a stove, and glass lies on the floor. The broken plates symbolize a broken system of "ordinances." Rats break into the food-filled cupboard labeled "City Treasury." A suffragist stands in the doorway to survey the scene and asks, "May I Help?" The man responds, "Avaunt! Man Alone Has the Capacity for These Great Affairs!" Society prized women's domestic expertise, but men refused to let them contribute it. Through this cartoon and other campaign materials, like suffrage cookbooks, reformers addressed concerns about their kitchen expertise.[12] If Bradley had not met Addams, he had certainly read about the famed fellow Chicagoan. His cartoon signaled the gradual shift among mainstream newspapers—papers aimed at a broad audience rather than solely reformers—to support suffrage, especially their public motherhood vision.

While some suffragists truly aspired to the public motherhood ideal, others—especially the publicity professionals that NAWSA hired—recognized the imagery as central to their efforts to win supporters.[13] They insisted that the modern political woman was young and attractive and embraced family life. State campaigns helped suffragists refine their mass advertising and publicity strategies. After women won the ballot in Washington in 1910, Californians became the first to pioneer mass publicity strategies during their successful campaign in 1911.[14] To make sure their message reached the public, NAWSA founded departments to coordinate the movement's public face. In 1913, NAWSA started the National Woman Suffrage Publishing Company to print their flyers, pamphlets, and posters. Printed catalogs listed their supplies so that supporters and state associations could purchase them for their campaigns.[15]

Suffragists wanted the public to forget the stereotypes of masculine old maids, and popular pictures demonstrate that their efforts paid off.[16] In

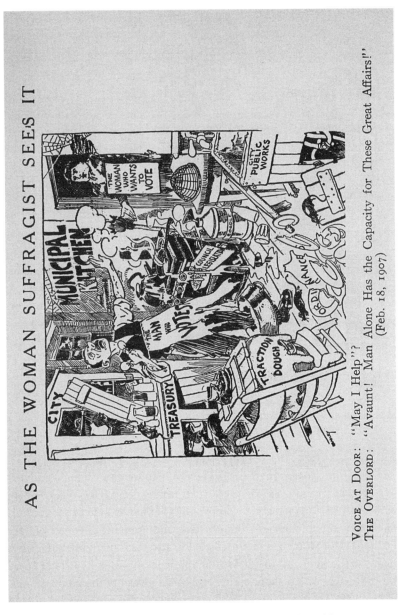

6.2: Luther Daniels (L. D.) Bradley, *Public Housekeeping*, published in *Cartoons by Bradley* (1917), page 46. Also published in the *Chicago Daily News*, February 18, 1907. Courtesy of the Whitney Museum of American Art, Frances Mulhall Achilles Library.

THE TYPE HAS CHANGED.

6.3: Boardman Robinson, *The Type Has Changed*, 1911, published in the *New York Tribune*, February 24, 1911, page 7. Courtesy of the Library of Congress, Chronicling America: Historic American Newspapers.

1911, the *New York Tribune* printed a cartoon of two white women called *The Type Has Changed* (figure 6.3). Each woman wears a ribbon signifying her allegiance to suffrage. On the left, a frowning, spectacled, older woman with short hair and a plain hat stands with her hands in her coat pockets. She looks unapproachable, unattractive, and ignorant of contemporary fashions. This woman, so uninterested in attracting men, might be a lesbian. On the right, a younger, fashionable woman with a stylish hat poses for the viewer with a slight smile. Her corset gives her the popular hourglass shape, and her delicate heels contrast with the flats worn by the old suffragist type. Far more alluring to the opposite sex, she represents the idealized feminine type. The artist, Boardman Robinson, demonstrated the femininity of modern activists and pointed to the cause's popularity among the middle- and upper-class women who were the face of the movement.[17] Suffrage was no longer a lifestyle; it was a fashion.

NAWSA president Catt also noticed the change in the mainstream press. Previously "anti-suffragists were good-looking, fashionably dressed, highly respectable women," while suffragists "were made to look like escapers from insane asylums." For years cartoonists had portrayed Susan B. Anthony "with a dress hanging in uneven scallops and carrying a large umbrella," as on the front page of the *Daily Graphic* in 1873 (figure 3.16 on p. 85). But, by the turn of the century, Catt noted that even satirists depicted suffragists as "fashionable."[18]

Black suffragists, however, received little support from the mainstream press, even from papers that supported votes for women. Their erasure from public imagery demonstrated that suffragists and editors wanted to alter the gender hierarchy but protect white supremacy. White suffrage organizations continued to implement a strategy to win support from Southern officials by focusing on white women's votes. Despite this, the National Association of Colored Women built up their organization and, by 1906, had committees dedicated to the press, art, and literature.[19] In addition to supporting suffrage, they aimed to improve black communities by founding kindergartens, promoting temperance, and advocating against lynching. In 1912, NACW president Elizabeth Carter presided over a roundtable to educate convention attendees on the progress of women's suffrage. She also oversaw the establishment of the Committee on Public Posters and Prints.[20] The NACW's first president, Mary Church Terrell, no longer headed the group, but the NACW still claimed her and the vision of refined black political womanhood that she continued to represent.

Antisuffragists organized in response to the growing power of the suffrage movement. In 1911, they banded together to create the National Association Opposed to Woman Suffrage. Locals formed state associations in 1895, but antis needed to counter the reformers' sophisticated nationwide campaigns with their own.[21] According to antis, since men voted on behalf of their families, wives would only replicate their votes. Voting, therefore, would cost taxpayers double with no meaningful change. This argument encouraged suffragists to underscore gender difference. Even with a comparatively undeveloped organization, antisuffragists still had politically powerful, wealthy backers. Opponents worried about the suffragists' promise that moral female voters really would have greater consideration for the public good. The liquor industry feared they would enact the prohibition of alcohol, while businesses thought they would support legislation for shorter workdays and child labor laws. Racist leaders and Southern Democrats who continued to disenfranchise black men, furthermore, feared a world with more African American voters.[22]

Antis gradually lost the support of the press in the 1910s, but some influential editors still opposed suffrage. As in earlier decades, they argued that women had more social power as nonpartisan wives and mothers than they would with the ballot.[23] Artist Laura Foster designed an illustration for a 1912 issue of *Life*, a dedicated anti magazine, that features a woman climbing stairs toward a cup labeled "FAME" (figure 6.4).[24] A different facet of life is written on each of the risers. The bottom stairs—"LOVE," "MARRIAGE," and "CHILDREN"—are covered with flowers. A happy girl and boy play together. In contrast, cracks break up the top stairs marked "LONELINESS," "ANXIETY," and "SUFFRAGE," representing the dangerous breakdown of society. The higher the ambitious woman climbed above her station, the image implied, the unhappier she would become. Foster herself might not have agreed with the message, since she also drew cartoons in support of the vote.[25] She represents a wave of professional female artists—like Nina Allender, Blanche Ames, Rose O'Neill, and Mary Ellen Sigsbee—who published more suffrage imagery than ever before.[26]

Despite their innovative campaigns, suffragists employed traditional ideas about gender and society in their visions of political power. NAWSA glorified motherhood and promoted moral, white, feminine domesticity, while the NACW claimed respect for elegant, elite black women in their communities, not just in their homes. Newly organized antisuffragists competed to convince the public that feminine influence remained women's strongest tool. Whether prizing established race, class, or gender hierarchies, the groups stressed their aim to work within an existing social hierarchy, not redefine it.

PHOTOGRAPHS AND PUBLIC PROTESTS

Photographs of militant suffragists presented a strong challenge to existing norms. Like Mary Church Terrell, Alice Paul was among a rising generation of college-educated, professional young women. In 1905, Paul graduated from Swarthmore and then completed an MA in sociology at the University of Pennsylvania. In 1907, she went to Britain to pursue social work, a career path forged by leaders like Jane Addams. Paul joined the Women's Social and Political Union and, as their motto required, did "deeds" to advance the cause. Paul lectured to passersby on street corners and sold copies of *Votes for Women*, the group's newspaper.[27] Along with Lucy Burns, she protested meetings led by Winston Churchill. Police arrested Paul and Burns multiple times. They went on hunger strikes and jailers force-fed them. Photographic halftones made their demonstrations and faces famous overseas and in the United States.[28]

6.4: Laura E. Foster, *Looking Backward*, halftone, 1912, published in
Life, August 22, 1912, page 1638. Courtesy of the Library of Congress,
LC-DIG-ppmsca-02940.

Paul's mother only learned about her daughter's final imprisonment in Britain from American newspaper headlines.[29]

"Suffragettes," the epithet hurled at militant British suffragists, staged public protests to attract photojournalists and bystanders. British activists designed their events to appeal to the public before Americans did. In addition to publicity photographs, suffragists—militant and nonmilitant—founded the Artists' Suffrage League and Suffrage Atelier specifically to create imagery. As in the United States, suffragists circulated formal portraits of revered leaders as well as prints, postcards, and illustrated publications. They, too, countered cartoons that mocked political women as masculine social revolutionaries. While some imagery emphasized the themes of public motherhood as NAWSA's did, the British visual campaign often focused on justice and equality.[30]

In 1908, Paul marched in her first parade. Each section of the procession featured different organizations (militant and nonmilitant alike), regions of origin, and professions. The Artists' Suffrage League created elaborate banners that praised historical women, including Queen Elizabeth, Queen Victoria, Joan of Arc, Florence Nightingale, and American suffragist Lucy Stone.[31] Marchers carried banners and displayed them in the Council Chamber of Caxton Hall in Westminster to attract publicity. Newspapers printed halftones of the parade and its banners, which were lauded for their "most exquisite and elaborate style." Articles noted that the needlework "should convince the most sceptical that it is possible for a woman to use a needle even when she is also wanting a vote."[32] Suffragists forged a public and political path, but the press praised them for their domesticity and beauty.

Photographs and news of British spectacles circulated across the Atlantic, and American papers largely condemned public suffrage demonstrations, militant or not. The *New York Tribune* declared the "scenes" at the 1908 procession "disorderly and disgraceful."[33] Months later, a *Chicago Tribune* headline announced that British suffragists' "turbulent behavior," which by then included storming the House of Commons, would "result in a loss of support."[34] NAWSA leadership agreed. In 1909, the *New York Times* ran the headline "Mrs. Catt Disapproves," reporting, "Anna Shaw also frowns on Americans who paraded with suffragettes."[35]

Despite NAWSA's stance, some liked the ambitious model of engaged political womanhood they saw. While Paul completed her PhD in economics at the University of Pennsylvania, Harriot Stanton Blatch introduced parades, a tactic also employed by working women and labor activists, to the American suffrage movement.[36] In 1894, Jacob Coxey led America's

6.5: Dale, *Official Program Woman Suffrage Procession*, halftones, 1913.
Courtesy of the Library of Congress, LC-DIG-ppmsca-12512.

first major march on Washington, DC. His group of unemployed men,
nicknamed "Coxey's Army," went from Ohio to the capital to demand work
after the Panic of 1893.[37] After that, labor activists regularly participated in
similar protests. Blatch, a daughter of Elizabeth Cady Stanton, often col-
laborated with working women, which likely inspired her to adopt tactics
like parades. Blatch organized the first major processions in New York City
annually from 1910 through 1913.[38]

   Paul hoped that the first suffrage procession in Washington, DC, would
attract even more press attention. In 1913, Paul and Burns teamed up as
NAWSA's Congressional Committee, a defunct national organ based in
the capital city. Their official program, which doubled as a souvenir, visu-
alizes their aims, explains their cause, and lists participants' biographies.
A vibrant illustration on the cover features a female herald with a trumpet
on a white horse, calling for women to fall in line behind her to demand
the vote. The herald recalls allegorical female figures of Justice and Liberty, but she sports the bobbed hair of the New Woman (figure 6.5). She
wears an elaborate purple costume, perhaps inspired by medieval designs,
accented by suffrage yellow, instead of a classical, draped dress. Two suffragists with patriotic red, white, and blue sashes march behind her. The

illustration celebrates the cause with a sense of pride. Standing tall beyond the trees in the background, the rotunda of the US Capitol Building signals the protestors' demand for a constitutional amendment. Inside the booklet, formal portraits publicize the faces of the parade's organizers. The idealized image on the cover, by contrast, envisions a unified national movement led by an ambitious political woman, a modern Joan of Arc.

For suffrage and mainstream publications alike, the parade's real herald, Inez Milholland, was an appealing icon.[39] At twenty-six, she personified NAWSA's elite, educated, reform-minded, and beautiful white New Woman. Milholland, who also served as a herald in Blatch's New York parade, graduated from Vassar and completed a law degree from New York University, one of the few law schools that accepted women. The *Woman's Journal* reproduced a popular photograph of her on its front page (figure 6.6). She wears a white dress, cape, and crown as she sits astride a white horse with the Capitol rotunda in the background.[40] While the illustration inspires suffragists, the photograph demonstrates that they achieved the model they promoted. Smiling, Milholland rides past the crowds. Her white costume implies purity, and its classical draping recalls female symbols of liberty. The *Washington Post* called her "'the most beautiful suffragist.'"[41]

The press capitalized on the interest in the procession. "The pageant," according to the *Washington Post*, was "one of the greatest arguments in favor of suffrage because it has brought the pleas of women before the public in an attractive way when they would not read the propaganda put out."[42] Even when reporting on this political protest, writers emphasized feminine beauty. Photographs captured the "attractive" sections of the parade that highlighted the variety of women who wanted the vote.[43] Costumed or uniformed women represented college graduates, homemakers, actresses, and women from different countries. A postcard by the Leet Brothers features a group of nurses marching in front of NAWSA's striped grandstand (figure 6.7). Like the British suffragists, they carry a banner emblazoned with the name of Florence Nightingale, the British woman who paved the way for female nurses during the Civil War.

Photographs also captured something that Paul and Burns had not intended: riots. Men had marched in the streets before, but the presence of female protestors on the nation's main political avenue was unprecedented. They challenged gender hierarchies inscribed in public space and, the photographs demonstrated, were met with violence.[44] Even though suffragists had more supporters than ever, opponents still proved powerful. One postcard, printed by a local photography studio, depicts suffragists

6.6: Inez Milholland as herald, halftone photograph, published in the *Woman's Journal*, March 5, 1913, page 73. Courtesy of the Library of Congress, LC-DIG-ppmsca-02970.

6.7: Leet Brothers, *Contingent of Trained Nurses*, halftone photograph postcard, 1913. Ellen A. Webster Papers, Schlesinger Library, Radcliffe Institute, Harvard University.

trying to maneuver their float through the masses (figure 6.8). Entitled *Crowd Braking [sic] Parade Up at 9th St.*, the photograph captures the violent resistance to women's demand for power. The police did little to protect the marchers, so the cavalry was called in. Two hundred people reported injuries that day.[45] For opponents, photographs of the riots likely confirmed fears that political women disrupted society. On the other hand, the violence ensured that the parade made and remained in the news as officials investigated the way police had managed the situation. Ultimately, a Senate investigation led to the firing of the police superintendent.

Pictures of the protest forced Americans across the country to consider suffrage and NAWSA's marching women. Agencies sent their photographs to newspapers by wire.[46] As far away as California, the *San Jose Mercury* printed pictures with the story.[47] The *Chicago Daily Tribune* published a cartoon of a suffragist stealing the spotlight from the new President Woodrow Wilson.[48] Locally, the *Washington Post* split its front page to cover both events (figure 6.9).[49] The headline reads: "Woman's Beauty, Grace, and Art, Miles of Fluttering Femininity Present Entrancing Suffrage Appeal." Beneath it, a snapshot captures the tableau (described as a "dramatic symbolization of women's aspirations for political freedom") that took place on the steps of the Treasury Building. A group of girls and women wear classical robes behind a woman with her arm outstretched as a plea for justice. Idealized women in classical robes had represented liberty

6.8: Taylor Studio, "*Crowd Braking* [*sic*] *Parade Up at 9th St. Mch 3 1913*," 1913, halftone photograph postcard. Courtesy of the Library of Congress, LC-USZ62-95606.

and justice in American imagery since the nation's founding. Unlike the threatening photographs of women marching in the streets, photographs of these women in robes would have seemed more familiar to viewers. The picture of "fluttering femininity" contrasts with a more familiar vision of American political power: formal portraits of Wilson and his vice president.[50] Even as they praised the demonstration, the *Post* emphasized female beauty and male political leadership.

Nearly all of the news photographs feature white women marching in the segregated parade. During the days leading up to the march, a group of suffragists hiked from New York City to Washington, DC. Newspapers across the country wrote about and photographed them. Along the way, suffragists of color tried to join the group. The leaders of the hikers, "General" Rosalie Jones and "Colonel" Ida Crafts, told the *Washington Post*, "If the negroes attempt to march with us into Washington, I will not."[51] Paul and NAWSA kept the parade segregated because of these threats and their fear that allying with black women would keep officials from endorsing suffrage.[52]

The president of the National Association of Colored Women, Margaret Murray Washington, must have had this kind of racism in mind when she discussed the parade. Washington, who advocated for industrial education alongside her husband, Booker T. Washington, declared that the NACW's "attitude toward the suffrage is of the conservative kind." NACW members

6.9: Halftone photographs on the front page of the *Washington Post*,
March 4, 1913. Courtesy of the Library of Congress.

had not "blown any houses with dynamite" and have not been "parading in
the streets in men's attire." She added that she was "not at all certain" that
members would participate in the parade. Instead they would be "reading
and studying" so that they would be ready to cast ballots "intelligently"
when given the chance.[53]

Mary Church Terrell and Ida B. Wells-Barnett were not willing to read on
the sidelines. Terrell, still an honorary NACW president and living in Wash-

ington, DC, approved of "proper, dignified agitation," and certainly would not miss this.[54] Even though diagrams of the parade's sections did not note their groups, black women did march.[55] In her memoir, Terrell praised the herald, Inez Milholland, for insisting that the parade include black women from Howard University.[56] The sorority that Terrell had helped found there, Delta Sigma Theta, marched with fellow college women.[57] Black women were supposed to march at the back of the parade, but antilynching leader Wells-Barnett refused to do so. She integrated the delegation from Illinois, and the *Chicago Daily Tribune* printed a photograph of her marching with her peers. Like the others, she wears an Illinois sash, a white hat covered with stars, and a flag with a similar design. The caption noted some "differences" among the suffragists regarding her presence, but suggests that they took her "under their wing."[58] Later that month, the *Chicago Defender*, a local paper aimed at a black audience, lauded Wells-Barnett as "Queen of our race."[59] She was a leader, not someone who needed to be taken under anyone's wing.

Political cartoons mocked white suffragists for their refusal to march alongside black suffragists. Two weeks after the parade, the illustrated weekly humor magazine *Puck* printed a cartoon that illustrated racial tensions (figure 6.10).[60] A group of three black women with "VOTES FOR COLORED LADIES" sashes and a flag approach a white suffragist, who looks aghast. The white woman holding a hiking stick references the hikers. *Puck* ridiculed the white suffragist for excluding fellow supporters, but the cartoon also caricatures the black marchers, who resemble racist stereotypes. In addition to appearing masculine and unfashionable, the black suffragists are hunched over and have large lips and protruding mouths. They lack the silhouette, dress, and fine features of the white New Woman. The larger woman in the center appears as a politicized version of the familiar mammy stereotype. She has abandoned her usual domestic labors and defiantly holds a banner in front of a well-dressed white woman, the type of woman who might have employed her.

The cartoon reflects the anxiety that women's votes might upset white supremacy in its efforts to erode the patriarchy. Despite such attacks, suffrage organizations dominated by white women, NAWSA and the National Woman's Party, did not counter with positive images of African American suffragists. Politically, they wanted support from officials who supported laws that disenfranchised people of color. White women wanted to be equal to white men, not to fight for equality with black women. Suffrage leaders might have also feared such images would compromise the long-

6.10: L. M. G., *Well, Missy! Heah We Is!*, 1913, engraving, published in *Puck*, March 19, 1913, page 5. Courtesy of the Library of Congress, LC-USZC2-1059.

standing association of elite white womanhood with purity and morality. White women were willing to sacrifice the vote for "colored ladies" in order to win it for themselves.

After the 1913 parade, more photographs—and halftones of them—of protesting political women circulated widely. Photographic halftones of activists marching in parades, speaking on street corners, or on pilgrimages became common in periodicals, postcards, and other publications. Suffragists designed the events, but NAWSA's publicity departments had little control over the photographs taken by professional agencies like the Bain News Service, Harris & Ewing, and Underwood and Underwood.[61] They benefited from the coverage, and professional photography studios—and the editors that purchased their pictures—profited from sales. Most important, the visual publicity surrounding the parade made the public and politicians pay attention.

Suffragists also split over their visions of political womanhood. Though they made their procession appear attractive and feminine, the parade defied the ideals of domestic womanhood that NAWSA still promoted. NAWSA decided that they did not want to associate themselves with protests that resembled those of militant British suffragists. Alice Paul and her supporters, however, viewed news coverage as key to their success. In 1913, they broke with NAWSA and founded the Congressional Union, which became the National Woman's Party in 1917. (In this chapter, I will refer to Paul's group as the NWP to keep the various suffrage organizations clearer.[62]) Instead of promoting an idealized vision of public motherhood like NAWSA, Paul and her supporters argued that men and women had an equal right to the ballot. They ensured that pictures of women claiming power in traditionally masculine spaces made the news.

DOUBLING DOWN ON FEMININITY

Suffragists, especially NAWSA, and their opponents launched unprecedented visual campaigns to stress gender difference in their visions of modern political womanhood. Anna Howard Shaw ran NAWSA until 1915, when Carrie Chapman Catt, the group's previous president, reclaimed the presidency.[63] Catt oversaw dramatic improvements in NAWSA's visual campaign. She advocated for an unprecedented comprehensive strategy: the "Winning Plan." Suffragists sought more wins at the state level, especially in regions without suffrage states (the Northeast and South). At the same time, NAWSA increased financial support to lobby for a federal amendment. The executive council reined in state associations and directed them to follow their lead.[64]

NAWSA embraced bureaucracy and expertise, like other Progressive Era organizations, as they built their visual campaign. They founded a publicity department in 1914 and an art publicity committee in 1916.[65] By 1916, advertising professional Charles T. Heaslip was leading the NAWSA Press Committee. He also started a publicity council with members in twenty-six states.[66] A few years earlier, he had written about publicity as the "lively profession of disguising advertisements as news," a concept he applied to the suffrage movement.[67] By 1917, though, Heaslip had defected to work with Paul and the NWP, and Arthur Dunn, a newspaper correspondent for thirty years, took his place.[68] Charles Hallinan, "an experienced newspaperman," also became chairman of the press bureau because of his experience with "the latest methods of publicity work."[69] Male professionals were doing the work that dedicated female activists had once done.

At NAWSA's annual meeting in 1916, Heaslip articulated his strategy for attracting the press. Suffragists needed "to give them [newspapers] what *they* want, *weaving it in with as much as possible of the news and information that we want to reach the public.*"[70] Heaslip told NAWSA, "I am fanatical about pictures because they are far more important to a publicity campaign than the average person realizes." He did not want "artistic" or "attractive" photographs; he wanted newsworthy images of any "stunts" that NAWSA could distribute as high-quality halftones.[71] Suffragists needed to wear light-colored dresses—they chose white—for demonstrations so that they would stand out in halftone news photographs. Heaslip, furthermore, thought prosuffrage cartoons were "one of the most effective instruments in any campaign." He emphasized the importance of visual propaganda for appealing to voting men. He noted, "Few men will read a suffrage story or a story that bears any of the ear-marks of the suffrage propaganda, but they will look at a cartoon."[72] They needed more streetcar signs, more posters, more billboards, and more window displays.

In addition to news pictures, NAWSA produced appealing visual propaganda. They often stuck to their public motherhood message and regularly depicted babies and young girls to remind viewers that suffragists were (or could be) mothers.[73] Children appeared much less threatening than the women who marched in the streets. In 1915, artist Rose O'Neill illustrated NAWSA propaganda. O'Neill initially designed the popular Kewpie doll for the *Ladies' Home Journal*, a conservative magazine.[74] One of her posters, also printed as a postcard, features four Kewpies donning suffrage yellow and marching in step (figure 6.11). The lead Kewpie holds a "VOTES FOR OUR MOTHERS" flag. With their large eyes and pleading looks they declare, "GIVE MOTHER THE VOTE—WE NEED IT." The poster lists issues that women's votes would improve: schools, health, food, and homes. The familiar imagery of feminine domesticity, long associated with white women, aimed to appeal to mainstream audiences.

For the first time, reformers could rely on publications unassociated with the movement to print suffrage pictures, marking a major shift in popular imagery. Over the course of the 1910s, the informal network of prosuffrage publications began to resemble the network of opponents that had dominated print culture throughout the nineteenth century. After decades of satirical cartoons, the illustrated weekly humor magazine *Puck* endorsed suffrage and reproduced O'Neill's pictures. In 1915, they printed a series of prosuffrage illustrations, including a simplified version of her

6.11: Rose O'Neill, *Give Mother the Vote*, ca. 1915. Poster Collection, Schlesinger Library, Radcliffe Institute, Harvard University.

poster. The tide was turning, and *Puck* thought the shift would be profitable. The editor directed readers to cut out the pictures and pin them
to their walls. Suffrage organizations were given free copies. According to
the editor, "The skilled 'campaigner' has learned the enormous value of
a clever cartoon, a pithy editorial, used immediately and with telling effect." Supporters should "see that *Puck* comes into your home regularly"
because "its propaganda value alone will balance the cost many times
over."[75] NAWSA's vision of public motherhood was winning over editors
and readers alike.

In addition to cute cartoon children, suffrage imagery emphasized that
voting women would be ideal mothers. Boston artist Blanche Ames drew
Double the Power of the Home—Two Good Votes Are Better Than One, which
features a young, angelic-faced woman surrounded by three children
(figure 6.12).[76] A baby lies on her shoulder, and her son reads a book in
her lap. Her daughter leans in to listen. The composition recalls imagery
of the Madonna and child, the exemplary Christian pair. A "God Bless
Our Home" sign completes the idyllic kitchen. The knitting on the floor, a
white cat, a neat stack of plates, and a steaming kettle imply the mother's
domestic skills. Ames argues that a white, privileged mother like this one
will cast a "good" vote. The title implies that Americans who did not have
homes and families like this one, including immigrants, people of color,
and poor Americans, cast "bad" votes. Some suffragists hoped that white
women's votes would counter such votes. The illustration appeared in the
Boston Transcript, in the *Woman's Journal*, and on a separate flyer.[77] The
Woman's Journal believed Ames' cartoons attracted attention to the cause
and subscribers to their paper.

Ames originally designed *Double the Power of the Home* for the 1915
campaign to win suffrage in New York state.[78] The campaign likely influenced *Puck*, printed in New York, to support the cause. The state's suffrage association had a press and publicity infrastructure unparalleled
by other states.[79] They purchased many of their—mostly illustrated and
colorful—materials from NAWSA's catalog. Suffragists reported to NAWSA
that they sold or gave away almost eleven million pieces of literature,
nearly 300,000 novelties (such as pennants, fans, and buttons), and over
seven million posters.[80] The quantity of the materials distributed by New
York suffragists—along with the time and money required to get them—
demonstrate the centrality of propaganda to the movement. The 1915
campaign failed, but it prepared suffragists for a successful one in 1917.

Since antisuffragists could no longer rely on the popular press to mock
suffragists, they fought back with their own campaign. In the 1910s, the

6.12: Blanche Ames, *Double the Power of the Home—Two Good Votes Are Better Than One*, 1915, engraving. Originally published in the *Woman's Journal*, October 23, 1915, page 335 (front page) and the *Boston Transcript*, September 1915. Sophia Smith Collection, Smith College.

Massachusetts Association Opposed to the Further Extension of Suffrage started distributing illustrated flyers. On one, a man with a lunch pail returns home from work to find his daughter, doll in hand, unsupervised and in tears (figure 6.13). A child sitting on the floor reaches out to him. A "VOTES FOR WOMEN" poster hangs on the wall alongside a handwritten note. His wife will be "Back Some Time This Evening." As in earlier eras, the illustration argues that political women would lead to angry husbands and abandoned, unhappy children. Americans disagreed about whether votes would help or hurt the home. Suffragists mocked their opponents—who held their own meetings and conventions—with cartoons with titles like *Anti-Suffragist Off to Lecture on "Why Women Should Stay at Home."*[81]

Drawings remained appealing, but photographs still provided especially convincing evidence. Photographs are often perceived as an index or a representation of a real scene, despite an awareness of the ways that they can be manipulated. In 1916, Heaslip, still the head of the NAWSA Press Committee, wrote to a suffragist named Mrs. Alger, likely a state publicity representative, asking her to send him "the story of Mrs. Dunbar and her nineteen children." Most of all, Heaslip needed a photograph of her "pose[d] with as many of the nineteen about her as possible." He believed "one such picture would do more to knock the props from under the anti contention that only spinsters and advanced feminists are interested in suffrage than anything I know of." NAWSA sent these photographs to papers to demonstrate that political women cared for their families.[82]

NAWSA and antisuffragists both fought to present themselves as the most beautiful, motherly, modern women. Suffragists worked against a century of prejudice to portray themselves as womanly, but antis did not have to overcome such ideas. One female figure on their 1916 calendar wears a long pink and black dress with flounces (figure 6.14). She shyly looks at the viewer from under her fashionable hat. She resembles the stylish women who appeared in fashion magazines. The pink roses on her muff symbolize the anti cause, while yellow roses indicate suffrage support. The same illustration appeared on calendars and postcards recruiting new members for the anti groups.

Antisuffragists also employed photographs to testify to the dangers of women's votes. The Massachusetts Anti-Suffrage Committee, for example, printed a series of over a dozen flyers with halftones of election scenes. They probably commissioned them at the height of suffrage debates during the mid- to late 1910s. Each caption provides an antisuffrage interpretation of the scene. In one, *Papa Minds the Baby*, a man pushes a carriage covered with campaign posters (figure 6.15). A young child stands next to

6.13: Massachusetts Association Opposed to the Further Extension of
Suffrage, *Home!*, 1910s, flyer. Miscellaneous collection of antisuffrage
material assembled by an officer of the Massachusetts Association
Opposed to Further Extension of Suffrage to Women, Collection of
the Massachusetts Historical Society.

6.14: *Anti-Suffrage Calendar—1916*, 1916. The caption for January and February reads, "Four and twenty Suffragists went to win a male, / Their costumes were the newest, but their arguments were stale. / He shook his weary head at them and made a lovely bow, / "My State has voted NO," he said, "I cannot help you now." Collection of the Massachusetts Historical Society.

PAPA MINDS THE BABY

A common sight in Chicago on election day. Mother is out "whooping it up" for her candidate. Women make better pleaders for votes than men. Consequently papa minds the baby while mama hunts for votes, even though papa is not "equal" to mama in making baby happy.

Issued for Massachusetts Anti-Suffrage Committee
J. A. Desmond
56 Crescent Avenue, Dorchester

6.15: *Papa Minds the Baby*, 1910s, flyer. Miscellaneous collection of anti-suffrage material, Collection of the Massachusetts Historical Society.

him. The mother, according to the caption, had abandoned her family to promote a political candidate. Since women "make better pleaders for votes than men," the photograph captures a "common sight in Chicago on election day." The interpretation relies on the long-standing visual trope that men caring for children signaled the end of American family values. Some might not have interpreted the image as problematic, but the caption highlighted the threat. As in the case of Heaslip and Mrs. Alger, antis likely also staged the scenes they pictured, or interpreted existing images to support their cause.

White suffragists and their opponents agreed on one thing: women of color did not belong in their visions of political womanhood. The NACW never circulated as much suffrage-themed visual propaganda as NAWSA or the NWP. Still, they knew its value in their own fight for equality. In 1914, Katherine Tillman presented an update on her "baby" Department of Public Posters and Prints to the NACW. She wanted to counter "ugly caricatures" of African Americans by circulating images that would "develop race pride." She wrote to editors and advertisers to remove the "ugly-faced colored women from their columns and from the bill boards." She also specifically wanted to distribute "pretty pictures of colored children," which aligned with the NACW's aim to improve family life. Despite the size and newness of her committee, she stated her goal as "the uplift of humanity."[83]

Even with publicity committees, reform publications remained the most important advocates of the vote for women of color. In 1912 and 1915, the *Crisis*, the official paper of the National Association for the Advancement of Colored People (NAACP), dedicated entire issues to winning suffrage. Activists printed portraits of prominent leading reformers to construct a more complex, inspiring narrative of the past. The 1912 issue featured a photographic portrait of Frederick Douglass on its cover and an engraving of Sojourner Truth on its interior pages.[84] Similarly, the 1915 issue depicted an imagined 1864 meeting between Truth and Abraham Lincoln (figure 6.16). Based on an 1892 painting by Frank Courtner, the image features Truth sitting at a table. By the time it appeared in the *Crisis*, photographic reproductions had made the scene familiar to many. In 1914, the year before this issue, the NACW had distributed fans printed with a version of the picture.[85] Truth wears her white head wrap and shawl over her plain Quaker clothing. Lincoln stands behind her and looks over her shoulder. Both examine an open Bible, symbolizing the one given to Lincoln by the formerly enslaved people of Baltimore, Maryland. Truth remained an icon of black political womanhood, while Lincoln symbolized the ideal supportive political leader.[86]

The *Crisis* also printed an image that became perhaps the only piece of suffrage propaganda that portrayed black women as good mothers. In an undated broadside entitled *The South's Battalion of Death*, a black woman is poised to smash an eagle labeled "JIM-CROW LAW" with a bat labeled "FEDERAL CONSTITUTION" (figure 6.17). The woman, in a plain dress with her hair in motion, looks like a baseball player swinging her bat. Two

VOTES FOR WOMEN

6.16: *Votes for Women*, 1915, halftone, published in the *Crisis*, August
1915, cover page. Courtesy of the *Crisis*/National Association for the
Advancement of Colored People.

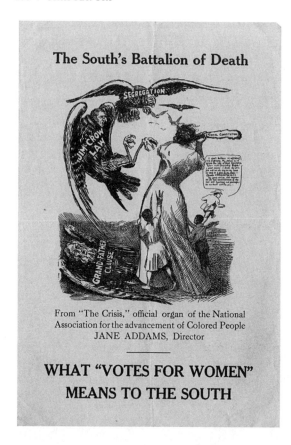

6.17: John Henry Adams, *The South's Battalion of Death*, ca. 1910s, flyer. Miscellaneous collection of antisuffrage material assembled by an officer of the Massachusetts Association Opposed to Further Extension of Suffrage to Women, Collection of the Massachusetts Historical Society.

children hide in her skirts. A desire to protect her family fuels her powerful swing. She has already knocked "GRAND-FATHER CLAUSE" to the ground and must end "SEGREGATION," "SEDUCTION," and "MOB" next. On the right, a black man in a suit and hat—a reference to the professional New Negro type—runs from the scene. He has ceded his place as the family protector. He calls out, "I don't believe in agitating and fighting. My policy is to pursue the line of least resistance. To h— with Citizenship Rights. I want money. I think the white folk will let me stay on my land as long as I stay in my place."[87] Some black men might have been ashamed of or even condemned this illustration, drawn by the black artist John Henry Adams, who had represented the New Negro Man and Woman in *Voice of the Negro* a decade earlier (figure 5.11 on p. 154). However, the picture might have inspired black women to join the growing number of local women's voluntary organizations that sought to improve black communities.

The image demanded that black female readers of the *Crisis* claim the moral superiority long associated with white women and fight for their families. Black women needed to be seen as expanding their domestic concerns rather than demanding power. They needed to win the power denied to black men, who had been disenfranchised in Southern states since 1890. The illustration condemns black men for seeming to focus more on education and jobs—strategies promoted by leaders like W. E. B. Du Bois and Booker T. Washington—than securing political power.

When the *Crisis* originally printed the illustration in May 1916, the editors made no explicit tie between the image and votes. The magazine featured only the picture with the title *Woman to the Rescue!*[88] In contrast, the broadside, perhaps printed by the NAACP or another group, enlisted the familiar argument that enfranchised women would care for their families. Unlike illustrations of white women in their homes with their children, however, the broadside portrays this black woman as a physically powerful, active protector. She contrasts with the pictures often circulated by the NACW and other civil rights publications that preferred refined, well-dressed black women. This picture engages with stereotypes about aggressive black women, yet demonstrates their commitment to enact change.

For white supremacists, John Henry Adams's picture illustrated their fear that black female voters would challenge discriminatory legislation. The bottom of the broadside offers another title for the piece: *What "Votes for Women" Means to the South*. Antisuffragists relied on this anxiety about black female voters to fuel opposition to the Nineteenth Amendment. For example, the Massachusetts Association Opposed to Further Extension of Suffrage to Women collected this piece of propaganda for reference. In contrast, white suffragists' visual campaign implicitly promoted white women's votes. They needed to appeal to enough white supremacists to win the ballot and sidestep concerns about black female voters as much as possible.

The black press and the *Crisis* tended to present their visions for the respectable New Negro as embodied by leading male and female activists. The NACW's efforts to work with the black press demonstrates their focus on winning suffrage support from African Americans. The 1912 issue's "Men of the Month" praised Mary Church Terrell, "well known to readers of *The Crisis*," alongside an elegant profile portrait.[89] In her article "The Justice of Woman Suffrage," Terrell stated, "If I were a colored man, and were unfortunate enough not to grasp the absurdity of opposing suffrage

6.18: National Woman Suffrage Publishing Company, *Votes for Women a Success*, ca. 1917, poster. Schlesinger Library, Radcliffe Institute, Harvard University.

because of the sex of a human being, I should at least be consistent enough never to raise my voice against those who have disfranchised my brothers and myself on account of race."[90] Black women realized their fight was inextricably linked to efforts to remove restrictions that prevented black men from voting. Other NACW leaders, such as Adella Hunt Logan, espoused arguments similar to NAWSA's. Logan, who headed the NACW's first suffrage department in 1899, argued that moral women would use the vote to improve education and uplift society.[91]

Logan also praised NAWSA for their "diligent . . . spread of propaganda," and she especially admired the maps that documented suffrage wins, state by state.[92] Suffragists developed publicity tactics in state campaigns, and those wins provided fodder for this data-driven visual propaganda. Since larger western states granted the ballot first, the vast map area where suffrage had been won offered a powerful image that suggested the inevitability of their victory. In 1908, the California Equal Suffrage Headquarters sold some of the earliest maps for one cent each.[93] One popular design, titled *Votes for Women a Success*, has the subtitle *The Map Proves It* (figure 6.18). The white states signify full women's suffrage, shaded states indicate partial suffrage, and black states are those that allowed male suffrage only.

NAWSA printed this version on a poster, but they also reproduced maps on letterheads, postcards, stamps, flyers, billboards, and newspapers. During their 1915 campaign, New York suffragists sold 35,000 fans illustrated with a suffrage map.[94] In a list of NAWSA's available materials, the manager of the New York State Woman Suffrage Association's sales department wrote about six items (including postcards, flyers, and posters) that featured maps.[95] She encouraged readers to purchase them by noting, "All of the map literature is excellent propaganda, and could be used to advantage in practically all kinds of work." In *Puck*'s suffrage issue that year, artist Henry Mayer created an iconic image of Liberty striding across the map, bringing voting rights from the West to the desperate women in the East (figure 6.19). Photographs show that suffragists hung maps in their headquarters and windows, pasted them on billboards, and even strung them across streets (figure 6.20).[96]

Antisuffragists thought map propaganda was so compelling that they needed to refute it. The National Association Opposed to Woman Suffrage produced imagery that pointed out the low populations of equal-suffrage states. One poster featured men with heights corresponding to their state's population (figure 6.21). Antis printed this poster sometime after 1913 and before New York women won the vote in 1917. In the image, yellow modern suits indicate a "double suffrage" state, while black historical costumes signify a "man suffrage" state. Illinois granted women partial suffrage in 1913, so their representative wears both colors. The poster connects modern attire with the evolving gender roles of equal-suffrage states. On the far left, the "New York" man wears late eighteenth-century attire, perhaps symbolizing a preference for traditional ideas of manhood and womanhood.

With the help of publicity professionals and specialized committees, NAWSA produced and distributed a range of propaganda. Their work proved so compelling and popular that this vision of modern political womanhood dominated the movement's public imagery through the passage of the Nineteenth Amendment. Suffragists made money from their publicity efforts, which allowed them to print even more. Though suffragists and opponents disagreed about whether women should contribute supposed moral superiority to politics, they both created visual campaigns to emphasize that women—especially middle- and upper-class white women—had these attributes. The often colorful, compelling pictures of white women belied a deep anxiety, shared by many white suffragists and opponents, about the downfall of the racial hierarchy as they sought to dismantle male dominance.

6.19: Henry Mayer, *The Awakening*, 1915, chromolithograph, published in *Puck*, February 20, 1915. Courtesy of the Library of Congress, LC-USZC2-1206.

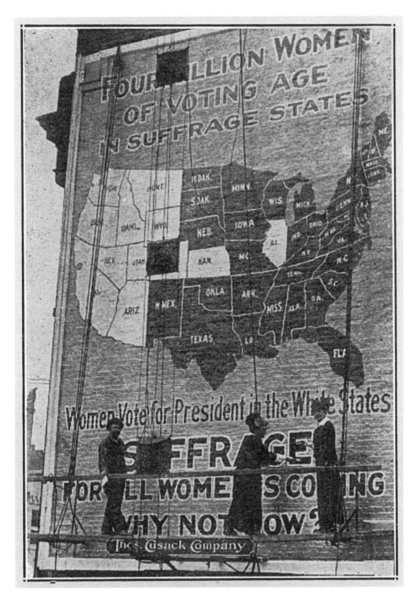

6.20: *Making Walls Talk*, 1916, halftone, published in the National
American Woman Suffrage Association's *Headquarters Newsletter*, June
22, 1916, page 16. Text on the map reads, "FOUR MILLION WOMEN OF
VOTING AGE IN SUFFRAGE STATES—WOMEN VOTE FOR PRESIDENT IN
THE WHITE STATES—SUFFRAGE FOR ALL WOMEN IS COMING—WHY
NOT NOW?" Sophia Smith Collection, Smith College.

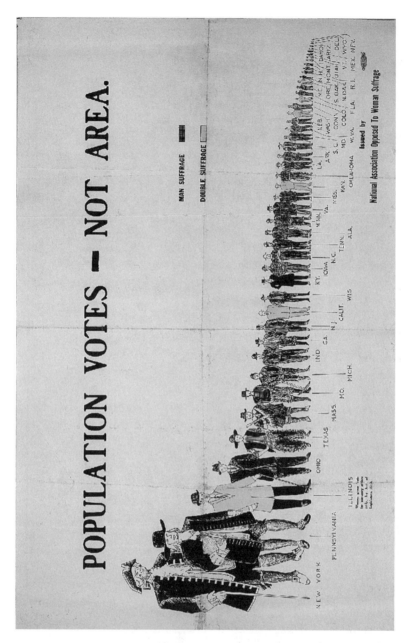

6.21: National Association Opposed to Woman Suffrage, *Population Votes—Not* Area, between 1913 and 1917, poster. Collection of the Massachusetts Historical Society.

PROTEST PHOTOGRAPHS IN THE POPULAR PRESS

Alice Paul wanted news photographs to show Americans the faces of many young, modern political women, not just a few favored older leaders. Photographs of suffrage protests demonstrated that great numbers of women wanted the ballot, educated the public about the movement, and emboldened more women to join. Even before she officially broke with NAWSA, Paul wanted control over the cause's public image. Months after the 1913 parade, she established her own organization, press bureau, and weekly newspaper, the *Suffragist*. NAWSA's leaders did not want her to compete with them, but Paul refused to share her press bureau or her lobbying strategies. In February 1914, less than a year after the parade, a NAWSA official declared, "A divided house cannot stand."[97] That same month, the *Suffragist* featured an unsigned article, likely written by Paul, to define her new organization's goals. The piece stated that the point of the recent pageants, processions, and protests was to "visualize to the reluctant and unimaginative public the greatly increasing strength of the suffrage movement."[98] The *Suffragist* announced plans for a demonstration in every state as well as another procession in Washington, DC.

Paul aimed for the photographs to reach a national audience, which corresponded to the NWP's advocacy for a constitutional amendment. She also lobbied against political candidates who did not support women's votes, but NAWSA wanted to remain nonpartisan. NAWSA presidents Shaw and Catt, then in their fifties and sixties, had known the suffrage pioneers personally. In comparison, Paul, Burns, and other young leaders had far less experience. Even though young women often represented the NWP to the public, older suffragists—especially Alva Belmont—provided crucial financial support.[99] Furthermore, with the help of Harriot Stanton Blatch, the NWP recruited working-class women with the promise that the ballot would lead to better conditions and wages.[100] Like NAWSA, however, the NWP did not seek to ally themselves with African American supporters.

Paul selected a headquarters within blocks of the White House and started planning protests to draw professional photographers. Her organization never grew as large as NAWSA, but a casual newspaper reader might not have known that. In 1916, she highly publicized a cross-country road trip to deliver a suffrage petition to Congress. The "Suffrage Special" officially launched her group as the National Woman's Party. Suffragists rode a train for six weeks, stopping to speak to locals and pose for photographs along the way.

NAWSA saw the value of publicity of highly orchestrated demonstrations that were not as controversial as Paul's. In 1916, Paul and her fellow NWP members marched with NAWSA in Chicago during the Republican convention. NAWSA advertised the parade with a cartoon of marching suffragists that told readers: "One Marcher in Line Is Worth Ten Petitions in the Waste Basket." Like Paul, they aimed to show that "the women of this country **do** want suffrage."[101] NAWSA also publicized the event using "newspapers, the 'movies,' electric signs, bill boards and practically every other advertising medium available." "Moving picture houses" advertised the parade with slides, and "a hugh [sic] electric sign" on Michigan Avenue flashed the message "Help nail the suffrage plank." NAWSA stated that they hired "all of the leading moving picture companies" to film the parade so that it could be shown "in picture houses around the country."[102] Although the organizations' visions differed, some suffragists supported both NAWSA and the NWP. Californian Alice Park, for example, adopted NAWSA rhetoric to design a "Votes for Mothers" postcard, but she also supported militant suffragists on both sides of the Atlantic.[103]

After the parade, halftones on the front page of the *Chicago Daily Tribune* demonstrated women's dedication to the cause (figure 6.22). The headline trumpeted: "Clothing Wet, Ardor Undampened, 5,000 Women March."[104] In the top image, women with sashes, signs, and umbrellas carry the suffrage plank for the Republican platform. The large text made their message visible to crowds and newspaper readers. In the bottom image, a woman salutes the viewer in front of an American flag, while two others carry banners. Unlike in pictures of fashionably dressed suffragists, the rain has prompted these women to wear practical raincoats. Umbrellas, rather than elegant muffs, are their accessories. The subtitle, "Suffrage Army Storms G. O. P. Fort," likened suffragists to soldiers.[105] The militarized language reinforces the shock of seeing women marching on this scale, especially in such terrible weather. The article notes that "no person would be so bold as to say that the 5,000 women who marched along Michigan Avenue yesterday do not want suffrage." The *Chicago American* similarly asserted that "no moderately intelligent man could see that parade yesterday and doubt that woman suffrage will soon be a reality." The rain "helped do the work," the *Chicago Herald* ventured, because it showed suffragists were "a force to be reckoned with."[106]

Halftones of militaristic, masculine marchers made NAWSA leaders anxious, but Paul made her demonstrations even more aggressive. In January 1917, the NWP launched their first picket at the White House. Paul chose the spot to attract crowds, the press, and, of course, President Wilson. The NWP must have approved of Charles Heaslip's publicity work

6.22: Halftone photographs on the front page of section 2, 1916, published in the *Chicago Daily Tribune*, June 8, 1916, page 17. Courtesy of the Library of Congress.

with NAWSA because Alice Paul hired him. Heaslip endorsed the picket because he thought it would provide "excellent photographic possibilities." He instructed Paul to "get six of your prettiest pickets" to the White House gates.[107] Local studio Harris and Ewing often photographed the NWP's public protests to sell their work to the press or the NWP for distribution (figure 6.23). Soon after the pickets began, the International Film Service

6.23: Harris & Ewing, *Penn[sylvania] on the Picket Line—1917*, 1917, photograph. The banner reads, "MR. PRESIDENT HOW LONG MUST WOMEN WAIT FOR LIBERTY." Courtesy of the Library of Congress, http://hdl.loc .gov/loc.mss/mnwp.160022.

circulated a photographic halftone, which appeared in papers like the *Los Angeles Times* (figure 6.24). In the picture, a handful of suffragists stand at the fence flanking the road to the White House. The caption notes that the women wear purple, white, and yellow sashes, the NWP's colors. They hold banners reading "Mr. President, What Will You Do for Woman Suffrage?" The stillness of the winter scene does not make them look threatening; nonetheless, the text reinforces the militancy of these "Suffragist Sentinels." The halftone gave viewers a chance to make up their own minds about the protests.

Some suffragists saw picketing as the only path forward, while others viewed the protest as unpatriotic. Not even men had picketed the White House before. The NWP had overtly attacked Wilson and, by extension, the Democratic Party. In their January newsletter, the National Association of Colored Women remarked, "We hope that America is not to have the Militant Suffragets [*sic*]. Let us get what we want in another way."[108] White women might have felt safe enough to march in the streets, but black women lacked the same level of security. The article beneath the note reiterated the NACW's commitment to extend women's success in housekeeping "to encompass the city."[109] Not all of their supporters agreed: Mary Church Terrell and her daughter picketed with the NWP several times. In

6.24: International Film Service, *Suffragist Sentinels Doing "Guard Mount" at White House Grounds*, 1917, halftone photograph, published in the *Los Angeles Times*, January 16, 1917, page 3. Courtesy of Widener Library, Harvard University.

her memoir, Terrell remembered standing on hot bricks in "bitter cold" and narrowly missing arrest.[110]

In April, tensions over whether suffragists should be picketing intensified. After three years of bloodshed overseas, the United States decided to enter World War I. Wilson proclaimed that he wanted to make the world "safe for democracy."[111] When Britain declared war in 1914, militant suffragists stopped their protests. Similarly, NAWSA affiliates largely ended public spectacles that could appear unpatriotic. The NWP, however, doubled down on their protests.[112] They wanted to hold Wilson to his democratic promise. NAWSA President Catt asked Paul to remove the pickets because of the "serious antagonism" they provoked, especially among congressional representatives.[113] Catt wrote letters to the press that declared

Scene before the White House portals. last Thursday morning. just prior to the destruction of the suffrage banner.

6.25: Harris and Ewing, *Scene before the White House Portals Last Thursday Morning Just prior to the Destruction of the Suffrage Banner*, 1917, halftone photograph, published in the *Washington Post*, June 24, 1917, page SM1. Courtesy of Widener Library, Harvard University.

that picketers were not "representative of the suffrage movement." She asked news editors to "emphasize the distinction between the two organizations" for the public.[114] Antisuffragists and politicians condemned the picketers as unpatriotic.[115]

Catt's disgust for the picketers reflected some of the public's as well. By June, photographs recorded violence against the suffragists. A halftone printed in the *Washington Post* features a male-dominated crowd menacing a handful of picketers with banners (figure 6.25). The Washington studio Harris and Ewing took the photograph, as the caption notes, "just prior to the destruction of the suffrage banner." In the image, a group of men and women crowd the sidewalk and spill into the street. The photograph provides evidence of interest in the protest, but captures no unrest. Similarly, halftones in the *Chicago Tribune* tell the story of a sailor tearing down a banner (figure 6.26). A halftone of the ripped cloth attests to the violence of the scene. The banner addresses "Kaiser Wilson" and reads "HAVE YOU FORGOTTEN YOUR SYMPATHY WITH THE POOR GERMANS BECAUSE THEY ARE NOT SELF-GOVERNED? 20,000,000 AMERICAN WOMEN ARE NOT SELF-GOVERNED. TAKE THE BEAM OUT OF YOUR OWN EYE."[116] The *Tribune* printed portraits of the Chicagoans involved: the young suffragist with a fashionable hat who went to jail and the well-groomed sailor who attacked her.

6.26: *First Spoils of "War,"* 1917, halftone photograph, published in the *Chicago Tribune*, August 19, 1917, page 3. Courtesy of the Library of Congress.

However, picketing, jailed white women did win attention. In November 1917, many newspapers, including the *Boston Globe*, *Chicago Tribune*, and *Los Angeles Times*, printed a halftone of eight women: seven jailed picketers and the jail's night officer (figure 6.27). Police arrested picketers for obstructing the sidewalk. Rather than pay fines, suffragists—including Alice Paul—went to the workhouse. They went on hunger strikes, were force-fed, and endured miserable conditions. Newspapers printed their testimonies, and the debacle became an embarrassment to the president, law enforcement officials, and courts. In the jail halftone, solemn suffragists wear light-colored, shapeless clothing, their hair pulled back without the stylish accessories that often accompanied them. Most place their hands in their laps, a passive pose. The suffragists sit together, while their jailer stands in the back. Captions comment on their appearance, particularly their "jail garb" and "prison styles."[117] Even when the suffragists were prisoners, writers instructed readers to evaluate them as though they were society ladies. In contrast, articles discussed Paul's thrice-daily force-feeding and

PRISON STYLES FOR WASHINGTON SUFFRAGISTS

Prominent Leaders in Picketing the White House as They Appeared in the Occoquan Jail.

In the front row, left to right—Miss Julia Hurlburt, Miss Nina Samaridin, Miss Elizabeth Stuyvesant. Back row—Mrs. John Winters Brennan, Mrs. John Rogers, Mrs. Lawrence, Philadelphia; Mrs. J. A. H. Hopkins, New Jersey, Chairman. The woman standing is Mrs. Bovee, the night officer of the jail.

6.27: Underwood and Underwood, *Prison Styles for Washington Suffragists*, 1917, halftone photograph, published in the *Chicago Daily Tribune*, November 19, 1917, page 5. Courtesy of Widener Library, Harvard University.

inhumane prison conditions. The text clashed with the expectation of feminine beauty.

Photographs of the jailed suffragists offered a sterner portrayal than the lively illustrations in the NWP's publication the *Suffragist*. The magazine featured photographs of their leaders, demonstrations, and political cartoons. Artists Nina Allender and Lou Rogers regularly drew for the publication.[118] On October 27, 1917, soon after the police first arrested Paul for picketing, Allender illustrated suffragists in line for jail (figure 6.28). The title reads "Headquarters for the Next Six Months." The picketers look unconcerned; one even smiles to another. Perhaps these women have been jailed before. One carries a small cage, labeled "TRAP," perhaps to catch the rats in the dilapidated building. They carry banners and flags emblazoned

6.28: Nina Allender, *Headquarters for the Next Six Months*, 1917, published in the *Suffragist*, October 27, 1917, cover page. Schlesinger Library, Radcliffe Institute, Harvard University.

with their challenges to Wilson. All of the women appear pretty and well dressed with elaborate hats and NWP sashes. These women represent Paul's idealized, triumphal vision of modern political womanhood. She saw no conflict between her demand for equality and her preference for white feminine beauty, and she hoped her audience would feel the same.

CALL ISSUED FOR FARMERETTES TO SAVE NATION'S CORN CROP

THREE OF THE MAUD MULLER ARMY ❖

All the Maud Mullers that can be marshalled toge her for farm work will be needed to gather in the corn throughout the United States, according to bulletins issued by the National American Woman Suffrage Association, New York city. Recruiting stations are to be opened everywhere by the organization, the first being already established in New York city, where women may enroll for farm work at the Working Women's Protective Union. It is to be an army of volunteers, and the farmers want representatives of any trade or profession, provided the recruits are physically able to do the work. They must pass a physical examination equivalent to that given the soldier. Experienced women farmers will be given jobs as supervisors. The others will work under the farmer's training.

6.29: *Call Issued for Farmerettes to Save Nation's Corn Crop*, 1918, halftone photograph, published in the *Washington Post*, April 21, 1918, page 8. Courtesy of Widener Library, Harvard University.

While the *Suffragist* and mainstream press printed pictures of the picketers, the *Woman's Journal* refused to acknowledge the protest. Most suffragists, including the NACW and NAWSA, publicly supported the war effort.[119] NAWSA ensured that news photographs represented white suffragists as patriotic mothers. In 1917, newspaper editor Mrs. Frank Leslie died and left money for NAWSA to establish the Leslie Woman Suffrage Commission, which took over the duties of the press committee.[120] Her donation made her the largest single donor to the movement, and NAWSA honored her wishes to build up their campaigns.[121] They circulated photographs of suffragists working as farmers and nurses in overseas hospitals founded by NAWSA. In April 1918, for example, the *Washington Post* ran two halftones of suffrage "farmerettes" (figure 6.29). In one, three women work in fields. On the left, a suffragist pushes a plow and another holds a rake. On the right, a farmerette holds a wheelbarrow filled with ears of corn. All three wear loose pants, long-sleeved oversized shirts, and wide-brimmed hats. The farmerettes were referred to in militaristic terms, as were the picketers, because they took on masculine tasks. They were an "army" of women who had to "pass a physical examination equivalent to that given the soldier."[122] The language emphasized their self-sacrificing patriotism.

Suffrage propaganda helped make self-sacrificing women in service to the nation into a popular image type. During World War I, the United States government, especially the Committee on Public Information, developed its own propaganda campaigns, perhaps inspired by the suffragists' successful work.[123] One famous lithographed poster distributed by the American Red Cross builds on suffrage imagery of idealized white mothers. In *The Greatest Mother in the World*, artist Alonzo Foringer depicted a larger-than-life young white female nurse, eyes lifted upward, holding a wounded soldier on a stretcher (figure 6.30). She wears a white cap with a red cross at her forehead, and flowing white robes. The pose and costume recall imagery of the Virgin Mary, Christianity's "Greatest Mother." Artists created similar posters and even songs based on this theme.[124] Though unaffiliated with NAWSA, the imagery reiterated the importance of women using their supposedly innate skills to support the nation.

Despite disapproval from fellow suffragists, Paul and her picketers continued through 1917. In January 1918, a year after the pickets began, President Wilson officially backed a federal amendment.[125] The House of Representatives quickly voted in support of the measure, but it stalled in the Senate. In the fall of 1918, Wilson addressed the Senate and labeled the amendment a "vitally necessary war measure," adding, "We shall need them in our vision of affairs as we have never needed them before, the sympathy and insight and clear moral instinct of the women of the world."[126] Still, the Senate delayed. While NAWSA lobbied representatives, Paul and the NWP continued their demonstrations. In December, NWP suffragists started fires in the park across from the White House. Protestors burned papers inscribed with Wilson's broken promises of democracy. Like the pickets, these "watchfires" attracted widespread publicity. The process of arrests, imprisonment, hunger strikes, and official retreat continued. After several more months, the Senate passed the Nineteenth Amendment in June 1919 and sent it to the states for ratification.

Although they disagreed on their aims, NAWSA and NWP suffragists designed highly visual campaigns to construct a modern, progressive vision of womanhood. Both wanted the public to replace older gendered norms with fresh ideas. The explosion of visual propaganda and news imagery during the movement's final decades demonstrates the suffragists' eagerness

6.30: Alonzo Earl Foringer, *The Greatest Mother in the World*, 1918, lithograph poster. Courtesy of the Library of Congress, LC-DIG-ppmsca-50981.

to embrace new forms of publicity and technology to alter the relationship between women and the state. Although they disagreed over tactics and their visions, their campaigns complemented each other. Paul's unceasing public protests and photographic halftones of poorly treated suffragists forced Americans to address the issue. Neither politicians nor voters could ignore the women who claimed these public, political spaces as their own.

Despite the NWP's success at winning the public's attention, NAWSA's version of womanhood held more widespread appeal, especially among the white, wealthy political elite. When Wilson made his case to Congress and the public, he articulated NAWSA's vision of public motherhood to make his case. On August 18, 1920, after a dramatic battle, Tennessee became the thirty-sixth and final state needed for ratification.[127] At the last minute, state legislator Harry Burn changed his vote, which proved decisive. His mother had sent him a letter encouraging him to support suffrage. He told the press that he had changed his mind because "I know a mother's advice is always safest for her boy to follow, and my mother wanted me to vote for ratification."[128] Politicians answered the arguments and images of society's breakdown, long touted by antisuffragists, with the vision of political womanhood that took NAWSA over two decades to develop.

THE SUFFRAGISTS' FLAWED VISIONS

When the Nineteenth Amendment passed, the single-issue suffrage coalitions collapsed. Activists who had disagreed on the best political strategies throughout the movement debated which cause to pursue next. They refused to fight for the ballot for women of color. Even with the Nineteenth Amendment, the literacy tests, poll taxes, grandfather clauses, and violence that prevented black men from voting also prevented black women from casting a ballot.[129] In March 1919, NAWSA officials had written several leading black suffragists to justify NAWSA's refusal to let their clubs into the organization. Ida Husted Harper, on behalf of Catt, wrote to former NACW president Elizabeth Carter. Harper suggested that she was not racist because her parents were abolitionists, and she had entertained Ida B. Wells-Barnett and Booker T. Washington. Yet Harper believed that if NAWSA admitted more black women, "the defeat of the amendment [would] be assured." She closed by remembering the "many personal sacrifices" made by activists over the years and asked, "Can you not accept this as the one laid upon you?"[130] In other words, black women needed to give up their demand for the vote so that white women could have it. Harper ignored the sacrifices that women of color made to work with white suffragists. She typed her letter on the press department's letterhead, leaving no question that the movement's public image was her top priority.

Though Alice Paul worked with black leaders like Mary Church Terrell, Paul also sacrificed black women's votes. In March 1919, the National Association for the Advancement of Colored People's secretary, Walter White, wrote to Terrell condemning a racist statement made by Paul. He wrote, "Just as you say . . . if they could get the Suffrage Amendment though without enfranchising colored women, they would do it in a moment."[131] Terrell's original letter does not survive, but she publicly praised the NWP's "heroic devotion." After the passage of the Nineteenth Amendment, she asked the NWP to investigate the "flagrant violations" of the law. Terrell declared, "No women are free until all are free."[132] Paul refused her request.

Terrell and Paul fought for social justice for the rest of their lives. Terrell advocated for civil rights and picketed segregated restaurants in Washington, DC, into her eighties. She died in 1954, eleven years before the passage of the Voting Rights Act, which established federal oversight to ensure access to the polls, especially for African Americans. More American women gained greater access to the polls through other laws like the Indian Citizenship Act of 1924 and the repeal of the Chinese Exclusion Act in 1943, but women in some states still faced limitations like poll taxes and literacy tests. Puerto Rico granted women the vote in 1929. Paul continued to focus on women's rights, authoring the Equal Rights Amendment in 1923 to constitutionally prohibit discrimination based on sex. She fought to pass it until her death in 1977. Congress passed the amendment in 1972, but not enough states ratified it, and it remains unratified today.

On the national level, the political status of many women changed suddenly with the ratification of the Nineteenth Amendment. Seemingly just as quickly, public mothers appeared outdated, as did political protestors. By the 1920s, the fun-loving flapper held far more appeal.[133] The flapper rejected Victorian constructions of femininity and flaunted her sexuality and freedom. Public imagery circulated by reformers throughout the nineteenth century aimed to liberate women from restrictive constructions of femininity, both visual and cultural: the flapper type, made possible by the suffragists' visual campaign to transform conceptions of American womanhood, represented one consequence of their success.

Even though it did not mark the end of the fight, the Nineteenth Amendment requires recognition as a step toward women's political equality. All the women who dedicated their lives, money, and expertise to the cause provided an opportunity for others to live their own vision of political life. Suffragists won women greater visibility and power to shape their own public image, especially as more female artists and editors influenced America's public pictures. Nineteenth-century reformers had very few female leaders to look to when they started their campaign. By 1920, political women had a wider range of female leaders and visual types of womanhood to emulate, yet the limited visual grammar of femininity promoted by suffragists remains prominent even in the twenty-first century.

EPILOGUE

Sojourner Truth and Susan B. Anthony sat for portraits by professional photographers when they wished. Truth maintained a copyright on her photographs and did not allow studios to sell them. Anthony burned everything she did not want later generations to see. Mary Church Terrell similarly visited professionals for the photographs that became famous. Alice Paul hired studio photographers to take the pictures of orchestrated tableaus and pickets for newspapers. Each of these women decided what the public would see. They worked to leave out the parts that did not fit their vision.

A century later, politicians and activists still seek to cultivate a specific public image. Improved image technology, however, means that politicians have to embody their favored persona almost constantly. Nearly everyone has a phone with a quality camera that can take a quick, covert photograph. Anyone with access to a public library can upload an image to social media and distribute it worldwide. Traditionally, voters have wanted politicians to live up to their branding. So, from Watergate to Benghazi, secret documents that betray a politician's message have often led to falls from power.

But do Americans want politicians with polished public images anymore? The visual strategies pioneered by suffragists a century ago might be going out of fashion. In the 2016 election, for example, Hillary Clinton's highly controlled presidential campaign contrasted with the unpredictability of Donald Trump's, whose controversial late-night tweets and uncovered film footage attracted voters.

The same question applies to representations of women's political activism. In 2017, official imagery of the Women's March, the largest protest in United States history, differed from popular pictures circulated by participants. Planning for the march began immediately after Trump's election. A wave of women invited friends on social media to march in Washington, DC, the day after the inauguration. Interest exploded overnight. The initial instigators handed off the preparations to four cochairs with experience in social justice advocacy: Bob Bland, Tamika Mallory, Carmen Perez, and

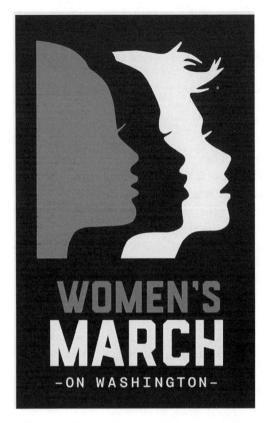

E.1: Nicole LaRue, *Women's March on Washington*, 2017, digital image. Courtesy of the Women's March.

Linda Sarsour. Local activists planned protests in major cities throughout the nation and on all seven continents.

Organizers wanted the march to appeal to as many supporters as possible, and their official logo reflected their aim to attract a diverse audience (figure E.1). The graphic, by designer Nicole LaRue, features three women in profile. Their silhouettes appear in three colors: a rusty red, navy, and cream. Outlines trace their upturned faces with elongated eyelashes and slightly parted lips. The trio looks patriotic, feminine, hopeful, and peaceful. For a book later published by the Women's March organizers, Artistic Director Paola Mendoza emphasized that she wanted the art to "change the hearts of folks, and to reinspire people to keep them engaged." She wanted love to drive people, "not anger, not revenge, not fear."[1] Organizers embraced a social movement's most valuable resource: hope and a belief in change. The logo, however, did not mirror the rage that many participants felt. At least one alternative version emerged to reflect such anger. That graphic depicted profiles of three people—without an

E.2: Liza Donovan, *Hear Our Voice*, 2017, digital image. Courtesy of the Amplifier Foundation in partnership with the Women's March.

obvious gender—with their mouths open wide as they yell in protest.[2] The Women's March also created free, similarly styled, hopeful imagery that attendees could download and print as posters to hold at the demonstration (figure E.2). Some pictures celebrated women of color, and others featured women who eschewed a typically feminine appearance. The imagery emphasized collaboration across racial lines, contrasting with historical movements focused on white women's rights. Mendoza declared, "The images that we chose were very specific around the communities that we were trying to protect. It was all very intentional."[3]

Suffragists would have preferred the professional, mass-produced graphics, but twenty-first-century marchers and news outlets did not. The most popular images from the march showed protestors with their signs,

E.3: Kelly Benvenuto, *[Pennsylvania Avenue during the Women's March in Washington, DC, January 21, 2017]*, 2017, digital photograph. Many marchers preferred to make their own signs, including posters of women's rights leaders like Susan B. Anthony, Eleanor Roosevelt, and Ruth Bader Ginsburg. Courtesy of Kelly Benvenuto.

often handmade with witty quips and earnest requests scrawled on poster board and cardboard scraps (figure E.3). Pictures of the signs littered social media and filled viral "best of" lists. Two books that focused solely on images from the march became *New York Times* bestsellers by the end of that year.[4] Professional photographers and videographers captured the action, but any marcher could make their own account visible to a broad audience through social media.

The photographs featured by marchers and the media differed from the official logo. Posters testified to the variety of political aims and visions of modern political participation that marchers embraced. After the protest, Women's March organizers immediately responded by posting a #SignOfResistance to social media each day. The images, some still made by professionals, captured aspects of everyday twenty-first century feminism that the original logo did not.

The Women's March represents one of the many challenges to the suffragists' visions for modern political womanhood. Even before the passage of the Nineteenth Amendment, alliances among female activists had begun to dissolve. A rising generation rebelled against their predecessors' embrace of traditional gender norms and iconography. The image of the flapper, with her short hair, preference for cocktails, and little concern for politics or domesticity, emerged. Decades later, photographs featured women wearing pants and Afros to march in favor of civil rights legislation and the Equal Rights Amendment. Shirley Chisholm brought her outspoken style to Congress and to a presidential candidacy in 1972. And Dolores Huerta organized protests of farm workers and feminists during that decade as well. "The personal is political," a mantra of feminists in the 1970s, most explicitly laid the foundation for today's vibrant, yet challenging, diversity of feminist visions.

Especially among those on the national political stage, however, the image of American political womanhood that suffragists engineered remains powerful. Public figures, feminist and antifeminist alike, continue to use their beauty, femininity, and motherhood as currency to win support. From Phyllis Schlafly, anti–Equal Rights Amendment leader of the 1970s, to women's rights advocate and former First Lady Michelle Obama, prominent leaders employ aspects of this image to temper fears about powerful women. Widely circulated photographs feature them in tailored and stylish feminine clothes with their children. They tend to emphasize agendas that seek to improve the lives of families. Journalists, in response, continue to ask prominent women how they juggle their duties as politicians and mothers. Mary Church Terrell, for example, would likely recognize Obama's image of educated femininity and respectability. She might have supported Obama's strategy for handling opponents during the 2016 election: "When they go low, we go high."[5] Similar to the suffrage picketers' challenge to advocates of patriotic, public motherhood, the recent feminist protests signify resistance to a traditionally feminine vision. Protestors dominate news cycles, but women who present a more traditional vision of womanhood tend to occupy visible government positions.

A familiar vision of political womanhood remains powerful because criticism of women as political leaders has changed little. Comments on the Women's March recalled the visual rhetoric of the 1869 Currier & Ives print *The Age of Brass, or The Triumphs of Woman's Rights* (figure I.1 on p. vi). Some people commented on social media, for example, that attendees were ugly spinsters. Former Nebraska State Senator Bill Kintner retweeted a photograph of marchers carrying anti–sexual assault posters, accompanied by a message implying that the women were too ugly for anyone to sexually assault them.[6] His constituents and fellow party members forced him to resign, but he was only one of many who vocalized this sentiment. The day after the march, the *New York Times* printed an article that chronicled the husbands who had struggled to maintain their households and care for children while their wives were away for the day.[7] Furthermore, some white women continue to advocate for more women to embrace domestic values like motherhood to uphold white supremacy.[8] Even after centuries of satirical cartoons, the fear of ugly feminists who abandon their families to attack American values remains strong.

Suffragists accomplished dramatic transformations in American politics and culture. They created an iconography of political women for later generations to emulate and a vision of female political power that many still find useful. A century later, my students have trouble believing women had to fight for the vote. Why would anyone oppose female voters? In 1894, Susan B. Anthony predicted their response. She told a crowd of suffragists, "Everybody will think it was always so.... They have no idea how every single inch of ground that she stands upon to-day has been gained by the hard work of some little handful of women in the past."[9] We cannot calculate the number of miles they traveled, speeches they delivered, dollars they invested, organizations they formed, or images they published so that women's votes would be an unremarkable part of American life. While this lack of awareness obscures their work, it also signifies the triumph of their vision.

Outdated notions of political womanhood need to be replaced by fresh images of female leadership. Despite gains in political equality, few people would confess the same surprise at the lack of parity in Congress or lack of a female president. Women have made dramatic strides toward political power over the past century. Yet, as of 2019, women hold 127 (23.7 percent) of the 535 seats in the United States Congress. This group represents the largest, most diverse group of women yet. Three female justices, the greatest number to date, serve on the Supreme Court of the United States. These women and their supporters have fought, as Anthony said, for "every single inch of ground."

Suffragists worked within established visual conventions for representing political power, long coded as masculine. Since then, each generation of feminists has seemed to reject the political styles of their predecessors to counter the still popular idea that feminists are serious, sexless, man-hating harridans. Instead of redefining womanhood as many have done before them, can the rising generation of political leaders redefine American imagery of political power? Rather than rewarding prominent elite white women who perform a complicated balancing act of femininity and political power, a modern vision could require less engagement with outdated gender, racial, and class norms.[10]

In the midst of commemorations honoring the centennial of the Nineteenth Amendment, historical imagery continues to define the ways we remember the movement. The enfranchisement of women deserves celebration, but the strategic use of racism, classism, and dated gender norms used by many suffragists requires a critical eye. Though the suffrage movement seems distant, their visual campaign illuminates the roots of today's gendered political imagery and its constraints. It is time for new visions of women and power.

ACKNOWLEDGMENTS

This book began when I browsed the Library of Congress's digitized photographs of suffrage picketers posing for the camera. The pictures are striking, even iconic, and I wanted to learn more about these bold women and their strategies. I did not have the Nineteenth Amendment centennial in mind, and I could not have imagined that a hundred years after the unprecedented picketing of the White House in January 1917, the nation's largest protest, also led by women, would pass the same location in January 2017. I hope that by examining this history we can see the generations of American women who have fought for equality, and learn from their mistakes and successes.

Institutional funding and many generous experts made this work possible. At Brandeis University, the Rose and Irving Crown Fellowship provided crucial support, as did the Sachar Award, two Mellon Dissertation Research Grants, a Provost Award, a History Department Prize Instructorship, and the Andrew W. Mellon Foundation Dissertation Year Fellowship. Two scholarships to participate in the Victorian Society of America's Summer Schools, one in England and another in Newport, Rhode Island, fueled my love and knowledge of nineteenth-century visual and material culture. The American Antiquarian Society's Center for Historic American Visual Culture summer seminar "Picturing Reform" provided an important starting place for my research and an introduction to Joshua Brown, a brilliant and generous visual culture scholar who offered valuable suggestions that shaped this project.

Historians eager to train a rising generation made this work worthwhile too. Thanks to my undergraduate honors thesis adviser at the University of Georgia, Stephen Mihm, for supporting a young historian's graduate-school ambitions. The publication of the *History of Woman Suffrage* by the advocates of octagonal houses was a delightful link between my first major history project and this one. At Brandeis University, I had my own bold women to look to. Joyce Antler and Karen Hansen's eye-opening class on the history of US feminisms drew me to the complex field of women's history. Susan Ware, who led a terrific Graduate Consortium of Women's

Studies writing group, offered meaningful encouragement, and I am grateful for her support. David Engerman provided valuable professional expertise and crucial guidance beginning with his first seminar. The inimitable Jane Kamensky encouraged me to write a book about gender, images, and power that encompassed far more than those picketing photographs. She taught me to write with intention and to have ambitions and see them through.

In addition, numerous archives also provided experts and crucial fellowships to further this project. Beginning with my first fellowship at the American Antiquarian Society (sponsored by the American Historical Print Collectors Society), Gigi Barnhill, Paul Erickson, and Lauren Hewes taught me to treasure a spectacular staff. Lauren's expertise has been invaluable. Thank you to Cornelia King, Erika Piola, Sarah Weatherwax, and the William H. Helfand Fellowship in American Visual Culture from the Library Company of Philadelphia. The New England Regional Fellowship Consortium Fellowship granted me time to research at the Boston Athenæum, Massachusetts Historical Society, Schlesinger Library, and Sophia Smith Collection. Thanks for the guidance from the excellent staffs at each institution, including Catherine Allgor, Anna Clutterbuck-Cook, Peter Drummey, Sarah Hutcheon, Catharina Slautterback, Mary Warnement, and Conrad Wright. At the Library of Congress, Martha Kennedy encouraged me to take special note of the female artists while researching with the support of the Caroline and Erwin Swann Foundation for Caricature and Cartoon Fellowship. David Mihaly and Diann Benti offered essential insights into the Huntington Library's collections, thanks to the Helen L. Bing Fellowship.

At the Wentworth Institute of Technology, I am part of an especially kind group of humanities and social sciences faculty who encouraged me throughout this process. Thank you to my department chair, Ron Bernier, for financial support to secure permissions for the 105 images in this book. Thanks also to Mary Carnell, who completed the administrative work that made it possible. I have enjoyed the support of our department's writing group, including my delightful officemate Paul Firenze, Jody Gordon, Mark John Isola, Juval Racelis, and Allen Wong. We are led by Ella Howard, a smart and witty historian who has taught me so much about teaching and the profession. I am grateful to Kelly Parrish and the committee, who have helped me highlight women's history on campus, efforts that our students valued enough to award me the Center for Diversity & Social Justice's Faculty Excellence Award. My students taught me the value of making academic history accessible to broader audiences, and working with them has transformed the way I communicate about my research. This book especially benefited from my university's support for my National Endowment for the Humanities summer stipend, which granted me a summer of leave from teaching to research and reconceptualize the book.

My work in public history shaped the ways that I present my research too. The terrific team of Ronald Grim and Stephanie Cyr taught me to develop exhibitions and write one-hundred-word labels about the American Revolution that spoke to current scholarship and to students visiting the Boston Public Library's Leventhal Map Center exhibitions. Working with them prepared me to curate an exhibition at the Massachusetts Historical Society called *Can She Do It? Massachusetts Debates a Woman's Right to Vote* as well as a suffrage exhibition at Harvard's Schlesinger Library in 2020. Thanks to Anna Clutterbuck-Cook, Gavin Kleepsies, Tamar Gonen Brown, Meg Rotzel, and the exhibition committees for their work. My fall 2018 and spring 2019 classes produced impressive women's suffrage documentaries for the Massachusetts Historical Society with the help of the MHS staff, Wentworth's librarians (especially Margaret Bean and Rhonda Postrel), and the always helpful Don Tracia.

Generous feedback helped me move this project forward. Comments on an early chapter by Mary Kelley and feedback from Lori Ginzberg on my talk at the Library Company proved formative. Thanks also to the anonymous reviewers for the University of Chicago Press, who provided valuable suggestions. Delightful and stimulating conversations on what we might call the "suffrage centennial circuit" with Barbara Berenson, Corinne T. Field, Kate Lemay, Laura Prieto, Lisa Tetrault, Susan Ware, and others spurred me on through the final stretch.

My gratitude also goes to the excellent team at the University of Chicago Press, especially Tim Mennel, Susannah Engstrom, Tamara Ghattas, Tyler McGaughey, and Rachel Kelly Unger. Tim offered support early on in this project and encouraged me to convey that these historical themes are relevant today. Thanks also to Tim and the press for publishing 105 images with funding from the Neil Harris Endowment Fund. I am grateful for the opportunity to produce this book with all of you.

Over the years, various writing groups have fostered wonderful friendships and new insights. My Brandeis group often included Cassandra Berman, Ian Campbell, Sascha Cohen, April French, John Hannigan, Matthew Linton, Michelle Mann, Lincoln Mullen, and Anne Marie Reardon. Fellow Brandeis grad students, especially Clara Altman, Yoni Appelbaum, Joshua

Cracraft, Joby DeCoster, Simone Diender, Rob Heinrich, Shane Landrum, Alex Wagner Lough, Amaryah Orenstein, and Craig Smith, made graduate school fun. A talented writer and great friend, Sarah Sutton helped me revise the book (and came up with the title!). Feedback from the brilliant Eva Payne and Casey Riley helped me put the final pieces in place.

The best of friends have stuck with me and this project for many, many years: Kelly Benvenuto, Cassandra Berman, Laine Cidlowski, Gwen Fernandez, Katherine Jensen, Brittany Sanders, and Caitlin Verboon. This book would not exist without our breaks for ballet brunches, India travels, *Downton* marathons, and late-night Café Intermezzo dates. My Boston book club with Kelly, Cassandra, Pauline Lewis, Zoë Samels, Sydney Shaw, Brooke Williams, and Emily Zevon is the best, as are Willa Brown and the Smart Women Eating Pasta crew.

Long before I encountered the photograph of the suffrage picketers, my marvelous aunt Marion Metzow taught me the value of historical images and objects with her museum-like home and family archive. She completed her PhD in history when far fewer women secured the degree, and she always pushed me to keep going. My loving grandmothers, Alice Harrmann—who said she would run away if her parents did not allow her to attend high school—and Blanche Lange—who late in life lamented the social pressures that pushed her to leave a job that she loved—helped me appreciate my own opportunities.

My family provided unwavering support and lots of love along the way, regularly in the form of puppy snaps. I'm grateful for my smart sisters, Maggie and Bethany, and the life adventures that we get to have together. My exceptional parents, Mark and Ellen, always believed in me. Thank you for sending me women's history memorabilia and asking what my next talk will be on, as though I talk about anything but suffrage right now. Most of all, thanks to my husband, James, who made me laugh on the challenging days and celebrated with me on the best ones. He could deliver a spectacular women's history talk of his own by now. I am excited to navigate our next chapters together.

NOTES

INTRODUCTION

1. Liette Gidlow, "The Sequel: The Fifteenth Amendment, the Nineteenth Amendment, and Southern Black Women's Struggle to Vote," *Journal of the Gilded Age and Progressive Era* 17, no. 3 (2018): 433–49.

2. See Thomas Nast, "Get Thee behind Me, (Mrs.) Satan!," *Harper's Weekly*, February 17, 1872, 140, 143.

3. For a discussion of Clinton's experience of this "balancing act," see Hillary Rodham Clinton, "On Being a Woman in Politics," in *What Happened* (New York: Simon & Schuster, 2017). See also Susan Bordo, *The Destruction of Hillary Clinton* (Brooklyn: Melville House, 2017).

4. Robin Givhan, "Why Washington's Most Powerful Women Are Wearing This Jacket," *Washington Post*, June 26, 2016, http://wapo.st/29bUTal; Mary Beard, "Women and Power," in *Women and Power: A Manifesto* (London: Profile Books, 2017).

5. Jose A. DelReal, "Trump Draws Rebuke from Clinton Campaign for Saying She Lacks 'a Presidential Look,'" *Washington Post*, September 6, 2016, http://wapo.st/2bRmU6P.

6. See for example, American Association of University Women, "Barriers and Bias: The Status of Women in Leadership" (Washington, DC: American Association of University Women, 2016); Pew Research Center, "Women and Leadership: Public Says Women Are Equally Qualified, but Barriers Persist" (Washington, DC: Pew Research Center, 2015); Elizabeth McClean et al., "The Social Consequences of Voice: An Examination of Voice Type and Gender on Status and Subsequent Leader Emergence," *Academy of Management Journal* 61, no. 5 (2018), 1869–91; Heather Murphy, "Picture a Leader. Is She a Woman?," *New York Times*, July 13, 2018, https://nyti.ms/2Dwi1xJ.

7. For more analysis of the perception of Clinton's "shrill" voice and idealized femininity, see Anne Helen Petersen, "Too Shrill: Hillary Clinton," in *Too Fat, Too Slutty, Too Loud: The Rise and Reign of the Unruly Woman* (New York: Plume, 2017).

8. Abby Ohlheiser, "Yes, #Repealthe19th Trended—but Not for the Reasons You Think," *Washington Post*, October 13, 2016, https://www.washingtonpost.com/news/the-intersect/wp/2016/10/13/yes-repealthe19th-trended-but-not-for-the-reasons-you-think/.

9. This is similar to the rise of national languages established and then circu-

lated in print culture, as described in Benedict Anderson, *Imagined Communities: Reflections on the Origin and Spread of Nationalism*, 2nd ed. (New York: Verso, 1991).

10. Significant historical works that argue for an expanded definition of politics include T. H. Breen, *The Marketplace of Revolution: How Consumer Politics Shaped American Independence* (New York: Oxford University Press, 2005); Joanne B. Freeman, *Affairs of Honor: National Politics in the New Republic* (New Haven, CT: Yale University Press, 2001); Steven Hahn, *A Nation under Our Feet: Black Political Struggles in the Rural South, from Slavery to the Great Migration* (Cambridge, MA: Belknap, 2003); Jeffrey L. Pasley, *"The Tyranny of Printers": Newspaper Politics in the Early American Republic* (Charlottesville: University of Virginia Press, 2001); David Waldstreicher, *In the Midst of Perpetual Fetes: The Making of American Nationalism, 1776–1820* (Chapel Hill: University of North Carolina Press, 1997). For recent histories of politics and visual and material culture, see Zara Anishanslin, *Portrait of a Woman in Silk: Hidden Histories of the British Atlantic World* (New Haven, CT: Yale University Press, 2016); David Brody, *Visualizing American Empire: Orientalism and Imperialism in the Philippines* (Chicago: University of Chicago Press, 2010); Joshua Brown, *Beyond the Lines: Pictorial Reporting, Everyday Life, and the Crisis of Gilded-Age America* (Berkeley: University of California Press, 2003); Sarah Anne Carter, *Object Lessons: How Nineteenth-Century Americans Learned to Make Sense of the Material World* (New York: Oxford University Press, 2018); Justin T. Clark, *City of Second Sight: Nineteenth-Century Boston and the Making of American Visual Culture* (Chapel Hill: University of North Carolina Press, 2018); Catherine E. Kelly, *Republic of Taste: Art, Politics, and Everyday Life in Early America* (Philadelphia: University of Pennsylvania Press, 2016); Susan E. Klepp, "Beauty and the Bestial: Images of Women," in *Revolutionary Conceptions: Women, Fertility, and Family Limitation in America, 1760–1820* (Chapel Hill: University of North Carolina Press, 2009); Amy K. DeFalco Lippert, *Consuming Identities: Visual Culture in Nineteenth-Century San Francisco* (New York: Oxford University Press, 2018); Hayes Peter Mauro, *The Art of Americanization at the Carlisle Indian School* (Albuquerque: University of New Mexico Press, 2011); Bonnie M. Miller, *From Liberation to Conquest: The Visual and Popular Cultures of the Spanish-American War of 1898* (Amherst: University of Massachusetts Press, 2011); Anna Pegler-Gordon, *In Sight of America: Photography and the Development of U.S. Immigration Policy* (Berkeley: University of California Press, 2009); Laura Wexler, *Tender Violence: Domestic Visions in an Age of U.S. Imperialism* (Chapel Hill: University of North Carolina Press, 2000).

11. For more on suffragists and their commercialized campaign, see Margaret Mary Finnegan, *Selling Suffrage: Consumer Culture and Votes for Women* (New York: Columbia University Press, 1999).

12. Recent works on race and visual politics include Martin A. Berger, *Seeing through Race: A Reinterpretation of Civil Rights Photography* (Berkeley: University of California Press, 2011); Maurice Berger, *For All the World to See: Visual Culture and the Struggle for Civil Rights* (New Haven, CT: Yale University Press, 2010); Jasmine Nichole Cobb, *Picture Freedom: Remaking Black Visuality in the Early Nineteenth*

Century (New York: New York University Press, 2015); Matthew Fox-Amato, *Exposing Slavery: Photography, Human Bondage, and the Birth of Modern Visual Politics in America* (New York: Oxford University Press, 2019); Matthew Pratt Guterl, *Seeing Race in Modern America* (Chapel Hill: University of North Carolina Press, 2013); Philip Lapansky, "Graphic Discord: Abolitionist and Antiabolitionist Images," in *The Abolitionist Sisterhood: Women's Political Culture in Antebellum America*, ed. Jean Fagan Yellin and John C. Van Horne (Ithaca, NY: Cornell University Press, 1994); Maurie Dee McInnis, *Slaves Waiting for Sale: Abolitionist Art and the American Slave Trade* (Chicago: University of Chicago Press, 2011); Leigh Raiford, *Imprisoned in a Luminous Glare: Photography and the African American Freedom Struggle* (Chapel Hill: University of North Carolina Press, 2011); Agnes Lugo-Ortiz and Angela Rosenthal, *Slave Portraiture in the Atlantic World* (New York: Cambridge University Press, 2013); Cherene Sherrard-Johnson, *Portraits of the New Negro Woman: Visual and Literary Culture in the Harlem Renaissance* (New Brunswick, NJ: Rutgers University Press, 2007); Shawn Michelle Smith, *Photography on the Color Line: W. E. B. Du Bois, Race, and Visual Culture* (Durham, NC: Duke University Press, 2004); John Stauffer, Zoe Trodd, and Celeste-Marie Bernier, *Picturing Frederick Douglass: An Illustrated Biography of the Nineteenth Century's Most Photographed American* (New York: Liveright, 2015); Maurice O. Wallace and Shawn Michelle Smith, eds., *Pictures and Progress: Early Photography and the Making of African American Identity* (Durham, NC: Duke University Press, 2012); Marcus Wood, *Blind Memory: Visual Representations of Slavery in England and America, 1780–1865* (New York: Routledge, 2000).

13. *Picturing Political Power* expands on insights into specific collections of suffrage imagery to construct a broader story. Kristin Allukian and Ana Stevenson, "The Suffrage Postcard Project," 2016, https://thesuffragepostcardproject.omeka .net/; Anne Biller Clark, "The Mighty Pen," in *My Dear Mrs. Ames: A Study of Suffragist Cartoonist Blanche Ames Ames* (New York: Peter Lang, 2001); Robert Cooney, *Winning the Vote: The Triumph of the American Woman Suffrage Movement* (Santa Cruz, CA: American Graphic Press, 2005); Kenneth Florey, *Women's Suffrage Memorabilia: An Illustrated Historical Study* (Jefferson, NC: McFarland, 2013); Kenneth Florey, *American Woman Suffrage Postcards: A Study and Catalog* (Jefferson, NC: McFarland, 2015); Kate Clarke Lemay, ed., *Votes for Women: A Portrait of Persistence* (Princeton, NJ: Princeton University Press, 2019); Cathleen Nista Rauterkus, *Go Get Mother's Picket Sign: Crossing Spheres with the Material Culture of Suffrage* (Lanham, MD: University Press of America, 2010); Alice Sheppard, *Cartooning for Suffrage* (Albuquerque: University of New Mexico Press, 1994); James Glen Stovall, *Seeing Suffrage: The 1913 Washington Suffrage Parade, Its Pictures, and Its Effects on the American Political Landscape* (Knoxville: University of Tennessee Press, 2013).

14. Significant scholarship on women's political participation before suffrage and the public-private divide includes Catherine Allgor, *Parlor Politics: In Which the Ladies of Washington Help Build a City and a Government* (Charlottesville: University of Virginia Press, 2000); Paula Baker, "The Domestication of Politics:

Women and American Political Society, 1780–1920," *American Historical Review* 89, no. 3 (1984): 620–47; Susan Branson, *These Fiery Frenchified Dames: Women and Political Culture in Early National Philadelphia* (Philadelphia: University of Pennsylvania Press, 2011); Lori D. Ginzberg, *Untidy Origins: A Story of Woman's Rights in Antebellum New York* (Chapel Hill: University of North Carolina Press, 2005); Nancy Isenberg, *Sex and Citizenship in Antebellum America* (Chapel Hill: University of North Carolina Press, 1998); Carol Lasser, *Antebellum Women: Private, Public, Partisan* (Lanham, MD: Rowman & Littlefield, 2010); Mary Kelley, *Learning to Stand and Speak: Women, Education, and Public Life in America's Republic* (Chapel Hill: University of North Carolina Press, 2006); Mary P. Ryan, *Women in Public: Between Banners and Ballots, 1825–1880* (Baltimore: Johns Hopkins University Press, 1990); Susan Zaeske, *Signatures of Citizenship: Petitioning, Antislavery, and Women's Political Identity* (Chapel Hill: University of North Carolina Press, 2003); Rosemarie Zagarri, *Revolutionary Backlash: Women and Politics in the Early American Republic* (Philadelphia: University of Pennsylvania Press, 2007).

15. For recent histories that offer a fresh look at suffrage, see Barbara F. Berenson, *Massachusetts in the Woman Suffrage Movement: Revolutionary Reformers* (Cheltenham, UK: History Press, 2018); Joan Marie Johnson, *Funding Feminism: Monied Women, Philanthropy, and the Women's Movement, 1870–1967* (Chapel Hill: University of North Carolina Press, 2017); Brooke Kroeger, *The Suffragents: How Women Used Men to Get the Vote* (Albany, NY: Excelsior Editions, 2017); Johanna Neuman, *Gilded Suffragists: The New York Socialites Who Fought for Women's Right to Vote* (New York: Washington Mews, 2017); Lisa Tetrault, *Myth of Seneca Falls: Memory and the Women's Suffrage Movement, 1848–1898.* (Chapel Hill: University of North Carolina Press, 2014). For examples of earlier influential suffrage histories, see Harriot Stanton Blatch and Alma Lutz, *Challenging Years: The Memoirs of Harriot Stanton Blatch* (New York: G. Putnam, 1940); Carrie Chapman Catt, *Woman Suffrage and Politics; the Inner Story of the Suffrage Movement,* (New York: Scribner, 1923); Nancy Cott, *The Grounding of Modern Feminism* (New Haven, CT: Yale University Press, 1987); Paulina W. Davis et al., *A History of the National Woman's Rights Movement, for Twenty Years: With the Proceedings of the Decade Meeting Held at Apollo Hall, October 20, 1870: From 1850 to 1870: With an Appendix Containing the History of the Movement during the Winter of 1871 in the National Capitol* (New York: Journeymen Printers' Co-operative Association, 1871); Ellen Carol DuBois, *Feminism and Suffrage: The Emergence of an Independent Women's Movement in America, 1848–1869* (Ithaca, NY: Cornell University Press, 1978); Eleanor Flexner, *Century of Struggle: The Woman's Rights Movement in the United States* (Cambridge, MA: Belknap, 1959); Ida Husted Harper, *The Life and Work of Susan B. Anthony*, 3 vols. (Indianapolis: Bowen-Merrill, 1898); Ida Husted Harper, *Story of the National Amendment for Woman Suffrage Movement* (New York: National Woman Suffrage Publishing, 1919); Aileen S. Kraditor, *The Ideas of the Woman Suffrage Movement, 1890–1920* (New York: Columbia University Press, 1965); Suzanne Marilley, *Woman Suffrage and the Origins of Liberal Feminism in the United States, 1820–1920* (Cam-

bridge, MA: Harvard University Press, 1996). Elizabeth Cady Stanton et al., eds., *History of Woman Suffrage*, 6 vols. (1881–1922; reprint, Salem, NH: Ayer, 1985).

16. A history of visual politics engages the distinct literatures on turn-of-the-century club movements that focus on white women and women of color. For more on black women's club movements, see Ann D. Gordon and Bettye Collier-Thomas, *African American Women and the Vote, 1837–1965* (Amherst: University of Massachusetts Press, 1997); Brittney C. Cooper, *Beyond Respectability: The Intellectual Thought of Race Women* (Urbana: University of Illinois Press, 2017); Evelyn Brooks Higginbotham, "African-American Women's History and the Meta-language of Race," *Signs* 17, no. 2 (1992): 251–74; Evelyn Brooks Higginbotham, *Righteous Discontent: The Women's Movement in the Black Baptist Church, 1880–1920* (Cambridge: Harvard University Press, 1993); Martha S. Jones, *All Bound Up Together: The Woman Question in African American Public Culture, 1830–1900* (Chapel Hill: University of North Carolina Press, 2007); Robin D. G. Kelley, *Race Rebels: Culture, Politics, and the Black Working Class* (New York: Free Press, 1994); Treva B. Lindsey, *Colored No More: Reinventing Black Womanhood in Washington, D.C.* (Urbana: University of Illinois Press, 2017); Alison M. Parker, *Articulating Rights: Nineteenth-Century American Women on Race, Reform, and the State* (DeKalb: Northern Illinois University Press, 2010); Rosalyn Terborg-Penn, *African American Women in the Struggle for the Vote, 1850–1920* (Bloomington: Indiana University Press, 1998); Deborah G. White, *Too Heavy a Load: Black Women in Defense of Themselves, 1894–1994* (New York: W. W. Norton, 1999).

17. *Picturing Political Power* draws on theory about the influence that images and objects can have on thought and action, including the power to shape popular understandings of gender. For more, see: Alfred Gell, *Art and Agency: An Anthropological Theory* (New York: Oxford University Press, 1998); Bruno Latour, *Pandora's Hope: Essays on the Reality of Science Studies* (Cambridge, MA: Harvard University Press, 1999); Bruno Latour, *Reassembling the Social: An Introduction to Actor-Network-Theory* (New York: Oxford University Press, 2005).

18. Deborah Cherry, *Beyond the Frame: Feminism and Visual Culture, Britain 1850–1900* (New York: Routledge, 2000); Colleen Denney, *The Visual Culture of Women's Activism in London, Paris and Beyond: An Analytical Art History, 1860 to the Present* (Jefferson, NC: McFarland, 2018); Miranda Garnett and Zoe Thomas, eds., *Suffrage and the Arts: Visual Culture, Politics, and Enterprise* (London: Bloomsbury, 2018); Lisa Tickner, *The Spectacle of Women: Imagery of the Suffrage Campaign, 1907–14* (London: Chatto & Windus, 1987).

CHAPTER ONE

1. For more analysis of the portrait, see Gwendolyn DuBois Shaw, *Portraits of a People: Picturing African Americans in the Nineteenth Century* (Seattle: University of Washington Press, 2006), 27.

2. For more on Wheatley, see Vincent Carretta, *Phillis Wheatley: Biography of a*

Genius in Bondage (Athens: University of Georgia Press, 2011); DuBois Shaw, "'On Deathless Glories Fix Thine Ardent View': Scipio Moorhead, Phillis Wheatley, and the Mythic Origins of Anglo-African Portraiture in New England," in *Portraits of a People*; Henry Louis Gates, *The Trials of Phillis Wheatley: America's First Black Poet and Her Encounters with the Founding Fathers* (New York: Basic Civitas Books, 2003); William Henry Robinson, ed., *Critical Essays on Phillis Wheatley* (Boston: G. K. Hall, 1982).

3. As quoted in DuBois Shaw, *Portraits of a People*, 31.

4. Linda J. Docherty, "Women as Readers: Visual Interpretations," in *Proceedings of the American Antiquarian Society* 107, part 2 (Worcester, MA: American Antiquarian Society, 1998), 348. For more on Wheatley as a public intellectual, see Mia Bay et al., "Phillis Wheatley, a Public Intellectual," in *Toward an Intellectual History of Black Women* (Chapel Hill: University of North Carolina Press, 2015), 35–51.

5. Margaretta M. Lovell, *Art in a Season of Revolution: Painters, Artisans, and Patrons in Early America* (Philadelphia: University of Pennsylvania Press, 2005), 159–63.

6. Richard Brilliant, *Portraiture*, Essays in Art and Culture (London: Reaktion, 1991); Lovell, "The Family: Painterly and Social Constructions," in *Art in a Season of Revolution*; Ellen G. Miles, "The Portrait in America, 1750–1776," in *American Colonial Portraits, 1700–1776*, ed. Richard H. Saunders and Ellen G. Miles (Washington, DC: Smithsonian Institution Press, 1987); Marcia R. Pointon, *Hanging the Head: Portraiture and Social Formation in Eighteenth-Century England* (New Haven, CT: Yale University Press, 1993); Susan Rather, *The American School: Artists and Status in the Late Colonial and Early National Era* (New Haven, CT: Yale University Press, 2016); Shearer West, *Portraiture* (New York: Oxford University Press, 2004).

7. Miles, "The Portrait in America," 43–44.

8. In the 1780s, frontispiece engravings in publications by formerly enslaved people, such Ignatius Sancho and Olaudah Equiano, similarly depicted them as dignified gentlemen. For more, see Vincent Carretta, *Equiano, the African: Biography of a Self-Made Man* (New York: Penguin Books, 2006), 280–93; DuBois Shaw, *Portraits of a People*, 33–34; Geoff Quilley, "Of Sailors and Slaves: Portraiture, Property, and the Trials of Circum-Atlantic Subjectivities, ca. 1750–1830," in *Slave Portraiture in the Atlantic World*, ed. Agnes Lugo-Ortiz and Angela Rosenthal (New York: Cambridge University Press, 2013), 171–99.

9. Cornelia King, Curator of Women's History at the Library Company of Philadelphia, catalogs the portraits of American female authors from their books. See "Portraits of American Women" at http://www.librarycompany.org/women/index .htm. See also Lugo-Ortiz and Rosenthal, *Slave Portraiture in the Atlantic World*.

10. For social expectations for women and writing, see Laurel Thatcher Ulrich, "Of Pens and Needles: Sources in Early American Women's History," *Journal of American History* 77, no. 1 (1990): 200–207. For more on how famous European women, especially female authors, managed fame, see Claire Brock, *The Feminization of Fame, 1750–1830* (New York: Macmillan, 2006). See also David D. Hall,

"Readers and Writers in Early New England," in *The Colonial Book in the Atlantic World*, ed. Hugh Amory and David D. Hall, vol. 1 of *A History of the Book in America* (Chapel Hill: University of North Carolina Press, 2007), 148–50. For more on idealized womanhood and the gaze in portraits, see Norman Bryson, *Vision and Painting the Logic of the Gaze* (New Haven, CT: Yale University Press, 1985); Whitney Davis, "Gender," in *Critical Terms for Art History*, ed. Robert S. Nelson and Richard Shiff (Chicago: University of Chicago Press, 2003); Margaret Olin, "Gaze," in Nelson and Shiff, *Critical Terms for Art History*; Griselda Pollock, *Vision and Difference: Femininity, Feminism and Histories of Art* (New York: Routledge, 2003); Angela Rosenthal, "Intersubjective Portrayal," in *Angelica Kauffman: Art and Sensibility* (New Haven, CT: Yale University Press, 2006); Angela Rosenthal, "She's Got the Look! Eighteenth-Century Female Portrait Painters and the Psychology of Potentially 'Dangerous Employment,'" in *Portraiture: Facing the Subject*, ed. Joanna Woodall (New York: St. Martin's Press, 1997).

11. "This Day Is Published," *Boston Gazette and Country Journal*, January 31, 1774, 1.

12. Catherine E. Kelly, "Picturing Race," in *Republic of Taste: Art, Politics, and Everyday Life in Early America* (Philadelphia: University of Pennsylvania Press, 2016).

13. Phillis Wheatley, "To the Publick," in *Poems on Various Subjects, Religious and Moral* (London: A. Bell, 1773). Italics in original.

14. Wheatley, *Poems*, iv–v.

15. See chap. 2 of this book and Allison Lange, "Picturing Tradition: Images of Martha Washington in Antebellum Politics," *Imprint* 37 (2012): 22–39.

16. Klepp, "Beauty and the Bestial."

17. For more on the Lansdowne portrait, see Carrie Rebora Barratt, *Gilbert Stuart* (New Haven, CT: Yale University Press, 2004). For more on Washington's presidential portraits, see Ellen Gross Miles, *George and Martha Washington: Portraits from the Presidential Years* (Washington, DC: Smithsonian Institution, 1999); Wendy Wick Reaves, *George Washington, an American Icon: The Eighteenth-Century Graphic Portraits* (Washington, DC: Smithsonian Institution, 1982).

18. For more on the importance of fine cloth in portraits, see Zara Anishanslin, *Portrait of a Woman in Silk: Hidden Histories of the British Atlantic World* (New Haven, CT: Yale University Press, 2016); Michael Zakim, "Sartorial Ideologies: From Homespun to Ready-Made," *American Historical Review* 106, no. 5 (2001): 1553–86; Michael Zakim, *Ready-Made Democracy: A History of Men's Dress in the American Republic, 1760–1860* (Chicago: University of Chicago Press, 2003).

19. For more on Washington's imagery and the development of his status as an icon, see Kelly, "Political Personae," in *Republic of Taste*. See also Edward G. Lengel, *Inventing George Washington* (New York: Harper Collins, 2011); Paul K. Longmore, *The Invention of George Washington* (Berkeley: University of California Press, 1988).

20. For examples, see William Spohn Baker, *The Engraved Portraits of Washington, with Notices of the Originals and Brief Biographical Sketches of the Painters*

(Philadelphia: Lindsay & Baker, 1880). Printed portraits of Washington's family, based on Edward Savage's painting, also proved popular. Scott Casper, "The First Family: Seventy Years with Edward Savage's The Washington Family," *Imprint* 24 (1999): 2–15.

21. Kelly, *Republic of Taste*, 211–12.

22. Wendy Bellion, *Citizen Spectator: Art, Illusion, and Visual Perception in Early National America* (Chapel Hill: University of North Carolina Press, 2011); Lovell, *Art in a Season of Revolution*; Maurie Dee McInnis and Louis P. Nelson, eds., *Shaping the Body Politic: Art and Political Formation in Early America* (Charlottesville: University of Virginia Press, 2011); Pointon, *Hanging the Head*, 94–104.

23. For a discussion of racist attacks on Wheatley, see Karen A. Weyler, "Mourning New England: Phillis Wheatley and the Broadside Elegy," in *Empowering Words: Outsiders and Authorship in Early America* (Athens: University of Georgia Press, 2013).

24. Notices numbered 18 and 19 from *Liberator*, October 27, 1837, 4. Reprinted in Robinson, *Critical Essays on Phillis Wheatley*, 54.

25. Georgia B. Barnhill, "Transformations in Pictorial Printing," in *An Extensive Republic: Print Culture, and Society in the New Nation, 1790–1840*, ed. Robert A. Gross and Mary Kelley, vol. 2 of *A History of the Book in America* (Chapel Hill: University of North Carolina Press, 2010), 433–37; Georgia B. Barnhill, "Business Practices of Commercial Nineteenth-Century American Lithographers," *Winterthur Portfolio* 48, no. 2/3 (2014): 213–32.

26. "Afric-American Picture Gallery—Fifth Paper," *Anglo-African Magazine*, July 1850, 218–18.

27. For a discussion of the symbolism of reversed gender roles in early modern Europe, for example, see Natalie Zemon Davis, "Women on Top," in *Society and Culture in Early Modern France: Eight Essays* (Stanford, CA: Stanford University Press, 1975). A similar genre of imagery featured women who dressed as men. The pictures often represented the women as curiosities, though accompanying texts offered reasons for their choices to dress and live as men. For examples, see Molly Gutridge, *A New Touch on the Times: Well Adapted to the Distressing Situation of Every Sea-Port Town* (Ezekiel Russell, 1779), American Antiquarian Society; Herman Mann, *The Female Review, or Memoirs of an American Young Lady* (Dedham, MA: Nathaniel and Benjamin Heaton, 1797); "Deborah Sampson" (H. Mann, 1797), Library Company of Philadelphia; Elizabeth M'Dougald, *The Life, Travels, and Extraordinary Adventures of Elizabeth M'Dougald* (Providence, RI: S. S. Southworth, 1834); Sophia Johnson, *The Friendless Orphan* (Pittsburgh: S. Johnson, 1842). For more on Deborah Sampson Gannett, the cross-dressing American Revolution soldier, see Alfred Fabian Young, *Masquerade: The Life and Times of Deborah Sampson, Continental Soldier* (New York: Knopf, 2004). For more on gender and public speaking, see Carolyn Eastman, *A Nation of Speechifiers: Making an American Public after the Revolution* (Chicago: University of Chicago Press, 2009); Jane Kamensky, *Governing the Tongue the Politics of Speech in Early New England* (New York: Oxford

University Press, 1997). For more on women in public, see Nancy Isenberg, *Sex and Citizenship in Antebellum America* (Chapel Hill: University of North Carolina Press, 1998); Glenna Matthews, *The Rise of Public Woman: Woman's Power and Woman's Place in the United States, 1630–1970* (New York: Oxford University Press, 1992); Mary P. Ryan, *Women in Public: Between Banners and Ballots, 1825–1880* (Baltimore: Johns Hopkins University Press, 1990).

28. For more on boycotts, see T. H. Breen, *The Marketplace of Revolution: How Consumer Politics Shaped American Independence* (New York: Oxford University Press, 2005); Mary Beth Norton, *Liberty's Daughters: The Revolutionary Experience of American Women, 1750–1800* (Boston: Little, Brown, 1980); Laurel Thatcher Ulrich, "Political Protest and the World of Goods," in *The Oxford Handbook of the American Revolution*, ed. Edward G. Gray and Jane Kamensky (New York: Oxford University Press, 2013). For more on this meeting, see Inez Parker Cumming, "The Edenton Ladies' Tea-Party," *Georgia Review* 8, no. 4 (1954): 389–95.

29. See Philip Dawe, *The Patriotick Barber of New York, or The Captain in the Suds* (London: R. Sayer & J. Bennett, 1775), mezzotint, Library of Congress Prints and Photographs; and Philip Dawe, *The Alternative of Williams-Burg* (London: R. Sayer & J. Bennett, 1775), Library of Congress Prints and Photographs.

30. For similar imagery that mocks women, see *Cornwallis Turned Nurse, and his Mistress a Soldier*, 1781, engraving, in *The Continental Almanac, for the year of our LORD, 1782*, American Antiquarian Society; *The Wife Acting the Soldier and the Husband Spinning and Nursing the Child*, 1780, engraving, in *The World Turned Upside Down or The Comical Metamorphoses*, opposite p. 31, Early American Imprints, Series 1, no. 43918; "The Wife Acting the Soldier," 1794, engraving, from *The World Turned Upside Down*, opposite p. 32, American Antiquarian Society.

31. Letter from Abigail Adams to John Adams, March 31–April 4, 1776, Adams Family Papers: An Electronic Archive, Massachusetts Historical Society.

32. Letter from John Adams to Abigail Adams, April 14, 1776, Adams Family Papers: An Electronic Archive, Massachusetts Historical Society.

33. By the 1780s, an estimated 60–90 percent of white men could vote. Robert J. Dinkin, *Voting in Revolutionary America: A Study of Elections in the Thirteen Original States, 1776–1789* (Westport, CT: Greenwood, 1982), 41–42; Alexander Keyssar, *The Right to Vote: The Contested History of Democracy in the United States* (New York: Basic Books, 2000); Donald Ratcliffe, "The Right to Vote and the Rise of Democracy, 1787–1828," *Journal of the Early Republic* 33, no. 2 (2013): 230, 248; Sean Wilentz, *The Rise of American Democracy: Jefferson to Lincoln* (New York: W. W. Norton, 2006). A 1790 New Jersey statute granted women the vote if they owned enough property to meet the state's requirement. Because women could not own property, female voters were probably widows. They voted until 1807, when a new law barred freed people of color and women from the ballot. Keyssar, *The Right to Vote*; Rosemarie Zagarri, *Revolutionary Backlash: Women and Politics in the Early American Republic* (Philadelphia: University of Pennsylvania Press, 2007), 30–37.

34. Simon P. Newman, *Parades and the Politics of the Street: Festive Culture*

in the Early American Republic (Philadelphia: University of Pennsylvania Press, 1997); David Waldstreicher, *In the Midst of Perpetual Fetes: The Making of American Nationalism, 1776–1820* (Chapel Hill: University of North Carolina Press, 1997); Susan Zaeske, *Signatures of Citizenship: Petitioning, Antislavery, and Women's Political Identity* (Chapel Hill: University of North Carolina Press, 2003); Zagarri, *Revolutionary Backlash.*

35. Jeanne E. Abrams, *First Ladies of the Republic: Martha Washington, Abigail Adams, Dolley Madison, and the Creation of an Iconic American Role* (New York: New York University Press, 2018); Catherine Allgor, *Parlor Politics: In Which the Ladies of Washington Help Build a City and a Government* (Charlottesville: University of Virginia Press, 2000); Catherine Allgor, *A Perfect Union: Dolley Madison and the Creation of the American Nation* (New York: Henry Holt, 2006); Susan Branson, *These Fiery Frenchified Dames: Women and Political Culture in Early National Philadelphia* (Philadelphia: University of Pennsylvania Press, 2011); Cynthia A. Kierner, *Beyond the Household: Women's Place in the Early South, 1700–1835* (Ithaca, NY: Cornell University Press, 1998); Clare A. Lyons, *Sex among the Rabble: An Intimate History of Gender and Power in the Age of Revolution, Philadelphia, 1730–1830* (Chapel Hill: University of North Carolina Press, 2006); Zagarri, *Revolutionary Backlash*, 62–68.

36. Mary Kelley, *Learning to Stand and Speak: Women, Education, and Public Life in America's Republic* (Chapel Hill: University of North Carolina Press, 2006); Lucia McMahon, *Mere Equals: The Paradox of Educated Women in the Early American Republic* (Ithaca, NY: Cornell University Press, 2012).

37. Mary Wollstonecraft, "A Vindication of the Rights of Woman," in *A Vindication of the Rights of Woman and A Vindication of the Rights of Men* (New York: Oxford University Press, 1993), 280–81.

38. Wollstonecraft, "A Vindication," 75.

39. David Hackett Fischer, *Liberty and Freedom: A Visual History of America's Founding Ideas* (New York: Oxford University Press, 2005), 234–37; E. McClung Fleming, "From Indian Princess to Greek Goddess the American Image, 1783–1815," *Winterthur Portfolio* 3 (1967): 37–66; Stephanie McKellop, "America, the 'Rebellious Slut': Gender & Political Cartoons in the American Revolution," *Common-Place* 17, no. 3 (2017), http://common-place.org/book/vol-17-no-3-mckellop/; Amelia Rauser, "Death or Liberty: British Political Prints and the Struggle for Symbols in the American Revolution," *Oxford Art Journal* 21, no. 2 (1998): 153–71; Frank Weitenkampf, "Our Political Symbols," *New York History* 33, no. 4 (1952): 371–78; Zagarri, *Revolutionary Backlash*, 104–14. For examples of Liberty, see William Charles, *Columbia Teaching John Bull His New Lesson*, 1813, etching, Library of Congress; Edward Savage, *Liberty*, 1796, engraving, Winterthur Museum.

40. "Explanation of the Frontispiece," *Lady's Magazine and Repository of Entertaining Knowledge*, vol. 1, 1792, v, American Antiquarian Society. Italics in original.

41. "Original Plan of the Ladies Magazine," *Lady's Magazine and Repository*, vol. 1, v.

42. "On Female Authorship: From the Trifler," *Lady's Magazine and Repository*, vol. 1, 68–69.

43. For more on the copy, see Kenneth Neill Cameron, *Shelley and His Circle, 1773–1822* (Cambridge, MA: Harvard University Press, 1961), 323–31. The National Portrait Gallery in London holds the original painting by John Opie, completed around 1797.

44. See John Opie, *Portrait of Mary Wollstonecraft*, ca. 1790–1791, oil on canvas, Tate.

45. For examples, see William T. Annis after John Opie, *Mary Wollstonecraft Godwin*, 1802, mezzotint, British Museum; unknown engraver after John Opie, *Mrs. Mary Wollstonecraft*, ca. 1800–1830, engraving, British Museum. For more on Wollstonecraft and her portraits, see Lucy Peltz, "Living Muses: Constructing and Celebrating the Professional Woman in Literature and the Arts," in Elizabeth Eger and Lucy Peltz, *Brilliant Women: 18th-Century Bluestockings* (London: National Portrait Gallery, 2008), 105–15. See figure 4.16 on p. 116: Wollstonecraft's portrait is the highest print in the picture on the wall above Susan B. Anthony's desk.

46. For more on *Memoirs*, see Andrew R. L. Cayton, *Love in the Time of Revolution: Transatlantic Literary Radicalism and Historical Change, 1793–1818* (Chapel Hill: University of North Carolina Press, 2013).

47. Allgor, *Parlor Politics*; Paula Baker, "The Domestication of Politics: Women and American Political Society, 1780–1920," *American Historical Review* 89, no. 3 (1984): 620–47; Branson, *These Fiery Frenchified Dames*; Nancy F. Cott, *The Bonds of Womanhood: "Woman's Sphere" in New England, 1780–1835* (New Haven, CT: Yale University Press, 1977); Kelley, *Learning to Stand & Speak*; Mary Kelley, *Private Woman, Public Stage: Literary Domesticity in Nineteenth-Century America* (New York: Oxford University Press, 1984); Linda K. Kerber, *Women of the Republic: Intellect and Ideology in Revolutionary America* (Chapel Hill: University of North Carolina Press, 1980); Kierner, *Beyond the Household*; Lyons, *Sex among the Rabble*; Newman, *Parades and the Politics of the Street*; Norton, *Liberty's Daughters*; Ryan, *Women in Public*; Waldstreicher, *In the Midst of Perpetual Fetes*; Zagarri, *Revolutionary Backlash*.

48. For more on ideals of womanhood, particularly the so-called cult of domesticity, see Barbara Welter, "The Cult of True Womanhood," *American Quarterly* 18 (1966): 151–74; and Linda Kerber, "Separate Spheres, Female Worlds, Woman's Place: The Rhetoric of Women's History," *Journal of American History* 75 (1988): 9–39. For discussions of women's benevolent societies and other organizations, see Lori D. Ginzberg, *Women and the Work of Benevolence: Morality, Politics, and Class in the Nineteenth-Century United States* (New Haven, CT: Yale University Press, 1990); Kelley, *Learning to Stand & Speak*; Jeanne Boydston, "Civilizing Selves: Public Structures and Private Lives in Mary Kelley's *Learning to Stand and Speak*," *Journal of the Early Republic* 28, no. 1 (2008): 47–60; John L. Brooke, "Spheres, Sites, Subjectivity, History: Reframing Antebellum American Society," *Journal of the Early Republic* 28, no. 1 (2008): 75–82; Philip Gould, "Civil Society and the Public

234 : NOTES TO PAGES 22–28

Woman," *Journal of the Early Republic* 28, no. 1 (2008): 29–46; Mary Kelley, "'The Need of Their Genius': Women's Reading and Writing Practices in Early America," *Journal of the Early Republic* 28, no. 1 (2008): 1–22; Zagarri, *Revolutionary Backlash*.

49. Georgia B. Barnhill, "Transformations in Pictorial Printing," 424–25.

CHAPTER TWO

1. See John Wollaston, *Martha (Dandridge Custis) Washington*, 1757, oil on canvas, Lee Chapel and Museum, Washington and Lee University.

2. Jeanne E. Abrams, *First Ladies of the Republic: Martha Washington, Abigail Adams, Dolley Madison, and the Creation of an Iconic American Role* (New York: New York University Press, 2018); Catherine Allgor, *Parlor Politics: In Which the Ladies of Washington Help Build a City and a Government* (Charlottesville: University of Virginia Press, 2000).

3. For more on Washington's portrait beyond this chapter, see Allison Lange, "Picturing Tradition: Images of Martha Washington in Antebellum Politics," *Imprint* 37 (2012): 22–39.

4. "The Use of Engravings," *Ballou's Pictorial Drawing-Room Companion*, Dec. 20, 1856, 11.

5. "The Use of Engravings," 11.

6. Joshua Brown, *Beyond the Lines: Pictorial Reporting, Everyday Life, and the Crisis of Gilded-Age America* (Berkeley: University of California Press, 2003), 14–15.

7. Brown, *Beyond the Lines*, 11–14.

8. Scott E. Casper, "Introduction," in *The Industrial Book, 1840–1880*, ed. Casper et al., vol. 3 of *A History of the Book in America* (Chapel Hill: University of North Carolina Press, 2007); Michael Winship, "Manufacturing and Book Production," in Casper et al., *The Industrial Book*, 64.

9. Georgia B. Barnhill, "Transformations in Pictorial Printing," in *An Extensive Republic: Print Culture, and Society in the New Nation, 1790–1840*, ed. Robert A. Gross and Mary Kelley, vol. 2 of *A History of the Book in America* (Chapel Hill: University of North Carolina Press, 2010), 430–33.

10. David Henkin, "The Urban World of Print," in Casper et al., *The Industrial Book*, 334.

11. "Circulation," *Ballou's Pictorial Drawing-Room Companion*, January 6, 1855, 11.

12. Brown, *Beyond the Lines*, 23.

13. Casper, "Introduction," 10–13.

14. Winship, "Manufacturing and Book Production," 65–66.

15. David M. Henkin, *The Postal Age: The Emergence of Modern Communications in Nineteenth-Century America* (Chicago: University Of Chicago Press, 2006); Scott E. Casper, "The Census, the Post Office, and Governmental Publishing," in Casper et al., *The Industrial Book*, 183.

16. Brown, *Beyond the Lines*, 9.

17. Christopher J. Lukasik, *Discerning Characters: The Culture of Appearance in Early America* (Philadelphia: University of Pennsylvania Press, 2011).

18. "The Use of Engravings."

19. "Afric-American Picture Gallery—Second Paper," *Anglo-African Magazine*, March 1859, 87.

20. "The Approaching Presidential Election," *Frank Leslie's Illustrated Newspaper*, July 12, 1856, 65–66.

21. George Bingham, *County Election* (New York: Goupil & Cie, 1854). Bingham's work carries on a tradition of election scene satire and imagery, such as William Hogarth's *Election* series of four paintings from 1754 to 1755.

22. For more on cultural ideals of womanhood, see Barbara Welter, "The Cult of True Womanhood," *American Quarterly* 18 (1966): 151–74; and Linda Kerber, "Separate Spheres, Female Worlds, Woman's Place: The Rhetoric of Women's History," *Journal of American History* 75 (1988): 9–39. For discussions of how women redefined their influence on and participation in society through benevolent societies and other organizations, see Ginzberg, *Women and the Work of Benevolence*; Kelley, *Learning to Stand & Speak*; Jeanne Boydston, "Civilizing Selves: Public Structures and Private Lives in Mary Kelley's Learning to Stand and Speak," *Journal of the Early Republic* 28, no. 1 (2008): 47–60; John L. Brooke, "Spheres, Sites, Subjectivity, History: Reframing Antebellum American Society," *Journal of the Early Republic* 28, no. 1 (2008): 75–82; Philip Gould, "Civil Society and the Public Woman," *Journal of the Early Republic* 28, no. 1 (2008): 29–46; Mary Kelley, "'The Need of Their Genius': Women's Reading and Writing Practices in Early America," *Journal of the Early Republic* 28, no. 1 (2008): 1–22; Zagarri, *Revolutionary Backlash*.

23. Laura McCall, "'The Reign of Brute Force Is Now Over': A Content Analysis of 'Godey's Lady's Book,' 1830–1860," *Journal of the Early Republic* 9, no. 2 (1989): 221.

24. *Mutual Admiration—Godey's Fashion Plate for the Month*, in *Godey's Lady's Book*, February 1850, 154.

25. For more on women and the gaze, see Kathleen Adler and Marcia R. Pointon, *The Body Imaged: The Human Form and Visual Culture since the Renaissance* (New York: Cambridge University Press, 1993); Margaret Olin, "Gaze," in *Critical Terms for Art History*, ed. Robert S. Nelson and Shiff Richard (Chicago: University of Chicago Press, 2003); Griselda Pollock, *Vision and Difference: Femininity, Feminism and Histories of Art* (New York: Routledge, 2003); Angela Rosenthal, "She's Got the Look! Eighteenth-Century Female Portrait Painters and the Psychology of Potentially 'Dangerous Employment,'" in *Portraiture: Facing the Subject*, ed. Joanna Woodall (New York: St. Martin's Press, 1997); Angela Rosenthal, "Intersubjective Portrayal," in *Angelica Kauffman: Art and Sensibility* (New Haven, CT: Yale University Press, 2006).

26. For examples of Lind's portrait, see *Jenny Lind* (New York: John Neale, ca. 1850); *Jenny Lind*, in Frederika Bremer, *The Gem of the Season: A Souvenir for*

MDCCCLI (New York: Leavitt, 1851), frontispiece; W. L. Ormsby, *Jenny Lind*, in Mrs. L. G. Abell, *Gems by the Wayside or an Offering of Purity and Truth* (New York: William Holdredge, 1850), frontispiece; J. C. McRae, *Jenny Lind*, in *The Ladies' Wreath and Parlor Annual* (New York: Burdick and Scovill, ca. 1856), facing p. 57; I. B. Forrest, *Jenny Lind*, in *The Family Circle and Parlor Annual* (New York: James G. Reed, 1852), preceding p. 61; Albert Newsam, *Jenny Lind's Songs* (New York: W. Dubois, between 1851 and 1857); Wolf, *Miss Jenny Lind* (New York: Hermann J. Meyer, ca. 1850). The American Antiquarian Society houses all of these images.

27. *The Mothers Joy* in *The Jenny Lind Album* (New York: J. C. Riker, ca. 1850s), frontispiece, American Antiquarian Society.

28. See, for example, *Empress Eugenie, Queen Victoria* (New York: Currier & Ives, undated), American Antiquarian Society; J. Cochran, *Princess Victoria*, in *The Christian Keepsake and Missionary Manual*, William Ellis (London: Fisher, Son & Co., 1835), frontispiece, American Antiquarian Society; William Drummond, *Her Majesty* the Queen" in *Heath's Book of Beauty*, ed. Countess of Blessington (New York: Appleton), frontispiece, American Antiquarian Society.

29. J. M. Ridley, *Her Majesty Queen Victoria and Members of the Royal Family* (New York: Frank Leslie, 1877); William Drummond, "Her Majesty the Queen: The Prince of Wales & the Princess Royal," in *Heath's Book of Beauty* (New York: Appleton, 1842), frontispiece; J. Cochran, *Princess Victoria*, in *The Christian Keepsake, and Missionary Annual*, ed. William Ellis (New York: W. Jackson, 1835), frontispiece; *Empress Eugenie, Queen Victoria* (New York: Currier and Ives, 1857).

30. For example, see Edward Williams Clay, *The Oregon and Texas Question* (New York: A. Donnelly, 1844), American Antiquarian Society.

31. Nancy Isenberg, *Sex and Citizenship in Antebellum America* (Chapel Hill: University of North Carolina Press, 1998); Glenna Matthews, *The Rise of Public Woman: Woman's Power and Woman's Place in the United States, 1630–1970* (New York: Oxford University Press, 1992); Mary P. Ryan, *Women in Public: Between Banners and Ballots, 1825–1880* (Baltimore: Johns Hopkins University Press, 1990).

32. Patricia Cline Cohen, Timothy Gilfoyle, and Helen Lefkowitz Horowitz, *The Flash Press: Sporting Male Weeklies in 1840s New York* (Chicago: The University of Chicago Press, 2008), 10. For examples of these images, see *The Harlot*, in *Dixon's Polyanthos*, Sept. 18, 1841, 1; *Sketches of Characters,—-No 8: Female Landsharks; or, The Sailor Caught*, in *Whip, and Satirist of New-York and Brooklyn*, Feb. 12, 1842, 1; *Grand Trial Dance between Nance Holmes and Suse Bryant, on Long Wharf, Boston*, in *Whip, and Satirist of New-York and Brooklyn*, June 25, 1842, 1; *Sketches of Characters—-No. 15: The Pretty Serving Maid*, in *Whip, and Satirist of New-York and Brooklyn*, April 2, 1842, 1; *The Chambermaid*, in *Whip, and Satirist of New-York and Brooklyn*, April 9, 1842; *Our Picture Gallery: The Upper Ten And the Lower Twenty*, in *Broadway Belle, and Mirror of the Times*, January 29, 1855, 1. The American Antiquarian Society houses these images.

33. Alfred Hoffy, *Ellen Jewett* (New York: H. R. Robinson, 1836), American Antiquarian Society. Henry Robinson published numerous sensational prints like

this. Georgia B. Barnhill, "The Pictorial Context for Nathaniel Currier: Prints for the Elite and Middle Class," *Imprint* 31, no. 2 (2006): 34–35.

34. The short publication was published separately and as a serial in the *National Police Gazette* (whose editor authored the work) over a year from September 1848 through September 1849. George Wilkes, *The Lives of Helen Jewett, and Richard P. Robinson* (New York: H. Long & Brother, 1849). Advertisements for the publication include *The Great American Work*, in *Monthly Cosmopolite*, March 1, 1850, 2; *In Press, the Life of Helen Jewett Illustrated*, in *National Police Gazette*, November 24, 1849. Patricia Cline Cohen, *The Murder of Helen Jewett: The Life and Death of a Prostitute in Nineteenth-Century New York* (New York: Vintage, 1999).

35. *The Female Abortionist*, in *National Police Gazette*, March 13, 1847, 212; *Wonderful Trial of Caroline Lohman, alias Restell* (New York: Burgess, Stringer, 1847), 32, American Antiquarian Society; and "Circulation Figures," *National Police Gazette*, January 1, 1847, 1. A more realistic portrait of her (apparently of how she appeared on the first day of her trial) showed a resolute woman, lips pursed, eyes averted but steady. *Wonderful Trial of Caroline Lohman*, cover, 2. See also Susan E. Klepp, *Revolutionary Conceptions: Women, Fertility, and Family Limitation in America, 1760–1820* (Chapel Hill: University of North Carolina Press, 2009).

36. *The Female Abortionist.*

37. For a discussion of early nineteenth-century woman's political activism and women in public, see Allgor, *Parlor Politics*; Paula Baker, "The Domestication of Politics: Women and American Political Society, 1780–1920," *American Historical Review* 89, no. 3 (1984): 620–47; Anne M. Boylan, *The Origins of Women's Activism: New York and Boston, 1797–1840* (Chapel Hill: University of North Carolina Press, 2002); Susan Branson, *These Fiery Frenchified Dames: Women and Political Culture in Early National Philadelphia* (Philadelphia: University of Pennsylvania Press, 2011); Lori D. Ginzberg, *Women in Antebellum Reform* (Wheeling, IL: Harlan Davidson, 2000); Ginzberg, *Women and the Work of Benevolence*; Lori D. Ginzberg, *Untidy Origins: A Story of Woman's Rights in Antebellum New York* (Chapel Hill: University of North Carolina Press, 2005); Nancy A. Hewitt, *Women's Activism and Social Change: Rochester, New York, 1822–1872* (Ithaca, NY: Cornell University Press, 1984); Isenberg, *Sex and Citizenship in Antebellum America*; Kelley, *Learning to Stand & Speak*; Carol Lasser, *Antebellum Women: Private, Public, Partisan* (Lanham, MD: Rowman & Littlefield, 2010); Matthews, *The Rise of Public Woman*; Ryan, *Women in Public*; Susan Zaeske, *Signatures of Citizenship: Petitioning, Antislavery, and Women's Political Identity* (Chapel Hill: University of North Carolina Press, 2003); Zagarri, *Revolutionary Backlash.*

38. Carol Faulkner, *Lucretia Mott's Heresy: Abolition and Women's Rights in Nineteenth-Century America* (Philadelphia: University of Pennsylvania Press, 2011); Ginzberg, *Untidy Origins*; Zaeske, *Signatures of Citizenship.*

39. Ellen Carol DuBois, *Feminism and Suffrage: The Emergence of an Independent Women's Movement in America, 1848–1869* (Ithaca, NY: Cornell University Press, 1978). For more on the efforts of these early activists, see Alice Stone Blackwell,

Lucy Stone: Pioneer of Woman's Rights (Charlottesville: University of Virginia Press, 1930); Faulkner, *Lucretia Mott's Heresy*; Andrea Moore Kerr, *Lucy Stone Speaking Out for Equality* (New Brunswick, NJ: Rutgers University Press, 1992); Kristen Tegtmeier Oertel and Marilyn S. Blackwell, *Frontier Feminist: Clarina Howard Nichols and the Politics of Motherhood* (Lawrence: University Press of Kansas, 2010); Christine L Ridarsky and Mary Margaret Huth, *Susan B. Anthony and the Struggle for Equal Rights*, 2012; Dorothy Sterling, *Ahead of Her Time: Abby Kelley and the Politics of Anti-Slavery* (New York: W. W. Norton, 1994).

40. Elizabeth Cady Stanton, Susan B. Anthony, and Matilda Joslyn Gage, eds., *History of Woman Suffrage*, vol. 1 (New York: Fowler and Wells, 1881; Salem, NH: Ayer, 1985; citations refer to the 1985 edition), 53–62.

41. Isenberg, *Sex and Citizenship in Antebellum America*; Zaeske, *Signatures of Citizenship*; Zagarri, *Revolutionary Backlash*.

42. Lori Ginzberg examines the local conditions surrounding this petition in Ginzberg, *Untidy Origins*.

43. "Petition for Woman's Rights," published in William G. Bishop and William H. Attree, *Report of the Debates and Proceedings of the Convention for the Revision of the Constitution of the State of New-York*, 1846 (Albany, NY: Evening Atlas, 1846), 646.

44. Alexander Keyssar, *The Right to Vote: The Contested History of Democracy in the United States* (New York: Basic Books, 2000), 174; Susan B. Anthony and Ida Husted Harper, *History of Woman Suffrage*, vol. 4 (Indianapolis: Hollenbeck, 1902; Salem, NH: Ayer, 1985; citations refer to the 1985 edition), 73.

45. "Resolutions," Second Worcester Convention, 1851. Reprinted in Stanton, Anthony, and Gage, *History of Woman Suffrage*, 1:825.

46. "Declaration of Rights and Sentiments," adopted by the Seneca Falls Convention, July 19–20, 1848.

47. Sylvia D. Hoffert, *When Hens Crow: The Woman's Rights Movement in Antebellum America* (Bloomington: Indiana University Press, 1995), 127; Isenberg, *Sex and Citizenship in Antebellum America*, 20–21; Stanton, Anthony, and Gage, *History of Woman Suffrage*.

48. Among the first postconvention images was *Leaders of the Woman's Rights Convention Taking an Airing* (New York: James S. Baillie, 1848), Schlesinger Library. Isenberg, *Sex and Citizenship in Antebellum America*, 44–46.

49. For more on David Claypoole Johnston and his art, see Clarence S. Brigham, "David Claypoole Johnston, the American Cruikshank," *Proceedings of the American Antiquarian Society* 50 (1940): 98–110; Jennifer A. Greenhill, "David Claypoole Johnston and the Menial Labor of Caricature," *American Art* 17, no. 3 (2003): 32–51; Jack Larkin, "What He Did for Love," *Common-Place* 13, no. 3 (2013).

50. See, for example, *Patent Democratic Republican Steam Shaving Shop* (New York: Willis & Probst, 1844), lithograph, Library of Congress Prints and Photographs Division. For more, see Sean Trainor, *Groomed for Power: A Cultural Economy of the Male Body in Nineteenth-Century America* (PhD diss, Pennsylvania State University, 2015).

51. *Woman's Emancipation*, in *Harper's New Monthly Magazine*, August 1851, 424.

52. The print was plate 17 in Nagel & Weingärtner's *Humbug's American Museum Series*, published in 1851. Thanks to Lauren Hewes and the American Antiquarian Society staff for research on this series. Signed "AW," the print was likely completed by Adam Weingärtner himself.

53. See plate from the series called *Halloo! Turks in Gotham*, which has been digitized by the Library of Congress.

54. Margaret Fuller, *Woman in the Nineteenth Century* (New York: Greeley & McElrath, 1845), 23.

55. Fuller, *Woman in the Nineteenth Century*, 24.

56. Frances Willard and Mary Livermore, eds., "Lucy Stone," in *American Women* (New York: Mast, Crowell, and Kirkpatrick, 1897), 693–94; Alice Stone Blackwell, "Pioneers of the Woman's Movement," *Zion's Herald*, August 14, 1918, 1044.

57. *Lucy Stone*, in *Illustrated News*, May 28, 1853.

58. *Splinters*, in *Ballou's Pictorial Drawing-Room Companion*, March 17, 1855.

59. T. W. Higginson, "Woman and Her Wishes," in *Series of Women's Rights Tracts*, 26. Sophia Smith Collection Women's Rights Collection, Box 1, Folder 2.

60. For more on dress and the ways fashion and vanity undercut women's status in the eighteenth century (through images and texts), see Kate Haulman, *The Politics of Fashion in Eighteenth-Century America* (Chapel Hill: University of North Carolina Press, 2011).

61. Zara Anishanslin, *Portrait of a Woman in Silk: Hidden Histories of the British Atlantic World* (New Haven, CT: Yale University Press, 2016); Linda Baumgarten, *What Clothes Reveal: The Language of Clothing in Colonial and Federal America* (New Haven, CT: Yale University Press, 2002); Haulman, *The Politics of Fashion*; Michael Zakim, *Ready-Made Democracy: A History of Men's Dress in the American Republic, 1760–1860* (Chicago: University of Chicago Press, 2003).

62. Patricia A. Cunningham, *Reforming Women's Fashion, 1850–1920: Politics, Health, and Art* (Kent, OH: Kent State University Press, 2003), 11–15.

63. Baumgarten, *What Clothes Reveal: The Language of Clothing in Colonial and Federal America*, 64.

64. Gayle Fischer, *Pantaloons and Power: A Nineteenth-Century Dress Reform in the United States* (Kent, OH: Kent State University Press, 2001), 20.

65. *An "Awful Gardener,"* in *Nick-Nax for All Creation*, May 1859, 30; *Painful and Sad Warning*, in *Nick-Nax for All Creation*, April 1857, 381.

66. For more on mid-nineteenth-century comic monthlies, see Richard Samuel West, "Collecting Lincoln in Caricature," *Rail Splitter*, December 1995, 15–17.

67. *Expedient of the Long-Absent and Just-Returned Algernon Fitzimplies to Shake Hands with Lettice, His Betrothed: With the Hook of His Umbrella Handle around a Lamp-Post, He Is Enabled to Reach across the Hoops, and Take That Darling Hand into His*, in *Nick-Nax for All Creation*, February 1857, 307.

68. *To a Lady*, in *Nick-Nax for All Creation*, December 1857, American Antiquarian Society.

69. *Nick-Nax for All Creation*, January 1860, 272.

70. Fischer, *Pantaloons and Power*, 79.

71. Letter from Gerrit Smith to Elizabeth Cady Stanton, December 1, 1855, American Antiquarian Society.

72. Cunningham, *Reforming Women's Fashion*, 33–37; Fischer, *Pantaloons and Power*, chap. 2. For more on laws against cross-dressing: Clare Sears, *Arresting Dress: Cross-Dressing, Law, and Fascination in Nineteenth-Century San Francisco* (Durham, NC: Duke University Press, 2015).

73. Cunningham, *Reforming Women's Fashion*, 32–33; Zakim, *Ready-Made Democracy*.

74. See Leora Auslander's discussion of the sans-culottes during the French Revolution in Auslander, "Making French Republicans: Revolutionary Transformation of the Everyday," in *Cultural Revolutions: The Politics of Everyday Life in Britain, North America and France* (Berkeley: University of California Press, 2009). For more on trousers as symbol of democracy in America, see Zakim, *Ready-Made Democracy*, 200–201; Hoffert, *When Hens Crow*, 22–31.

75. Cunningham, *Reforming Women's Fashion*, 35; Fischer, *Pantaloons and Power*, chaps. 1–3.

76. Some pictures of women in bloomers resembled the fashion plates from *Godey's* and *Frank Leslie's Gazette*. Examples include Mathias Keller, *The New Costume Polka* (Philadelphia: Lee & Walker, 1851) and *The Bloomer Polka & Schottisch* (Baltimore: F. D. Benteen, 1851); Charles Vincent, *Bloomer Sett of Waltzes* (Philadelphia: Couenfoven & Duffy, 1851); Charles Grobe, *The Bloomer Quick Step* (Baltimore: F. D. Benteen, 1851); Edward Le Roy, *Bloomer, or New Costume Polka* (New York: Firth Pond, 1851); William Dressler, *The Bloomer Schottisch* (New York: William Hall & Son, 1851). The American Antiquarian Society holds examples of these works.

77. *The Attractive Points of a Woman's Rights Lecture*, in *Nick-Nax for All Creation*, June 1856, 28.

78. *Old Fashion*, in *Frank Leslie's Ladies Gazette of Paris, London, and New York Fashions*, July 1856, 10. See also Auslander, "Making French Republicans."

79. Stanton, Anthony, and Gage, *History of Woman Suffrage*, 1:469.

80. Letter from Elizabeth Cady Stanton and Susan B. Anthony to Lucy Stone, February 16, 1854, as quoted in Fischer, *Pantaloons and Power*, 103.

81. Letter from Gerrit Smith to Elizabeth Cady Stanton, December 1, 1855, American Antiquarian Society.

82. Gerrit Smith to Reform Dress Association, May 18, 1857, American Antiquarian Society.

83. Fellow New York supporter Matilda Joslyn Gage saw the letter printed in a newspaper, carefully cut it out, and then pasted it into a scrapbook of text on the progress of the movement. "Letter to Gerrit Smith, Seneca Falls, Dec. 21" in Matilda Joslyn Gage Scrapbook, Rare Books and Manuscripts, Library of Con-

gress; and reprinted in Stanton, Anthony, and Gage, *History of Woman Suffrage*, 1:839–42.

84. West, "Collecting Lincoln in Caricature," 16.

85. *The Capture of Jeff. Davis of the C.S.A.*, in *Phunny Phellow*, July 1865, 1.

86. For more on the denial of Davis wearing women's clothing, see *Life and Imprisonment of Jefferson Davis, Together with the Life and Military Career of Stonewall Jackson* (New York: M. Doolady, 1866), 140; *Life and Reminiscences of Jefferson Davis* (Baltimore: R. H. Woodward, 1890), 278–79; William P. Stedman and James Harrison Wilson, "Pursuit and Capture of Jefferson Davis," *Century Illustrated Monthly Magazine*, vol. 39 (New York: Century, 1890), 586–196.

87. Although women worked in the publishing and printing industries, they usually performed more menial tasks. Casper, "Introduction," 10–17.

88. Lange, "Picturing Tradition."

89. The term "court" has monarchical associations, but Griswold may have chosen this term because he associated it with elegance. He asserted this group had "as much refinement of manners ... as could be found perhaps in any foreign society." The term reflects the delicate balance that leaders and their wives struck between republican virtue and European worldliness to establish the government's credibility. Rufus Griswold, *The Republican Court, or American Society in the Days of Washington* (New York: D. Appleton, 1855), 7. See also Allgor, *Parlor Politics*; Catherine Allgor, *A Perfect Union: Dolley Madison and the Creation of the American Nation* (New York: Henry Holt, 2006).

90. Griswold, *The Republican Court*, 367.

91. Griswold, *The Republican Court*, 370.

92. Griswold, *The Republican Court*, 370.

93. Griswold, *The Republican Court*, 369.

94. The American Antiquarian Society's copy of the 1851 *The Golden Keepsake*, for example, contains an inscription from a niece to an aunt. Mrs. S. T. Martyn, ed., *The Golden Keepsake* (New York: J. M. Fletcher, 1851). For more on gift books, see Lorraine Janzen Kooistra, *Poetry, Pictures, and Popular Publishing: The Illustrated Gift Book and Victorian Visual Culture, 1855–1875* (Athens: Ohio University Press, 2011).

95. Martyn, *The Golden Keepsake*, 35.

96. Martyn, *The Golden Keepsake*, 212.

97. See A. H. Ritchie (after a painting by D. Huntington), *Lady Washington's Reception*, 1865, engraving, American Antiquarian Society. The original painting is Daniel Huntington, *The Republican Court (Lady Washington's Reception Day)*, oil on canvas, 1861, Brooklyn Museum.

98. *Description of Mr. Huntington's Picture of the Republican Court in the Time of Washington* (New York: Emil Seitz, Fine Art Galleries, 1865).

99. Allgor notes that Thomas Jefferson was concerned about Martha Washington's status and potential for power because of her status as a queenlike figure.

She argues, however, that Washington never accepted even the title of "Lady Washington" because of concerns about the administration's monarchical leanings. Allgor, *Parlor Politics*, 20–21, 74–75.

100. *Description of Mr. Huntington's Picture*.

101. See, for example, George Spohni, *Washington's Reception at the White House, 1776* (New York: Thomas Kelly, 1867), American Antiquarian Society; *Lady Washington Reception, April 6ᵗʰ, 1875, at the New York Academy of Music—Ladies Distributing Tea and Cakes Among the Veterans of 1812*, engraving, in *Frank Leslie's Illustrated Almanac for 1876*, 1876, 33.

102. Leopold Grozelier, *Representative Women*, 1857, lithograph, Women's Rights Collection, Box 51, Sophia Smith Collection, Smith College.

103. Leopold Grozelier, *Heralds of Freedom: Truth, Love, Justice*, 1857, lithograph, Boston: C. H. Brainerd, Boston Athenaeum. In 1870, L. Prang published an updated version.

104. Ralph Waldo Emerson, *Representative Men: Seven Lectures*. (London: John Chapman, 1850), 5.

CHAPTER THREE

1. For more on Prophet Matthias, see G. Vale, *Fanaticism: Its Source and Influence* (New York: G. Vale, 1835); Nell Irvin Painter, "In the Kingdom of Matthias," in *Sojourner Truth: A Life, a Symbol* (New York: W. W. Norton, 1997); Paul E. Johnson and Sean Wilentz, *The Kingdom of Matthias* (New York: Oxford University Press, 1994).

2. Sojourner Truth and Olive Gilbert, *Narrative of Sojourner Truth*, ed. Nell Painter (New York: Penguin Books, 1998); Darcy Grimaldo Grigsby, *Enduring Truths: Sojourner's Shadows and Substance* (Chicago: University of Chicago Press, 2015); Painter, *Sojourner Truth*.

3. For more on suffragists on the lecture circuit after the Civil War, see Lisa Tetrault, "The Incorporation of American Feminism: Suffragists and the Postbellum Lyceum," *Journal of American History* 96, no. 4 (2010): 1027–56.

4. Augusta Rohrbach, "Shadow and Substance: Sojourner Truth in Black and White," in *Pictures and Progress: Early Photography and the Making of African American Identity*, ed. Maurice O. Wallace and Shawn Michelle Smith (Durham, NC: Duke University Press, 2012), 85.

5. Jeffrey C. Stewart, "Introduction," in Olive Gilbert and Sojourner Truth, *Narrative of Sojourner Truth, a Bondswoman of Olden Time: With a History of Her Labors and Correspondence Drawn from Her "Book of Life"* (New York: Oxford University Press, 1991), xxxviii–xxxix.

6. Michael A. Chaney, *Fugitive Vision: Slave Image and Black Identity in Antebellum Narrative* (Bloomington: Indiana University Press, 2009), 26–29; Lynn Casmier-Paz, "Slave Narratives and the Rhetoric of Author Portraiture," *New Literary History* 34, no. 1 (2003): 98.

7. For more on Frederick Douglass's portraits, see John Stauffer, "Creating an

Image in Black," in *The Black Hearts of Men: Radical Abolitionists and the Transformation of Race* (Cambridge, MA: Harvard University Press, 2001); John Stauffer, Zoe Trodd, and Celeste-Marie Bernier, *Picturing Frederick Douglass: An Illustrated Biography of the Nineteenth Century's Most Photographed American* (New York: Liveright, 2015).

8. For more on the theory on objects and agency: Alfred Gell, *Art and Agency: An Anthropological Theory* (New York: Oxford University Press, 1998); Bruno Latour, *Pandora's Hope: Essays on the Reality of Science Studies* (Cambridge, MA: Harvard University Press, 1999); Bruno Latour, *Reassembling the Social: An Introduction to Actor-Network-Theory* (New York: Oxford University Press, 2005).

9. For more on this topic, see Grigsby, *Enduring Truths*; Painter, *Sojourner Truth*; Teresa Zackodnik, "The 'Green-Backs of Civilization': Sojourner Truth and Portrait Photography," *American Studies* 46, no. 2 (2005): 117–43.

10. For more on the visual politics of the antislavery movement, see Chaney, *Fugitive Vision*; Philip Lapansky, "Graphic Discord: Abolitionist and Antiabolitionist Images," in *The Abolitionist Sisterhood: Women's Political Culture in Antebellum America*, ed. Jean Fagan Yellin and John C. Van Horne (Ithaca, NY: Cornell University Press, 1994); Maurie Dee McInnis, *Slaves Waiting for Sale: Abolitionist Art and the American Slave Trade* (Chicago: University of Chicago Press, 2011); Agnes Lugo-Ortiz and Angela Rosenthal, *Slave Portraiture in the Atlantic World* (New York: Cambridge University Press, 2013); Catherine Molineux, *Faces of Perfect Ebony: Encountering Atlantic Slavery in Imperial Britain* (Cambridge, MA: Harvard University Press, 2012); Gwendolyn DuBois Shaw, *Portraits of a People: Picturing African Americans in the Nineteenth Century* (Seattle: University of Washington Press, 2006); Wallace and Smith, *Pictures and Progress*; Marcus Wood, *Blind Memory: Visual Representations of Slavery in England and America, 1780–1865* (New York: Routledge, 2000); Jean Fagan Yellin, *Women and Sisters: The Antislavery Feminists in American Culture* (New Haven, CT: Yale University Press, 1989).

11. For more on the image of the supplicating female slave, see Yellin, *Women and Sisters*.

12. See Josiah Wedgwood, *Antislavery Medallion*, 1787, The British Museum; Maurie D. McInnis, *Slaves Waiting for Sale: Abolitionist Art and the American Slave Trade* (Chicago: University of Chicago Press, 2011), 29. See also Philip Lapansky, "Graphic Discord"; Robin Reilly, *Wedgwood*, vol. 1 (New York: Stockton, 1989), 114–16. For more on this image, see Cynthia S. Hamilton, "Hercules Subdued: The Visual Rhetoric of the Kneeling Slave," *Slavery & Abolition* 34, no. 4 (2013): 631–52; Sam Margolin, "'And Freedom to the Slave': Antislavery Ceramics 1787–1865," in *Ceramics in America*, ed. Robert Hunter (New York: Chipstone, 2002); McInnis, *Slaves Waiting for Sale*, 31; Lugo-Ortiz and Rosenthal, "Introduction," in *Slave Portraiture*; Yellin, *Women and Sisters*, 5–7. For more on abolition in Britain, see Christopher Leslie Brown, *Moral Capital: Foundations of British Abolitionism* (Chapel Hill: University of North Carolina Press, 2006); Elizabeth J. Clapp and Julie Roy Jeffrey, *Women, Dissent and Anti-Slavery in Britain and America, 1790–1865*

(New York: Oxford University Press, 2011); Paul Michael Kielstra, *The Politics of Slave Trade Suppression in Britain and France, 1814–48: Diplomacy, Morality and Economics* (New York: St. Martin's Press, 2000); John R. Oldfield, *Popular Politics and British Anti-Slavery: The Mobilisation of Public Opinion Against the Slave Trade, 1787–1807* (New York: St. Martin's Press, 1995); Charlotte Sussman, *Consuming Anxieties: Consumer Protest, Gender, and British Slavery, 1713–1833* (Stanford, CA: Stanford University Press, 2000).

13. Benjamin Franklin to Josiah Wedgwood, May 15, 1787, *The Papers of Benjamin Franklin*, sponsored by the American Philosophical Society and Yale University, http://franklinpapers.org.

14. George Bourne, *Slavery Illustrated in Its Effects Upon Woman and Domestic Society* (Boston: Isaac Knapp, 1837). The image also appeared engraved on a copper token; see Hard Times Token, *Am I Not a Woman and a Sister?*, 1838, Smithsonian Institution, National Numismatic Collection.

15. George Bourne, *Slavery Illustrated in Its Effects upon Woman and Domestic Society*. Reprint ed. (Freeport, NY: Books for Libraries Press, 1972), 27.

16. See, for example, Henry W. Williams to Stephen S. Foster, February 28, 1846, Abby Kelley Foster Papers, American Antiquarian Society.

17. Angelina Grimké, *Appeal to the Christian Women of the South* (New York: American Anti-Slavery Society, 1836), 34.

18. Grimké, *Appeal to the Christian Women*, 33.

19. Yellin, *Women and Sisters*, 14.

20. For more on this series, see Jasmine Nichole Cobb, "Racing the Transatlantic Parlor: Blackness at Home and Abroad," in *Picture Freedom: Remaking Black Visuality in the Early Nineteenth Century* (New York: New York University Press, 2015).

21. Douglass wrote a second version of "Pictures and Progress" in 1865, showing his continued interest in the topic. Laura Wexler, "'A More Perfect Likeness': Frederick Douglass and the Image of the Nation," in Wallace and Smith, *Pictures and Progress*. For more on Douglass's work and discussions of photography, see Marcy J. Dinius, "Seeing Slave as a Man: Frederick Douglass, Racial Progress and Daguerrian Portraiture," in *The Camera and the Press* (Philadelphia: University of Pennsylvania Press, 2012).

22. Frederick Douglass, "Pictures and Progress: An Address Delivered in Boston, Massachusetts, on 3 December 1861," in *The Frederick Douglass Papers. Series One: Speeches, Debates, and Interviews.*, vol. 3, *1855–63*, ed. John Blassingame (New Haven, CT: Yale University Press, 1985), 461.

23. Douglass, "Pictures and Progress," 456.

24. Douglass, "Pictures and Progress," 457.

25. Douglass, "Pictures and Progress," 458.

26. Joshua Brown, *Beyond the Lines: Pictorial Reporting, Everyday Life, and the Crisis of Gilded-Age America* (Berkeley: University of California Press, 2003), 39–40.

27. Brown, *Beyond the Lines*, 36–39.

28. Stauffer, Trodd, and Bernier, *Picturing Frederick Douglass*, ix–xvii; Stauffer, "Creating an Image in Black," in *The Black Hearts of Men*.

29. Frederick Douglass, "Age of Pictures," in Stauffer, Trodd, and Bernier, *Picturing Frederick Douglass*, 142–43.

30. For more on the visual culture of the Civil War and the rise of photography, see Keith Davis, "A Terrible Distinctness: Photography of the Civil War Era," in *Photography in Nineteenth-Century America*, ed. Martha A. Sandweiss (Fort Worth, TX: Amon Carter Museum, 1991); Sarah Burns and Daniel Greene, "The Home at War, the War at Home: The Visual Culture of the Northern Home Front," in *Home Front: Daily Life in the Civil War North*, ed. Peter John Brownlee, et al. (Chicago: University of Chicago Press, 2013); William A. Frassanito, *Gettysburg: A Journey in Time* (New York: Scribner, 1975); William A. Frassanito, *Antietam: The Photographic Legacy of America's Bloodiest Day* (New York: Scribner, 1978); Eleanor Jones Harvey, *The Civil War and American Art* (New Haven, CT: Yale University Press, 2012); Mark E. Neely, *The Confederate Image: Prints of the Lost Cause* (Chapel Hill: University of North Carolina Press, 1987); Mark E. Neely and Harold Holzer, *The Union Image: Popular Prints of the Civil War North* (Chapel Hill: University of North Carolina Press, 2000); Anthony W. Lee and Elizabeth Young, *On Alexander Gardner's Photographic Sketch Book of the Civil War* (Berkeley: University of California Press, 2007); Mary Panzer, *Mathew Brady and the Image of History* (Washington, DC: Smithsonian Institution Press, 1997); Jeff L. Rosenheim, *Photography and the American Civil War* (New York: Metropolitan Museum of Art, 2013); Shirley Samuels, *Facing America: Iconography and the Civil War* (New York: Oxford University Press, 2004); Alan Trachtenberg, *Reading American Photographs: Images as History, Mathew Brady to Walker Evans* (New York: Hill and Wang, 1989).

31. "American Photographs," *Photographic News*, September 5, 1862, 429.

32. "Talk in the Studio," *Photographic News*, February 2, 1863, 96.

33. G. Boritt, Mark Neely, and Harold Holzer, *The Lincoln Image: Abraham Lincoln and the Popular Print* (Urbana: University of Illinois Press, 2001), xvi; William Culp Darrah, *Cartes de Visite in Nineteenth Century Photography* (Gettysburg, VA: W.C. Darrah, 1981); David M. Henkin, *The Postal Age: The Emergence of Modern Communications in Nineteenth-Century America* (Chicago: University of Chicago Press, 2006); Carol Wichard and Robin Wichard, *Victorian Cartes-de-Visite* (Princes Risborough, UK: Shire, 1999).

34. For literature on cartes de visite, see Darrah, *Cartes de Visite*, 2, 7; Andrea Volpe, *Cheap Pictures: Cartes De Visite Portrait Photographs and Visual Culture in the United States, 1860–1877* (PhD diss., Rutgers University, 1999); Wichard and Wichard, *Victorian Cartes-de-Visite*. To keep up with demand, the number of photographers tripled from 3,154 to 9,990 between 1860 and 1880. Darrah, *Cartes de Visite*, 12.

35. Darrah, *Cartes de Visite*, 19.

36. Oliver Wendell Holmes, "Doings of the Sunbeam," *Atlantic Monthly*, July 1863, 8.

37. Darrah, *Cartes de Visite*, 8–9.

38. See E. Anthony and H. T. Anthony, *Catalogue of Card Photographs* (New York: E. & H. T. Anthony, 1862), 7.

39. Anthony and Anthony, *Catalogue of Card Photographs*, 18; Anthony Berger, *[Abraham Lincoln, U.S. President, Looking at a Photo Album with His Son, Tad Lincoln, Feb. 9, 1864]*, 1864, photograph, Library of Congress.

40. Laura McCall, "'The Reign of Brute Force Is Now Over': A Content Analysis of 'Godey's Lady's Book,' 1830–1860," *Journal of the Early Republic* 9, no. 2 (July 1989): 221.

41. "Photography and Its Album," *Godey's Lady's Book*, March 1864, 302.

42. For more analysis on photography as science or art, see Dinius, *The Camera and the Press*; Sean Ross Meehan, *Mediating American Autobiography: Photography in Emerson, Thoreau, Douglass, and Whitman* (Columbia: University of Missouri Press, 2008), 26–40.

43. Gail Hamilton, "Brady's Gallery," *National Era*, March 24, 1859, 46.

44. "Brady's Photographs," *New York Times*, October 20, 1862, 5.

45. As noted in Kathleen Collins, "The Scourged Back," *History of Photography* 9, no. 1 (1985): 43–45.

46. *Harper's Weekly* published the engraving on July 4, 1863, with a description of the gruesome physical punishments endured by slaves. *Harper's* asserted the authenticity of the engravings by noting were "from photographs, by McPherson and Oliver." "A Typical Negro," *Harper's Weekly*, July 4, 1863, 429. For more on Gordon's portraits, see Collins, "The Scourged Back"; Wood, *Blind Memory*, 263–71.

47. Boritt, Neely, and Holzer, *The Lincoln Image*, 11; Allen Thorndike Rice, *Reminiscences of Abraham Lincoln by Distinguished Men of His Time* (North American Publishing, 1886), 593; Alan Trachtenberg, *Lincoln's Smile and Other Enigmas* (New York: Hill and Wang, 2007), 76.

48. Philip B. Kunhardt III, Peter W. Kunhardt, and Peter W. Kunhardt Jr., *Lincoln, Life-Size* (New York: Knopf, 2009), 34; Mathew B. Brady Studio, *Abraham Lincoln on the Day of His Speech at the Cooper Union, February, 27, 1860*, 1860, James Wadsworth Family Papers, Manuscript Division., Library of Congress.

49. Darrah, "Portraits of Celebrities," in *Cartes de Visite*.

50. George Alfred Townsend, "Still Taking Pictures: Brady, the Grand Old Man of American Photography, Hard at Work At Sixty-Seven (Interview), Reprinted from *The World*, April 12, 1891," in *Photography in Print: Writings from 1816 to the Present*, ed. Vicki Goldberg (Albuquerque: University of New Mexico Press, 1981), 204. Many artists translated Brady's photograph into an engraving as well. Frederick Douglass, "Age of Pictures," 262.

51. Carol Faulkner, *Lucretia Mott's Heresy: Abolition and Women's Rights in Nineteenth-Century America* (Philadelphia: University of Pennsylvania Press, 2011).

52. The photograph appears nearly identical to an engraved portrait from 1844, perhaps the first she made public, that appeared as the frontispiece to the antislavery gift book *The Liberty Bell*. John Sartain (engraver) after a painting by

J. Kyle, *Lucretia Mott*, 1844, engraving and mezzotint, published in *The Liberty Bell* (Boston: Massachusetts Anti-Slavery Fair, 1844).

53. Marcus A. Root, *The Camera and the Pencil* (Philadelphia: J. B. Lippincott, 1864), 253.

54. Harriet Beecher Stowe, "Sojourner Truth, The Libyan Sibyl," *Atlantic Monthly*, April 1863, 473–81.

55. Stowe, "Sojourner Truth," 478; Grigsby, "The Libyan Sibyl," in *Enduring Truths*.

56. Gage recounted Truth's speech at the 1851 Woman's Rights Convention. While Gage told a compelling story, her tale differed from an 1851 recounting of Truth's speech and is most likely her own creation. Painter, "Ar'n't I a Woman?," in *Sojourner Truth*; Susan B. Anthony and Ida Husted Harper, *History of Woman Suffrage*, vol. 4 (Indianapolis: Hollenbeck, 1902; Salem, NH: Ayer, 1985; citations refer to the 1985 edition), 114–17.

57. Frances Dana Gage, "Ar'n't I a Woman?," *Antislavery Standard*, April 23, 1863. Reprinted in Painter, *Sojourner Truth*, 168.

58. Rohrbach, "Shadow and Substance," 89.

59. Truth regularly reproduced this photograph, and Grigsby agrees that this was Truth's favorite portrait. Grigsby, "Truth's Captioned Cartes de Visite after 1864," in *Enduring Truths*. An engraving of this portrait appeared as *Sojourner Truth, the Eloquent Negress*, in *Frank Leslie's Illustrated Newspaper*, December 25, 1869, 245.

60. "Sojourner Truth," *Revolution*, January 21, 1869, 44.

61. Rohrbach, "Shadow and Substance," 85.

62. Painter, *Sojourner Truth*, 198.

63. For more on Truth's portraits, see Kathleen Collins, "Shadow and Substance: Sojourner Truth," *History of Photography* 7, no. 3 (1983): 183–205; Grigsby, "Truth's Captioned Cartes de Visite"; Painter, "Truth in Photographs," in *Sojourner Truth*; Carla L. Peterson, "'A Sign unto This Nation': Sojourner Truth, History, Orature, and Modernity," in *"Doers of the Word": African-American Women Speakers and Writers in the North (1830–1880)* (New Brunswick, NJ: Rutgers University Press, 1998); Zackodnik, "The 'Green-Backs of Civilization.'"

64. Stereotypes of African American women include exaggerated facial features, including large lips and nose, and open mouths, which marked the person as ignorant and lower-class. See Eric Lott, *Love and Theft: Blackface Minstrelsy and the American Working Class* (New York: Oxford University Press, 1993). For an example of a servant image and these tropes, see *A Lucky Coincidence—Fast Day in Richmond*, in *Frank Leslie's Illustrated Newspaper*, October 25, 1862, 80. For an example of a black woman as a curiosity, see *Greatest Natural & National Curiosity in the World: Joice Heth*, 1835, Harvard Fine Arts Library. For more on popular images of black women, see Dinius, *The Camera and the Press*, 223–32; Deborah Willis, *The Black Female Body: A Photographic History* (Philadelphia: Temple University Press, 2002).

65. *Sojourner Truth: I Sell the Shadow to Support the Substance*, 1864, photograph carte de visite, Boston Athenaeum. The back of this carte de visite states that Truth secured the copyright in the Eastern District of Michigan, where she lived at the time. For more on her copyrights, see Grigsby, *Enduring Truths*.

66. Anthony and Harper, *History of Woman Suffrage*, 4:927.

67. "Sojourner Truth," *Revolution*, 44.

68. *[Untitled Advertisement]*, in Robert Cooney, *Winning the Vote: The Triumph of the American Woman Suffrage Movement* (Santa Cruz, CA: American Graphic Press, 2005), 11; Collins, "Shadow and Substance," 189, 200; Olive Gilbert, *Narrative of Sojourner Truth: A Bondswoman of Olden Time, Emancipated by the New York Legislature in the Early Part of the Present Century; with a History of Her Labors and Correspondence, Drawn from Her "Book of Life"* (Battle Creek, MI: published by the author, 1878), 258–59; "Sojourner Truth," *Revolution*, 44; Rohrbach, "Shadow and Substance," 90.

69. Gilbert, *Narrative of Sojourner Truth*, 201, 203, 224, 261; Collins, "Shadow and Substance," 199.

70. "Sojourner Truth," *Revolution*, 44.

71. Painter, *Sojourner Truth*, 230–33; Margaret Washington, *Sojourner Truth's America* (Urbana: University of Illinois Press, 2009).

72. While Nell Painter argues Anthony showed a photograph of Truth leaning on a cane, the original account does not include this detail. Painter, *Sojourner Truth*, 187.

73. Elizabeth Cady Stanton, Susan B. Anthony, and Matilda Joslyn Gage, eds., *History of Woman Suffrage*, vol. 2 (New York: Fowler and Wells, 1882; Salem, NH: Ayer, 1985; citations refer to the 1985 edition), 898.

74. Lori D. Ginzberg, *Elizabeth Cady Stanton: An American Life* (New York: Hill and Wang, 2009); Michele Mitchell, "'Lower Orders,' Racial Hierarchies, and Rights Rhetoric: Evolutionary Echoes in Elizabeth Cady Stanton's Thought during the Late 1860s," in *Elizabeth Cady Stanton, Feminist as Thinker: A Reader in Documents and Essays*, ed. Ellen Carol DuBois and Richard Cándida Smith (New York: New York University Press, 2007); Rosalyn Terborg-Penn, *African American Women in the Struggle for the Vote, 1850–1920* (Bloomington: Indiana University Press, 1998).

75. Faye E. Dudden, *Fighting Chance: The Struggle over Woman Suffrage and Black Suffrage in Reconstruction America* (New York: Oxford University Press, 2011), chaps. 4–5.

76. For more on the split among suffragists and the establishment of these organizations, see Ellen Carol DuBois, *Feminism and Suffrage: The Emergence of an Independent Women's Movement in America, 1848–1869* (Ithaca, NY: Cornell University Press, 1978); Dudden, *Fighting Chance*.

77. Wendy Hamand Venet, *A Strong-Minded Woman: The Life of Mary Livermore* (Amherst: University of Massachusetts Press, 2005), 168.

78. "The Revolution, for 1870," *Revolution*, December 9, 1869, 360.

79. Bonnie J. Dow, "The *Revolution*, 1868–1870: Expanding the Woman Suffrage

Agenda," in *A Voice of Their Own: The Woman Suffrage Press, 1840–1910*, ed. Martha Solomon (Tuscaloosa: University of Alabama Press, 1991), 71, 75.

80. "Political Organization," *Woman's Journal*, January 8, 1870, 8.

81. Letter from Susan B. Anthony, dated February 4, 1871, *Woodhull and Claflin's Weekly*, January 25, 1873, 10.

82. Susan Schultz Huxman, "The *Woman's Journal*, 1870–1890: Torchbearer for Suffrage," in Solomon, *A Voice of Their Own*, 89–91.

83. Henry Brown Blackwell, "Boston and New York," *Woman's Journal*, April 9, 1870, 105.

84. Susan B. Anthony in Ann Dexter Gordon, ed., *The Selected Papers of Elizabeth Cady Stanton and Susan B. Anthony*, vol. 2, *Against an Aristocracy of Sex, 1866 to 1873* (New Brunswick, NJ: Rutgers University Press, 2000), 308.

85. James Parton et al., *Eminent Women of the Age: Being Narratives of the Lives and Deeds of the Most Prominent Women of the Present Generation* (Hartford, CT: S. M. Betts, 1869), 349–50.

86. For analysis of photographs of men who did pose together, see John Ibson, *Picturing Men: A Century of Male Relationships in Everyday American Photography* (Chicago: University of Chicago Press, 2006).

87. See Sarony & Co, *Susan B. Anthony & E. Cady Stanton*, 1870–1871, photograph, Boston Athenaeum.

88. Elizabeth Cady Stanton, *Revolution*, August 12, 1869, 88.

89. Parton et al., *Eminent Women of the Age*, v.

90. Parton et al., *Eminent Women of the Age*, 358.

91. "The Chicago Convention," *Revolution*, February 25, 1869, 113–15.

92. Parton et al., *Eminent Women of the Age*, 349–50.

93. Parton et al., *Eminent Women of the Age*, 359–60.

94. "Agents Wanted," *Godey's Lady's Book*, January 1871, 112–13.

95. "Eminent Women of the Age," *Revolution*, October 8, 1868, 218.

96. The artist of the engraving sold in the paper was the same as the artist who created the portrait for *Eminent Women*. "Given Away! A Grand Work of Art!," *Revolution*, June 2, 1870, 349.

97. "Given Away! A Grand Work of Art!," 349.

98. "The New Justice of the Peace," *Revolution*, March 17, 1870, 170; "Mrs. Esther Morris," *Woman's Journal*, April 9, 1870, 110.

99. Venet, *A Strong-Minded Woman*, 164–69.

100. "'The Revolution' and the Revolutionists," *Revolution*, May 13, 1869, 301.

101. "The Revolution at Home," *Revolution*, July 14, 1870, 23.

102. "The Anti-Female Suffrage Movement," *Woman's Journal*, June 18, 1870, 187.

103. For more on the ways Stanton and Anthony promoted their narrative of the movement, see Lisa Tetrault, *Myth of Seneca Falls: Memory and the Women's Suffrage Movement, 1848–1898* (Chapel Hill: University of North Carolina Press, 2014).

104. For more on women's suffrage in the west, see Beverly Beeton, *Women Vote in the West: The Woman Suffrage Movement, 1869–1896* (New York: Garland, 1986);

Alan Pendleton Grimes, *The Puritan Ethic and Woman Suffrage* (New York: Oxford University Press, 1967); Holly J. McCammon and Karen E. Campbell, "Winning the Vote in the West: The Political Successes of the Women's Suffrage Movements, 1866–1919," *Gender and Society* 15, no. 1 (2001): 55–82; Rebecca Mead, "Pioneers at the Polls: Woman Suffrage in the West," in *Votes for Women: The Struggle for Suffrage Revisited*, ed. Jean Baker (New York: Oxford University Press, 2002); Rebecca Mead, *How the Vote Was Won: Woman Suffrage in the Western United States, 1868–1914* (New York: New York University Press, 2004); Allison Sneider, *Suffragists in an Imperial Age: U.S. Expansion and the Woman Question, 1870–1929* (New York: Oxford University Press, 2008).

105. "Republican Party Platform of 1872," in The American Presidency Project, ed. Gerhard Peters and John T. Woolley, https://www.presidency.ucsb.edu/node /273303.

106. For a more complete list of female voters, see Ann D. Gordon, ed., "Appendix C: Women Who Went to the Polls, 1868–1873," in *The Selected Papers of Elizabeth Cady Stanton and Susan B. Anthony*, vol. 2, *Against an Aristocracy of Sex, 1866–1873* (New Brunswick, NJ: Rutgers University Press, 2000), 645–54.

107. Victoria Woodhull, "Manifesto, from the New York Herald, April 2, 1870," in *The Human Body and the Temple of God; or, the Philosophy of Sociology* (London, 1890), 86.

108. Elizabeth Cady Stanton to Lucretia Mott, April 1, 1871, Box 13, Folder 25, Sophia Smith Collection.

109. Elizabeth Cady Stanton to Lucretia Mott.

110. For more on Victoria Woodhull, see Amanda Frisken, *Victoria Woodhull's Sexual Revolution: Political Theater and the Popular Press in Nineteenth-Century America* (Philadelphia: University of Pennsylvania Press, 2004); Barbara Goldsmith, *Other Powers: The Age of Suffrage, Spiritualism, and the Scandalous Victoria Woodhull* (New York: Knopf, 1998).

111. For more on the Beecher-Tilton scandal, see Richard Wightman Fox, *Trials of Intimacy: Love and Loss in the Beecher-Tilton Scandal* (Chicago: University of Chicago Press, 1999).

112. For photographs that capture similar themes, see, for example, C. H. Schute & Son, *Woman's Suffrage, No. 354*, ca. 1875–1876, stereograph, Library of Congress Prints and Photographs; William Culp Darrah, *The World of Stereographs* (Gettysburg, PA: Darrah, 1977). For other discussions of *The Woman Who Dared*, see Gary Bunker, "The Art of Condescension," *Common-Place* 7, no. 3 (April 2007), http://www.common-place.org/vol-07/no-03/bunker/; Ann D. Gordon, "Knowing Susan B. Anthony: The Stories We Tell of a Life," in *Susan B. Anthony and the Struggle for Equal Rights*, ed. Christine L. Ridarsky and Mary Margaret Huth (Rochester: University of Rochester Press, 2012), 204–5.

113. For examples, see H. Balling, *Mrs. Woodhull Asserting Her Right to Vote*, in *Harper's Weekly*, November 25, 1871; "Washington, D. C.: The Judiciary Committee of the House of Representatives Receiving a Deputation of Female Suffragists,

January 11th—A Lady Delegate Reading Her Argument in Favor of Woman's Voting, on the Basis of the Fourteenth and Fifteenth Constitutional Amendments," *Frank Leslie's Illustrated Newspaper*, February 4, 1871; *Elizabeth Cady Stanton before the Senate Committee on Privileges and Elections*, in *New York Daily Graphic*, January 16, 1878, 501.

114. Mary Ann Shadd Cary, "Speech to the Judiciary re: the Rights of Woman to Vote," January 1872, Mary Ann Shadd Cary Papers, Moorland-Spingarn Research Center, Howard University. Published in Teresa C. Zackodnik, *African American Feminisms, 1828–1923* (New York: Routledge, 2007), 411–14.

115. Terborg-Penn, *African American Women*, 38–39.

116. Truth and Gilbert, *Narrative of Sojourner Truth*, 232.

CHAPTER FOUR

1. *Frank Leslie's Illustrated Historical Register of the Centennial Exposition, 1876* (New York: Frank Leslie, 1876).

2. Dolores Pfeuffer-Scherer, "Remembrance and the American Revolution: Women and the 1876 Centennial Exhibition" (PhD diss., Temple University, 2016), 1–3.

3. Elizabeth Duane Gillespie, *A Book of Remembrance* (Philadelphia: J. B. Lippincott, 1901), 284–85.

4. Pfeuffer-Scherer, "Remembrance and the American Revolution," 126–29.

5. Sally G. McMillen, *Lucy Stone: An Unapologetic Life* (New York: Oxford University Press, 2015), 204–5.

6. Ida Husted Harper, *The Life and Work of Susan B. Anthony*, vol. 1 (Indianapolis: Bowen-Merrill, 1898), 474–76.

7. Susan B. Anthony, "From the Diary of SBA," in Ann D. Gordon, ed., *The Selected Papers of Elizabeth Cady Stanton and Susan B. Anthony*, vol. 3, *National Protection for National Citizens, 1873–1880* (New Brunswick, NJ: Rutgers University Press, 2003), 226–27.

8. National Woman Suffrage Association, "Declaration of Rights of the Women of the United States," p. 3, Claremont Colleges Digital Library, http://ccdl.libraries .claremont.edu/cdm/ref/collection/p15831coll5/id/1114.

9. Lisa Tetrault, "We Shall Be Remembered: Susan B. Anthony and the Politics of Writing History," in *Susan B. Anthony and the Struggle for Equal Rights*, ed. Christine L. Ridarsky and Mary Margaret Huth (Rochester: University of Rochester Press, 2012), 17–18.

10. Tetrault, "We Shall Be Remembered," 23–24; Lisa Tetrault, *Myth of Seneca Falls: Memory and the Women's Suffrage Movement, 1848–1898* (Chapel Hill: University of North Carolina Press, 2014).

11. "Elizabeth Cady Stanton to Olympia Brown, July 29, 1882," in Gordon, *Selected Papers*, 4:145–46.

12. "Susan B. Anthony to Elizabeth Boynton Harbert, September 12, 1885," in Gordon, *Selected Papers*, 4:197–98.

13. "Woman-Suffrage," *Chicago Daily Tribune*, July 9, 1881, 9.

14. Lori D. Ginzberg, *Elizabeth Cady Stanton: An American Life* (New York: Hill and Wang, 2009), 184; Tetrault, *Myth of Seneca Falls*.

15. Elizabeth Cady Stanton, Susan B. Anthony, and Matilda Joslyn Gage, eds., *History of Woman Suffrage*, vol. 1 (New York: Fowler and Wells, 1881; Salem, NH: Ayer, 1985; citations refer to the 1985 edition), 7.

16. Stanton, Anthony, and Gage, *History of Woman Suffrage*, 1:15.

17. Stanton, Anthony, and Gage, *History of Woman Suffrage*, 1:15.

18. For a discussion of the connotations of the profile portrait, see Jennifer L. Roberts, "Copley's Cargo: Boy with a Squirrel and the Dilemma of Transit," *American Art* 21, no. 2 (2007): 29–32; Marcia R. Pointon, *Hanging the Head: Portraiture and Social Formation in Eighteenth-Century England* (New Haven, CT: Yale University Press, 1993), 86.

19. Richard Brilliant, *Portraiture* (London: Reaktion, 1991), 112.

20. "Susan B. Anthony to Elizabeth Boynton Harbert, February 4, 1882," in Gordon, *Selected Papers*, 4:150–51.

21. "Clarina Howard Nichols to Susan B. Anthony, December 17, 1880," Microfilm M-42 Reel 1, Schlesinger Library on the History of Women in America; "Susan B. Anthony to Clara Barton, September 19, 1876," in Gordon, *Selected Papers*, 3:262–64; "Susan B. Anthony to Clara Barton, February 14, 1881," in Gordon, *Selected Papers*, 4:49–50; "Susan B. Anthony to Lillie Devereux Blake, July 9, 1881," Gordon, *Selected Papers*, 4:99; "Susan B. Anthony to Amelia Jenks Bloomer, November 30, 1880," in Gordon, *Selected Papers*, 4:23; Ginzberg, *Elizabeth Cady Stanton*, 154–57.

22. "Susan B. Anthony to Amelia Jenks Bloomer, November 30, 1880," 23.

23. Susan B. Anthony and Ida Husted Harper, *History of Woman Suffrage*, vol. 4 (Indianapolis: Hollenbeck, 1902; Salem, NH: Ayer, 1985; citations refer to the 1985 edition), vii; Tetrault, "We Shall Be Remembered," 25.

24. "Susan B. Anthony to Lillie Devereux Blake, July 9, 1881," 99; "Susan B. Anthony to Amelia Jenks Bloomer, November 30, 1880," 23–24; "Franklin G. Adams to Susan B. Anthony, December 13, 1881," in Gordon, *Selected Papers*, 4:125. Anthony paid for the engravings of activists who were already dead. Tetrault, "We Shall Be Remembered," 24.

25. "Susan B. Anthony to Lillie Devereux Blake, July 9, 1881," 99.

26. Rosalyn Terborg-Penn notes that she had a version of volume four that features a portrait of Harriet Purvis Jr. She notes that the portrait was removed from subsequent editions. I have yet to find a copy with Purvis. Rosalyn Terborg-Penn, *African American Women in the Struggle for the Vote, 1850–1920* (Bloomington: Indiana University Press, 1998).

27. Frances Ellen Watkins Harper, "Speech at the Eleventh Annual Woman's Rights Convention," in *Proceedings of the Eleventh Woman's Rights Convention, May, 1866* (New York: Robert Johnston, 1866), 45–48.

28. Stanton, Anthony, and Gage, *History of Woman Suffrage*, 1:175, 185, 200; Kris-

ten Tegtmeier Oertel and Marilyn S. Blackwell, *Frontier Feminist: Clarina Howard Nichols and the Politics of Motherhood* (Lawrence: University Press of Kansas, 2010).

29. "Clarina Howard Nichols to Susan B. Anthony," December 17, 1880, Susan B. Anthony Papers, M-42, reel 1, Schlesinger Library; "Susan B. Anthony to Franklin G. Adams, December 18, 1881," in Gordon, *Selected Papers*, 4:127.

30. "Clarina Howard Nichols to Susan B. Anthony."

31. "Clarina Howard Nichols to Susan B. Anthony."

32. "Lucy Stone to Elizabeth Cady Stanton, Aug. 3, 1876," in Gordon, *Selected Papers*, 3:249–50; "Susan B. Anthony to Clara Barton, September 19, 1876," in Gordon, *Selected Papers, 3:262–64*; Ginzberg, *Elizabeth Cady Stanton*, 154–57.

33. "Lucy Stone to Elizabeth Cady Stanton, August 3, 1876," 249-250.

34. ["Untitled"], *Woman's Journal*, May 26, 1888, 167.

35. Originally, the editors planned to publish with a larger publisher, D. Appleton of New York. As the length of the project grew and the nation plunged into recession in the late 1870s, Appleton decided not to publish the work. "Susan B. Anthony to Caroline Healey Dall, November 24, 1876," in Gordon, *Selected Papers*, 3:273–74; Susan B. Anthony, "'The History,' Toledo Ballot Box, February 1877," in Gordon, *Selected Papers*, 3:290; "Susan B. Anthony to Amelia Jenks Bloomer, November 30, 1880," in Gordon, *Selected Papers*, 4:24; Tetrault, "We Shall Be Remembered," 20.

36. The editors likely had a previous relationship with the publishers, since one of the women they dedicated the book to, Lydia F. Fowler, M.D., was part of the Fowler family who owned the publishing company. Examples of work published by the company includes Orson Squire Fowler, *A Home for All, or The Gravel Wall and Octagon Mode of Building* (New York: Fowlers and Wells, 1854); *The Water-Cure Journal* (New York: Fowler and Wells, 1845); *The Phrenological Journal and Science of Health* (New York: Fowler & Wells, 1889).

37. Ginzberg, *Elizabeth Cady Stanton*, 157; Anthony and Harper, *History of Woman Suffrage*, 4:viii; "Elizabeth Cady Stanton to the Editor of the *New York Sun*, December 1881," Gordon, *Selected Papers*, 4:122–24; "Susan B. Anthony to Franklin G. Adams, December 18, 1881," in Gordon, *Selected Papers*, 4:127; "Susan B. Anthony to Olivia Bigelow Hall, January 6, 1889," in Gordon, *Selected Papers*, 5:164–65; Tetrault, "We Shall Be Remembered," 38–39.

38. "Recent Prominent Publications," *Literary News*, July 1881, 216; "Recent Prominent Publications," *Literary News*, October 1882, 312.

39. "Notices of New Books," *Godey's Lady's Book*, July 1887, 81; "Our Book Table," *Godey's Lady's Book and Magazine*, November 1882, 477; "History of Woman Suffrage," *Boston Daily Globe*, September 17, 1882, 3; "Our Book Table," *Zion's Herald*, October 25, 1882, 338.

40. "Literature and Art," *Potter's American Monthly*, July 1881, 87; "Our Book Table," *Godey's Lady's Book and Magazine*, August 1881, 188; "Library," *Phrenological Journal and Science of Health* 73, no. 1 (July 1881): 56.

41. "Our Book Table," *Godey's Lady's Book*, August 1881, 188; "Our Book Table,"

Godey's Lady's Book, November 1882, 477; "Woman Suffrage: From the New York Herald," *Literary News*, July 1881, 200; "Woman in France," *Washington Post*, August 28, 1881, 2; "Woman-Suffrage," *Chicago Daily Tribune*, July 9, 1881, 9; "Editor's Table," *Chautauquan*, November 1881; "Library," 56; "Article 1—No Title," *Independent*, January 12, 1882, 1; "History of Woman Suffrage," *Boston Daily Globe*, September 17, 1882, 3; "History of Woman Suffrage: From the *Boston Globe*," *Literary News*, October 1882, 300; Tetrault, "We Shall Be Remembered," 25–26.

42. "Our Book Table," *Zion's Herald*, October 25, 1882, 338.

43. Lucy Stone, "The History of Woman Suffrage," *Woman's Journal*, June 11, 1881, 188.

44. "Books Received," *Woman's Journal*, September 16, 1882, 296.

45. Pocahontas supposedly appeared on a bill in 1875, but I have yet to find a copy. Washington also became the first woman to appear on a postage stamp, in 1902. In 2016, the US Treasury announced that in 2020, American currency will feature portraits of women, including Harriet Tubman, Lucretia Mott, Anthony, and Stanton.

46. Anthony, for example, wrote to Stanton that Belva Lockwood, who ran for president in 1884 and 1888, wore her hair styled "ala [*sic*] Martha Washington" at an 1884 campaign speech. "Susan B. Anthony to Elizabeth Cady Stanton, October 23, 1884," in Gordon, *Selected Papers*, 4:371–72.

47. See also Allison Lange, "Picturing Tradition: Images of Martha Washington in Antebellum Politics," *Imprint* 37 (2012): 22–39.

48. For another example from *Puck*, see Joseph Keppler, "A Female Suffrage Fancy," *Puck*, July 14, 1880, 342–43.

49. Charles Taylor, "A Squelcher for Woman Suffrage," *Puck*, June 6, 1894, 241; "Concerning an Unmanly Fad," *Puck*, June 6, 1894, 242.

50. "Susan B. Anthony to the Editor, *Cincinnati Commercial Gazette*, December 29, 1883," in Gordon, *Selected Papers*, 4:321.

51. "Susan B. Anthony," *Cincinnati Commercial Gazette*, December 23, 1883, sec. Extra Sheet; "Elizabeth Cady Stanton," *Cincinnati Commercial Gazette*, December 23, 1883, sec. Extra Sheet.

52. Allison Sneider, *Suffragists in an Imperial Age: U.S. Expansion and the Woman Question, 1870–1929* (New York: Oxford University Press, 2008); Rebecca Mead, "Pioneers at the Polls: Woman Suffrage in the West," in *Votes for Women: The Struggle for Suffrage Revisited*, ed. Jean Baker (New York: Oxford University Press, 2002).

53. Rebecca Mead, *How the Vote Was Won: Woman Suffrage in the Western United States, 1868–1914* (New York: New York University Press, 2004), 43; Mead, "Pioneers at the Polls," 91–92; Lola Van Wagenen, *Sister-Wives and Suffragists: Polygamy and the Politics of Woman Suffrage, 1870–1896* (Provo, UT: Joseph Fielding Smith Institute for Latter-Day Saint History, 2003).

54. Alexander Keyssar, *The Right to Vote: The Contested History of Democracy in the United States* (New York: Basic Books, 2000), 365–68.

55. See also "Women Voting at the Municipal Election in Boston on December 11," *Harper's Weekly*, December 15, 1881, 965; and "Female Suffrage in Kansas," *Frank Leslie's Illustrated Newspaper*, April 16, 1887, 133.

56. Suffragists' rebuttals to attacks on women's suffrage in the West include Hon. James S. Clarkson, "How Women Voted in Colorado," December 1894, Box 4, Folder 4, Suffrage Collection, Sophia Smith Collection; "Woman Suffrage in Wyoming," May 1, 1889, Box 4, Folder 5, Suffrage Collection, Sophia Smith Collection; "Colorado Speaks for Herself," January 1897, Box 4, Folder 4, Suffrage Collection, Sophia Smith Collection; Alice Stone Blackwell, "Miss Cracken on Colorado," July 1904, Box 4, Folder 4, Suffrage Collection, Sophia Smith Collection; Governor Davis H. Waite and Governor Lorenzo Crounse, "Woman Suffrage in Practice," *North American Review*, June 1894, Box 3, Folder 7, Sophia Smith Collection.

57. "Woman Suffrage in Wyoming Territory," *Frank Leslie's Illustrated Newspaper*, November 24, 1888, 233–34.

58. "Women Voting at the Municipal Election," *Harper's Weekly*, 965.

59. Joshua Brown, *Beyond the Lines: Pictorial Reporting, Everyday Life, and the Crisis of Gilded-Age America* (Berkeley: University of California Press, 2003), 172; ["Untitled"], *Frank Leslie's Illustrated Newspaper*, November 24, 1888, 230.

60. Brown, *Beyond the Lines*, 173.

61. Brown, *Beyond the Lines*, 234; Rose Young, *The Record of the Leslie Woman Suffrage Commission, Inc., 1917–1929* (New York: Leslie Woman Suffrage Commission, 1929), 64.

62. Eleanor Flexner, *Century of Struggle: The Woman's Rights Movement in the United States*, Enlarged edition (Cambridge, MA: Belknap, 1996), 211; Tetrault, "We Shall Be Remembered," 40–42.

63. Theda Skocpol, "Extending the Separate Sphere," in *Protecting Soldiers and Mothers: The Political Origins of Social Policy in the United States* (Cambridge, MA: Belknap, 1992).

64. For more on the work of progressive reformers, see Roy Rosenzweig and Elizabeth Blackmar, *The Park and the People: A History of Central Park* (Ithaca, NY: Cornell University Press, 1992); Miroslava Chavez-Garcia, *States of Delinquency: Race and Science in the Making of California's Juvenile Justice System* (Berkeley: University of California Press, 2012); Maureen A Flanagan, *America Reformed: Progressives and Progressivisms, 1890s—1920s* (New York: Oxford University Press, 2007); Lawrence Goldstone, *Inherently Unequal: The Betrayal of Equal Rights by the Supreme Court, 1865–1903* (New York: Walker, 2011); Richard Hofstadter, *The Age of Reform: From Bryan to F.D.R.* (New York: Vintage, 1960); Karl Jacoby, *Crimes against Nature: Squatters, Poachers, Thieves, and the Hidden History of American Conservation* (Berkeley: University of California Press, 2001); Alison M. Parker, *Articulating Rights: Nineteenth-Century American Women on Race, Reform, and the State* (DeKalb: Northern Illinois University Press, 2010); Donald Wayne Rogers,

Making Capitalism Safe: Work Safety and Health Regulation in America, 1880–1940 (Urbana: University of Illinois Press, 2009); Daniel T. Rodgers, *Atlantic Crossings: Social Politics in a Progressive Age* (Cambridge, MA: Belknap, 1998); Skocpol, *Protecting Soldiers and Mothers*; Robert H. Wiebe, *The Search for Order, 1877–1920* (New York: Hill and Wang, 1967); Deborah Valenze, *Milk: A Local and Global History* (New Haven, CT: Yale University Press, 2011).

65. Skocpol, "Extending the Separate Sphere."

66. Patricia G. Holland and Ann D. Gordon, eds., *The Papers of Elizabeth Cady Stanton and Susan B. Anthony: Guide and Index to the Microfilm Edition* (Wilmington, DE: Scholarly Resources, 1992), 67.

67. Corinne Field, "Elizabeth Cady Stanton and the Gendered Politics of Aging," *Iris*, April 30, 2001; Corinne T. Field, *Grand Old Women and Modern Girls: Generational and Racial Conflict in the US Women's Rights Movement, 1870–1920*, forthcoming; Elizabeth Cady Stanton, "The Pleasures of Age," in Gordon, *Selected Papers*, 4:452–63.

68. "A Leader of Women," *Evening Star*, December 28, 1889, 9.

69. Harper, *The Life and Work*, 2:660–61.

70. "Elizabeth Cady Stanton to Susan B. Anthony, ca. June 1891," in Gordon, *Selected Papers*, 5:385.

71. The first photographic reproduction processes were developed in the 1860s and 1870s, but they were too expensive for widespread use. Michael L. Carlebach, *The Origins of Photojournalism in America* (Washington, DC: Smithsonian Institution Press, 1992), 160–61; Carl F. Kaestle and Janice A. Radway, "A Framework for the History of Publishing and Reading in the United States, 1880–1940," in *Print in Motion: The Expansion of Publishing and Reading in the United States, 1880–1940*, ed. Kaestle and Radway, vol. 4 of *A History of the Book in America* (Chapel Hill: The University of North Carolina Press, 2009), 12–13.

72. Kaestle and Radway, "A Framework," 13; Megan Benton, "Unruly Servants: Machines, Modernity, and the Printed Page," in Kaestle and Radway, *Print in Motion*, 155.

73. Benton, "Unruly Servants," 153–54.

74. Sarah Kennel, Diane Waggoner, and Alice Carver-Kubik, *In the Darkroom: An Illustrated Guide to Photographic Processes before the Digital Age* (Washington, DC: National Gallery of Art, 2010), 55–57.

75. Jacob A. Riis, *How the Other Half Lives: Studies among the Tenements of New York* (New York: Scribner, 1890). See also Gregory S. Jackson, "Cultivating Spiritual Sight: Jacob Riis's Virtual-Tour Narrative and the Visual Modernization of Protestant Homiletics," *Representations* 83, no. 1 (2003): 126–66; Carol Quirke, "Picturing the Poor: Jacob Riis's Reform Photography," *Reviews in American History* 36, no. 4 (2008): 557–65.

76. Alice Stone Blackwell, "Lucy Stone," *Woman's Journal*, April 15, 1893, 113.

77. *Portrait of Lucy Stone*, ca. 1888–1893, Schlesinger Library on the History of Women in America; *Portrait of Lucy Stone* (New Jersey, ca. 1888–1893), Scrapbook

for Catherine W. M. C. S. Vol. I, Schlesinger Library on the History of Women in America; Blackwell, "Lucy Stone," 113–14.

78. "Lucy Stone, in 1893," *Woman's Journal*, October 28, 1893, 337.

79. "Lucy Stone in 1855," *Woman's Journal*, March 24, 1894, 89; "Lucy Stone in 1855," *Woman's Column*, March 24, 1894, 1.

80. "Circulate Suffrage Papers," *Woman's Column*, November 25, 1893; Alice Stone Blackwell, "To the Friends of The Woman's Journal," *Woman's Journal*, December 2, 1893, 4; "Portraits of Lucy Stone," *Woman's Column*, January 13, 1894, 4; Alice Stone Blackwell, "Photographs of Lucy Stone," *Woman's Journal*, November 25, 1893, 372.

81. "Photographs of Lucy Stone," *Woman's Column*, December 9, 1893.

82. "Lucy Stone's Portrait," *Woman's Journal*, January 2, 1897, 264.

83. E. M. H. Merrill, "The Typical Woman Suffragist," *Woman's Column*, November 19, 1892, 3, Massachusetts Historical Society; E. M. H. Merrill, "The Typical Woman Suffragist," *Woman's Journal*, November 19, 1892, 378.

84. See chap. 3 of this book as well as "The Chicago Convention," *Revolution*, February 25, 1869, 113–15; and James Parton et al., *Eminent Women of the Age: Being Narratives of the Lives and Deeds of the Most Prominent Women of the Present Generation* (Hartford, CT: S. M. Betts, 1869), 358.

85. Photograph from the Friends Historical Library (RG6, S.6/12) reproduced in Robert Cooney, *Winning the Vote: The Triumph of the American Woman Suffrage Movement* (Santa Cruz, CA: American Graphic Press, 2005), 70–71, 464.

86. See, for example, *I Go for All Sharing Privileges of Government Who Assist in Bearing Its Burdens, by No Means Excluding Women*; *Abraham Lincoln in 1836* (James H. Barry, ca. 1903–1926), 183. Alice Park Posters, Schlesinger Library on the History of Women in America.

87. Mary T. W. McTeer, "Tennessee Remembers Lucy Stone," *Woman's Journal*, April 21, 1894, 122.

88. I. H. S., "Mrs. Stanton Remembered in Maine," *Woman's Journal*, November 30, 1895, 377; F. M. A., "A Yellow Ribbon Reception," *Woman's Journal*, April 14, 1894, 120.

89. F. B. Chamberlin might be the incorrect initials for prominent Florida suffragist Ella Chamberlain, who founded and became the first president of the Florida Woman Suffrage Association. She worked on representations of the suffrage movement in the press. A. Elizabeth Taylor, "The Woman Suffrage Movement in Florida," *Florida Historical Quarterly* 36, no. 1 (1957): 42–60; Harriet Taylor Upton, ed., *The Hand Book of the National American Woman Suffrage Association and Proceedings of the Twenty-Fifth Annual Convention of the National American Woman Suffrage Association* (Washington, DC: Stormont & Jackson, 1893), 164.

90. Mrs. H. B. Kells, "What Southern Women Say," *Woman's Column*, October 1, 1892, 3.

91. Frances B. Johnston, *Susan B. Anthony at Her Desk*, 1900, Susan B. Anthony Papers, Box 1, Folder 12, Sophia Smith Collection.

92. Johnston, *Susan B. Anthony at Her Desk*.

93. Holland and Gordon, *Papers*, 65.

94. Bettina Berch, *The Woman behind the Lens: The Life and Work of Frances Benjamin Johnston, 1864–1952* (Charlottesville: University of Virginia Press, 2000), 11.

95. Berch, *The Woman behind the Lens*; Frances Johnston, *Frances Benjamin Johnston, Full-length Self-portrait Dressed as a Man with False Moustache, Posed with Bicycle, Facing Left*, ca. 1890–1900, Frances Benjamin Johnston Collection, Library of Congress Prints and Photographs.

96. Berch, *The Woman behind the Lens*, 100.

97. Catharine M. Fleming, *The Anthony Home Calendar*, 1900, 8, Susan B. Anthony Papers, 1815–1961, Susan B. Anthony Memorabilia, A-143, Folder 31, Schlesinger Library on the History of Women in America, http://nrs.harvard.edu /urn-3:RAD.SCHL:8920789.

98. Fleming, *The Anthony Home Calendar*; *Miss Susan B. Anthony at Her Desk*, ca. 1900, Postcard Box 1, Women's Library.

99. Fleming, *The Anthony Home Calendar*, 2–3.

100. Rachel Foster Avery, ed., *Proceedings of the Thirtieth Annual Convention of the National American Woman Suffrage Association of the Fiftieth Anniversary of the First Woman's Rights Convention* (Philadelphia: Alfred J. Ferris, 1898), 2.

101. Carrie Chapman Catt, "Beautiful Woman Suffrage Calendars," *Woman's Journal*, December 19, 1896, 401.

102. Alice Stone Blackwell, "The Suffrage Fair," *Woman's Journal*, December 15, 1894, 396; Alice Stone Blackwell, "The Suffrage Fair," *Woman's Journal*, December 1, 1894, 380.

103. The Anthony pin might have resembled those from the 1908 NAWSA meeting that feature portraits of Stanton and Mott. *60th Anniversary Pin with Portraits of Lucretia Mott and Elizabeth Cady Stanton* (Whitehead and Hoag Company Badges, Newark, 1908), Suffrage Memorabilia, Box 2 Tray 1, Schlesinger Library on the History of Women in America; Rachel Foster Avery, ed., *Proceedings of the Thirty-Second Annual Convention of the National American Woman Suffrage Association* (Philadelphia: Alfred J. Ferris, 1900), 12–13.

104. Ida Husted Harper, ed., *History of Woman Suffrage*, vols. 5–6 (New York: J. J. Little & Ives, 1922; Salem, NH: Ayer, 1985).

105. Harper, *The Life and Work*. Anthony burned papers in a bonfire in her backyard for days. Tetrault, "We Shall Be Remembered," 42–45.

106. Sara Hunter Graham, *Woman Suffrage and the New Democracy* (New Haven, CT: Yale University Press, 1996), 44.

107. Graham, *Woman Suffrage*, 44–52.

108. J. E. Hale, *Failure Is Impossible*, early twentieth century, Susan B. Anthony Papers, Box 1, Folder 10, Sophia Smith Collection.

109. "Catalogue and Price List" (National Woman Suffrage Publishing, 1917), 10, Suffrage Collection, Box 5, Folder 10, Sophia Smith Collection.

CHAPTER FIVE

1. Mary Church Terrell, *A Colored Woman in a White World* (Washington, DC: Ransdell, 1940), 120–21.

2. "Mary Church Terrell," *Woman's Era*, September 1896, 3; "To Improve Their People," *Chicago Daily News*, August 14, 1899, Mary Church Terrell Papers, Library of Congress; "Mrs. Terrell Wins," *Chicago Record*, August 17, 1899, Mary Church Terrell Papers, Library of Congress; J. H. Cunningham, "Mrs. Mary Church Terrell," *Colored American*, February 17, 1900, Library of Congress.

3. Joshua Brown, *Beyond the Lines: Pictorial Reporting, Everyday Life, and the Crisis of Gilded-Age America* (Berkeley: University of California Press, 2003).

4. For more on the founding of women's colleges by wealthy female donors, see Joan Marie Johnson, "An Education for Women Equal to That of Men," in *Funding Feminism: Monied Women, Philanthropy, and the Women's Movement, 1870–1967* (Chapel Hill: University of North Carolina Press, 2017).

5. "Dr. M. A. Majors to Mary Church Terrell, July 6, 1892," Mary Church Terrell Papers, Reel 3, Library of Congress.

6. *Our Famous Women*, advertisement, 1892, Mary Church Terrell Papers, Reel 3, Library of Congress.

7. Rosalyn Terborg-Penn, *African American Women in the Struggle for the Vote, 1850–1920* (Bloomington: Indiana University Press, 1998), 51–52.

8. Brittney C. Cooper, *Beyond Respectability: The Intellectual Thought of Race Women* (Urbana: University of Illinois Press, 2017), 134.

9. Mrs. N. F. [Gertrude Bustill] Mossell, *The Work of the Afro-American Woman* (Philadelphia: G. S. Ferguson, 1894), frontispiece, 4, http://archive.org/details /workofafroameric00moss. Her book does not identify the figures, but *Evidences of Progress* features the same photograph with a label. G. F. Richings, *Evidences of Progress among Colored People* (Philadelphia: George S. Ferguson, 1902), 418.

10. Mossell, *The Work of the Afro-American Woman*, 115, 123.

11. Alison M. Parker, *Articulating Rights: Nineteenth-Century American Women on Race, Reform, and the State* (DeKalb: Northern Illinois University Press, 2010), 181.

12. Terrell, *A Colored Woman*, 32.

13. Terrell, *A Colored Woman*, 99.

14. Terrell, *A Colored Woman*, 140; Parker, *Articulating Rights*, 184–85.

15. Parker, *Articulating Rights*, 139.

16. May Wright Sewall, ed., *The World's Congress of Representative Women: A Historical Résumé for Popular Circulation of the World's Congress of Representative Women* (Chicago: Rand, McNally, 1894), 6, http://archive.org/details /worldscongressof00worluoft.

17. Sewall, *The World's Congress*, 3–4.

18. Sewall, *The World's Congress*, 5.

19. Terrell, *A Colored Woman*, 109.

20. "Editorial Notes," *Woman's Journal*, July 15, 1893, 217.

21. "Editorial Notes," 217.

22. Henrietta Briggs-Wall, "American Woman and Her Political Peers," 1899, Research file, Kansas Museum of History.

23. S. Soloman, "That Picture," *Woman's Journal*, December 30, 1893, 416.

24. Soloman, "That Picture," 416.

25. The *Woman's Tribune* publicized the piece as well. "World's Fair Notes," *Woman's Journal*, April 22, 1893, 126; "Editorial Notes," 217; Lucy S. Richardson, "Dr. Buckley as an Art Critic," *Woman's Journal*, September 15, 1894, 290; Briggs-Wall, "American Woman and Her Political Peers." Briggs-Wall's letter can be found in Henrietta Briggs-Wall, "Woman's Political Peers," *Woman's Column*, September 9, 1893; Henrietta Briggs-Wall, "Idiots, Lunatics, Felons and Women," *Woman's Journal*, September 9, 1893, 287.

26. Sheridan Ploughe, *History of Reno County, Kansas: Its People, Industries and Institutions*, vol. 2 (B.F. Bowen, 1917), 692–95.

27. Briggs-Wall, "American Woman."

28. "Please Keep This Card," ca. 1890s, Research file, Kansas Museum of History.

29. *Hearing before the Committee on Woman Suffrage, February 21, 1894* (Washington, D. C: G.P.O., 1894), 12. See also the copy of Briggs-Wall, "American Woman and Her Political Peers," at the American Antiquarian Society, which has inscribed on the back: "Photograph of oil painting exhibited in the Kansas building at the World's Fair. Presented to the U.S. Senate Special Committee on Woman Suffrage by Clara Bewick Colby of Nebraska at hearing of National American Woman Suffrage Association before the Committee Feb. 21, 1894."

30. *Hearing before the Committee*, 22.

31. *Hearing before the Committee*, 12.

32. *Hearing before the Committee*, 22.

33. "Ethel Ingalls to Wed," *Washington Post*, October 22, 1894, 2.

34. Ethel Ingalls, "A Bright One," *Los Angeles Times*, September 10, 1893, 17.

35. For more on the rise of the public motherhood message and shifts in suffrage arguments, see Jessica Derleth, "'Kneading Politics': Cookery and the American Woman Suffrage Movement," *Journal of the Gilded Age and Progressive Era* 17, no. 3 (2018): 450–74; Eleanor Flexner, *Century of Struggle: The Woman's Rights Movement in the United States*, enlarged ed. (Cambridge, MA: Belknap, 1996); Sara Hunter Graham, *Woman Suffrage and the New Democracy* (New Haven, CT: Yale University Press, 1996); Aileen S. Kraditor, *The Ideas of the Woman Suffrage Movement, 1890–1920* (New York: Columbia University Press, 1965); Suzanne Marilley, *Woman Suffrage and the Origins of Liberal Feminism in the United States, 1820–1920* (Cambridge, MA: Harvard University Press, 1996); Holly J. McCammon, Lyndi Hewitt, and Sandy Smith, "'No Weapon Save Argument': Strategic Frame Amplification in the U.S. Woman Suffrage Movements," *Sociological Quarterly* 45, no. 3 (July 1, 2004): 529–56; Theda Skocpol, *Protecting Soldiers and Mothers: The Political Origins of Social Policy in the United States* (Cambridge, MA: Belknap, 1992).

36. For more on the association between black women, sexual promiscuity, and the Jezebel stereotype, see Cooper, *Beyond Respectability*; Patricia Hill Collins, *Black Feminist Thought: Knowledge, Consciousness, and the Politics of Empowerment* (New York: Routledge, 2009); Treva B. Lindsey, *Colored No More: Reinventing Black Womanhood in Washington, D.C.* (Urbana: University of Illinois Press, 2017); Dorothy E. Roberts, *Killing the Black Body: Race, Reproduction, and the Meaning of Liberty* (New York: Pantheon, 1997); Deborah Gray White, *Ar'n't I a Woman?: Female Slaves in the Plantation South* (New York: W. W. Norton, 1999); Deborah Willis, *The Black Female Body: A Photographic History* (Philadelphia: Temple University Press, 2002); Deborah Willis, *Posing Beauty: African American Images from the 1890s to the Present* (New York: W. W. Norton, 2009).

37. *Hearing before the Committee*, 12.

38. Fannie Barrier Williams, "The Intellectual Progress of the Colored Women of the United States since the Emancipation Proclamation," in *The World's Congress of Representative Women*, vol. 2, ed. May Wright Sewall (New York: Rand, McNally, 1894), 701.

39. For more on the relationship between the Baptist organizations and the NACW, see Evelyn Brooks Higginbotham, *Righteous Discontent: The Women's Movement in the Black Baptist Church, 1880–1920* (Cambridge: Harvard University Press, 1993); Terborg-Penn, *African American Women*.

40. On disenfranchisement during this era, see Alexander Keyssar, *The Right to Vote: The Contested History of Democracy in the United States* (New York: Basic Books, 2000), 83–93. For more on black women's efforts to regain the voting rights of black men, see Liette Gidlow, "The Sequel: The Fifteenth Amendment, The Nineteenth Amendment, and Southern Black Women's Struggle to Vote," *Journal of the Gilded Age and Progressive Era* 17, no. 3 (2018): 433–49.

41. *Constitution of the State of Mississippi, Adopted November 1, 1890* (Jackson, MI: Clarion-Ledger Establishment, 1891), 54.

42. Teresa Holden, "'Earnest Women Can Do Anything': The Public Career of Josephine St. Pierre Ruffin, 1842–1904" (PhD diss., St. Louis University, 2005).

43. *A History of the Club Movement among the Colored Women of the United States of America* (Washington, DC: National Association of Colored Women's Clubs, 1978), 16.

44. "Let Us Confer Together," *Woman's Era*, June 1895, 8; "A Charge to Be Refuted," *Woman's Era*, June 1895, 9.

45. Significant scholarship on the National Association of Colored Women includes Mia Bay et al., eds., *Toward an Intellectual History of Black Women* (Chapel Hill: University of North Carolina Press, 2015); Nikki Brown, *Private Politics and Public Voices: Black Women's Activism from World War I to the New Deal* (Bloomington: Indiana University Press, 2006); Cooper, *Beyond Respectability*; Martha S. Jones, *All Bound Up Together: The Woman Question in African American Public Culture, 1830–1900* (Chapel Hill: University of North Carolina Press, 2007); Lindsey, *Colored No More*; Terborg-Penn, *African American Women*; Deborah Gray

White, *Too Heavy a Load: Black Women in Defense of Themselves* (New York: W. W. Norton, 1999).

46. "Additional Convention Notes," *Woman's Era*, July 1896, Mary Church Terrell Papers, Reel 30, Library of Congress.

47. Parker, *Articulating Rights*, 137, 190–93; White, *Too Heavy a Load*, 33.

48. *A History of the Club Movement*, 35.

49. Terborg-Penn, *African American Women*, 110–11; Sharon Harley and Rosalyn Terborg-Penn, *The Afro-American Woman: Struggles and Images* (Black Classic Press, 1997), 24.

50. White, *Too Heavy a Load*, 41–42.

51. Mary Greenleaf Clement Leavitt, ed., *Report Made to the First Convention of the World's Women's Christian Temperance Union* (Boston: Alfred Mudge, 1891), 12.

52. "For God & Home And Every Land, Boston, 1891" (Woman's Temperance Publishing Association, 1891), Susan B. Anthony Ephemera Collection, Box 6, Folder 5, Huntington Library; *Minutes of the National Woman's Christian Temperance Union* (Chicago: Woman's Temperance Publishing Association, 1891), cover.

53. Parker, *Articulating Rights*, 124.

54. Parker, *Articulating Rights*, 166–76.

55. Mrs. N. F. [Gertrude Bustill] Mossell, *The Work of the Afro-American Woman*, 9; Rosetta E. Lawson, "Colored Women in the Reform Movement," *National Notes*, January 1899, 2, National Association of Colored Women's Clubs Papers (microfilm).

56. Margaret Murray Washington, "Notes from Tuskegee," *National Notes*, June 1899, 3, National Association of Colored Women's Clubs Papers (microfilm).

57. "Minutes of the Eleventh Biennial Convention of the National Association of Colored Women," 1918, 51, National Association of Colored Women's Clubs Papers (microfilm).

58. Other leading civil rights figures of the era, such as W. E. B. Du Bois, employed imagery contest racial stereotypes as well. Shawn Michelle Smith, *Photography on the Color Line: W. E. B. Du Bois, Race, and Visual Culture* (Durham, NC: Duke University Press, 2004).

59. Mary Church Terrell, "Washington," *Woman's Era*, May 1895, 3.

60. "Corrections," *Woman's Era*, June 1895, 8–9.

61. Mary Church Terrell, "What Colored Women Have Done," *National Notes*, November 1900, 3, National Association of Colored Women's Clubs Papers (microfilm).

62. "The Secret of Attraction," *National Association Notes*, June 1899, 2, Mary Church Terrell Papers, Box 102-18, Moorland-Spingarn Research Center, Howard University. For more on editor Margaret Murray Washington's views on her vision for the New Negro Woman, see Martha Patterson, "Margaret Murray Washington, Pauline Hopkins, and the New Negro Woman," in *Beyond the Gibson Girl: Reimagining the American New Woman, 1895–1915* (Chicago: University of Illinois Press, 2005).

63. "Scott's Magic Hair Straightener and Grower," *Colored American*, February 17, 1900, 2.

64. "Have It Straight, 'What?' Your Hair," *Colored American*, February 17, 1900, 5.

65. Thomas B. Crane, "Black Skin Remover," *Colored American*, February 17, 1900, 16.

66. For more on the history of colorism in the US, see Laila Haidarali, *Brown Beauty: Color, Sex, and Race from the Harlem Renaissance to World War II* (New York: New York University Press, 2018); Audrey Elisa Kerr, *The Paper Bag Principle: Class, Colorism, and Rumor and the Case of Black Washington, D.C.* (Knoxville: University of Tennessee Press, 2006); Kimberly Jade Norwood, *Color Matters: Skin Tone Bias and the Myth of a Postracial America* (New York: Routledge, 2014).

67. Terrell, *A Colored Woman*, 427, 372–96.

68. For more on black women's hair during this era, see Lindsey, "Make Me Beautiful: Aesthetic Discourses of New Negro Womanhood," in *Colored No More*; Noliwe M. Rooks, "Beauty, Race, and Black Pride," in *Hair Raising: Beauty, Culture, and African American Women* (New Brunswick, NJ: Rutgers University Press, 1996).

69. "Light Color Bar to Office," *Baltimore Afro-American*, July 21, 1906, 1.

70. "Tumult of Hisses Mars Convention," *Detroit Journal*, 1906, Mary Church Terrell Papers, Reel 31, Library of Congress.

71. Mary Church Terrell, *The Progress of Colored Women* (Washington, DC: Smith Brothers, 1898), 7.

72. Darlene Hine, "Rape and the Inner Lives of Black Women in the Middle West: Preliminary Thoughts on the Culture of Dissemblance," *Signs* 14, no. 4 (1989): 912–20.

73. For more on Idár, see Jessica Enoch, "Claiming Cultural Citizenship: Jovita Idar, Marta Peña, Leonor Villegas de Magnón, and La Crónica," in *Refiguring Rhetorical Education: Women Teaching African American, Native American, and Chicano/a Students, 1865–1911* (Carbondale: Southern Illinois University Press, 2008); Gabriela González, "Jovita Idar: The Ideological Origins of a Transnational Advocate for La Raza," in *Redeeming La Raza: Transborder Modernity, Race, Respectability, and Rights*, ed. Elizabeth Hayes Turner, Stephanie Cole, and Rebecca Sharpless (Athens: University of Georgia Press, 2015). For more on Lee, see "Chinese Girl Wants Vote," *New York Tribune*, April 13, 1912.

74. Keyssar, *The Right to Vote*, 91.

75. Terrell, *A Colored Woman*, 163.

76. "Comment of the Press upon Mary Church Terrell's Address," *National Notes*, April 1900, 4, Mary Church Terrell Papers, Moorland-Spingarn Research Center, Howard University.

77. White, *Too Heavy a Load*, 60–68.

78. W. E. B. Du Bois, "The Work of Negro Women in Society," *Spelman Messenger*, February 1902, 1–2, The Spelman Messenger, Box 2, Spelman College Archives.

79. Garth E. Pauley, "W. E. B. Du Bois on Woman Suffrage: A Critical Analysis of His Crisis Writings," *Journal of Black Studies* 30, no. 3 (2000): 383–410.

80. Hill Collins, *Black Feminist Thought*; Roberts, *Killing the Black Body*; Patricia A. Turner, *Ceramic Uncles & Celluloid Mammies: Black Images and Their Influence on Culture* (New York: Anchor, 1994); White, *Ar'n't I a Woman?*; Willis, *The Black Female Body*, 128–29; Willis, *Posing Beauty*.

81. David W. Blight, *Race and Reunion: The Civil War in American Memory* (Cambridge, MA: Belknap, 2001).

82. Cooper, *Beyond Respectability*, 41.

83. Ida B. Wells-Barnett, "The Model Woman: A Pen Picture of the Typical Southern Girl, printed in the *New York Freeman*, February 18, 1888," in *The Memphis Diary of Ida B. Wells* (Boston: Beacon, 1995), 188–89.

84. Ida B. Wells, *The Reason Why the Colored American Is Not in the World's Columbian Exposition*, ed. Robert W. Rydell (Urbana: University of Illinois Press, 1999). First published 1893.

85. Terrell, *A Colored Woman*, 145. For more on women of color as "diplomats," see Glenda Gilmore, *Gender and Jim Crow: Women and the Politics of White Supremacy in North Carolina, 1896–1920* (Chapel Hill: University of North Carolina Press, 1996).

86. These female reformers complicate the civil rights narrative that pits Booker T. Washington's advocacy of industrial education against W. E. B. Du Bois's belief that the educated "talented tenth" of black society should lead. Margaret Murray Washington, the wife of Booker T. Washington, edited and printed the NACW's *National Notes* for over two decades and served as the group's president from 1912 to 1916. The NACW supported industrial education initiatives, but its extraordinarily well-educated officers also believed needed to lead the black community. For recent work that considers the significance of the debate between Du Bois and Washington, see Thomas Aiello, "The First Fissure: The Du Bois-Washington Relationship from 1898–1899," *Phylon* 51, no. 1 (2014): 76–87; Reginald K. Ellis, *Between Washington and Du Bois: The Racial Politics of James Edward Shepard* (Gainesville: University Press of Florida, 2017); Anna Pochmara, *The Making of the New Negro: Black Authorship, Masculinity, and Sexuality in the Harlem Renaissance* (Amsterdam: Amsterdam University Press, 2011). For more on Margaret Murray Washington, see Elizabeth Lindsay Davis, *Lifting as They Climb* (Washington, DC: National Association of Colored Women, 1933), 209–10; Sheena Harris, "Margaret Murray Washington: A Southern Reformer and the Black Women's Club Movement," in *Alabama Women: Their Lives and Times*, ed. Susan Youngblood Ashmore and Lisa Lindquist Dorr (Athens: University of Georgia Press, 2017); Patterson, "Margaret Murray Washington."

87. Jane L. McKeever, "The Woman's Temperance Publishing Association," *Library Quarterly* 55, no. 4 (1985): 367.

88. Johnson, *Funding Feminism*.

89. "Proceedings of the Executive Committee," *National Notes*, December 1900, 1, National Association of Colored Women's Clubs Papers (microfilm).

90. Rebecca Mead, "Suffrage and Populism in the Silver State of Colorado,"

in *How the Vote Was Won: Woman Suffrage in the Western United States, 1868–1914* (New York: New York University Press, 2004); Holly J. McCammon, "Stirring up Suffrage Sentiment: The Formation of the State Woman Suffrage Organizations, 1866–1914," *Social Forces* 80, no. 2 (2001): 456–57; Holly J. McCammon et al., "How Movements Win: Gendered Opportunity Structures and U.S. Women's Suffrage Movements, 1866 to 1919," *American Sociological Review* 66, no. 1 (2001): 49–70.

91. Washington territory had women's suffrage from 1883 through 1888 when the Supreme Court of the territory overturned the law. Women did not win suffrage in the state until 1910. Mead, *How the Vote Was Won*, 43–45; Andrea G. Radke-Moss, "Mormon Women, Suffrage, and Citizenship at the 1893 Chicago World's Fair," in *Gendering the Fair: Histories of Women and Gender at World's Fairs*, ed. T. J. Boisseau and Abigail M. Markwyn (Urbana: University of Illinois Press, 2010).

92. Marjorie Julian Spruill, "Race, Reform, and Reaction at the Turn of the Century: Southern Suffragists, the NAWSA, and the 'Southern Strategy' in Context," in *Votes for Women: The Struggle for Suffrage Revisited*, ed. Jean Baker (New York: Oxford University Press, 2002); Elna Green, *Southern Strategies: Southern Women and the Woman Suffrage Question* (Chapel Hill: University of North Carolina Press, 1997).

93. Harriet Taylor Upton, ed., *Proceedings of the Twenty-Seventh Annual Convention of the National American Woman Suffrage Association* (Warren, OH: William Ritezel, 1895), 14–15.

94. Upton, *Proceedings of the Twenty-Seventh*, 15.

95. Rachel Foster Avery, ed., *Proceedings of the Twenty-Ninth Annual Convention of the National American Woman Suffrage Association* (Philadelphia: Alfred J. Ferris, 1897), 73.

96. Avery, *Proceedings of the Twenty-Ninth*, 70.

97. Rachel Foster Avery, ed., *Proceedings of the Thirty-Second Annual Convention of the National American Woman Suffrage Association* (Philadelphia: Alfred J. Ferris, 1900), 23, 26.

98. Rachel Foster Avery, ed., *Proceedings of the Twenty-Eighth Annual Convention of the National-American Woman Suffrage Association* (Philadelphia: Alfred J. Ferris, 1896), 1.

99. Alice Stone Blackwell, "Why the Yellow?," *Woman Citizen*, June 16, 1917; and Laura M. Johns, "The Origin of Our Badge," *Woman's Tribune*, 1896. Both articles were pasted into Clippings, Volume 14, Susan B. Anthony Library, Huntington Library, page 42. For more on choosing yellow, see Margaret Mary Finnegan, *Selling Suffrage: Consumer Culture and Votes for Women* (New York: Columbia University Press, 1999), 115–16.

100. Rachel Foster Avery, ed., *Proceedings of the Thirty-First Annual Convention of the National-American Woman Suffrage Association* (Warren, OH: Press of Perry, 1899), 16.

101. "Press Bureau to Friend, December 19, 1897," Garrison Family Papers, Box 109, Folder 26, Sophia Smith Collection.

102. Avery, *Proceedings of the Thirty-Second*, 24–25. Babcock reported on the success of this work a year later. Alice Stone Blackwell, ed., *Proceedings of the Thirty-Third Annual Convention of the National American Woman Suffrage Association* (Warren, OH: Press of Perry, 1901), 35.

103. Avery, *Proceedings of the Thirty-Second*, 29.

104. Avery, *Proceedings of the Thirty-Second*, 23.

105. Margaret Finnegan's *Selling Suffrage* examines the suffragists' adoption of advertising practices and a commercialized style of politics. Other works analyze the growth of advertising at the turn of the century. Finnegan, *Selling Suffrage*; *The Culture of Consumption: Critical Essays in American History, 1880–1980* (New York: Pantheon, 1983); T. J. Jackson Lears, *Fables of Abundance: A Cultural History of Advertising in America* (New York: Basic Books, 1994); Roland Marchand, *Advertising the American Dream: Making Way for Modernity, 1920–1940* (Berkeley: University of California Press, 1985); Charles McGovern, *Sold American: Consumption and Citizenship, 1890–1945* (Chapel Hill: University of North Carolina Press, 2006).

106. Catharine Esther Beecher, *Woman's Profession as Mother and Educator, with Views in Opposition to Woman Suffrage* (Philadelphia: G. Maclean, 1872), 5.

107. Beecher, *Woman's Profession*, 7.

108. Beecher, *Woman's Profession*, dedication.

109. Anne Myra Goodman Benjamin, *A History of the Anti-Suffrage Movement in the United States from 1895 to 1920: Women against Equality* (Lewiston, NY: Edwin Mellen Press, 1991), 1–42; Barbara F. Berenson, *Massachusetts in the Woman Suffrage Movement: Revolutionary Reformers* (History Press, 2018); Jane Jerome Camhi, *Women against Women: American Anti-Suffragism, 1880–1920* (Brooklyn: Carlson, 1994), 77–89; Flexner, *Century of Struggle*, 286–99; Susan Goodier, *No Votes for Women: The New York State Anti-Suffrage Movement* (Urbana: University of Illinois Press, 2012), 40–66; Graham, *Woman Suffrage and the New Democracy*, 7–22; Thomas J. Jablonsky, *The Home, Heaven, and Mother Party: Female Anti-Suffragists in the United States, 1868–1920* (Brooklyn: Carlson, 1994).

110. Keyssar, *The Right to Vote*, 365.

111. "The Massachusetts 'Referendum,'" *Remonstrance*, ca. 1896, 1, Collection Development Department, Widener Library.

112. "The Massachusetts 'Referendum,'" 1.

113. "The Massachusetts 'Referendum,'" 1; Goodier, *No Votes for Women*, 50–51; Susan E Marshall, *Splintered Sisterhood: Gender and Class in the Campaign against Woman Suffrage* (Madison: University of Wisconsin Press, 1997), 25–26.

114. Marshall, *Splintered Sisterhood*, 25.

115. "The Massachusetts 'Referendum,'" 1.

116. Scholars argue that the New Woman stemmed from the popularity of the strong female characters in literature, but do not acknowledge the root of these visual types in antisuffrage imagery. Melody Davis, "The New Woman in American Stereoviews, 1871–1905," in *The New Woman International: Representations in Pho-*

tography and Film from the 1870s through the 1960s, ed. Elizabeth Otto and Vanessa Rocco (Ann Arbor: University of Michigan Press, 2011); Melody Davis, "Doubling the Vision: Women and Narration Stereography, the United States, 1870–1910" (PhD diss., City University of New York, 2004); Elizabeth Otto and Vanessa Rocco, "Introduction: Imagining and Embodying New Womanhood," in Otto and Rocco, *The New Woman International*; Patterson, *Beyond the Gibson Girl.*

117. Davis, "Doubling the Vision," 332.

118. For additional examples, see C. H. Shrute and Son, *Woman Suffrage No. 354*, stereograph (Edgartown, MA, 1870s), Library of Congress Prints and Photographs Division; Littleton View Company, *What is Home without a Husband?* stereograph (Baltimore, 1899), Library Company of Philadelphia; Keystone View Company, *Sew on Your Own Buttons, I'm Going for a Ride*, stereograph (Meadowville, PA, 1899), Library Company of Philadelphia.

119. For a discussion of how the New Woman challenged prevailing heterosexual identities, see Carroll Smith Rosenberg, "The New Woman as Androgyne: Social Disorder and Gender Crisis, 1870–1936," in *Disorderly Conduct: Visions of Gender in Victorian America* (New York: Knopf, 1985). For more on the New Woman, see also Martha Banta, *Imaging American Women: Idea and Ideals in Cultural History* (New York: Columbia University Press, 1987); Lois W. Banner, *American Beauty* (Chicago: University of Chicago Press, 1984); Davis, "The New Woman in American Stereoviews"; Rosemary Hennessy, *Materialist Feminism and the Politics of Discourse* (New York: Routledge, 1993); Patricia Marks, *Bicycles, Bangs, and Bloomers: The New Woman in the Popular Press* (Lexington: University Press of Kentucky, 1990); Otto and Rocco, *The New Woman International*; Patterson, *Beyond the Gibson Girl.*

120. Davis, "Doubling the Vision," 342–44; Davis, "The New Woman in American Stereoviews," 31–32. For more on sexuality at the turn of the century, see Margot Canaday, *The Straight State: Sexuality and Citizenship in Twentieth-Century America* (Princeton, NJ: Princeton University Press, 2009); George Chauncey, *Gay New York: Gender, Urban Culture, and the Making of the Gay Male World, 1890–1940* (New York: Basic Books, 2008); Lillian Faderman, *Odd Girls and Twilight Lovers: A History of Lesbian Life in Twentieth-Century America* (New York: Columbia University Press, 1991); Jay Hatheway, *The Gilded Age Construction of Modern American Homophobia* (New York: Palgrave Macmillan, 2003); Leila Rupp, *A Desired Past* (Chicago: University of Chicago Press, 1999).

121. Theodore Roosevelt, "The Manly Virtues and Practical Politics," *Forum*, July 1894, 555.

122. Roosevelt, "The Manly Virtues," 555.

123. Gail Bederman, *Manliness and Civilization* (Chicago: University of Chicago Press, 1995); Kristin L. Hoganson, *Fighting for American Manhood: How Gender Politics Provoked the Spanish-American and Philippine-American Wars* (New Haven, CT: Yale University Press, 1998); Kevin P. Murphy, *Political Manhood: Red Bloods,*

Mollycoddles, and the Politics of Progressive Era Reform (New York: Columbia University Press, 2008).

124. "Cartoons and Comments," *Puck*, July 27, 1898, 7.

125. John Henry Adams, "Rough Sketches: 'The New Negro Man,'" *Voice of the Negro*, October 1904, 447.

126. Adams, "The New Negro Man," 447–52.

127. Adams, "The New Negro Man," 450–52. For more on masculinity and race during this era, see Gilmore, "Race and Manhood," in *Gender and Jim Crow*.

128. Patterson, *Beyond the Gibson Girl*, 22, 28, 32. For more on the New Woman as a visual type, see Banta, "American Girls and the New Woman," in *Imaging American Women*; Patterson, "Selling the American New Woman as Gibson Girl," in *Beyond the Gibson Girl*.

129. Charlotte Perkins Gilman, *Women and Economics: A Study of the Economic Relation between Men and Women as a Factor in Social Evolution* (Boston: Small, Maynard, 1898), 148–49.

130. For a discussion of the New Woman as an icon of change and the global implications of this visual and cultural type, see Otto and Rocco, "Introduction"; Patterson, *Beyond the Gibson*, 8.

131. John Henry Adams, "Rough Sketches: A Study of the Features of the New Negro Woman," *Voice of the Negro*, August 1904, 323–26.

132. For more on the New Negro Woman as embodied by Margaret Murray Washington, see Patterson, "Margaret Murray Washington." Examples of Terrell's public portraits include *Mrs. Mary Church Terrell*, in *Colored American*, August 13, 1904, 1; *Mrs. Mary Church Terrell*, in *Afro-American Ledger*, April 15, 1905, 1; *Noted Colored Women Coming to Detroit to Attend Convention*, in *Detroit Free Press*, June 29, 1906, 2; *Mary Church Terrell* (Rochester: Central P&E, ca. 1900s), Mary Church Terrell Papers, Box 102-14, Folder 265, Moorland-Spingarn Research Center, Howard University; *'The Bright Side of a Dark Subject' Discussed by Mrs. Mary C. Terrell*, 1907, Mary Church Terrell Papers, Reel 29, Library of Congress.

133. Adams, "The New Negro Man."

134. Mary Church Terrell, "The International Congress of Women," *Voice of the Negro*, October 1904, 453–61, Howard University Box 102–5, Folder 140.

135. Terrell, *A Colored Woman*, 200.

136. "Light on Life in Germany," *Washington Post*, July 19, 1904, 6.

137. Terrell, *A Colored Woman*, 204–5.

138. For more on the rise of New Negro Womanhood in the 1890s, see Lindsey, *Colored No More*.

139. Carl F. Kaestle and Janice A. Radway, "A Framework for the History of Publishing and Reading in the United States, 1880–1940," in *Print in Motion: The Expansion of Publishing and Reading in the United States, 1880–1940*, ed. Kaestle and Radway, vol. 4 of *A History of the Book in America* (Chapel Hill: University of North Carolina Press, 2009), 13; Megan Benton, "Unruly Servants: Machines, Modernity, and the Printed Page," in Kaestle and Radway, *Print in Motion*, 155.

CHAPTER SIX

1. Alice Paul, *Conversations with Alice Paul: Woman Suffrage and the Equal Rights Amendment*, ed. Amelia Fry (Berkeley: University of California Berkeley, 1976), 72–73.

2. Paul, *Conversations*, 52–53, 56–57.

3. Paul, *Conversations*, 72–73.

4. "Women Win in House," *Washington Post*, March 2, 1913, 7.

5. Belinda A. Stillion Southard, "Mimesis and Political Ritual: The National Woman Suffrage Parade," in *Militant Citizenship: Rhetorical Strategies of the National Woman's Party, 1913–1920* (College Station: Texas A&M University Press, 2011).

6. Paul, *Conversations*, 329.

7. Paul, *Conversations*, 34–39, 48. For more on American suffragists who worked with British suffragists, see Jane S. Gabin, "Suffrage and Suffering: The American Woman Responds," in *American Women in Gilded Age London: Expatriates Rediscovered* (Gainesville: University Press of Florida, 2006).

8. For more on the Women's Social and Political Union, see Barbara Green, *Spectacular Confessions: Autobiography, Performative Activism, and the Sites of Suffrage, 1905–1938* (New York: St. Martin's Press, 1997); Laura E. Nym Mayhall, *The Militant Suffrage Movement: Citizenship and Resistance in Britain, 1860–1930* (New York: Oxford University Press, 2003); Lisa Tickner, *The Spectacle of Women: Imagery of the Suffrage Campaign, 1907–14* (London: Chatto & Windus, 1987).

9. Carl F. Kaestle and Janice A. Radway, eds., *Print in Motion: The Expansion of Publishing and Reading in the United States, 1880–1940*, vol. 4 of *A History of the Book in America* (Chapel Hill: University of North Carolina Press, 2009), 12, 152–55.

10. For more on Addams, see Victoria Brown, *The Education of Jane Addams* (Philadelphia: University of Pennsylvania Press, 2004); Maurice Hamington, ed., *Feminist Interpretations of Jane Addams* (University Park: Pennsylvania State University Press, 2010); Louise W. Knight, *Citizen: Jane Addams and the Struggle for Democracy* (Chicago: University of Chicago Press, 2005); Louise W. Knight, *Jane Addams: Spirit in Action* (New York: W. W. Norton, 2010).

11. Jane Addams, "Women and Public Housekeeping" (National Woman Suffrage Publishing, early twentieth century), Suffrage Collection, Box 5, Folder 9, Sophia Smith Collection. NAWSA printed flyers with excerpts from an article Addams wrote for the generally antisuffrage *Ladies' Home Journal*. NAWSA also reprinted the *Ladies' Home Journal* article as a booklet and sold it for ten cents per dozen. Jane Addams, "Why Women Should Vote" (National Woman Suffrage Publishing, 1910s), Suffrage Collection, Box 5, Folder 10, Sophia Smith Collection.

12. Jessica Derleth, "'Kneading Politics': Cookery and the American Woman Suffrage Movement," *Journal of the Gilded Age and Progressive Era* 17, no. 3 (2018): 450–74.

13. For a discussion on the effectiveness of the expediency or public housekeep-

ing arguments in comparison to the justice argument, see Holly J. McCammon, Lyndi Hewitt, and Sandy Smith, "'No Weapon Save Argument': Strategic Frame Amplification in the U.S. Woman Suffrage Movements," *Sociological Quarterly* 45, no. 3 (2004): 529–56. For more on the intellectual history of the justice and expediency arguments, see Eleanor Flexner, *Century of Struggle: The Woman's Rights Movement in the United States,* reprint ed. (Cambridge, MA: Belknap, 1996); Sara Hunter Graham, *Woman Suffrage and the New Democracy* (New Haven, CT: Yale University Press, 1996); Aileen S. Kraditor, *The Ideas of the Woman Suffrage Movement, 1890–1920* (New York: Columbia University Press, 1965); Suzanne Marilley, *Woman Suffrage and the Origins of Liberal Feminism in the United States, 1820–1920* (Cambridge, MA: Harvard University Press, 1996).

14. For more on the California suffragists' publicity campaign, see the Alice Park Papers at the Huntington Library, as well as Susan Englander, *Class Coalition and Class Conflict in the California Woman Suffrage Movement, 1907–1912: The San Francisco Wage Earners' Suffrage League* (San Francisco: Mellen Research University Press, 1992); Gayle Ann Gullett, *Becoming Citizens: The Emergence and Development of the California Women's Movement, 1880–1911* (Urbana: University of Illinois Press, 2000); Rebecca Mead, *How the Vote Was Won: Woman Suffrage in the Western United States, 1868–1914* (New York: New York University Press, 2004); Selina Solomons, *How We Won the Vote in California* (San Francisco: New Woman Publishing, 1912); Ann Marie Wilson et al., *California Women and Politics from the Gold Rush to the Great Depression* (Lincoln: University of Nebraska Press, 2011); Una Richardson Winter, *Alice Park of California: Worker for Woman Suffrage and for Children's Rights* (Upland, CA: Susan B. Anthony Memorial Committee of California, 1948).

15. See, for example, "Catalogue and Price List" (National Woman Suffrage Publishing, 1917), Suffrage Collection, Box 5, Folder 10, Sophia Smith Collection. For more on NAWSA's catalogs and the items they sold, see Margaret Mary Finnegan, "From Sunflower Badges to Kewpie Dolls: Woman Suffrage Commodities and the Embrace of Consumer Capitalism," in *Selling Suffrage: Consumer Culture and Votes for Women* (New York: Columbia University Press, 1999).

16. Corinne Field provides a deeper discussion of the ways age shaped the public image of the suffrage movement in *Grand Old Women and Modern Girls: Generational and Racial Conflict in the US Women's Rights Movement, 1870–1920,* forthcoming.

17. For more on the ways that elite New York women influenced the movement's public face, see Johanna Neuman, *Gilded Suffragists: The New York Socialites Who Fought for Women's Right to Vote* (New York: Washington Mews, 2017).

18. Jacqueline Van Voris, *Carrie Chapman Catt: A Public Life* (New York: Feminist Press at CUNY, 1996), 33. "Only Yesterday," incomplete typescript, Carrie Chapman Catt Papers, Sophia Smith Collection.

19. "Minutes of the Fourth Biennial of the National Association of Colored Women," 1906, 8–9, National Association of Colored Women's Clubs Papers (microfilm).

20. "Minutes of the Eighth Biennial of the National Association of Colored Women," 1912, 48, 61, National Association of Colored Women's Clubs Papers (microfilm).

21. Anne Myra Goodman Benjamin, *A History of the Anti-Suffrage Movement in the United States from 1895 to 1920: Women against Equality* (Lewiston, NY: Edwin Mellen Press, 1991); Jane Jerome Camhi, *Women against Women: American Anti-Suffragism, 1880–1920* (Brooklyn: Carlson, 1994); Flexner, *Century of Struggle*, 286–99; Graham, *Woman Suffrage and the New Democracy*, 7–22; Elna Green, *Southern Strategies: Southern Women and the Woman Suffrage Question* (Chapel Hill: University of North Carolina Press, 1997); Thomas J. Jablonsky, *The Home, Heaven, and Mother Party: Female Anti-Suffragists in the United States, 1868–1920* (Brooklyn: Carlson, 1994).

22. Benjamin, "Not Officially Connected," in *A History of the Anti-Suffrage Movement*; Camhi, "Antisuffrage Allies," in *Women against Women*; Flexner, *Century of Struggle*, 286–97; Green, "Origins of the Southern Antisuffrage Movement," in *Southern Strategies*; Jablonsky, "Friends and Associates," in *The Home, Heaven, and Mother Party*.

23. Camhi, "Antisuffrage Assumptions Regarding Woman's Sphere and Anti-suffrage Theories of Government," in *Women against Women*; Graham, *Woman Suffrage and the New Democracy*, 12–21.

24. Alice Sheppard, *Cartooning for Suffrage* (Albuquerque: University of New Mexico Press, 1994), 89.

25. Laura R. Prieto, *At Home in the Studio: The Professionalization of Women Artists in America* (Cambridge, MA: Harvard University Press, 2001), 175. For an example of a prosuffrage cartoon, see Laura Foster, *Dreaming Dreams No Mortal Ever Dared Dream Before*, in *Life*, February 5, 1914.

26. Sheppard, "Becoming a Suffrage Cartoonist," in *Cartooning for Suffrage*. For more on female illustrators, including Laura Foster, see Martha H. Kennedy, *Drawn to Purpose: American Women Illustrators and Cartoonists* (Jackson: University Press of Mississippi, 2018).

27. Paul, *Conversations*, 45.

28. A scrapbook of newspaper clippings, presumably created by a British suffragist, presents a glimpse of their demonstrations and the illustrated newspaper coverage of them. *Votes for Women: A Picture Book of the Campaign during Recent Years Compiled Principally from Newspaper Photography*, 1930/1907, Fawcett Library Scrapbooks and Press Cuttings, Box 10/04, Women's Library; Sandie Brothers, *Mrs. Drummond opposite the Terrace of the House of Commons Addressing M.P.'s, Inviting Them to the Hyde Park Demonstration*, June 21, 1908, Postcards, Box 3, Demonstrations, England, Women's Library.

29. J. D. Zahniser and Amelia R. Fry, *Alice Paul: Claiming Power* (New York: Oxford University Press, 2014), 96–97.

30. See, for example, portrait postcards of suffrage leaders such as Charlotte Despard, Flora Drummond, Emmeline Pankhurst, Christabel Pankhurst, Sylvia

Pankhurst, Emmeline Pethick-Lawrence, and others circulated by their respective organizations at the Women's Library. See imagery by the Suffrage Atelier or the Artists' Suffrage League for examples of prosuffrage cartoons, including JHD, *Young New Zealand Cartoon* (Artists' Suffrage League, circa 1910), Postcards, Box 2, Women's Library. For examples of mocking imagery of suffragists comparable to that in the United States, see *Votes for Women—While in the Act of Voting Mrs. Jones Remembers That She Has Left a Cake in the Oven!* (J. Salmon, ca. 1913), Postcards, Box 2, Women's Library; *At the Suffragette Meetings You Can Hear Some Plain Things—And See Them Too!* (ca. 1910), Postcards, Box 2, Women's Library; *Is Your Wife a Suffragette?* (Eustace Watkins, ca. 1910), Postcards, Box 2, Women's Library. For more on the visual culture of British suffragists, see Colleen Denney, *The Visual Culture of Women's Activism in London, Paris and Beyond: An Analytical Art History, 1860 to the Present* (Jefferson, NC: McFarland, 2018); Miranda Garnett and Zoë Thomas, eds., *Suffrage and the Arts: Visual Culture, Politics, and Enterprise* (London: Bloomsbury, 2018); Tickner, *The Spectacle of Women.*

31. For more on the symbolism of Joan of Arc and Florence Nightingale for British suffragettes, see Denney, "Allegory in Suffrage Propaganda," in *The Visual Culture of Women's Activism*; Mayhall, "Embodying Citizenship, 1908–1914," in *The Militant Suffrage Movement.*

32. *Press Reports of the Banners Designed by The Artists' Suffrage League* (Vacher & Sons, ca. 1908), Records of the Artists' Suffrage League, Women's Library. For an example of an image of this parade in the news, see Max Cowper, *The Woman Militant: The Great Suffragist Procession,* in *Illustrated London News,* June 20, 1908, 893, 904. Women's Social and Political Union leader Sylvia Pankhurst collected press pictures of this parade and other suffragist spectacles in Sylvia Pankhurst, *The Suffragette* (New York: Sturgis and Walton, 1911).

33. I.N.F., "Big Suffrage Parade," *New York Tribune,* June 14, 1908. The article was cut and pasted into a scrapbook. *Woman Suffrage in Great Britain: With particular reference to British militants,* book 1, p. 10, Massachusetts Historical Society.

34. "Rows Hurt Cause of Suffragettes," *Chicago Tribune,* October 18, 1908. The article was cut and pasted into a scrapbook. *Woman Suffrage in Great Britain: With particular reference to British militants,* book 1, p. 12, Massachusetts Historical Society.

35. "Mrs. Catt Disapproves," *New York Times,* April 26, 1909, 1. The article was cut and pasted into a scrapbook. See also *Woman Suffrage in Great Britain: with particular reference to British militants,* book 1, Massachusetts Historical Society.

36. Ellen Carol DuBois, "Working Women, Class Relations, and Suffrage Militance: Harriot Stanton Blatch and the New York Woman Suffrage Movement, 1894–1909," *Journal of American History* 74, no. 1 (1987): 34; Ellen Carol DuBois, *Harriot Stanton Blatch and the Winning of Woman Suffrage* (New Haven, CT: Yale University Press, 1997).

37. Women supported the group but were not allowed to march with the men. Carlos A. Schwantes, "Western Women in Coxey's Army in 1894," *Arizona and the West* 26, no. 1 (1984): 5–20.

38. Stillion Southard, *Militant Citizenship*, 62.

39. The Leet Brothers also printed a postcard with a halftone of Milholland on it. Three years after the march, Milholland died giving a suffrage speech and became a martyr for the cause. Suffragists commemorated her with a lithographed poster of her as a herald. "Inez Milholland Boissevain Who Died for the Freedom of Women," 1916, Alice Paul Papers, Schlesinger Library on the History of Women in America; Leet Brothers, *Miss Inez Milholland, Herald* (March 3, 1913), Ellen A. Webster Papers, Schlesinger Library on the History of Women in America.

40. Stillion Southard, *Militant Citizenship*, 62.

41. "5,000 of Fair Sex Ready to Parade," *Washington Post*, March 3, 1913, 1; "Vote an Aid to Beauty," *Washington Post*, March 3, 1913, 10; Ann Marie Nicolosi, "'The Most Beautiful Suffragette': Inez Milholland and the Political Currency of Beauty," *Journal of the Gilded Age and Progressive Era* 6, no. 3 (2007): 286–309.

42. "Vote an Aid to Beauty," 10.

43. For a detailed discussion of the sections of the parade and comparisons between the suffrage parade and the inaugural parade, see Stillion Southard, "Mimesis and Political Ritual: The National Woman Suffrage Parade," in *Militant Citizenship*.

44. For more on the significance of women and suffragists claiming public spaces, see DuBois, "Working Women"; Marianne Hansen, "Suffrage Pageants and Parades: Fashioning a Central and Socially Integrated Identity," in *Re-Framing Representations of Women: Figuring, Fashioning, Portraiting, and Telling in the "Picturing" Women Project* (Burlington, VT: Ashgate, 2008), 61–68; Holly J. McCammon, "'Out of the Parlors and into the Streets': The Changing Tactical Repertoire of the U.S. Women's Suffrage Movements," *Social Forces* 81, no. 3 (2003): 787–818; Mary P. Ryan, *Women in Public: Between Banners and Ballots, 1825–1880* (Baltimore: Johns Hopkins University Press, 1990); Stillion Southard, "Mimesis and Political Ritual." For more on photographs of suffrage pageants and parades collected by Carrie Chapman Catt, see Hansen, "Suffrage Pageants and Parades," 61–68.

45. Stillion Southard, *Militant Citizenship*, 87.

46. Kaestle and Radway, "A Framework for the History of Publishing and Reading in the United States, 1880–1940," in *Print in Motion*, 13; Michael Winship, "The Rise of a National Book Trade System in the United States," in Kaestle and Radway, *Print in Motion*, 76.

47. "Women Protest against the Treatment Accorded Them by the Washington Police," *San Jose Mercury*, March 10, 1913, Susan B. Anthony Memorial Collection, Huntington Library.

48. John T. McCutcheon, "In the Nation's Spot Light," *Chicago Daily Tribune*, March 4, 1913, 1.

49. "Woman's Beauty, Grace, and Art Bewilder the Capital, Miles of Fluttering Femininity Present Entrancing Suffrage Appeal," *Washington Post*, March 4, 1913, 1.

50. "Women's Beauty, Grace, and Art."

51. "Race Barrier Is Up: Suffragist Army May Abandon Its March Today If Colored Women Join It," *Washington Post*, February 27, 1913, 1.

52. Graham, *Woman Suffrage and the New Democracy*, 21–25.

53. Margaret Murray Washington, "National Association of Colored Women's Clubs," *National Notes*, June 1913, 7, National Association of Colored Women's Clubs Papers (microfilm). Given the June date and Washington's specificity about the March 3 parade, *Notes* likely reproduced a speech given by Washington earlier that year, which was a common practice.

54. Brittney C. Cooper, "'Proper, Dignified Agitation': The Evolution of Mary Church Terrell," in *Beyond Respectability: The Intellectual Thought of Race Women* (Urbana: University of Illinois Press, 2017).

55. Winsor McCay, "Suffrage March Line—How Thousands of Women Parade Today at Capitol," *New York Evening Journal*, March 4, 1913; Treva B. Lindsey, *Colored No More: Reinventing Black Womanhood in Washington, D.C.* (Urbana: University of Illinois Press, 2017), 103–4.

56. Mary Church Terrell, *A Colored Woman in a White World* (Washington, DC: Ransdell, 1940), 252; Zahniser and Fry, *Alice Paul*, 141–42.

57. Lindsey, *Colored No More*, 105. See the rest of the chapter "Performing and Politicizing 'Ladyhood': Black Washington Women and New Negro Suffrage Activism" for additional analysis of race and suffrage in Washington, DC, during that era.

58. Stillion Southard, *Militant Citizenship*, 84–85.

59. *[Ida B. Wells in Washington, DC Parade]*, in *Chicago Defender*, March 22, 1913.

60. For a similar cartoon, see Boardman Robinson, *Just Like the Men*, in *New York Tribune*, March 1, 1913.

61. The Library of Congress Prints and Photographs Division holds the Bain News Service Collection of photographs of the 1913 parade.

62. For more on the Congressional Union and NWP, see Nancy Cott, *The Grounding of Modern Feminism* (New Haven, CT: Yale University Press, 1987); Stillion Southard, *Militant Citizenship*.

63. Ida Husted Harper, ed., *History of Woman Suffrage*, vol. 5 (New York: J. J. Little & Ives, 1922; Salem, NH: Ayer, 1985; citations refer to the 1985 edition), 455–57.

64. Flexner, *Century of Struggle*, 272–75; Graham, *Woman Suffrage and the New Democracy*, 89–93.

65. The publicity and art publicity committees gave their first reports at annual meetings in 1914 and 1916, respectively. Harper, *History of Woman Suffrage*, 5:372, 405; Hannah J. Patterson, ed., *The Handbook of the National American Woman Suffrage Association and Proceedings of the Forty-Eighth Annual Convention* (New York: National Woman Suffrage Publishing, 1916), 118.

66. Patterson, *Proceedings of the Forty-Eighth Annual Convention*, 139; Harper, *History of Woman Suffrage*, 5:494.

67. "Literary," *American Educational Review: A Monthly Review of the Progress of*

Higher Education 31, no. 9 (1910): 570. See also the original article, "The Gentle Art of Publicity," *Colliers* 45, no. 17 (1910).

68. Mary Walton, *A Woman's Crusade: Alice Paul and the Battle for the Ballot* (New York: Macmillan, 2010), 156.

69. Harper, *History of Woman Suffrage*, 5:418.

70. Italics in original. Patterson, *Proceedings of the Forty-Eighth Annual Convention*, 141.

71. Patterson, *Proceedings of the Forty-Eighth Annual Convention*, 149–50.

72. Patterson, *Proceedings of the Forty-Eighth Annual Convention*, 150–51.

73. Mariea Caudill Dennison, "Babies for Suffrage: 'The Exhibition of Painting and Sculpture by Women Artists for the Benefit of the Woman Suffrage Campaign,'" *Woman's Art Journal* 24, no. 2 (2003): 24–30; Cathleen Nista Rauterkus, "Madonna and Child," in *Go Get Mother's Picket Sign: Crossing Spheres with the Material Culture of Suffrage* (Lanham, MD: University Press of America, 2010).

74. For more on Rose O'Neill, see Kennedy, *Drawn to Purpose*, 29–30, 111–13.

75. "A Note to Our Suffrage Friends," *Puck*, February 20, 1915, 3.

76. For more on Blanche Ames' suffrage advocacy and her cartoons, see Anne Biller Clark, "The Mighty Pen," in *My Dear Mrs. Ames: A Study of Suffragist Cartoonist Blanche Ames Ames* (New York: Peter Lang, 2001).

77. Blanche Ames, *Double the Power of the Home—Two Good Votes Are Better Than One*, in *Boston Transcript*, September 1915, 335; Kenneth Florey, *Women's Suffrage Memorabilia: An Illustrated Historical Study* (Jefferson, NC: McFarland, 2013), 150. For more on the *Woman's Journal*'s comments on artists Ames and Fredrikke Palmer, see Agnes E. Ryan, *The Torch Bearer: A Look Forward and Back at the Woman's Journal, the Organ of the Woman's Movement* (Woman's Journal and Suffrage News, 1916), 31.

78. An early copy of the image includes text written in pencil, presumably by Ames, promoting the November 2, 1915, New York vote on women's suffrage. Blanche Ames, *Vote Yes on Suffrage, Nov. 2. Double the Power of the Home—Two Good Votes Are Better Than One* (1915), Ames Family Papers, Oversize Drawer 28, Sophia Smith Collection.

79. Rachel Foster Avery, ed., *Proceedings of the Thirty-Second Annual Convention of the National American Woman Suffrage Association* (Philadelphia: Alfred J. Ferris, 1900), 23.

80. *Annual Report of the New York State Suffrage Association*, 1915, 157, Suffrage Collection, Box 12, Folder 4, Sophia Smith Collection.

81. J. Banks, "Anti-Suffragist off to Lecture on 'Why Women Should Stay at Home,'" *Woman Voter*, February 1912, 8.

82. "Charles Heaslip to Mrs. Dunbar, September 18, 1916," Manuscript Division, National American Woman Suffrage Association Papers, Box 1, Reel 1, Library of Congress.

83. Katherine D. Tillman, "Report of the Public Posters and Prints Department,"

National Notes, 1914, 18–20, National Association of Colored Women's Clubs Papers (microfilm).

84. *Woman's Suffrage Number*, in *Crisis*, September 1912.

85. "Minutes from the Biennial Meeting of the National Association of Colored Women," 1914, 31, National Association of Colored Women's Clubs Papers (microfilm).

86. In 1902, Courtner's painting burned in a fire. J. S. Jackson painted a new one, based on photographs of it in 1913. Although the *Crisis* notes the composite photograph was by journalist Hinton Gilmore, it is more likely based on a photograph of the original painting or a second version painted in 1913. See Kathleen Collins, "Shadow and Substance: Sojourner Truth," *History of Photography* 7, no. 3 (1983): 192–93.

87. The text also references Wilmington, North Carolina, where in 1898 white supremacists violently drove black people from the city and took over the city's government. John Henry Adams suggests that even if people of color play by the rules, they will be subject to discrimination and violence.

88. John Henry Adams, "Woman to the Rescue," *Crisis*, May 1916. For more analysis of this image and other art in the *Crisis*, see Anne Elizabeth Carroll, *Word, Image, and the New Negro: Representation and Identity in the Harlem Renaissance* (Bloomington: Indiana University Press, 2005); Amy Helene Kirschke, "DuBois and 'The Crisis' Magazine: Imaging Women and Family," *Source: Notes in the History of Art* 24, no. 4 (2005): 35–45; Amy Helene Kirschke, *Art in Crisis: W. E. B. Du Bois and the Struggle for African American Identity and Memory* (Bloomington: Indiana University Press, 2007); Jenny Woodley, *Art for Equality—The NAACP's Cultural Campaign for Civil Rights* (Lexington: University Press of Kentucky, 2014).

89. Crisis Publishing, *Men of the Month* (Baltimore: Crisis Publishing, 1912), 223.

90. Mary Church Terrell, "The Justice of Woman Suffrage," *Crisis*, September 1912, 243.

91. Adella Hunt Logan, "Colored Women as Voters," *Crisis*, September 1912, 242–43.

92. *Minutes of the Eighth Biennial Convention of the National Association of Colored Women*, 1912, 48; Logan, "Colored Women as Voters," 243.

93. The map, entitled *Votes for Women*, was sold by the California Equal Suffrage Headquarters during or after 1908. The original is in the Sophia Smith Collection's United States Suffrage Series and was reprinted in Robert Cooney, *Winning the Vote: The Triumph of the American Woman Suffrage Movement* (Santa Cruz, CA: American Graphic Press, 2005), 85.

94. *Annual Report of the New York State Suffrage Association*, 25.

95. NAWSA's catalog from that year includes the same descriptions of the materials for sale. "Catalogue and Price List." Ethel Hall, "Letter from Ethel Hall to Suffragists," June 23, 1917, Papers of Portia Willis Fitzgerald, Box 1, Folder 7, Sophia Smith Collection.

96. See, for example, *Nevada Women's Street-Banner, 1914, Showing "the Black*

Spot," from the Carrie Chapman Catt Photo Albums at Bryn Mawr College, and a window display in *Congressional Union for Woman's Suffrage National Summer Headquarters*, 1914, Library of Congress Prints and Photographs Division. Both are reproduced in Cooney, *Winning the Vote*, 237, 244–45.

97. Mrs. Medill McCormick, "Statement," February 3, 1914, Papers of the National American Woman Suffrage Association, microfilm reel 33, Library of Congress.

98. "National Demonstration, May 2d and 9th," *Suffragist*, February 14, 1914, 3, Nineteenth Century Collections Online.

99. Paul, *Conversations*, 189–90; Cott, *The Grounding of Modern Feminism*, 55–57; Sylvia D. Hoffert, *Alva Vanderbilt Belmont: Unlikely Champion of Women's Rights* (Bloomington: Indiana University Press, 2012); Joan Marie Johnson, *Funding Feminism: Monied Women, Philanthropy, and the Women's Movement, 1870–1967* (Chapel Hill: University of North Carolina Press, 2017). For more on Alva Belmont and the influence of New York socialites on the suffrage movement, see Neuman, *Gilded Suffragists*.

100. Jewish, Chinese, and other immigrant groups formed their own associations and worked within the organizations when they could. Melissa R. Klapper, *Ballots, Babies, and Banners of Peace: American Jewish Women's Activism, 1890–1940* (New York: New York University Press, 2013); Marilley, "Race and Nativism in the Woman Suffrage Movement," in *Woman Suffrage and the Origins of Liberal Feminism*.

101. Boldface in original. *One Marcher in Line Is Worth Ten Petitions in the Waste Basket*, 1916, flyer, published by NAWSA, Suffrage Collection, Sophia Smith Collection. The illustration circulated on flyers, in NAWSA's *Headquarters Newsletter*, and in the *Woman's Journal*. "Planks for Women. On to Chicago and Saint Louis. (Courtesy Headquarters Newsletter)," *Woman's Journal*, May 6, 1916, 145, Ames Family Papers, Box 94, Folder 10, Sophia Smith Collection.

102. "A Peek at Organized Publicity," *Headquarters Newsletter*, June 22, 1916, 3.

103. See the Alice Park Papers at the Huntington Library. Her papers include correspondence, especially about the 1911 California suffrage campaign, as well as a variety of visual material used in the campaign (much of which she designed and distributed).

104. George Morris, "Clothing Wet, Ardor Undampened, 5,000 Women March," *Chicago Daily Tribune*, June 8, 1916, 17.

105. Journalists used similar language to describe the 1913 parade as well. See, for example, "Suffrage Invasion Is on in Earnest," *New York Times*, March 2, 1913, 15; "Suffragists Take City for Pageant," *Washington Post*, March 2, 1913, 1; "Suffrage Pageant Today's Spectacle," *Boston Daily Globe*, March 3, 1913, 1.

106. "Ten Thousand Plucky Women Marching in the Cold Rain," *Chicago American*, June 8, 1916; "The Suffrage Victory," *Chicago Herald*, June 9, 1916. Both articles were reprinted in the June 22, 1916, issue of the *Headquarters Newsletter*, 8–9.

107. Heaslip left two months later, and the NWP hired a woman in his place.

Unlike NAWSA, they seem to have preferred have women in these roles. "Charles Heaslip to Alice Paul, January 1917," Alice Paul Papers, Schlesinger Library; Walton, *A Woman's Crusade*, 156–57.

108. *National Association Notes*, January 1917, 11, Neighborhood Union Collection, Box 8, Robert W. Woodruff Library of the Atlanta University Center, Inc.

109. M. S. Pearson, "The Home," *National Association Notes*, January 1917, 11, Neighborhood Union Collection, Box 8, Robert W. Woodruff Library of the Atlanta University Center, Inc.

110. Mary Church Terrell, *A Colored Woman in a White World* (Amherst: Humanity Books, 2005), 355.

111. Address Delivered at Joint Session of the Two Houses of Congress. U.S. 65th Congress, 1st Session, Senate Document 5, April 2, 1917.

112. Mayhall, *The Militant Suffrage Movement*; Angela K. Smith, *Suffrage Discourse in Britain during the First World War* (Burlington, VT: Ashgate, 2005).

113. "Carrie Chapman Catt to Alice Paul, May 24, 1917," Papers of the National American Woman Suffrage Association, microfilm reel 33, Library of Congress.

114. "Carrie Chapman Catt and Mr. James P. Hornaday, May 24, 1917," Papers of the National American Woman Suffrage Association, microfilm reel 33, Library of Congress.

115. For a discussion of the split among suffragists regarding the war effort and related imagery, see Rachel Schreiber, "She Will Spike War's Gun: Suffrage Citizenship and War," in *Gender and Activism in a Little Magazine: The Modern Figures of the Masses* (Burlington, VT: Ashgate, 2011); Rachel Schreiber, "'She Will Spike War's Gun': The Anti-War Graphic Satire of the American Suffrage Press," in *Modern Print Activism in the United States* (Burlington, VT: Ashgate, 2013).

116. "First Spoils of 'War,'" *Chicago Tribune*, August 19, 1917, 3.

117. Underwood and Underwood, *Suffrage Pickets, Just Freed from Imprisonment, in the Jail Garb*, in *Boston Daily Globe*, November 10, 1917, 14; Underwood and Underwood, *Prison Styles for Washington Suffragists*, in *Chicago Daily Tribune*, November 19, 1917, 5; Underwood and Underwood, *How the Suffragettes Look after Their Jail Terms*, in *Los Angeles Daily Times*, November 14, 1917, 4.

118. For a collection of cartoons from the *Suffragist*, see Sheppard, *Cartooning for Suffrage*.

119. For more on the National Association of Colored Women's efforts during World War I, see Nikki Brown, *Private Politics and Public Voices: Black Women's Activism from World War I to the New Deal* (Bloomington: Indiana University Press, 2006).

120. For a record of the Commission's activities, see Rose Young, *The Record of the Leslie Woman Suffrage Commission, Inc., 1917–1929* (New York: Leslie Woman Suffrage Commission, 1929).

121. For more on Leslie and her donation, see Johnson, *Funding Feminism*, 39, 72–79.

NOTES TO PAGES 205–213 : 279

122. "Call Issued for Farmerettes to Save Nation's Corn Crop," *Washington Post*, April 21, 1918, 8.

123. See also Susan A. Brewer, *Why America Fights: Patriotism and War Propaganda from the Philippines to Iraq* (New York: Oxford University Press, 2009); Brett Gary, *The Nervous Liberals: Propaganda Anxieties from World War I to the Cold War* (New York: Columbia University Press, 1999); Pearl James, *Picture This: World War I Posters and Visual Culture* (Lincoln: University of Nebraska Press, 2009); Celia Malone Kingsbury, *For Home and Country: World War I Propaganda on the Home Front* (Lincoln: University of Nebraska Press, 2010).

124. See, for example, Lawrence Wilbur, *Join! Yesterday-Today-Always—The Greatest Mother*, lithograph poster, ca. 1917, New York: Snyder & Black, Inc., Library of Congress; and Stanley Brothers, "Little Red Cross Mother, You're the Greatest Mother of All," sheet music, 1918, Library of Congress.

125. "Wilson Backs Amendment for Woman Suffrage," *New York Times*, January 10, 1918, 1.

126. Woodrow Wilson, "Address to the Senate on the 19th Amendment," September 30, 1918.

127. For more on the ratification process in Tennessee, see Elaine Weiss, *The Woman's Hour: The Great Fight to Win the Vote* (New York: Viking, 2018).

128. Ida Husted Harper, ed., *History of Woman Suffrage*, vol. 6 (New York: J. J. Little & Ives, 1922; Salem, NH: Ayer, 1985; citations refer to the 1985 edition), 624.

129. Brown, "National Party Politics through the Depression," in *Private Politics and Public Voices*; Liette Gidlow, "The Sequel: The Fifteenth Amendment, The Nineteenth Amendment, and Southern Black Women's Struggle to Vote," *Journal of the Gilded Age and Progressive Era* 17, no. 3 (2018): 433–49; Glenda Gilmore, *Gender and Jim Crow: Women and the Politics of White Supremacy in North Carolina, 1896–1920* (Chapel Hill: University of North Carolina Press, 1996).

130. "Ida Husted Harper to Elizabeth C. Carter, March 18, 1919," Mary Church Terrell Papers (microfilm), Reel 4, Library of Congress.

131. "Walter White to Mary Church Terrell, March 14, 1919," Mary Church Terrell Papers (microfilm), Reel 4, Library of Congress.

132. "Mary Church Terrell, 1920," Mary Church Terrell Papers (microfilm), Reel 17, Library of Congress.

133. Martha Patterson, *Beyond the Gibson Girl: Reimagining the American New Woman, 1895–1915* (Chicago: University of Illinois Press, 2005), 22, 28.

EPILOGUE

1. Kateri Akiwenzie-Damm et al., *Together We Rise: Behind the Scenes at the Protest Heard Round the World* (New York: Dey Street, 2018), 84.

2. *Women's March on Washington Alternate Design*, CustomInk, January 2017, https://www.booster.com/real-faces-of-the-womens-march-on-washington.

3. Akiwenzie-Damm et al., *Together We Rise*, 89.

4. *Why We March: Signs of Protest and Hope—Voices from the Women's March* (New York: Artisan, 2017); *Why I March: Images from the Woman's March around the World* (New York: Harry N. Abrams, 2017).

5. Will Drabold, "Read Michelle Obama's Emotional Speech at the Convention," *Time*, July 25, 2016, http://time.com/4421538/democratic-convention-michelle -obama-transcript/.

6. "Nebraska Lawmaker Quits after Tweet about Women's March Protesters Sparks Outrage," *Los Angeles Times*, January 25, 2017, http://www.latimes.com /nation/nationnow/la-na-nebraska-state-legislator-resigns-tweet-20170125-story .html.

7. Filip Bondy, "How Vital Are Women? This Town Found Out as They Left to March," *New York Times*, January 22, 2017, https://nyti.ms/2kfLQJM.

8. Annie Kelly, "The Housewives of White Supremacy," *New York Times*, June 8, 2018, https://nyti.ms/2xAMnkW.

9. Ida Husted Harper and Susan B. Anthony, eds., *History of Woman Suffrage*, vol. 4 (Indianapolis: Hollenbeck, 1902; Salem, NH: Ayer, 1985; citations refer to the 1985 edition), 223.

10. Mary Beard suggests redefining power structures instead of women. Fresh imagery would be part of this redefinition. Mary Beard, "Women in Power," in *Women and Power: A Manifesto* (London: Profile Books, 2017), 82–87.

BIBLIOGRAPHY

ARCHIVAL COLLECTIONS

American Antiquarian Society
    David Claypoole Johnston Family Collection

Boston Athenaeum
    Genre Prints

The Huntington Library
    Alice (Locke) Park Papers
    Anthony Family Collection
    Caroline Severance Papers
    Clara Bewick Colby Papers
    Elizabeth Boynton Harbert Papers
    Susan B. Anthony Ephemera Collection
    Susan B. Anthony Memorial Library
    Una Richardson Winter Papers

Kansas Museum of History
    Henrietta Briggs-Wall, *American Woman and Her Political Peers*, research file

Lamont Library, Harvard University
    National Association of Colored Women's Clubs Papers (microfilm)

Library Company of Philadelphia
    American Celebrities Album
    James Barton Longacre Collection
    John Cheney Wells Collection
    New Woman Stereographs
    Political Cartoons Collection

Library of Congress
    Bain Collection, Women's Suffrage Movement in the United States
    Blackwell Family Papers
    Elizabeth Cady Stanton Papers
    Mary Church Terrell Papers
    Matilda Joslyn Gage Scrapbook
    Men's League for Woman Suffrage Scrapbook

National American Woman Suffrage Association Papers
National Photo Company Collection
News Photographs, 1912–1920, Relating to U.S. Woman Suffrage
People and Activities of the National Woman's Party 1884–ca. 1965
Photographs and Postcards of the Women's Suffrage Procession Held in
    Washington, D.C. on March 3rd and April 7th, 1913
Scenes from a Tableau Held on the Treasury Steps in Washington, D.C.,
    in Conjunction with the Women's Suffrage Procession on March 3, 1913
Susan B. Anthony Papers
Woman Suffrage Movement in Great Britain Collection

Massachusetts Historical Society
Massachusetts Association Opposed to the Further Extension of Suffrage
    to Women Records, 1895–1920
Miscellaneous Collection of Anti-Suffrage Material Assembled by an Officer
    of the Massachusetts Association Opposed to Further Extension of
    Suffrage to Women
Portraits of American Abolitionists
Scrapbook of Newspaper Clippings Pertaining to the Women's Suffrage
    Movement, Primarily from Boston, Mass. Newspapers, 1896–1904
Woman Suffrage in Great Britain, with particular reference to British
    militants
Volume of Pamphlets on Woman Suffrage
Warren-Adams Papers

Moorland-Spingarn Research Center, Howard University
Mary Ann Shadd Cary Papers
Mary Church Terrell Papers

Robert W. Woodruff Library of the Atlanta University Center, Inc.
Neighborhood Union Collection

Schlesinger Library on the History of Women in America, Harvard University
Alice Park Posters
Antoinette Brown Blackwell Collection
Clara Goldberg Schiffer Papers
Ellen A. Webster Papers
Suffrage Memorabilia
Susan B. Anthony Papers
Woman's Rights Collection

Belmont-Paul Women's Equality National Monument
National Woman's Party Papers

Sophia Smith Collection
  Ames Family Papers
  Carrie Chapman Catt Papers
  Garrison Family Papers
  Portia Willis Fitzgerald Papers
  Suffrage Collection
  Susan B. Anthony Papers
  Woman's Rights Collection

Spelman College Archives, Spelman College
  The Spelman Messenger

The Women's Library
  Collection of Suffrage Ephemera
  Fawcett Library Scrapbooks and Press Cuttings
  Suffrage Photographs
  Suffrage Postcards
  Records of the Artists' Suffrage League
  Scrapbook of Emmeline Pethick Lawrence
  Scrapbook of Press Cuttings Related to Women's Suffrage Campaigns, 1907–1938
  Scrapbook of Suffrage Campaigns
  Suffrage Atelier Correspondence
  Suffrage Press Cuttings
  Votes for Women: A Picture Book of the Campaign during Recent Years Compiled Principally from Newspaper Photography, by Alex Sydney Millward, ca. 1907–1930

PERIODICALS

  The Afro-American Ledger
  The American Educational Review
  The Anglo-African Magazine
  The Atlantic Monthly
  Ballou's Pictorial Drawing-Room Companion
  The Baltimore Afro-American
  Boston Daily Globe
  The Boston Gazette and Country Journal
  Boston Transcript
  The Broadway Belle, and Mirror of the Times
  The Chautauquan
  Chicago American
  Chicago Daily News
  Chicago Defender
  Chicago Herald
  The Chicago Record

Chicago Tribune
Cincinnati Commercial Gazette
The Colored American
The Crisis
The Daily Graphic
Demorest's Illustrated Monthly Magazine
Detroit Free Press
Detroit Journal
Dixon's Polyanthos
Frank Leslie's Budget of Fun
Frank Leslie's Illustrated Newspaper
Frank Leslie's Ladies Gazette of Paris London and New York Fashions
Frank Leslie's Lady's Magazine
Gleason's Pictorial Drawing-Room Companion
Godey's Lady's Book
The Guardian
Harper's Monthly
Harper's Weekly
Headquarters Newsletter
Humphrey's Journal of Photography
Illustrated London News
The Independent
Jolly Joker
Judge
The Ladies' Magazine
The Lady's Magazine and Repository of Entertaining Knowledge
Leslie's Weekly
The Libertine
Life
The Lily
The Literary News
Little Joker
Los Angeles Times
The Monthly Mirror
National Anti-Slavery Standard
The National Citizen and Ballot Box
The National Era
National Notes
The National Police Gazette
The New-York Illustrated News
The New York Times
The New York Tribune
The New Yorker
Nick-Nax for All Creation
The Photographic News
The Phrenological Journal and Science of Health

Phunny Phellow
Potter's American Monthly
Puck
Punch
The Remonstrance
The Revolution
Royal American Magazine
San Francisco Chronicle
The Spelman Messenger
The Suffragette
The Suffragist
The Una
Voice of the Negro
The Vote
Votes for Women
The Washington Post
The Water-Cure Journal
The Western Woman Voter
The Whip, and Satirist of New-York and Brooklyn
The Woman Citizen
The Woman Voter
The Woman's Advocate
The Woman's Column
The Woman's Era
The Woman's Journal
The Woman's Tribune
Woodhull & Claflin's Weekly
Zion's Herald

PUBLISHED PRIMARY SOURCES

Description of Mr. Huntington's Picture of the Republican Court in the Time of Washington. New York: Emil Seitz, 1865.

The Exhibition of the Columbianum of American Academy of Painting, Sculpture, and Architecture, & Established at Philadelphia, 1795. Philadelphia: Francis & Robert Bailey, 1795.

Frank Leslie's Illustrated Historical Register of the Centennial Exposition, 1876. New York: Frank Leslie, 1876.

Forty-Fourth Annual Report of the National American Woman Suffrage Association Given at the Convention. New York: The Association, 1912.

Forty-Fifth Annual Report of the National American Woman Suffrage Association Given at the Convention. New York: The Association, 1913.

Hearing before the Committee on Woman Suffrage, February 21, 1894. Washington, DC: Government Printing Office, 1894.

Proceedings of the Eleventh Woman's Rights Convention, May, 1866. New York: Robert Johnston, 1866.

Report of the International Council of Women. Washington, DC: Rufus H. Darby, 1888.

The World Turned Upside Down, or The Comical Metamorphoses. Boston: John D. M'Dougall, 1780.

The World Turned Upside Down, or The Comical Metamorphoses. Boston: I. Normon, 1794.

Addams, Jane. *Twenty Years at Hull-House, with Autobiographical Notes*. New York: Macmillan, 1910.

Alcott, William A. *Gift Book for Young Ladies*. Auburn, NY: Miller, Orton & Mulligan, 1854.

Alexander, William. *The History of Women, from Earliest Antiquity to the Present Time; Giving an Account of Almost Every Interesting Particular concerning That Sex, among All Nations Ancient and Modern*. 2 vols. Philadelphia: J. Turner and I. H. Dobelbower, 1795–1796.

Anthony, Susan B., and Ida Husted Harper. *History of Woman Suffrage*. Vol. 4. Indianapolis: Hollenbeck, 1902. Reprint, Salem, NH: Ayer, 1985. Page references are to the 1985 edition.

Avery, Rachel Foster, ed. *Proceedings of the Twenty-Eighth Annual Convention of the National-American Woman Suffrage Association*. Philadelphia: Alfred J. Ferris, 1896.

———, ed. *Proceedings of the Twenty-Ninth Annual Convention of the National American Woman Suffrage Association*. Philadelphia: Alfred J. Ferris, 1897.

———, ed. *Proceedings of the Thirtieth Annual Convention of the National American Woman Suffrage Association of the Fiftieth Anniversary of the First Woman's Rights Convention*. Philadelphia: Alfred J. Ferris, 1898.

———, ed. *Proceedings of the Thirty-First Annual Convention of the National-American Woman Suffrage Association*. Warren, OH: Press of Perry, 1899.

———, ed. *Proceedings of the Thirty-Second Annual Convention of the National American Woman Suffrage Association*. Philadelphia: Alfred J. Ferris, 1900.

Baker, William Spohn. *The Engraved Portraits of Washington, with Notices of the Originals and Brief Biographical Sketches of the Painters*. Philadelphia: Lindsay & Baker, 1880.

Beecher, Catharine E. *The American Woman's Home: Or, Principles of Domestic Science*. New York: J. B. Ford, 1869.

———. *The New Housekeeper's Manual*. New York: J. B. Ford, 1874.

———. *A Treatise on Domestic Economy*. Boston: Thomas H. Webb, 1843.

———. *Woman's Profession as Mother and Educator*. Philadelphia: G. Maclean, 1872.

Beecher, Henry Ward. *Woman's Duty to Vote*. New York: American Equal Rights Association, 1867.

———. *Woman's Influence in Politics*. Boston: C. K. Whipple, 1869.

Blackwell, Alice Stone, ed., *Proceedings of the Thirty-Third Annual Convention of the National American Woman Suffrage Association*. Warren, OH: Press of Perry, 1901.

Brady, Mathew. *Gallery of Illustrious Americans*. New York: Wiley, 1850.

Cary, Mary Ann Shadd. "Speech to the Judiciary re: the Rights of Woman to

Vote," January 1872, Mary Ann Shadd Cary Papers, Moorland-Spingarn Research Center, Howard University.

Chapman, Maria Weston. *The Liberty Bell*. Boston: Massachusetts Anti-Slavery Fair, 1844.

Davis, Paulina W. *A History of the National Woman's Rights Movement, for Twenty Years*. New York: Journeymen Printers' Co-Operative Association, 1871.

Duyckinck, Evert A. *Portrait Gallery of Eminent Men and Women of Europe and America*. New York: Johnson & Miles, 1873.

Ellet, Elizabeth. *The Women of the American Revolution*. New York: Baker and Scribner, 1848.

Ellis, William, ed. *The Christian Keepsake, and Missionary Annual*. New York: W. Jackson, 1835.

Emerson, Ralph Waldo. *Representative Men: Seven Lectures*. London: John Chapman, 1850.

Fitzgerald, Susan W., ed. *The Hand Book of the National American Woman Suffrage Association and Proceedings of the Forty-Seventh Annual Convention*. New York: National Woman Suffrage Publishing, 1915.

Fuller, Margaret. *Woman in the Nineteenth Century*. New York: Greeley & McElrath, 1845.

Gilbert, Olive. *Narrative of Sojourner Truth: A Bondswoman of Olden Time, Emancipated by the New York Legislature in the Early Part of the Present Century; with a History of Her Labors and Correspondence*. Boston: Published by the author, 1875.

———. *Narrative of Sojourner Truth: A Bondswoman of Olden Time, Emancipated by the New York Legislature in the Early Part of the Present Century; with a History of Her Labors and Correspondence, Drawn from Her "Book of Life."* Battle Creek, MI: published by the author, 1878.

Gilbert & Bacon. *Catalogue of Theatrical and Public Celebrities*. Philadelphia: Gilbert & Bacon, 1880.

Gillespie, Elizabeth Duane. *A Book of Remembrance*. Philadelphia: J. B. Lippincott, 1901.

Gilman, Charlotte Perkins. *Women and Economics: A Study of the Economic Relation between Men and Women as a Factor in Social Evolution*. Boston: Small, Maynard, & Co., 1898.

Godwin, William. *Memoirs of the Author of "A Vindication of the Rights of Woman."* London: J. Johnson, 1798.

Goodrich, S. G, ed. *The Token and Atlantic Souvenir*. Boston: American Stationers' Co., 1838.

Grimké, Angelina. *Appeal to the Christian Women of the South*. New York: American Anti-Slavery Society, 1836.

Griswold, Rufus. *The Republican Court: Or, American Society in the Days of Washington*. New York: D. Appleton, 1864.

Gutridge, Molly. *A New Touch on the Times*. Danvers, MA: Ezekiel Russell, 1779.

Hale, Sarah Josepha Buell. *Woman's Record, or Sketches of All Distinguished Women: From the Creation to A.D. 1854*. New York: Harper & Brothers, 1855.

Harper, Ida Husted, ed. *The Life and Work of Susan B. Anthony*. Vols. 1–3. Indianapolis: Bowen-Merrill, 1898.

———. *Story of the National Amendment for Woman Suffrage Movement*. New York: National Woman Suffrage Publishing, 1919.

———, ed. *History of Woman Suffrage*. Vols, 5–6. New York: J. J. Little & Ives, 1922. Reprint, Salem, NH: Ayer, 1985. Page references are to the 1985 edition.

Heath, Charles, and Marguerite Blessington, eds. *Heath's Book of Beauty*. New York: Appleton, 1842.

Higginson, Thomas Wentworth. *Short Answers to Common Objections against Woman Suffrage*.

Boston: American Woman Suffrage Association, 1870–1890.

Holloway, Laura C. *The Ladies of the White House, or In the Home of the Presidents*. Philadelphia: Bradley, 1881.

Hutchinson, Enoch, ed. *Christian Keepsake, or Friendship's Memorial*. New York: J. C. Burdick, 1851.

Johnson, Sophia. *The Friendless Orphan*. Pittsburgh: S. Johnson, 1842.

Jones, A. D. *The Illustrated American Biography*. New York: J. Milton Emerson, 1855.

Lossing, Benson John. *The Pictorial Field-Book of the Revolution, or Illustrations, by Pen and Pencil, of the History, Biography, Scenery, Relics, and Traditions of the War for Independence*. New York: Harper & Brothers, 1859.

———. *Pictorial History of the Civil War in the United States of America*. Philadelphia: G. W. Childs, 1866.

Mann, Herman. *The Female Review, or Memoirs of an American Young Lady*. Dedham, MA: Nathaniel and Benjamin Heaton, 1797.

Martyn, S. T. *The Golden Keepsake, or Ladies' Wreath*. New York: J. M. Fletcher, 1851.

M'Dougald, Elizabeth. *The Life, Travels, and Extraordinary Adventures of Elizabeth M'Dougald*. Providence, RI: S. S. Southworth, 1834.

Miller, Francis Trevelyan, and Robert S. Lanier, eds. *The Photographic History of the Civil War in Ten Volumes*. New York: Review of Reviews, 1911.

Mossell, N. F. *The Work of the Afro-American Woman*. Philadelphia: George S. Ferguson, 1908.

Murray, Judith Sargent. "On the Equality of the Sexes." *Massachusetts Magazine*, vol. 2, 1790, 132–35, 223–26.

National Association of Colored Women's Clubs. *A History of the Club Movement among the Colored Women of the United States of America*. Washington, DC: National Association of Colored Women's Clubs, 1902. Reprint, Washington, DC: National Association of Colored Women's Clubs, 1978.

Pankhurst, Sylvia. *The Suffragette*. New York: Sturgis and Walton, 1911.

Parton, James, Horace Greeley, T. W. Higginson, J. S. C. Abbott, James M. Hoppin, William Winter, Theodore Tilton, Fanny Fern, Grace Greenwood, and Elizabeth Cady Stanton. *Eminent Women of the Age: Being*

Narratives of the Lives and Deeds of the Most Prominent Women of the Present Generation. Hartford, CT: S. M. Betts, 1869.

Patterson, Hannah J., ed. *The Handbook of the National American Woman Suffrage Association and Proceedings of the Forty-Eighth Annual Convention*. New York: National Woman Suffrage Publishing, 1916.

Ploughe, Sheridan. *History of Reno County, Kansas: Its People, Industries and Institutions*. Vol. 2. B. F. Bowen, 1917.

Reed, Esther de Berdt. *The Sentiments of an American Woman*. Philadelphia: John Dunlap, 1780.

Richings, G. F. *Evidences of Progress among Colored People*. Philadelphia: George S. Ferguson, 1902.

Riis, Jacob A. *How the Other Half Lives: Studies among the Tenements of New York*. New York: Scribner, 1890.

Rogers, Nettie. *The Hand Book of the National American Woman Suffrage Association and Proceedings of the Forty-Ninth Annual Convention*. New York: National Woman Suffrage Publishing, 1917.

Root, Marcus A. *The Camera and the Pencil*. Philadelphia: J. B. Lippincott, 1864.

Sewall, May Wright. *The World's Congress of Representative Women*. Vol. 2. New York: Rand, McNally & Co., 1894.

Sharp, Anthony. *The Continental Almanac, for the Year of Our Lord, 1782*. Philadelphia: Francis Bailey, 1781.

Solomons, Selina. *How We Won the Vote in California*. San Francisco: New Woman Publishing, 1912.

Stanton, Elizabeth Cady. "Address in Favor of Universal Suffrage for the Election of Delegates to the Constitutional Convention. Before the Judiciary Committees of the Legislature of New York, in the Assembly Chamber, January 23, 1867, in Behalf of the American Equal Rights Association." Albany, NY: Weed, Parsons & Co., 1867.

Stanton, Elizabeth Cady, Susan B. Anthony, and Matilda Joslyn Gage, eds. *History of Woman Suffrage*. Vol. 1. New York: Fowler and Wells, 1881. Reprint, Salem, NH: Ayer, 1985. Page references are to the 1985 edition.

———. *History of Woman Suffrage*. Vol. 2. New York: Fowler and Wells, 1882. Reprint, Salem, NH: Ayer, 1985. Page references are to the 1985 edition.

———. *History of Woman Suffrage*. Vol. 3. Rochester, NY: Susan B. Anthony, 1886. Reprint, Salem, NH: Ayer, 1985. Page references are to the 1985 edition.

Terrell, Mary Church. *A Colored Woman in a White World*. Washington, DC: Ransdell, 1940.

———. *The Progress of Colored Women*. Washington, DC: Smith Brothers, 1898.

Upton, Harriet Taylor, ed. *The Hand Book of the National American Woman Suffrage Association and Proceedings of the Twenty-Fifth Annual Convention of the National American Woman Suffrage Association*. Washington, D.C.: Stormont & Jackson, 1893.

———, ed. *Proceedings of the Twenty-Seventh Annual Convention of the*

National-American Woman Suffrage Association. Warren, OH: William
  Ritezel, 1895.

Vale, G. *Fanaticism: Its Source and Influence, Illustrated by the Simple Narrative
  of Isabella, in the Case of Matthias, Mr. and Mrs. B. Folger, Mr. Pierson,
  Mr. Mills, Catherine, Isabella, &c. &c.: A Reply to W.L. Stone, with Descrip-
  tive Portraits of All the Parties, While at Sing-Sing and at Third Street.—
  Containing the Whole Truth—and Nothing but the Truth*. New York: G. Vale,
  1835.

Wells, Ida B. *The Memphis Diary of Ida B. Wells*. Boston: Beacon Press, 1995.

———. *The Reason Why the Colored American Is Not in the World's Columbian
  Exposition*. Edited by Robert W. Rydell. Urbana: University of Illinois
  Press, 1999. First published 1893.

Wheatley, Phillis. *Poems on Various Subjects, Religious and Moral*. London:
  A. Bell, 1773.

Willard, Frances. *American Women*. New York: Mast, 1897.

Winter, Una Richardson. *Alice Park of California: Worker for Woman Suffrage
  and for Children's Rights*. Upland: Susan B. Anthony Memorial Committee
  of California, 1948.

Wollstonecraft, Mary. *A Vindication of the Rights of Woman*. Boston: Peter
  Edes, 1792.

Woodhull, Victoria C. *"And the Truth Shall Make You Free": A Speech on the
  Principles of Social Freedom*. New York: Woodhull, Claflin & Co., 1871.

Wright, Frances. *Course of Popular Lectures*. New York: Office of the Free
  Enquirer, 1831.

Young, Rose. *The Record of the Leslie Woman Suffrage Commission, Inc., 1917–
  1929*. New York: Leslie Woman Suffrage Commission, 1929.

SECONDARY SOURCES

Abrams, Jeanne E. *First Ladies of the Republic: Martha Washington, Abigail
  Adams, Dolley Madison, and the Creation of an Iconic American Role*. New
  York: New York University Press, 2018.

Adler, Kathleen, and Marcia R. Pointon. *The Body Imaged: The Human Form
  and Visual Culture since the Renaissance*. New York: Cambridge University
  Press, 1993.

Aiello, Thomas. "The First Fissure: The Du Bois-Washington Relationship
  from 1898–1899." *Phylon* 51, no. 1 (2014): 76–87.

Akiwenzie-Damm, Kateri, Rowan Blanchard, Melanie L. Campbell, Tammy
  Duckworth, America Ferrera, Roxane Gay, Ilana Glazer, et al. *Together We
  Rise: Behind the Scenes at the Protest Heard round the World*. New York: Dey
  Street, 2018.

Allgor, Catherine. *Parlor Politics: In Which the Ladies of Washington Help Build
  a City and a Government*. Charlottesville: University Press of Virginia,
  2000.

———. *A Perfect Union: Dolley Madison and the Creation of the American
  Nation*. New York: Henry Holt, 2006.

American Association of University Women. "Barriers and Bias: The Status of Women in Leadership." Washington, DC: American Association of University Women, 2016.

Amory, Hugh, and David D. Hall, eds. *The Colonial Book in the Atlantic World*. Vol. 1 of *A History of the Book in America*. Chapel Hill: University of North Carolina Press, 2007.

Anderson, Benedict. *Imagined Communities: Reflections on the Origin and Spread of Nationalism*. 2nd ed. New York: Verso, 1991.

Anishanslin, Zara. *Portrait of a Woman in Silk: Hidden Histories of the British Atlantic World*. New Haven, CT: Yale University Press, 2016.

Asleson, Robyn, ed. *A Passion for Performance: Sarah Siddons and Her Portraitists*. Los Angeles: J. Paul Getty Museum, 1999.

Auslander, Leora. *Cultural Revolutions: The Politics of Everyday Life in Britain, North America and France*. Berkeley: University of California Press, 2009.

Baker, Jean, ed. *Votes for Women: The Struggle for Suffrage Revisited*. New York: Oxford University Press, 2002.

Baker, Paula. "The Domestication of Politics: Women and American Political Society, 1780–1920." *American Historical Review* 89, no. 3 (1984): 620–47.

Banaszak, Lee Ann. *Why Movements Succeed or Fail: Opportunity, Culture, and the Struggle for Woman Suffrage*. Princeton, NJ: Princeton University Press, 1996.

Banner, Lois W. *American Beauty*. Chicago: University of Chicago Press, 1984.

Banta, Martha. *Imaging American Women: Idea and Ideals in Cultural History*. New York: Columbia University Press, 1987.

Barker-Benfield, G. J. *Abigail and John Adams: The Americanization of Sensibility*. Chicago: University of Chicago Press, 2010.

Barnett Cash, Floris Loretta. *African American Women and Social Action: The Clubwomen and Volunteerism from Jim Crow to the New Deal, 1896–1936*. Westport, CT: Greenwood Press, 2001.

Barnhill, Georgia B. "The Pictorial Context for Nathaniel Currier: Prints for the Elite and Middle Class." *Imprint* 31, no. 2 (2006): 31–42.

———. "Transformations in Pictorial Printing." In *An Extensive Republic: Print, Culture, and Society in the New Nation, 1790–1840*, ed. Robert A. Gross and Mary Kelley. Vol. 2 of *A History of the Book in America*. Chapel Hill: University of North Carolina Press, 2010.

Barratt, Carrie Rebora. *Gilbert Stuart*. New Haven, CT: Yale University Press, 2004.

Barthes, Roland. *Camera Lucida: Reflections on Photography*. New York: Hill and Wang, 1981.

Baumgarten, Linda. *What Clothes Reveal: The Language of Clothing in Colonial and Federal America*. New Haven, CT: Yale University Press, 2002.

Bay, Mia, Farah J. Griffin, Martha S. Jones, and Barbara D. Savage, eds. *Toward an Intellectual History of Black Women*. Chapel Hill: University of North Carolina Press, 2015.

Beard, Mary. *Women and Power: A Manifesto*. London: Profile Books, 2017.

Bederman, Gail. *Manliness and Civilization*. Chicago: University of Chicago Press, 1995.

Beeton, Beverly. *Women Vote in the West: The Woman Suffrage Movement, 1869–1896*. New York: Garland, 1986.

Bellion, Wendy. *Citizen Spectator: Art, Illusion, and Visual Perception in Early National America*. Chapel Hill: University of North Carolina Press, 2011.

———. "Illusion and Allusion: Charles Willson Peale's 'Staircase Group' at the Columbianum Exhibition." *American Art* 17, no. 2 (2003): 19–39.

Benjamin, Anne Myra Goodman. *A History of the Anti-Suffrage Movement in the United States from 1895 to 1920: Women against Equality*. Lewiston, NY: Edwin Mellen Press, 1991.

Benjamin, Walter. *The Arcades Project*. Cambridge, MA: Belknap, 1999.

———. *The Work of Art in the Age of Its Technological Reproducibility, and Other Writings on Media*. Cambridge, MA: Belknap, 2008.

Berch, Bettina. *The Woman behind the Lens: The Life and Work of Frances Benjamin Johnston, 1864–1952*. Charlottesville: University of Virginia Press, 2000.

Berenson, Barbara F. *Massachusetts in the Woman Suffrage Movement: Revolutionary Reformers*. Cheltenham, UK: History Press, 2018.

Bergen, Benjamin K. *Louder Than Words: The New Science of How the Mind Makes Meaning*. New York: Basic Books, 2012.

Berger, Martin A. *Seeing through Race: A Reinterpretation of Civil Rights Photography*. Berkeley: University of California Press, 2011.

Berger, Maurice. *For All the World to See: Visual Culture and the Struggle for Civil Rights*. New Haven, CT: Yale University Press, 2010.

Blackwell, Alice Stone. *Lucy Stone: Pioneer of Woman's Rights*. Charlottesville: University of Virginia Press, 1930.

Blatch, Harriot Stanton, and Alma Lutz. *Challenging Years: The Memoirs of Harriot Stanton Blatch*. New York: G. Putnam, 1940.

Boisseau, T. J., and Abigail M. Markwyn. *Gendering the Fair: Histories of Women and Gender at World's Fairs*. Urbana: University of Illinois Press, 2010.

Bordo, Susan. *The Destruction of Hillary Clinton*. Brooklyn: Melville House, 2017.

Boritt, G., Mark Neely, and Harold Holzer. *The Lincoln Image: Abraham Lincoln and the Popular Print*. Urbana: University of Illinois Press, 2001.

Boydston, Jeanne. "Civilizing Selves: Public Structures and Private Lives in Mary Kelley's *Learning to Stand and Speak*." *Journal of the Early Republic* 28, no. 1 (2008): 47–60.

Boylan, Anne M. *The Origins of Women's Activism: New York and Boston, 1797–1840*. Chapel Hill: University of North Carolina Press, 2002.

Branson, Susan. *These Fiery Frenchified Dames: Women and Political Culture in Early National Philadelphia*. Philadelphia: University of Pennsylvania Press, 2011.

Breen, T. H. *The Marketplace of Revolution: How Consumer Politics Shaped American Independence*. New York: Oxford University Press, 2005.

Brewer, Susan A. *Why America Fights: Patriotism and War Propaganda from the Philippines to Iraq*. New York: Oxford University Press, 2009.

Brigham, Clarence S. "David Claypoole Johnston, the American Cruik-shank." *Proceedings of the American Antiquarian Society* 50 (1940): 98–110.

Brilliant, Richard. *Portraiture: Essays in Art and Culture*. London: Reaktion, 1991.

Brock, Claire. *The Feminization of Fame, 1750–1830*. New York: Palgrave Macmillan, 2006.

Brody, David. *Visualizing American Empire: Orientalism and Imperialism in the Philippines*. Chicago: University of Chicago Press, 2010.

Brooke, John L. "Spheres, Sites, Subjectivity, History: Reframing Antebellum American Society." *Journal of the Early Republic* 28, no. 1 (2008): 75–82.

Brooks, Peter. *Realist Vision*. New Haven, CT: Yale University Press, 2005.

Brown, Christopher Leslie. *Moral Capital: Foundations of British Abolitionism*. Chapel Hill: University of North Carolina Press, 2006.

Brown, Joshua. *Beyond the Lines: Pictorial Reporting, Everyday Life, and the Crisis of Gilded-Age America*. Berkeley: University of California Press, 2003.

Brown, Nikki. *Private Politics and Public Voices: Black Women's Activism from World War I to the New Deal*. Bloomington: Indiana University Press, 2006.

Brown, Victoria. *The Education of Jane Addams*. Philadelphia: University of Pennsylvania Press, 2004.

Brownlee, Peter John, Sarah Burns, Diane Dillon, Daniel Greene, and Scott Manning Stevens, eds. *Home Front: Daily Life in the Civil War North*. Chicago: The University of Chicago Press, 2013.

Bunker, Gary. "The Art of Condescension." *Common-Place* 7, no. 3 (April 2007), http://www.common-place.org/vol-07/no-03/bunker/.

Bryson, Norman. *Vision and Painting the Logic of the Gaze*. New Haven, CT: Yale University Press, 1985.

Cameron, Kenneth Neill, ed. *Shelley and His Circle, 1773–1822*. Cambridge, MA: Harvard University Press, 1961.

Camhi, Jane Jerome. *Women against Women: American Anti-Suffragism, 1880–1920*. Brooklyn: Carlson, 1994.

Canaday, Margot. *The Straight State: Sexuality and Citizenship in Twentieth-Century America*. Politics and Society in Twentieth-Century America. Princeton, NJ: Princeton University Press, 2009.

Carlebach, Michael L. *The Origins of Photojournalism in America*. Washington, DC: Smithsonian Institution Press, 1992.

Carretta, Vincent. *Equiano, the African: Biography of a Self-Made Man*. New York: Penguin, 2006.

———. *Phillis Wheatley: Biography of a Genius in Bondage*. Athens: University of Georgia Press, 2011.

Carter, Sarah Anne. *Object Lessons: How Nineteenth-Century Americans*

Learned to Make Sense of the Material World. New York: Oxford University Press, 2018.

Casmier-Paz, Lynn. "Slave Narratives and the Rhetoric of Author Portraiture." *New Literary History* 34, no. 1 (2003): 91–116.

Casper, Scott. "The First Family: Seventy Years with Edward Savage's *The Washington Family*." *Imprint* 24 (1999): 2–15.

Casper, Scott E., Jeffrey D. Groves, Stephen W. Nissenbaum, and Michael Winship, eds. *The Industrial Book, 1840–1880*. Vol. 3 of *A History of the Book in America*. Chapel Hill: University of North Carolina Press, 2007.

Catt, Carrie Chapman. *Woman Suffrage and Politics: The Inner Story of the Suffrage Movement*. New York: Scribner, 1923.

Cayton, Andrew R. L. *Love in the Time of Revolution: Transatlantic Literary Radicalism and Historical Change, 1793–1818*. Chapel Hill: University of North Carolina Press, 2013.

Chaney, Michael A. *Fugitive Vision: Slave Image and Black Identity in Antebellum Narrative*. Bloomington: Indiana University Press, 2009.

Chauncey, George. *Gay New York: Gender, Urban Culture, and the Making of the Gay Male World, 1890–1940*. New York: Basic Books, 2008.

Chavez-Garcia, Miroslava. *States of Delinquency: Race and Science in the Making of California's Juvenile Justice System*. Berkeley: University of California Press, 2012.

Cherry, Deborah. *Beyond the Frame: Feminism and Visual Culture, Britain 1850–1900*. New York: Routledge, 2000.

Ciarlo, David. *Advertising Empire: Race and Visual Culture in Imperial Germany*. Cambridge, MA: Harvard University Press, 2011.

Clapp, Elizabeth J., and Julie Roy Jeffrey. *Women, Dissent and Anti-Slavery in Britain and America, 1790–1865*. New York: Oxford University Press, 2011.

Clark, Anne Biller. *My Dear Mrs. Ames: A Study of Suffragist Cartoonist Blanche Ames*. New York: Peter Lang, 2001.

Clark, Justin T. *City of Second Sight: Nineteenth-Century Boston and the Making of American Visual Culture*. Chapel Hill: University of North Carolina Press, 2018.

Clinton, Hillary Rodham. *What Happened*. New York: Simon & Schuster, 2017.

Cobb, Jasmine Nichole. *Picture Freedom: Remaking Black Visuality in the Early Nineteenth Century*. New York: New York University Press, 2015.

Cohen, Lizabeth. *A Consumer's Republic: The Politics of Mass Consumption in Postwar America*. New York: Knopf, 2003.

Cohen, Patricia Cline. *The Murder of Helen Jewett: The Life and Death of a Prostitute in Nineteenth-Century New York*. New York: Vintage, 1999.

Collins, Kathleen. "The Scourged Back." *History of Photography* 9, no. 1 (March 1985): 43–45.

———. "Shadow and Substance: Sojourner Truth." *History of Photography* 7, no. 3 (1983): 183–205.

Cook, James W. "Seeing the Visual in U.S. History." *Journal of American History* 95, no. 2 (2008): 432–41.

Cooney, Robert. *Winning the Vote: The Triumph of the American Woman Suffrage Movement*. Santa Cruz, CA: American Graphic Press, 2005.

Cooper, Brittney C. *Beyond Respectability: The Intellectual Thought of Race Women*. Urbana: University of Illinois Press, 2017.

Cott, Nancy. *The Bonds of Womanhood: "Woman's Sphere" in New England, 1780–1835*. New Haven, CT: Yale University Press, 1977.

———. *The Grounding of Modern Feminism*. New Haven, CT: Yale University Press, 1987.

Cowman, Krista. *Women of the Right Spirit: Paid Organisers of the Women's Social and Political Union (WSPU) 1904–18*. New York: Manchester University Press, 2011.

Cumming, Inez Parker. "The Edenton Ladies' Tea-Party." *Georgia Review* 8, no. 4 (1954): 389–95.

Cunningham, Patricia A. *Reforming Women's Fashion, 1850–1920: Politics, Health, and Art*. Kent, OH: Kent State University Press, 2003.

Darrah, William Culp. *Cartes de Visite in Nineteenth Century Photography*. Gettysburg, PA: W. C. Darrah, 1981.

———. *The World of Stereographs*. Gettysburg, PA: Darrah, 1977.

Davis, Melody. "Doubling the Vision: Women and Narration Stereography, the United States, 1870–1910." PhD diss., City University of New York, 2004.

Davis, Natalie Zemon. "Women on Top." In *Society and Culture in Early Modern France: Eight Essays*. Stanford, CA: Stanford University Press, 1975.

Denney, Colleen. *The Visual Culture of Women's Activism in London, Paris and Beyond: An Analytical Art History, 1860 to the Present*. Jefferson, NC: McFarland, 2018.

Derleth, Jessica. "'Kneading Politics': Cookery and the American Woman Suffrage Movement." *Journal of the Gilded Age and Progressive Era* 17, no. 3 (2018): 450–74.

Dinius, Marcy J. *The Camera and the Press*. Philadelphia: University of Pennsylvania Press, 2012.

Dinkin, Robert J. *Voting in Revolutionary America: A Study of Elections in the Thirteen Original States, 1776–1789*. Westport, CT: Greenwood, 1982.

Docherty, Linda J. "Women as Readers: Visual Interpretations." In *Proceedings of the American Antiquarian Society* 107, part 2. Worcester, MA: American Antiquarian Society, 1998.

Dorr, Rheta Louise Childe. *Susan B. Anthony: The Woman Who Changed the Mind of a Nation*. New York: Frederick A. Stokes, 1928.

Dow, Bonnie J. "The Revolution, 1868–1870: Expanding the Woman Suffrage Agenda." In *A Voice of Their Own: The Woman Suffrage Press, 1840–1910*, ed. Martha Solomon. Tuscaloosa: University of Alabama Press, 1991.

DuBois, Ellen Carol. *Feminism and Suffrage: The Emergence of an Independent Women's Movement in America, 1848–1869*. Ithaca, NY: Cornell University Press, 1978.

———. *Harriot Stanton Blatch and the Winning of Woman Suffrage*. New Haven, CT: Yale University Press, 1997.

———. "Working Women, Class Relations, and Suffrage Militance: Harriot Stanton Blatch and the New York Woman Suffrage Movement, 1894–1909." *Journal of American History* 74, no. 1 (1987): 176–209.

DuBois Shaw, Gwendolyn. *Portraits of a People: Picturing African Americans in the Nineteenth Century.* Seattle: University of Washington Press, 2006.

Dudden, Faye E. *Fighting Chance: The Struggle Over Woman Suffrage and Black Suffrage in Reconstruction America.* New York: Oxford University Press, 2011.

Eastman, Carolyn. *A Nation of Speechifiers: Making an American Public after the Revolution.* Chicago: University of Chicago Press, 2009.

Eger, Elizabeth, and Lucy Peltz. *Brilliant Women: 18th-Century Bluestockings.* London: National Portrait Gallery, 2008.

Ellis, Reginald K. *Between Washington and Du Bois: The Racial Politics of James Edward Shepard.* Gainesville: University Press of Florida, 2017.

Englander, Susan. *Class Coalition and Class Conflict in the California Woman Suffrage Movement, 1907–1912: The San Francisco Wage Earners' Suffrage League.* San Francisco: Mellen Research University Press, 1992.

Enoch, Jessica. *Refiguring Rhetorical Education: Women Teaching African American, Native American, and Chicano/a Students, 1865–1911.* Carbondale: Southern Illinois University Press, 2008.

Fagan Yellin, Jean. *Women and Sisters: The Antislavery Feminists in American Culture.* New Haven, CT: Yale University Press, 1989.

Fagan Yellin, Jean, and John C. Van Horne, eds. *The Abolitionist Sisterhood: Women's Political Culture in Antebellum America.* Ithaca, NY: Cornell University Press, 1994.

Faulkner, Carol. *Lucretia Mott's Heresy: Abolition and Women's Rights in Nineteenth-Century America.* Philadelphia: University of Pennsylvania Press, 2011.

Field, Corinne T. "Grand Old Women: Age, Race, and Power in the US Women's Rights Movement, 1870–1920." Unpublished manuscript.

Finnegan, Margaret Mary. *Selling Suffrage: Consumer Culture and Votes for Women.* New York: Columbia University Press, 1999.

Fischer, David Hackett. *Liberty and Freedom: A Visual History of America's Founding Ideas.* New York: Oxford University Press, 2005.

Fischer, Gayle V. *Pantaloons and Power: Nineteenth-Century Dress Reform in the United States.* Kent, OH: Kent State University Press, 2001.

Flanagan, Maureen A. *America Reformed: Progressives and Progressivisms, 1890s–1920s.* New York: Oxford University Press, 2007.

Fleming, E. McClung. "The American Image as Indian Princess, 1765–1783." *Winterthur Portfolio* 2 (1965): 65–81.

———. "From Indian Princess to Greek Goddess: The American Image, 1783–1815." *Winterthur Portfolio* 3 (1967): 37–66.

Flexner, Eleanor. *Century of Struggle: The Woman's Rights Movement in the United States.* Cambridge, MA: Belknap, 1959.

Florey, Kenneth. *American Woman Suffrage Postcards: A Study and Catalog.* Jefferson, NC: McFarland, 2015.

———. *Women's Suffrage Memorabilia: An Illustrated Historical Study*. Jefferson, NC: McFarland, 2013.

Foner, Eric. *Free Soil, Free Labor, Free Men: The Ideology of the Republican Party before the Civil War*. New York: Oxford University Press, 1995.

Fortune, Brandon Brame. "'Studious Men Are Always Painted in Gowns': Charles Willson Peale's Benjamin Rush and the Question of Banyans in Eighteenth-Century Anglo-American Portraiture." *Dress* 29, no. 1 (2002): 27–40.

Fowble, E. McSherry. *Two Centuries of Prints in America, 1680–1880: A Selective Catalogue of the Winterthur Museum Collection*. Charlottesville: University of Virginia Press, 1987.

Fox, Richard Wightman. *Trials of Intimacy: Love and Loss in the Beecher-Tilton Scandal*. Chicago: University of Chicago Press, 1999.

Fox, Richard Wightman, and T. J. Jackson Lears, eds. *The Culture of Consumption: Critical Essays in American History, 1880–1980*. New York: Pantheon Books, 1983.

Fox-Amato, Matthew. *Exposing Slavery: Photography, Human Bondage, and the Birth of Modern Visual Politics in America*. New York: Oxford University Press, 2019.

Frassanito, William A. *Antietam: The Photographic Legacy of America's Bloodiest Day*. New York: Scribner, 1978.

———. *Gettysburg: A Journey in Time*. New York: Scribner, 1975.

Freeman, Joanne B. *Affairs of Honor: National Politics in the New Republic*. New Haven, CT: Yale University Press, 2001.

Freund, Amy. "The Citoyenne Tallien: Women, Politics, and Portraiture during the French Revolution." *Art Bulletin* 93, no. 3 (2011): 325–44.

Frisken, Amanda. *Victoria Woodhull's Sexual Revolution: Political Theater and the Popular Press in Nineteenth-Century America*. Philadelphia: University of Pennsylvania Press, 2004.

Fry, Amelia, ed. *Conversations with Alice Paul: Woman Suffrage and the Equal Rights Amendment*. Suffragists Oral History Project. Berkeley: University of California, 1976.

Gabin, Jane S. *American Women in Gilded Age London: Expatriates Rediscovered*. Gainesville: University Press of Florida, 2006.

Gallagher, Julie A. *Black Women and Politics in New York City*. Urbana: University of Illinois Press, 2012.

Garnett, Miranda, and Zoë Thomas. *Suffrage and the Arts: Visual Culture, Politics, and Enterprise*. London: Bloomsbury, 2018.

Garvey, Ellen Gruber. *The Adman in the Parlor: Magazines and the Gendering of Consumer Culture, 1880s to 1910s*. New York: Oxford University Press, 1996.

Gary, Brett. *The Nervous Liberals: Propaganda Anxieties from World War I to the Cold War*. New York: Columbia University Press, 1999.

Gates, Henry Louis. *The Trials of Phillis Wheatley: America's First Black Poet and Her Encounters with the Founding Fathers*. New York: Basic Civitas Books, 2003.

Gell, Alfred. *Art and Agency: An Anthropological Theory*. New York: Oxford University Press, 1998.

Gidlow, Liette. "The Sequel: The Fifteenth Amendment, The Nineteenth Amendment, and Southern Black Women's Struggle to Vote." *Journal of the Gilded Age And Progressive Era* 17, no. 3 (2018): 433–49.

Giesberg, Judith Ann. *Civil War Sisterhood: The U.S. Sanitary Commission and Women's Politics in Transition*. Boston: Northeastern University Press, 2006.

Gillmore, Inez Haynes. *The Story of the Woman's Party*. New York: Harcourt, Brace, 1921.

Gilmore, Glenda Elizabeth. *Gender and Jim Crow: Women and the Politics of White Supremacy in North Carolina, 1896–1920*. Chapel Hill: University of North Carolina Press, 1996.

Ginzberg, Lori D. *Elizabeth Cady Stanton: An American Life*. New York: Hill and Wang, 2009.

———. *Untidy Origins: A Story of Woman's Rights in Antebellum New York*. Chapel Hill: University of North Carolina Press, 2005.

———. *Women and the Work of Benevolence: Morality, Politics, and Class in the Nineteenth-Century United States*. New Haven, CT: Yale University Press, 1990.

———. *Women in Antebellum Reform*. Wheeling, IL: Harlan Davidson, 2000.

Glickman, Lawrence B. *Buying Power: A History of Consumer Activism in America*. Chicago: University of Chicago Press, 2009.

Goldsmith, Barbara. *Other Powers: The Age of Suffrage, Spiritualism, and the Scandalous Victoria Woodhull*. New York: Knopf, 1998.

Goldstone, Lawrence. *Inherently Unequal: The Betrayal of Equal Rights by the Supreme Court, 1865–1903*. New York: Walker, 2011.

González, Gabriela. "Jovita Idar: The Ideological Origins of a Transnational Advocate for La Raza." In *Redeeming La Raza: Transborder Modernity, Race, Respectability, and Rights*, ed. Elizabeth Hayes Turner, Stephanie Cole, and Rebecca Sharpless. Athens: University of Georgia Press, 2015.

Goodier, Susan. *No Votes for Women: The New York State Anti-Suffrage Movement*. Urbana: University of Illinois Press, 2012.

Gordon, Ann D., ed. *The Selected Papers of Elizabeth Cady Stanton and Susan B. Anthony*. 6 vols. New Brunswick, NJ: Rutgers University Press, 1997–2009.

Gordon, Ann D., and Bettye Collier-Thomas, eds. *African American Women and the Vote, 1837–1965*. Amherst: University of Massachusetts Press, 1997.

Gould, Philip. "Civil Society and the Public Woman." *Journal of the Early Republic* 28, no. 1 (2008): 29–46.

Graham, Sara Hunter. *Woman Suffrage and the New Democracy*. New Haven, CT: Yale University Press, 1996.

Gray, Edward G., and Jane Kamensky, eds. *The Oxford Handbook of the American Revolution*. New York: Oxford University Press, 2013.

Green, Barbara. *Spectacular Confessions: Autobiography, Performative Activism, and the Sites of Suffrage, 1905–1938*. New York: St. Martin's Press, 1997.

Green, Elna. *Southern Strategies: Southern Women and the Woman Suffrage Question*. Chapel Hill: University of North Carolina Press, 1997.

Greenhill, Jennifer A. "David Claypoole Johnston and the Menial Labor of Caricature." *American Art* 17, no. 3 (2003): 32–51.

Grigsby, Darcy Grimaldo. *Enduring Truths: Sojourner's Shadows and Substance*. Chicago: University of Chicago Press, 2015.

Grimes, Alan Pendleton. *The Puritan Ethic and Woman Suffrage*. New York: Oxford University Press, 1967.

Gullett, Gayle Ann. *Becoming Citizens: The Emergence and Development of the California Women's Movement, 1880–1911*. Urbana: University of Illinois Press, 2000.

Guterl, Matthew Pratt. *Seeing Race in Modern America*. Chapel Hill: University of North Carolina Press, 2013.

Hahn, Steven. *A Nation under Our Feet: Black Political Struggles in the Rural South, from Slavery to the Great Migration*. Cambridge, MA: Belknap, 2003.

Haidarali, Laila. *Brown Beauty: Color, Sex, and Race from the Harlem Renaissance to World War II*. New York: New York University Press, 2018.

Hamilton, Cynthia S. "Hercules Subdued: The Visual Rhetoric of the Kneeling Slave." *Slavery & Abolition* 34, no. 4 (2013): 631–52.

Hamington, Maurice, ed. *Feminist Interpretations of Jane Addams*. University Park: Pennsylvania State University Press, 2010.

Harley, Sharon, and Rosalyn Terborg-Penn. *The Afro-American Woman: Struggles and Images*. Baltimore: Black Classic Press, 1997.

Harrison, Patricia Greenwood. *Connecting Links: The British and American Woman Suffrage Movements, 1900–1914*. Westport, CT: Greenwood, 2000.

Harvey, Eleanor Jones. *The Civil War and American Art*. New Haven, CT: Yale University Press, 2012.

Haulman, Kate. *The Politics of Fashion in Eighteenth-Century America*. Chapel Hill: University of North Carolina Press, 2011.

Henkin, David M. *The Postal Age: The Emergence of Modern Communications in Nineteenth-Century America*. Chicago: University of Chicago Press, 2006.

Hennessy, Rosemary. *Materialist Feminism and the Politics of Discourse*. New York: Routledge, 1993.

Hewitt, Nancy A. "Taking the True Woman Hostage." *Journal of Women's History* 14, no. 1 (2002): 156–62.

———. *Women's Activism and Social Change: Rochester, New York, 1822–1872*. Ithaca, NY: Cornell University Press, 1984.

Higginbotham, Evelyn Brooks. "African-American Women's History and the Metalanguage of Race." *Signs* 17, no. 2 (1992): 251–74.

———. *Righteous Discontent: The Women's Movement in the Black Baptist Church, 1880–1920*. Cambridge, MA: Harvard University Press, 1993.

Hine, Darlene. "Rape and the Inner Lives of Black Women in the Middle West: Preliminary Thoughts on the Culture of Dissemblance." *Signs* 14, no. 4 (1989): 912–20.

Hoffert, Sylvia D. *Alva Vanderbilt Belmont: Unlikely Champion of Women's Rights.* Bloomington: Indiana University Press, 2012.

———. *When Hens Crow: The Woman's Rights Movement in Antebellum America.* Bloomington: Indiana University Press, 1995.

Hofstadter, Richard. *The Age of Reform: From Bryan to F.D.R.* New York: Vintage, 1960.

Hoganson, Kristin L. *Fighting for American Manhood: How Gender Politics Provoked the Spanish-American and Philippine-American Wars.* New Haven, CT: Yale University Press, 1998.

Holden, Teresa. *"Earnest Women Can Do Anything": The Public Career of Josephine St. Pierre Ruffin, 1842–1904.* PhD diss., St. Louis University, 2005.

Holland, Patricia G., and Ann D. Gordon, eds. *The Papers of Elizabeth Cady Stanton and Susan B. Anthony: Guide and Index to the Microfilm Edition.* Wilmington, DE: Scholarly Resources, 1992.

Holton, Sandra Stanley. *Feminism and Democracy: Women's Suffrage and Reform Politics in Britain, 1900–1918.* Cambridge, UK: Cambridge University Press, 2002.

Holton, Woody. *Abigail Adams.* New York: Free Press, 2010.

Horn, James P., Jan Lewis, and Peter S. Onuf, eds. *The Revolution of 1800: Democracy, Race, and the New Republic.* Charlottesville: University of Virginia Press, 2002.

Hunter, Robert, ed. *Ceramics in America.* New York: Chipstone, 2002.

Huxman, Susan Schultz. "The *Woman's Journal*, 1870–1890: Torchbearer for Suffrage." In *A Voice of Their Own: The Woman Suffrage Press, 1840–1910*, ed. Martha Solomon. Tuscaloosa: University of Alabama Press, 1991.

Ibson, John. *Picturing Men: A Century of Male Relationships in Everyday American Photography.* Chicago: University of Chicago Press, 2006.

Isenberg, Nancy. *Sex and Citizenship in Antebellum America.* Chapel Hill: The University of North Carolina Press, 1998.

Jablonsky, Thomas J. *The Home, Heaven, and Mother Party: Female Anti-Suffragists in the United States, 1868–1920.* Brooklyn: Carlson, 1994.

Jackson, Gregory S. "Cultivating Spiritual Sight: Jacob Riis's Virtual-Tour Narrative and the Visual Modernization of Protestant Homiletics." *Representations* 83, no. 1 (2003): 126–66.

Jacobs, Meg. *Pocketbook Politics: Economic Citizenship in Twentieth-Century America.* Princeton, NJ: Princeton University Press, 2005.

Jacoby, Karl. *Crimes against Nature: Squatters, Poachers, Thieves, and the Hidden History of American Conservation.* Berkeley: University of California Press, 2001.

James, Pearl. *Picture This: World War I Posters and Visual Culture.* Lincoln: University of Nebraska Press, 2009.

Johnson, Claudia L., ed. *The Cambridge Companion to Mary Wollstonecraft.* New York: Cambridge University Press, 2002.

Johnson, Joan Marie. *Funding Feminism: Monied Women, Philanthropy, and the Women's Movement, 1870–1967.* Chapel Hill: University of North Carolina Press, 2017.

Johnson, Paul E., and Sean Wilentz. *The Kingdom of Matthias*. New York: Oxford University Press, 1994.

Jones, Martha S. *All Bound Up Together: The Woman Question in African American Public Culture, 1830–1900*. Chapel Hill: University of North Carolina Press, 2007.

Kaestle, Carl F., and Janice A. Radway, eds. *Print in Motion: The Expansion of Publishing and Reading in the United States, 1880–1940*. Vol. 4 of *A History of the Book in America*. Chapel Hill: University of North Carolina Press, 2009.

Kamensky, Jane. *Governing the Tongue the Politics of Speech in Early New England*. New York: Oxford University Press, 1997.

———. *A Revolution in Color: The World of John Singleton Copley*. New York: W. W. Norton, 2016.

Kelley, Mary. *Learning to Stand and Speak: Women, Education, and Public Life in America's Republic*. Chapel Hill: University of North Carolina Press, 2006.

———. "'The Need of Their Genius': Women's Reading and Writing Practices in Early America." *Journal of the Early Republic* 28, no. 1 (2008): 1–22.

———. *Private Woman, Public Stage: Literary Domesticity in Nineteenth-Century America*. New York: Oxford University Press, 1984.

Kelley, Robin D. G. *Race Rebels: Culture, Politics, and the Black Working Class*. New York: Free Press, 1994.

Kelly, Catherine E. *Republic of Taste: Art, Politics, and Everyday Life in Early America*. Philadelphia: University of Pennsylvania Press, 2016.

Kennedy, Martha H. *Drawn to Purpose: American Women Illustrators and Cartoonists*. Jackson: University Press of Mississippi, 2018.

Kennel, Sarah, Diane Waggoner, and Alice Carver-Kubik. *In the Darkroom: An Illustrated Guide to Photographic Processes before the Digital Age*. Washington, DC: National Gallery of Art, 2010.

Kerber, Linda K. "Separate Spheres, Female Worlds, Woman's Place: The Rhetoric of Women's History." *Journal of American History* 75, no. 1 (1988): 9–39.

———. *Women of the Republic: Intellect and Ideology in Revolutionary America*. Chapel Hill: University of North Carolina Press, 1980.

Kerr, Andrea Moore. *Lucy Stone Speaking Out for Equality*. New Brunswick, NJ: Rutgers University Press, 1992.

Keyssar, Alexander. *The Right to Vote: The Contested History of Democracy in the United States*. New York: Basic Books, 2000.

Kielstra, Paul Michael. *The Politics of Slave Trade Suppression in Britain and France, 1814–48: Diplomacy, Morality and Economics*. New York: St. Martin's Press, 2000.

Kierner, Cynthia A. *Beyond the Household: Women's Place in the Early South, 1700–1835*. Ithaca, NY: Cornell University Press, 1998.

Kingsbury, Celia Malone. *For Home and Country: World War I Propaganda on the Home Front*. Lincoln: University of Nebraska Press, 2010.

Kirschke, Amy Helene. *Art in Crisis: W.E.B. Du Bois and the Struggle for African*

American Identity and Memory. Bloomington: Indiana University Press, 2007.

———. "DuBois and 'The Crisis' Magazine: Imaging Women and Family." *Source: Notes in the History of Art* 24, no. 4 (2005): 35–45.

Klapper, Melissa R. *Ballots, Babies, and Banners of Peace: American Jewish Women's Activism, 1890–1940*. New York: New York University Press, 2013.

Klepp, Susan E. *Revolutionary Conceptions: Women, Fertility, and Family Limitation in America, 1760–1820*. Chapel Hill: University of North Carolina Press, 2009.

Knight, Louise W. *Citizen: Jane Addams and the Struggle for Democracy*. Chicago: University of Chicago Press, 2005.

———. *Jane Addams: Spirit in Action*. New York: W. W. Norton, 2010.

Kooistra, Lorraine Janzen. *Poetry, Pictures, and Popular Publishing the Illustrated Gift Book and Victorian Visual Culture, 1855–1875*. Athens: Ohio University Press, 2011.

Korshak, Yvonne. "The Liberty Cap as a Revolutionary Symbol in America and France." *Smithsonian Studies in American Art* 1, no. 2 (1987): 53–69.

Kraditor, Aileen S. *The Ideas of the Woman Suffrage Movement, 1890–1920*. New York: Columbia University Press, 1965.

Kroeger, Brooke. *The Suffragents: How Women Used Men to Get the Vote*. Albany, NY: Excelsior Editions, 2017.

Laird, Pamela Walker. *Advertising Progress: American Business and the Rise of Consumer Marketing*. Baltimore: Johns Hopkins University Press, 2001.

Lange, Allison. "Picturing Tradition: Images of Martha Washington in Antebellum Politics." *Imprint* 37 (2012): 22–39.

Larkin, Jack. "What He Did for Love: David Claypoole Johnston and the Boston Irish, 1825–1865." *Common-Place* 13, no. 3 (2013), http://www.common -place-archives.org/vol-13/no-03/larkin/.

Lasser, Carol. *Antebellum Women: Private, Public, Partisan*. Lanham, MD: Rowman & Littlefield, 2010.

Latour, Bruno. *Pandora's Hope: Essays on the Reality of Science Studies*. Cambridge, MA: Harvard University Press, 1999.

———. *Reassembling the Social: An Introduction to Actor-Network-Theory*. New York: Oxford University Press, 2005.

Lears, T. J. Jackson. *Fables of Abundance: A Cultural History of Advertising in America*. New York: Basic Books, 1994.

Lee, Anthony W., and Elizabeth Young. *On Alexander Gardner's Photographic Sketch Book of the Civil War*. Berkeley: University of California Press, 2007.

Lemay, Kate Clarke, ed. *Votes for Women: A Portrait of Persistence*. Princeton, NJ: Princeton University Press, 2019.

Lippert, Amy K. DeFalco. *Consuming Identities: Visual Culture in Nineteenth-Century San Francisco*. New York: Oxford University Press, 2018.

Lengel, Edward G. *Inventing George Washington*. New York: Harper Collins, 2011.

Lerner, Gerda. "The Lady and the Mill Girl: Changes in the Status of Women in the Age of Jackson." *American Studies* 10, no. 1 (1969): 5–15.

Lindsey, Treva B. *Colored No More: Reinventing Black Womanhood in Washington, D.C.* Urbana: University of Illinois Press, 2017.

Longmore, Paul K. *The Invention of George Washington.* Berkeley: University of California Press, 1988.

Lovell, Margaretta M. *Art in a Season of Revolution: Painters, Artisans, and Patrons in Early America.* Philadelphia: University of Pennsylvania Press, 2005.

Lubin, David M. *Picturing a Nation: Art and Social Change in Nineteenth-Century America.* New Haven, CT: Yale University Press, 1994.

Lugo-Ortiz, Agnes, and Angela Rosenthal *Slave Portraiture in the Atlantic World.* New York: Cambridge University Press, 2013.

Lukasik, Christopher J. *Discerning Characters: The Culture of Appearance in Early America.* Philadelphia: University of Pennsylvania Press, 2011.

Lunardini, Christine A. *From Equal Suffrage to Equal Rights: Alice Paul and the National Woman's Party, 1912–1928.* New York: New York University Press, 1986.

Lyons, Clare A. *Sex among the Rabble: An Intimate History of Gender and Power in the Age of Revolution, Philadelphia, 1730–1830.* Chapel Hill: University of North Carolina Press, 2006.

Marchand, Roland. *Advertising the American Dream: Making Way for Modernity, 1920–1940.* Berkeley: University of California Press, 1985.

Marilley, Suzanne. *Woman Suffrage and the Origins of Liberal Feminism in the United States, 1820–1920.* Cambridge, MA: Harvard University Press, 1996.

Marks, Patricia. *Bicycles, Bangs, and Bloomers: The New Woman in the Popular Press.* Lexington: University Press of Kentucky, 1990.

Matthews, Glenna. *The Rise of Public Woman: Woman's Power and Woman's Place in the United States, 1630–1970.* New York: Oxford University Press, 1992.

Mauro, Hayes Peter. *The Art of Americanization at the Carlisle Indian School.* Albuquerque: University of New Mexico Press, 2011.

Mayhall, Laura E. Nym. "Defining Militancy: Radical Protest, the Constitutional Idiom, and Women's Suffrage in Britain, 1908–1909." *Journal of British Studies* 39, no. 3 (2000): 340–71.

———. *The Militant Suffrage Movement: Citizenship and Resistance in Britain, 1860–1930.* New York: Oxford University Press, 2003.

McCall, Laura. "'The Reign of Brute Force Is Now Over': A Content Analysis of 'Godey's Lady's Book,' 1830–1860." *Journal of the Early Republic* 9, no. 2 (1989): 217–36.

McCammon, Holly J. "'Out of the Parlors and into the Streets': The Changing Tactical Repertoire of the U.S. Women's Suffrage Movements." *Social Forces* 81, no. 3 (2003): 787–818.

———. "Stirring up Suffrage Sentiment: The Formation of the State Woman Suffrage Organizations, 1866–1914." *Social Forces* 80, no. 2 (2001): 449–80.

McCammon, Holly J., and Karen E. Campbell. "Winning the Vote in the West: The Political Successes of the Women's Suffrage Movements, 1866–1919." *Gender and Society* 15, no. 1 (2001): 55–82.

McCammon, Holly J., Karen E. Campbell, Ellen M. Granberg, and Christine Mowery. "How Movements Win: Gendered Opportunity Structures and U.S. Women's Suffrage Movements, 1866 to 1919." *American Sociological Review* 66, no. 1 (2001): 49–70.

McCammon, Holly J., Lyndi Hewitt, and Sandy Smith. "'No Weapon Save Argument': Strategic Frame Amplification in the U.S. Woman Suffrage Movements." *Sociological Quarterly* 45, no. 3 (2004): 529–56.

McClean, Elizabeth, Sean R. Martin, Kyle J. Emich, and Todd Woodruff. "The Social Consequences of Voice: An Examination of Voice Type and Gender on Status and Subsequent Leader Emergence." *Academy of Management Journal* 61, no. 5 (2018): 1869–91.

McCreery, Cindy. *The Satirical Gaze: Prints of Women in Late Eighteenth-Century England*. Oxford, UK: Oxford University Press, 2004.

McGovern, Charles. *Sold American: Consumption and Citizenship, 1890–1945*. Chapel Hill: University of North Carolina Press, 2006.

McKeever, Jane L. "The Woman's Temperance Publishing Association." *Library Quarterly* 55, no. 4 (1985): 365–97.

McKellop, Stephanie. "America, the 'Rebellious Slut': Gender & Political Cartoons in the American Revolution." *Common-Place* 17, no. 3 (2017), http://common-place.org/book/vol-17-no-3-mckellop/.

McInnis, Maurie Dee. *Slaves Waiting for Sale: Abolitionist Art and the American Slave Trade*. Chicago: University of Chicago Press, 2011.

McInnis, Maurie Dee, and Louis P. Nelson, eds. *Shaping the Body Politic: Art and Political Formation in Early America*. Charlottesville: University of Virginia Press, 2011.

McMahon, Lucia. *Mere Equals: The Paradox of Educated Women in the Early American Republic*. Ithaca, NY: Cornell University Press, 2012.

McMillen, Sally G. *Lucy Stone: An Unapologetic Life*. New York: Oxford University Press, 2015.

Mead, Rebecca. *How the Vote Was Won: Woman Suffrage in the Western United States, 1868–1914*. New York: New York University Press, 2004.

Meehan, Sean Ross. *Mediating American Autobiography: Photography in Emerson, Thoreau, Douglass, and Whitman*. Columbia: University of Missouri Press, 2008.

Miles, Ellen Gross. *George and Martha Washington: Portraits from the Presidential Years*. Washington, DC: Smithsonian Institution, 1999.

Miller, Bonnie M. *From Liberation to Conquest: The Visual and Popular Cultures of the Spanish-American War of 1898*. Amherst: University of Massachusetts Press, 2011.

Mirzoeff, Nicholas, ed. *The Visual Culture Reader*. 3rd ed. New York: Routledge, 2013.

Mitchell, Michele. "'Lower Orders,' Racial Hierarchies, and Rights Rhetoric: Evolutionary Echoes in Elizabeth Cady Stanton's Thought during the Late 1860s." In *Elizabeth Cady Stanton, Feminist as Thinker: A Reader in Documents and Essays*, ed. Ellen Carol DuBois and Richard Cándida Smith. New York: New York University Press, 2007.

Molineux, Catherine. *Faces of Perfect Ebony: Encountering Atlantic Slavery in Imperial Britain*. Cambridge, MA: Harvard University Press, 2012.

Morris, Errol. *Believing Is Seeing: Observations on the Mysteries of Photography*. New York: Penguin Press, 2011.

Murphy, Kevin P. *Political Manhood: Red Bloods, Mollycoddles, and the Politics of Progressive Era Reform*. New York: Columbia University Press, 2008.

Myers, Sylvia Harcstark. *The Bluestocking Circle: Women, Friendship, and the Life of the Mind in Eighteenth-Century England*. Oxford, UK: Clarendon, 1990.

Neely, Mark E. *The Confederate Image: Prints of the Lost Cause*. Chapel Hill: University of North Carolina Press, 1987.

Neely, Mark E., and Harold Holzer. *The Union Image: Popular Prints of the Civil War North*. Chapel Hill: University of North Carolina Press, 2000.

Nelson, Robert S., and Richard Shiff, eds. *Critical Terms for Art History*. Chicago: University of Chicago Press, 2003.

Neuman, Johanna. *Gilded Suffragists: The New York Socialites Who Fought for Women's Right to Vote*. New York: Washington Mews, 2017.

Newman, Ewell L. "Graceful Vines, Common Scolds, and Shameless Devils: The Image of Woman in Nineteenth Century American Historical Prints." *Imprint* 6, no. 1 (1981): 2–18.

Newman, Simon P. *Parades and the Politics of the Street: Festive Culture in the Early American Republic*. Philadelphia: University of Pennsylvania Press, 1997.

Nochlin, Linda. *Representing Women*. New York: Thames and Hudson, 1999.

———. *Women, Art, and Power: And Other Essays*. New York: Harper & Row, 1988.

Norton, Mary Beth. *Liberty's Daughters: The Revolutionary Experience of American Women, 1750–1800*. Boston: Little, Brown & Co., 1980.

———. *Separated by Their Sex: Women in Public and Private in the Colonial Atlantic World*. Ithaca, NY: Cornell University Press, 2011.

Norwood, Kimberly Jade. *Color Matters: Skin Tone Bias and the Myth of a Postracial America*. New York: Routledge, 2014.

Oertel, Kristen Tegtmeier, and Marilyn S. Blackwell. *Frontier Feminist: Clarina Howard Nichols and the Politics of Motherhood*. Lawrence: University Press of Kansas, 2010.

Oldfield, John R. *Popular Politics and British Anti-Slavery: The Mobilisation of Public Opinion Against the Slave Trade, 1787–1807*. New York: St. Martin's Press, 1995.

Otto, Elizabeth, and Vanessa Rocco, eds. *The New Woman International: Representations in Photography and Film from the 1870s through the 1960s*. Ann Arbor: University of Michigan Press, 2011.

Painter, Nell Irvin. *Sojourner Truth: A Life, a Symbol*. New York: W. W. Norton, 1997.

Panzer, Mary. *Mathew Brady and the Image of History*. Washington, DC: Smithsonian Institution Press, 1997.

Parker, Alison M. *Articulating Rights: Nineteenth-Century American Women on*

Race, Reform, and the State. DeKalb: Northern Illinois University Press, 2010.

Parsons, Elaine Frantz. *Manhood Lost: Fallen Drunkards and Redeeming Women in the Nineteenth-Century United States*. Baltimore: Johns Hopkins University Press, 2003.

Pasley, Jeffrey L. *"The Tyranny of Printers": Newspaper Politics in the Early American Republic*. Charlottesville: University of Virginia Press, 2001.

Patterson, Martha. *Beyond the Gibson Girl: Reimagining the American New Woman, 1895–1915*. Chicago: University of Illinois Press, 2005.

Pauley, Garth E. "W.E.B. Du Bois on Woman Suffrage: A Critical Analysis of His Crisis Writings." *Journal of Black Studies* 30, no. 3 (2000): 383–410.

Pegler-Gordon, Anna. *In Sight of America: Photography and the Development of U.S. Immigration Policy*. Berkeley: University of California Press, 2009.

Petersen, Anne Helen. *Too Fat, Too Slutty, Too Loud: The Rise and Reign of the Unruly Woman*. New York: Plume, 2017.

Peterson, Carla L. *"Doers of the Word": African-American Women Speakers and Writers in the North (1830–1880)*. New Brunswick, NJ: Rutgers University Press, 1998.

Pew Research Center. "Women and Leadership: Public Says Women Are Equally Qualified, but Barriers Persist." Washington, DC: Pew Research Center, 2015.

Pochmara, Anna. *The Making of the New Negro: Black Authorship, Masculinity, and Sexuality in the Harlem Renaissance*. Amsterdam: Amsterdam University Press, 2011.

Pointon, Marcia R. *Hanging the Head: Portraiture and Social Formation in Eighteenth-Century England*. New Haven, CT: Yale University Press, 1993.

Pollack, Griselda. *Vision and Difference: Femininity, Feminism and Histories of Art*. New York: Routledge, 2003.

Prieto, Laura R. *At Home in the Studio: The Professionalization of Women Artists in America*. Cambridge, MA: Harvard University Press, 2001.

Pugh, Martin. *The March of the Women: A Revisionist Analysis of the Campaign for Women's Suffrage, 1866–1914*. Oxford, UK: Oxford University Press, 2002.

Quirke, Carol. "Picturing the Poor: Jacob Riis's Reform Photography." *Reviews in American History* 36, no. 4 (2008): 557–65.

Raiford, Leigh. *Imprisoned in a Luminous Glare: Photography and the African American Freedom Struggle*. Chapel Hill: University of North Carolina Press, 2011.

Ratcliffe, Donald. "The Right to Vote and the Rise of Democracy, 1787–1828." *Journal of the Early Republic* 33, no. 2 (2013): 219–54.

Rauser, Amelia. "Death or Liberty: British Political Prints and the Struggle for Symbols in the American Revolution." *Oxford Art Journal* 21, no. 2 (1998): 153–71.

Rauterkus, Cathleen Nista. *Go Get Mother's Picket Sign: Crossing Spheres with the Material Culture of Suffrage*. Lanham, MD: University Press of America, 2010.

Reaves, Wendy Wick. *George Washington, an American Icon: The Eighteenth-Century Graphic Portraits*. Washington, DC: Smithsonian Institution, 1982.

Reilly, Elizabeth Carroll. *A Dictionary of Colonial American Printers' Ornaments and Illustrations*. Worcester, MA: American Antiquarian Society, 1975.

Reilly, Robin. *Wedgwood*. New York: Stockton, 1989.

Ridarsky, Christine L., and Mary Margaret Huth, eds. *Susan B. Anthony and the Struggle for Equal Rights*. Rochester, NY: University of Rochester Press, 2012.

Roberts, Jennifer L. "Copley's Cargo: Boy with a Squirrel and the Dilemma of Transit." *American Art* 21, no. 2 (2007): 20–41.

Roberts, Mary Louise. "True Womanhood Revisited." *Journal of Women's History* 14, no. 1 (2002): 150–55.

Robertson, Stacey M. *Hearts Beating for Liberty: Women Abolitionists in the Old Northwest*. Chapel Hill: University of North Carolina Press, 2010.

Robinson, William Henry, ed. *Critical Essays on Phillis Wheatley*. Boston: G. K. Hall, 1982.

Rodgers, Daniel T. *Atlantic Crossings: Social Politics in a Progressive Age*. Cambridge, MA: Belknap, 1998.

Roeder, George H., Jr. "Filling in the Picture: Visual Culture." *Reviews in American History* 26, no. 1 (1998): 275–93.

Rogers, Donald Wayne. *Making Capitalism Safe: Work Safety and Health Regulation in America, 1880–1940*. Urbana: University of Illinois Press, 2009.

Romer, Grant B., Brian Wallis, Sally Pierce, and Wendy Wick Reaves, eds. *Young America: The Daguerreotypes of Southworth & Hawes*. New York: Steidl, 2008.

Rooks, Noliwe M. *Hair Raising: Beauty, Culture, and African American Women*. New Brunswick, NJ: Rutgers University Press, 1996.

Rosen, Andrew. *Rise Up, Women!: The Militant Campaign of the Women's Social and Political Union, 1903–1914*. London: Routledge, 1974.

Rosenberg, Carroll Smith. "Beauty, the Beast and the Militant Woman: A Case Study in Sex Roles and Social Stress in Jacksonian America." *American Quarterly* 23, no. 4 (1971): 562–84.

Rosenheim, Jeff L. *Photography and the American Civil War*. New York: Metropolitan Museum of Art, 2013.

Rosenthal, Angela. *Angelica Kauffman: Art and Sensibility*. New Haven, CT: Yale University Press, 2006.

Rosenzweig, Roy, and Elizabeth Blackmar. *The Park and the People: A History of Central Park*. Ithaca, NY: Cornell University Press, 1992.

Rupp, Leila. *A Desired Past*. Chicago: University of Chicago Press, 1999.

Ryan, Mary P. *Cradle of the Middle Class: The Family in Oneida County, New York, 1790–1865*. New York: Cambridge University Press, 1981.

———. *Women in Public: Between Banners and Ballots, 1825–1880*. Baltimore: Johns Hopkins University Press, 1990.

Samuels, Shirley. *Facing America Iconography and the Civil War*. New York: Oxford University Press, 2004.

Sandweiss, Martha A. *Print the Legend: Photography and the American West.* New Haven: Yale University Press, 2002.

Sandweiss, Martha A., and Alan Trachtenberg. *Photography in Nineteenth-Century America.* Fort Worth, TX: Amon Carter Museum, 1991.

Saunders, Richard H., and Ellen G. Miles *American Colonial Portraits, 1700–1776.* Washington, DC: Smithsonian Institution Press, 1987.

Schreiber, Rachel. *Gender and Activism in a Little Magazine: The Modern Figures of the Masses.* Burlington, VT: Ashgate, 2011.

Schreiber, Rachel, ed. *Modern Print Activism in the United States.* Burlington, VT: Ashgate, 2013.

Schultz, Jane E. *Women at the Front: Hospital Workers in Civil War America.* Chapel Hill: University of North Carolina Press, 2004.

Schwantes, Carlos A. "Western Women in Coxey's Army in 1894." *Arizona and the West* 26, no. 1 (1984): 5–20.

Schwartz, Vanessa R. "Walter Benjamin for Historians." *American Historical Review* 106, no. 5 (2001): 1721–43.

Schwartz, Vanessa R., and Jeannene M. Przyblyski, eds. *The Nineteenth-Century Visual Culture Reader.* New York: Routledge, 2004.

Sheppard, Alice. *Cartooning for Suffrage.* Albuquerque: University of New Mexico Press, 1994.

Sherrard-Johnson, Cherene. *Portraits of the New Negro Woman: Visual and Literary Culture in the Harlem Renaissance.* New Brunswick, NJ: Rutgers University Press, 2007.

Shifrin, Susan, ed. *Re-framing Representations of Women: Figuring, Fashioning, Portraiting, and Telling in the "Picturing" Women Project.* Burlington, VT: Ashgate, 2008.

Silber, Nina. *Daughters of the Union: Northern Women Fight the Civil War.* Cambridge, MA: Harvard University Press, 2011.

Skocpol, Theda. *Protecting Soldiers and Mothers: The Political Origins of Social Policy in the United States.* Cambridge, MA: Belknap, 1992.

Smith, Angela K. *Suffrage Discourse in Britain during the First World War.* Burlington, VT: Ashgate, 2005.

Smith, Shawn Michelle. *American Archives: Gender, Race, and Class in Visual Culture.* Princeton, NJ: Princeton University Press, 1999.

———. *Photography on the Color Line: W. E. B. Du Bois, Race, and Visual Culture.* Durham, NC: Duke University Press, 2004.

Smith Rosenberg, Carroll. *Disorderly Conduct: Visions of Gender in Victorian America.* New York: Knopf, 1985.

Sneider, Allison. *Suffragists in an Imperial Age: U.S. Expansion and the Woman Question, 1870–1929.* New York: Oxford University Press, 2008.

Solomon, Martha, ed. *A Voice of Their Own: The Woman Suffrage Press, 1840–1910.* Tuscaloosa: University of Alabama Press, 1991.

Stauffer, John, Zoe Trodd, and Celeste-Marie Bernier. *Picturing Frederick Douglass: An Illustrated Biography of the Nineteenth Century's Most Photographed American.* New York: Liveright, 2015.

Sterling, Dorothy. *Ahead of Her Time: Abby Kelley and the Politics of Anti-Slavery*. New York: W. W. Norton, 1994.

Stillion Southard, Belinda A. *Militant Citizenship: Rhetorical Strategies of the National Woman's Party, 1913–1920*. College Station: Texas A&M University Press, 2011.

Stovall, James Glen. *Seeing Suffrage: The 1913 Washington Suffrage Parade, Its Pictures, and Its Effects on the American Political Landscape*. Knoxville: University of Tennessee Press, 2013.

Sussman, Charlotte. *Consuming Anxieties: Consumer Protest, Gender, and British Slavery, 1713–1833*. Stanford, CA: Stanford University Press, 2000.

Taft, Robert. *Photography and the American Scene: A Social History, 1839–1889*. New York: Macmillan, 1938.

Taylor, A. Elizabeth. "The Woman Suffrage Movement in Florida." *Florida Historical Quarterly* 36, no. 1 (1957): 42–60.

Terborg-Penn, Rosalyn. *African American Women in the Struggle for the Vote, 1850–1920*. Bloomington: Indiana University Press, 1998.

Tetrault, Lisa. "The Incorporation of American Feminism: Suffragists and the Postbellum Lyceum." *The Journal of American History* 96, no. 4 (March 1, 2010): 1027–56.

———. *Myth of Seneca Falls: Memory and the Women's Suffrage Movement, 1848–1898*. Chapel Hill: University of North Carolina Press, 2014.

Tickner, Lisa. *The Spectacle of Women: Imagery of the Suffrage Campaign, 1907–14*. London: Chatto & Windus, 1987.

Trachtenberg, Alan. *Reading American Photographs: Images as History, Mathew Brady to Walker Evans*. New York: Hill and Wang, 1989.

Trainor, Sean. *Groomed for Power: A Cultural Economy of the Male Body in Nineteenth-Century America*. PhD diss, Pennsylvania State University, 2015.

Ulrich, Laurel Thatcher. "Of Pens and Needles: Sources in Early American Women's History." *The Journal of American History* 77, no. 1 (1990): 200–207.

Valenze, Deborah. *Milk: A Local and Global History*. New Haven, CT: Yale University Press, 2011.

Van Wagenen, Lola. *Sister-Wives and Suffragists: Polygamy and the Politics of Woman Suffrage, 1870–1896*. Provo, UT: Joseph Fielding Smith Institute for Latter-Day Saint History, 2003.

Varon, Elizabeth. *We Mean to Be Counted: White Women and Politics in Antebellum Virginia*. Chapel Hill: University of North Carolina Press, 1998.

Venet, Wendy Hamand. *A Strong-Minded Woman: The Life of Mary Livermore*. Amherst: University of Massachusetts Press, 2005.

Volpe, Andrea. *Cheap Pictures: Cartes de Visite Portrait Photographs and Visual Culture in the United States, 1860–1877*. PhD diss., Rutgers University, 1999.

Waldstreicher, David. *In the Midst of Perpetual Fetes: The Making of American Nationalism, 1776–1820*. Chapel Hill: University of North Carolina Press, 1997.

Wallace, Maurice O., and Shawn Michelle Smith, eds. *Pictures and Progress: Early Photography and the Making of African American Identity*. Durham, NC: Duke University Press, 2012.

Walton, Mary. *A Woman's Crusade: Alice Paul and the Battle for the Ballot*. New York: Macmillan, 2010.

Wardle, Ralph Martin, ed. *Collected Letters of Mary Wollstonecraft*. Ithaca, NY: Cornell University Press, 1979.

Ware, Caroline Farrar. *The Cultural Approach to History*. New York: Columbia University Press, 1940.

Ware, Susan. *Why They Marched: Untold Stories of the Women Who Fought for the Right to Vote*. Cambridge, MA: Harvard University Press, 2019.

Washington, Margaret. *Sojourner Truth's America*. Urbana: University of Illinois Press, 2009.

Weiss, Elaine. *The Woman's Hour: The Great Fight to Win the Vote*. New York: Viking, 2018.

Weitenkampf, Frank. "Our Political Symbols." *New York History* 33, no. 4 (1952): 371–78.

Welter, Barbara. "The Cult of True Womanhood: 1820–1860." *American Quarterly* 18, no. 2 (1966): 151–74.

West, Richard Samuel. "Collecting Lincoln in Caricature." *Rail Splitter*, December 1995, 15–17.

West, Shearer. *Portraiture*. New York: Oxford University Press, 2004.

Wexler, Laura. *Tender Violence: Domestic Visions in an Age of U.S. Imperialism*. Chapel Hill: University of North Carolina Press, 2000.

Weyler, Karen A. *Empowering Words: Outsiders and Authorship in Early America*. Athens: University of Georgia Press, 2013.

Wheeler, Marjorie Spruill. *New Women of the New South: The Leaders of the Woman Suffrage Movement in the Southern States*. New York: Oxford University Press, 1993.

White, Deborah G. *Too Heavy a Load: Black Women in Defense of Themselves, 1894–1994*. New York: W. W. Norton, 1999.

Wichard, Carol, and Robin Wichard. *Victorian Cartes-de-Visite*. Princes Risborough, UK: Shire, 1999.

Wiebe, Robert H. *The Search for Order, 1877–1920*. New York: Hill and Wang, 1967.

Wilentz, Sean. *The Rise of American Democracy: Jefferson to Lincoln*. New York: W. W. Norton, 2006.

Willis, Deborah. *The Black Female Body: A Photographic History*. Philadelphia: Temple University Press, 2002.

———. *Posing Beauty: African American Images from the 1890s to the Present*. New York: W. W. Norton, 2009.

Willrich, Michael. *City of Courts: Socializing Justice in Progressive Era Chicago*. Cambridge, UK: Cambridge University Press, 2003.

———. *Pox: An American History*. New York: Penguin, 2011.

Wilson, Ann Marie, Mary Ann Irwin, Robert W. Cherny, and Project Muse.

California Women and Politics from the Gold Rush to the Great Depression. Lincoln: University of Nebraska Press, 2011.

Wood, Marcus. *Blind Memory: Visual Representations of Slavery in England and America, 1780–1865.* New York: Routledge, 2000.

Woodall, Joanna, ed. *Portraiture: Facing the Subject.* New York: St. Martin's Press, 1997.

Woodley, Jenny. *Art for Equality: The NAACP's Cultural Campaign for Civil Rights.* Lexington: University Press of Kentucky, 2014.

Zackodnik, Teresa. "The 'Green-Backs of Civilization': Sojourner Truth and Portrait Photography." *American Studies* 46, no. 2 (2005): 117–43.

———, ed. *African American Feminisms, 1828–1923.* New York: Routledge, 2007.

Zaeske, Susan. *Signatures of Citizenship: Petitioning, Antislavery, and Women's Political Identity.* Chapel Hill: University of North Carolina Press, 2003.

Zagarri, Rosemarie. *Revolutionary Backlash: Women and Politics in the Early American Republic.* Philadelphia: University of Pennsylvania Press, 2007.

Zahniser, J. D., and Amelia R. Fry. *Alice Paul: Claiming Power.* New York: Oxford University Press, 2014.

Zakim, Michael. *Ready-Made Democracy: A History of Men's Dress in the American Republic, 1760–1860.* Chicago: University of Chicago Press, 2003.

———. "Sartorial Ideologies: From Homespun to Ready-Made." *American Historical Review* 106, no. 5 (2001): 1553–86.

INDEX

Page numbers in italics refer to figures.